Formosa, China, and the United Nations

FORMOSA, CHINA,

AND THE

UNITED NATIONS

Formosa in the World Community

LUNG-CHU CHEN

HAROLD D. LASSWELL

St. Martin's Press, New York

Preface

IN THIS POLICY-ORIENTED STUDY, we tackle the dilemma of Communist China for the United Nations and the United States by focusing on a most fundamental issue: Formosa. After examining the full range of policy alternatives open to American foreign policy makers and member states of the U.N., we conclude that a "one China, one Formosa" solution to Chinese participation in the U.N. and Formosa's dangerously ambiguous international status would best serve all our common interests. According to this formulation, Communist China would occupy "China's" seats in both the General Assembly and the Security Council in place of the Nationalist delegation; and simultaneously Formosa would be assured of admission to the U.N. after attaining independence through self-determination. We support this proposal with a detailed and anticipatory examination of the problems of implementation: the transition to an independent status and the ensuing task of building a viable and responsible Formosan nation. Our emphasis is on the present and the future, rather than the past.

In exploring, inventing, and evaluating alternative courses of action, we have operated within the framework of the policy sciences. The policy sciences are concerned with analyzing the decision process in government and society, and with mobilizing all available knowledge for use in these decisions. In this way we seek to make our contribution to the ultimate goal—a world community of human dignity. It is our first responsibility and pleasure to acknowledge the fundamental contributions to this method (and its many applications) by our colleague, Myres S. McDougal, but in no way does this imply accountability on his part for the details of the present analysis or the specific proposals that we endorse.

Practical assistance for which we return thanks has come from Deans Eugene V. Rostow and Louis H. Pollak and their administrative associates at the Yale Law School, and especially from the Ogden Foundation in Mountainville, New York. We are particularly obligated to Mr. H. Peter Stern, Vice President of the Foundation, for his unfailing encouragement of the candid exploration of complex issues of government, law, and social process.

Working drafts of the book were distributed to scholars and officials specializing in Asian studies or international law and relations. It would be difficult to exaggerate the courtesies or the aid forthcoming from either the scholarly or the official community. Harassed with teaching, research, or consultation, or driven by the pressure of recurring crises, many people have nevertheless taken time to challenge, amplify, or otherwise contribute to an informal dialogue—in writing or conversation—that, if institutionalized and made continuing, would be a brilliant instance of what we call a "decision seminar." At the risk of imputing a policy preference not necessarily theirs or an authentication of detail to which they dissent, we cannot refrain from giving explicit thanks to at least a few, notably (in alphabetical order): Hayward R. Alker, Jr., Massachusetts Institute of Technology; A. Doak Barnett, Columbia University; Inis L. Claude, University of Michigan; Karl W. Deutsch, Harvard University; John K. Fairbank, Harvard University; Rosalyn Higgins, the Royal Institute of International

Affairs; Neil H. Jacoby, University of California, Los Angeles; Charles E. Lindblom, Yale University; Lucian W. Pye, Massachusetts Institute of Technology; Oscar Schachter, United Nations Institute of Teaching and Research; Egon Schwelb, Yale Law School; and Burns Weston, University of Iowa. For obvious reasons we must content ourselves with a blanket acknowledgment to officials and political personalities of all shades of opinion who are responsibly involved in public affairs.

It is gratifying to be more specific in acknowledging the abundant assistance of Rosann H. Bonaldo, Isabel Malone, Dorothy Egan, and Doris Moriarty, who executed our secretarial requests.

We are particularly fortunate in the alert, perceptive editing of the manuscript by Joan Levinson of St. Martin's Press.

L.C.C.

H.D.L.

Yale University, July, 1967

Contents

wei

An Emerging Nation

Independence—And After

Contents   xi

If I am not for myself, who will be for me?
If I am for myself only, what am I?
If not now—when?

THE TALMUD.

Formosa, China, and the United Nations

The Issue

THE CHINESE QUESTION has been a major issue in the United Nations and a principal problem for the foreign policy of the United States since the launching of the U.N. and the transfer of power on the mainland to the Communists. The United Nations has continued to exclude Peking and accept Chiang Kai-shek's government on Formosa as authorized to speak for "China." During recent years misgivings about U.N. policy have increased as the Peking government retains its grip on the mainland and becomes a member of the nuclear club. In the perspective of many decision-makers and commentators it has become more and more incongruous that the most inclusive organization expressly concerned with world security should fail to include the effective rulers of the most populous nation on earth. More than incongruity is involved. How can a comprehensive world public order be achieved under such conditions? How can there be progress by noncommunication? How can the clouds of war, whether localized in Southeastern Asia or expanded to the globe, be dissipated under the present circumstances of nonparticipation?

The foreign policy of the United States is as embarrassed by

the Chinese question as is the United Nations. The initial support given by the government of the U.S. to Chiang's government
in exile was an expression of fidelity to an old if not altogether
satisfactory ally and of friendship for as many surviving elements
of the mainland cataclysm as could reach the sanctuary of Formosa. Years of close association between American society and
modernizing groups in China created a network of interlocking
interests that were threatened and frustrated by the Communist
takeover. The takeover itself came with unexpected suddenness to
the overwhelming majority of Americans, and it precipitated a
sequence of measures not necessarily calculated to serve the principal long-term interests of the United States.

The widespread expectation that the Communist regime would
prove transitory has withered, notwithstanding the current upheavals on the China mainland caused by the "great proletariat
cultural revolution." The long-term concern of American policy
with world security—the principal objective sought through the
United Nations—has seemed less and less adequately served by
earlier commitments. The chronic failure of years of intermittent
talks at the ambassadorial level in Warsaw is not to be accounted
for by a single factor or by the refractoriness of a single issue.
Nevertheless one issue persists like a giant landslide blocking the
road to understanding. It is the Formosan question.

When a whole spectrum of acute problems—ranging from the
status of Formosa, recognition, establishment of diplomatic relations, cultural exchange, trade, U.N. participation, wars of national
liberation, to nonproliferation of nuclear weapons—demands simultaneous solution, there seems to be no practicable order of priority
nor any guide out of the labyrinth. Policy advisors are baffled, and
decision-makers hesitate to act. Useful though mincing steps to
further common interests are put off again and again, in the elusive hope that a grandiose design aimed to "kill all birds with one
stone" can be found.

A fresh way to tackle the China dilemma is to start with the most fundamental issue by focusing on Formosa. If this perplexing problem can be illuminated, a much-needed sense of priority and proportion can be generated. Such an approach opens up the possibility of initiating a series of practical acts that would otherwise be postponed or overlooked, and which could make a timely contribution to solving an entanglement that defies a packaged solution.

The continuing victory of the United States in the Chinese participation question in the United Nations portends not solution but further gathering of the storm. Most certainly that issue will press for an early and serious solution in the immediate future. While the hostility generated by Peking's campaign of hatred and Washington's policy of "containment" may continue for some time, it is not out of the question that the U.N. may soon set out on a new course in regard to Chinese participation, even if strong U.S. opposition continues.

In seeking a solution to "China's" participation in the world body, attention immediately and inevitably centers on Formosa's status. Under these circumstances it is hardly advisable to continue the usual practice of treating the problem of Formosa casually. What is needed is a comprehensive study in depth of all that is at stake. Such a study can point to a wider range of policy options than are currently perceived either by leading figures in the U.N. or in Washington.

A thoroughgoing examination of Formosa's significance can contribute to the reconsideration of many relatively antiquated and unrealistic images presently shared by many leaders of American official and nonofficial life. For example, most Americans are under the impression that while Chiang Kai-shek can no longer be taken seriously as a spokesman for the hundreds of millions of mainland Chinese, he can at least be accepted as a genuine voice of Formosa. These Americans are sure to be shocked when they are presented with a critical re-evaluation of this "truth." But as usual Americans do not like to be fooled, and will eventually be grateful for a more realistic conception—that a neglected dimension of the Formosan problem, hence of the U.N. participation issue, is the principle of self-determination. When the situation is redefined, its problematic character will not dry up and blow away. On the contrary, new though manageable questions will arise. These issues, however, will be relevant to the reality; they will no longer depend on the dream world of defeated politicians and the impulsive generosity of well-meaning if misguided friends.

The present study must begin by scrutinizing the questions related to Chinese participation in the United Nations. In view of the legalistic tangle in which these matters are usually discussed, we shall chart a path through the current confusion before proceeding to the affirmative lines of policy that are, in fact, open in the situation. The agenda of our presentation, therefore, is: (1) the question of Chinese participation in the United Nations; (2) the applicability of the principle of self-determination to Formosa; (3) the provisional and transitional measures essential to Formosa's independence; and (4) a blueprint for building an independent Formosan nation state.

An Emerging Alternative: "One China, One Formosa"

CHAPTER ONE

China in the United Nations

"CHINA" WAS ONE of the four major powers that issued invitations to the founding conference of the United Nations at San Francisco in 1945. In power then was the Nationalist government headed by Generalissimo Chiang Kai-shek. But in October 1949, victors in the civil war with the Kuomintang, the Communist forces led by Mao Tse-tung established the Central People's Government of the "People's Republic of China."* In December 1949 the Nationalist government retreated to Taiwan—then a Japanese territory under Allied belligerent occupation—but continued to send a delegation to the United Nations.

On November 18, 1949, the Foreign Minister of the People's Republic of China sent a note to the President of the General

---

* Officially Communist China is called the "People's Republic of China" and Chiang Kai-shek's Nationalist China is the "Republic of China"; we shall not stick only to these official titles. Unless specified otherwise, "Formosa" includes the Pescadores and is used interchangeably with "Taiwan." The "people of Formosa" or the "Formosan people" refers to all the inhabitants on the island, regardless of origin. Exiles from the mainland are designated "mainland Chinese"; the eleven million native Formosans, including some 200,000 aborigines, are referred to as "native Formosans," "Formosans," or "natives."

Assembly, repudiating the legal status of the Nationalist delegation under T. F. Tsiang and denying his formal authority to speak on behalf of the Chinese people in the United Nations. On December 29, 1949, the representative of the Soviet Union in the Security Council, in support of Peking's claim, challenged the competence of the "representative of the Kuomintang group" to represent China and the Chinese people in the Council. No action was taken since the matter had not been included in the provisional agenda.

The question was again considered by the Security Council in 1950. Shortly after the arena of dispute was transferred to the General Assembly at its fifth session, 1950–51. Since then the question of Chinese participation has vexed every session of the General Assembly.

In 1950 the General Assembly dealt with the substantive question in both general and specific terms. From 1951 to 1960 annually the Assembly decided to postpone consideration of the Chinese participation question at each session by rejecting proposals to include the item officially in its agenda. This decade was known as the "moratorium period." In 1961 the strategy of a moratorium was abandoned, and the question of Chinese participation has since then been included in the Assembly's agenda and squarely considered in substance. Decisions thus far taken have been in favor of the Chinese Nationalist regime. The Nationalist regime has continued to represent the "Republic of China" in all organs of the United Nations, and Communist China continues to be excluded from participation in the United Nations.

The Claimants and
Types of Claim

BEFORE we specify the various claims, a brief remark on three theories of the participation question is in order: the "credentials" theory, the "representation" theory, and the "admission" theory.

In the perspective of the "credentials" theory, the question of "China's" participation is simply a matter of the "authority of a delegation" to represent a government—with special reference to the authenticity of the credentials, the identity of the delegates, and the scope of authorized powers. As a general rule, the problem of credentials is considered a "procedural matter" to be decided by simple majority in the General Assembly and not subject to "veto" in the Security Council.[1]

According to the "representation" theory, the question arises from a change of "government" in a particular member state. As expressly provided by the Charter, "China" is an original member of the United Nations and a permanent member of the Security Council (Article 23(1)); hence China's "membership" is not at issue. Unlike a credentials case, the question is not the "authority of a delegation" to "represent a government," but "the authority of a government" to "represent a particular member state." The problem is to choose which of the two rival governments really "represents" a particular member state. Whether or not this is entitled to be called an "important question" to be decided by a two-thirds majority in the General Assembly (Article 18(2) of the Charter) or a "substantive matter" subject to veto in the Security Council (Article 27(3) of the Charter) has caused considerable controversy. In 1961 the General Assembly decided that "any proposal to change the representation of China" was an important question, and this decision was reaffirmed in 1965 and 1966.

The "admission theory" holds that the question is a matter of "admission to membership" in the United Nations of a new nation —the "People's Republic of China." The assumption is that so many changes have occurred in the body politic on the mainland that Communist China is not the same entity which was an original member of the United Nations. According to Article 4 of the Charter, membership in the United Nations is open to "peace-loving" states, "able and willing" to carry out Charter obligations; and admission is to be decided by the General Assembly "upon the recommendation of the Security Council." This means that the veto power of the permanent members of the Security Council is applicable (Article 27(3)).

These legal theories have occasioned embittered debate; they fall short of clarifying the underlying community policies as guides to solving this complicated problem. Instead of couching their claims strictly in terms of legal technicality, the claimants have formulated them by referring to outcomes they seek to achieve. Hence the various claims can be summarized as follows:

1] The claim to substitute Communist China for Nationalist China has been the position of Communist China since 1949. The Soviet Union and India have at different times been active on behalf of Peking; most recently Albania and Cambodia have taken over this role. The claim seeks justification by asserting that the Communist government in Peking, presently in control over nearly all Chinese territory, is entitled to represent "China" and to replace the Nationalist delegation in all organs and specialized agencies of the United Nations.

2] The claim to continue to exclude Communist China's participation is the position of Nationalist China and has been strongly championed by the United States since the participation question arose. The claim seeks justification on the ground that despite the limited effective control presently exercised by the Nationalist government, it is still the authoritative government to represent "China" in the United Nations.[2]

3] The claim to include both Communist China and Nationalist China in the United Nations was suggested in 1961, notably by Nigeria and Sierra Leone. At the twenty-first Assembly in 1966, the Canadian delegation prominently articulated this position in considerable detail, though a formal proposal was withheld. This claim involves two alternatives: to continue Nationalist China in possession of seats in both the General Assembly and the Security Council and seat Communist China only in the General Assembly; or to give Communist China seats in both the General Assembly and the Security Council, leaving Nationalist China with a seat solely in the General Assembly. The claim seeks justification on the theory that two "successor" states are in existence as a result of the Chinese civil war of 1949—the People's Republic of China on the mainland and the Republic of China in Formosa. Which should be seated in the Security Council depends upon which China is believed to represent the original "China" as embodied in Article 23(1) of the Charter. Interpretation one way or another depends in part on the customary international law of state succession.

4] The claim to substitute Communist China for Nationalist China and to admit Formosa to membership in the United Nations assumes that Communist China is the authoritative representative of "China" and hence replaces the Nationalist delegation in all organs of the United Nations. But Peking's claim that Taiwan is part of China is to be rejected. Formosa is to become an independent state through self-determination and to be admitted to the United Nations. This alternative, based on the assumption that the legal status of Formosa in international law has remained undetermined since it was emancipated from Japan after World War II, has been advocated by native Formosans. To an increasing extent, the United Kingdom and France have displayed, implicitly if not explicitly, a sympathetic attitude to this alternative. Ireland was explicit when in 1966 its delegate stated in the Assembly that the question of "the representation of China" should be properly described as "the question of the representation of China and of Formosa in the United Nations."

5] There is a claim to defer decision on the question of China's participation pending adequate Charter amendment to eliminate China as a permanent member of the Security Council. It is argued that since a basic complication of the entire controversy arises from China's status as a permanent member of the Security Council, a Charter amendment to eliminate China's seat in the Security Council may facilitate the solution of the controversy.

6] The claim to exclude the participation of both Communist China and Nationalist China in the United Nations is made just because the question is so highly controversial. The issue is to be left entirely to resolution by direct negotiation between Communist China and Nationalist China outside the framework of the United Nations.

Authoritative Decision-Makers

THE CHINESE participation question was initially considered in substance by the Security Council. In January 1950 the Foreign Minister of Communist China informed the governments of states represented on the Security Council that the Kuomintang delegation in the Council was "illegal" and hence should be "expelled." Two days later, the representative of the Soviet Union formally requested the exclusion of the representative of "the Kuomintang group" from the Council. When this request was defeated, the delegation of the Soviet Union walked out of the Security Council, denying the validity of any decision the Security Council arrived at with the participation of representatives of the "Kuomintang group." Shortly after the outbreak of the Korean war, the Soviet delegation returned and assumed the presidency of the Security Council in August 1950. The ruling by President Malik to exclude the representatives of the "Kuomintang group" from the Council's meetings was challenged and overruled by the Council.

The consideration of the participation question by the Security Council was discontinued when the General Assembly on December 14, 1950, adopted a resolution that dealt with competing claims to participation in United Nations organs. The Resolution 396(V) reads in part:

The General Assembly,
    Considering that difficulties may arise regarding the representation of a Member State in the United Nations and that

there is a risk that conflicting decisions may be reached by its various organs, . . .

Considering that, in virtue of its composition, the General Assembly is the organ in the United Nations in which consideration can best be given to the views of all Member States in matters affecting the functioning of the Organization as a whole; . . .

2. *Recommends* that, when any such question arises, it should be considered by the General Assembly, or by the Interim Committee if the General Assembly is not in session;

3. *Recommends* that the attitude adopted by the General Assembly or its Interim Committee concerning any such question should be taken into account in other organs of the United Nations and in the specialized agencies; . . .

Although the General Assembly resolution was not designed to deprive the Security Council of competence to determine representation in that organ under its own rules of procedure, the arena of subsequent debate on China's participation was henceforth transferred to the General Assembly. Both the United States and the Soviet Union consider it politically expedient to confine the participation issue to the Assembly.

This perplexing question has been raised each year in various ways, not only in the General Assembly, but also in the other Councils, the specialized agencies, and in many subsidiary bodies, including subcommittees whose nature is purely technical.[3] In the analysis to follow, however, our attention will focus primarily on the General Assembly. Although it is generally accepted that each organ or body is the authoritative decision-maker in regard to its own membership, all components of the United Nations have given special deference to the Assembly, or postponed consideration out of a desire for the question to be decided by some "higher body."[4] To avoid the difficulties that might arise from conflicting decisions by different organs, the agencies will probably continue to hesitate to act until the Assembly has. So far as the Security

Council is concerned, given the complexities of the "veto," it appears unlikely that action by the Security Council will precede decision by the Assembly. As a matter of fact, major participants have found it prudent and expedient not to stir up emotion in the Council.

The role of the General Assembly has undergone a significant evolution since the founding of the United Nations. The United Nations was organized on the assumption that the primary responsibility for maintaining international peace and security rested with the major powers. In his report to Congress, Secretary Stettinius stated:

> Perhaps the basic difference between the constitutional arrangement of the United Nations and that of the League of Nations is that instead of the Assembly and the Council having identical functions, as was the case under the League, the General Assembly and the Security Council will each have different functions assigned to it. The General Assembly is primarily a body for deliberation and recommendation, while the Security Council is given powers to act in maintenance of international peace and security whenever it deems necessary.[5]

While the Security Council, charged with primary responsibility for maintaining minimum world public order, operated on a permanent basis to deal with any crisis or dispute, the General Assembly met in regular session once a year with a more limited scope of competence.

The effectiveness of the Security Council was soon paralyzed by the cold war—with the United States and the Soviet Union as chief opponents. In view of the deadlock in the Security Council, the General Assembly was asked to deal with important questions affecting international peace and security. The "uniting for peace" resolution in 1950 made it possible for the Assembly to convene within twenty-four hours in emergency session.[6] This was the opening of a new epoch for the General Assembly. Its role was significantly increased in 1956 in response to the Suez Canal crisis when the United Nations Emergency Force was created. By 1961 it was clear that in one way or another the United Nations was able to act to maintain world public order despite the paralysis of the Security Council. While such a shift was initially prompted by the efforts of the United States to nullify Soviet veto power in the Security Council, the rising assertiveness of most of the smaller powers was a factor in the change.[7] As a result of the influx of "nonaligned" nations, the major powers have concentrated their efforts in positive attempts to win friends and influence people in the General Assembly rather than in negative strategies designed to block Security Council action.

Though there is still a tendency to submit crucial issues in the first instance to the Security Council, inaction in the Council does not automatically preclude the Assembly from action. Therefore in 1967 the role of the General Assembly is more important than had been envisaged at San Francisco in 1945, despite the recent efforts of some powers during the arrears case to revert to 1945. The growth of the United Nations from its original 51 members in 1945 to 122 in 1967 emphasizes that the General Assembly is the only organ of the United Nations representing all members. The Assembly is the sole organ in which the expectations entertained by the entire membership can be directly articulated.

With this constitutive change in mind, it is reasonable to predict that the General Assembly will set the pace in settling the question of Chinese participation. Any decision taken by the Assembly will have a decisive effect on action by other U.N. organs and bodies. As long as the General Assembly supports the status quo, the chances are that all other bodies will withstand pressure to take action that would be regarded by their members as premature. Moreover, once the Chinese Communist regime is seated in the General Assembly a chain reaction will influence decisions in other organs or bodies. It is therefore warranted to devote primary attention to the decision process of the General Assembly.

Fundamental Community
Policies

THE INDISPENSABLE step toward a solution of the vital problem of Chinese participation in the U.N. must clarify the community policies that guide decision-makers. This task, difficult as it may appear, is intellectually possible. The several interests at stake can be identified, and if we address ourselves to the authoritative decision-makers—notably the Assembly—it is feasible to draw their attention to the community values and policies at stake.

Any decision on Chinese participation will have a far-reaching impact on world public order and the decision process of the United Nations in future years. At stake is whether one-fourth of the world's population can join in the formulation and execution of decisions in the world community. Though the role of the Security Council has not been constant, a permanent seat is still the most important source of authorized power in the United Nations. A seat in the General Assembly enables a participant to operate in a worldwide arena. Participation in other organs, bodies, and various specialized agencies affects activities in economic, welfare, and other areas, including the protection and promotion of human rights, the development of international law, economic development through the allocation of capital and technical assistance, the dissemination of skills and of knowledge related to well-being, improving international labor practice, the peaceful uses of atomic energy, and the cooperative ventures in space. Participation in the Secretariat not only affords an opportunity to affect administrative activities, but opens a wide channel for obtaining many kinds of intelligence.

Outside the framework of the United Nations, the potential values at stake in the membership controversy are equally great. The inclusion of a regime that has long been denied access to the world organization would greatly enhance its international prestige and its power position. The heaviest impact of a transfer of "China's" seat on the Security Council would be felt in Formosa, whose security is always threatened by Communist China. Other states neighboring Communist China would also be affected. While these nations and a majority of overseas Chinese will sooner or later reconcile themselves with the "shadow" presence of the giant of Communist China, formal participation in the United Nations would hasten this trend, particularly in Southeast Asia. Japan and India, long regarded as counterforces against Communist China's expansion, would be constrained to reappraise their policies accordingly. Participation in the U.N. would smooth the way to more relations at various levels, particularly trade between Communist China and Western or nonaligned nations. Within the Communist bloc, Peking's influence would be augmented. Developments of this kind, though upset by Peking's recent failures, have already been in the making, irrespective of the fact that the Peking government is excluded from the U.N. Mainland China's presence in the Council would make it necessary for the United States to re-examine its tactics if not its specific objectives in global politics.

This brief account facilitates a realistic grasp of the community policies at stake. Our fundamental goal is to find a solution that furthers the attainment by consent of a world public order in which values are shaped and shared on a wide scale, not a narrow one. An urgent task in moving toward a world of at least minimum public order is to create and nurture the predisposition of decision-makers to forego the unilateral use of military force in settling international disputes, particularly controversies over the acquisition of territory.

Ever since the founding of the United Nations, the government of the "Republic of China" has been the authoritative government representing China in the United Nations. Its authority, however, has been consistently challenged since the Nationalist government lost control of mainland China in 1949. The present situation, then, is that two rival governments confront each other with substantial military forces across the Formosan Straits, each claiming to be the authoritative government of all "China," and each threatening to conquer the territory presently controlled by the other. Each side has been assured by treaties of military assistance with one of the two major competing powers: the treaty of friendship, alliance, and mutual assistance between the Soviet Union and the People's Republic of China (February 15, 1950) on the one hand; and the mutual defense treaty between the United States and the Republic of China (December 2, 1954) on the other.[8]

As the Sino-Soviet rift reaches an irremediable point, it becomes a matter of speculation just how much if anything the existing paper alliance means to either Moscow or Peking. Nevertheless, it is beyond dispute that any question that affects public order in Asia is bound to affect the public order of the world at large. A conflict between Communist China and Formosa would almost inevitably escalate far beyond the Far East. Whatever arrangement is adopted, a principal point essential to the gradual attainment of the goal of minimum world order is that territorial changes must not be made in response to force or threat of force. This entirely excludes acquiescence by the U.N. in the addition of Formosa to the territory of mainland China, since Communist China has shown no sign of abandoning its claim to "liberate" Taiwan. Essential to any such solution is assurance of Formosa's security.

If the United Nations is to be the organ of world security, it should represent the world. To be effective it should reflect common demands and expectations on an inclusive and realistic basis. Universality is particularly necessary if we are to achieve a world order in which diverse social, political, and economic systems cooperate in peace and tolerance. One by-product of universality, and a result indispensable to the long-run aim of the U.N., is to establish a process of genuine communication. Without it, steps toward the peaceful settlement of disputes are bound to be faltering and inconclusive. Universality also brings with it the widest possible access to the base values required for the effective implementation of community policies. In an interdependent world the goal of wide shaping and sharing of all values ultimately calls for a scale of organized action that encompasses the globe.

Universality is a formalistic shell unless a degree of effective unity exists, a degree rather ambiguously known as the principle of "responsibility." This principle, derived from Article 4 of the Charter, assumes that participants should be "able" and "willing" to carry out Charter obligations. While the "ability" of a nation to discharge Charter obligations can be ascertained by the control the elite exercises over its resources, the test of "willingness" to fulfill Charter obligations is less a matter of fact judgment. However, the cause of unity is not served when the bases of inference for judging "willingness," and the procedures followed in arriving at an evaluation, are arbitrary. In the case of the two governments in this controversy over participation in the U.N., no objective third-party observer is likely to conclude that either government is not in control of its resources, such as they are in each case. The question of the degree of control over population is more open to question, as is "willingness" to fulfill obligations under the Charter. Estimates of willingness that have any validity for world order must point toward the future, and give weight to the possibility that a weak commitment may become stronger once the barriers to communication and collaboration have been reduced through formal participation in the United Nations. We are inclined to suggest that it is more important to gamble on the possibility of achieving a more responsible attitude by experience within the U.N. system than on the outside.

A fourth guide to the present case emerges from our examination of fundamental goals. Human rights are at stake—more specifically, the human rights of individuals under the rule of Communist China, of the people of Formosa, of the population of the world. Whatever policies are considered need to be evaluated according to their probable consequences for the human rights of all peoples affected. The human rights of the inhabitants of Formosa are not to be dismissed out of hand as though a "mere thirteen million people" are involved. A "mere thirteen million" is larger than two-thirds of the members of the United Nations. Our special concern with this aspect of the problem arises from the close linkage of the Chinese participation question and the status of Formosa, bearing in mind the uncertain legal status of Formosa after World War II and the persistent claims and threats of Communist China to "conquer" and "incorporate" Taiwan.

Any sound policy alternative in the Chinese participation question should be designed not only to enhance the United Nations as an instrument of the noncoercive settlement of controversies, but also as an instrument of human rights. The consideration of world public order, whether maximum or minimum,[9] obliges the U.N., and every serious commentator on world policy, to give full attention to the possible impacts of the U.N. participation question on the destinies of many people, including the populace of Formosa.

Trends in Past Decisions and Conditioning Factors

TO EXAMINE the trend of past decisions taken by the General Assembly on the question of Chinese participation, and to analyze the principal factors that have combined to produce the decisions, we shall make a contextual inquiry according to the following outline: active supporters; objectives; crisis factors in context; bases of power; strategies; outcomes; and effects.

Active Supporters

Since the participation question arose in 1950, while the United States has remained the staunchest champion of the continued participation of Nationalist China, the principal active supporters of Communist China have shifted. From 1950 to 1955 the Soviet Union was most active in Communist China's cause— no surprise in view of the close alliance between Moscow and Peking during the earlier years of Communist China's emergence. As a consequence of the Bandung Conference of April 1955, India became an active spokesman for Peking's participation by requesting that the question be placed on the General Assembly's agenda from 1956 to 1959, but it has ceased to do so since 1960 because of the Sino-Indian border conflicts. Thus in the following three years the U.S.S.R. again assumed the title role in urging Peking's participation in the U.N., though with every evidence of diminished enthusiasm. As the Sino-Soviet rift worsened, Albania loyally requested in 1963 the inclusion of an item entitled "Restoration of the lawful rights of the People's Republic of China in the United Nations." Joined by Cambodia, it introduced a draft resolution before the Assembly. In 1965 the proposal to seat Communist China was put forward jointly by twelve nations, which had attended the Conference of Heads of State or Government of Non-Aligned Countries held at Cairo in October 1964. In 1966 the proposal to seat Peking was cosponsored by eleven delegations: Albania, Algeria, Cambodia, Congo (Brazzaville), Cuba, Guinea, Mauritania, Mali, Pakistan, Romania, and Syria.

These changes signify the ideological and political estrangement between Communist China and the Soviet Union. The changing sponsorship of Communist China's cause is a significant reflection of the closeness or distance between Peking and the sponsoring powers.

Objectives

While strategies might differ in detail according to circumstances, the manifest objective sought by the United States as champion of Nationalist China is to exclude Communist China's participation in the United Nations and to enable the "Republic of China" to "challenge the claim of the Chinese Communists to represent the Chinese people."[10] This brief statement must be viewed in the wider context of United States policy toward Communist China since the outbreak of the Korean war. In order to "contain" Communist China, the United States has mobilized not only military instruments, but all other instruments of policy. As with the nonrecognition policy, the campaign to block Communist China's access to the world organization is evidently part of the overall effort to contain Chinese Communist expansionism.

On the other hand, for supporters of Peking's cause, while the manifest aim seems to replace Nationalist China by Communist China, it may not be quite so simple. For instance, it has sometimes been suggested that in spite of its efforts the Soviet Union might have no genuine interest in seeing Communist China seated in the world organization. Rather, it may prefer to perpetuate its monopoly position as the unchallenged spokesman of the Communist nations in the U.N.[11] Such an allegation, though beyond the possibility of immediate verification, is by no means farfetched, especially in light of the rift between Peking and Moscow.

While the proposal to include both Nationalist China (or Taiwan) and Communist China in the United Nations has not been formally submitted, a general drift in favor of this alternate has been apparent since 1961, and was highlighted by the articulate statement of the Canadian delegation in November 1966. This trend seems to have been prompted for the most part by the hope of stabilizing community expectations with full acknowledgment of the present realities of international life.

Crisis Factors in Context

The trends in the world situation that we have reviewed quickly depend for their continuation on various factor combinations that can be identified and evaluated. When the United

Nations came into being at the end of World War II, it was assumed that the concerted action of major powers was essential to maintain peace and security, and this view found expression in the special role conferred on the Security Council. It soon became clear, however, that such cooperation was hardly possible so long as the Russians remained obdurately opposed to free elections in the East European nations. The descending of an "iron curtain" across the European continent was met by a policy of "containment," which signified the coming of a new era—the "cold war." The implementation of the Truman Doctrine in March 1947 led to aid to Greece and Turkey, and to the defense against the Berlin blockade in June 1948; finally the North Atlantic Treaty Organization was formed in April 1949.

On the mainland of Asia, however, the story was different. After prolonged civil strife, the Chinese Communists eventually established the Central Government of the People's Republic of China and the Nationalists fled to Formosa. The conclusion of the alliance treaty between Moscow and Peking in February 1950 radically altered the balance of power in Asia. According to this treaty, a contracting party was committed to render "military and other assistance by all means at its disposal" to the other in the event that the other was attacked by Japan "or any state allied with it." Unmistakably the United States was the ultimate target.

The invasion of South Korea by Communist-dominated North Korea on June 25, 1950, heightened the tension in Asia. President Truman immediately proclaimed the "neutralization" of the Taiwan Straits and dispatched the United States Seventh Fleet, endeavoring not only to prevent an attack on Formosa by the Chinese Communists, but also to forestall invasion of mainland China by the Nationalist forces. Owing to the walkout of the Soviet representative in the Security Council, sending United Nations forces to repel aggression in Korea was formally authorized. The offensive launched by United Nations forces, however, was set back by the intervention of the armies of Communist China.

At the same time that Communist China brought formal complaints in the United Nations against the United States for "armed invasion of Taiwan," "bombing," and "violations of Chinese territory," Communist China was accused of "aggression against the Republic of Korea." Having previously condemned Communist China as an "aggressor," the United Nations passed a resolution on May 18, 1951, imposing an embargo on the export of "strategic materials" to Communist China. The resolution recommended that all member states "Apply an embargo on the shipment to areas under the control of the Central People's Government of the People's Republic of China and of the North Korean authorities of arms, ammunition and implements of war, atomic energy materials, petroleum, transportation materials of strategic value, and items useful in the production of arms, ammunition and implements of war."[12] At the initiative of the United States, a more extensive embargo against Communist China was subsequently imposed by the China Committee, consisting of fourteen Western nations and Japan. The war, which was not ended until July 1953, had the effect of hardening U.S. determination to support Chiang Kai-shek's regime in Formosa and prevent Communist China from "shooting [her] way into the United Nations."

In the meantime, the cold war took another turn. The nuclear monopoly of the United States was broken in August 1949 with a successful atomic test by the Soviet Union. Nuclear testing and the manufacture of nuclear armaments intensified on both sides, culminating in the launching of the Soviet Sputnik I in 1957.

Following the truce in Korea, international attention was drawn to the situation in Indochina, which soon became the concern of the Geneva Conference from April to July 1954. Indochina was divided into Cambodia, Laos, and Vietnam, and Vietnam was left a partitioned state.

In September 1954 the Chinese Communists began shelling the offshore islands held by the Chinese Nationalist forces. Efforts were made to bring about a cease-fire under United Nations' auspices, but no action was taken because of Communist China's insistence that the question was an "internal affair" of China.

In the hope of containing the expansion of Communist China in Southeastern Asia, the Southeast Asia Treaty Organization (SEATO) was formed on September 8, 1954. Formosa, however, was outside the treaty area. This gap was shortly filled by the conclusion of the mutual defense treaty between the United States and the Republic of China in December 1954, by the terms of which the United States would defend Formosa and the Pescadores and "such other territories as may be determined."[13] Because of the continuing crisis in the offshore islands, the U.S. Congress, even prior to the ratification of the mutual defense treaty, passed the so-called "Formosa resolution" authorizing the President to employ United States armed forces to protect Formosa and the Pescadores and related positions.[14]

The death of Stalin in March 1953 temporarily lessened international tension. The Afro-Asian Solidarity Conference at Bandung took place in April 1955, at which Chou En-lai played an important role by advocating the five principles of peaceful coexistence, even announcing his readiness to "enter into negotiation with the United States Government to discuss . . . especially the question of relaxing tension in the Taiwan area."[15] This paved the way for subsequent talks at Geneva from 1955 to 1957 between the United States and Communist China. As long as Communist China remained unwilling to renounce the use of force in the "liberation" of Taiwan, the United States was firm in refusing to withhold its forces from Taiwan. Subsequently, Peking offered the Nationalist regime an opportunity to negotiate the "peaceful liberation of Taiwan."[16]

On a higher level, the atmosphere of rapprochement with Russia also led to the abortive "summit" conference at Geneva in 1955. The "Geneva spirit," however, was soon disrupted by the dramatic events of 1956. In October of that year the Soviet Union suppressed by force a large-scale revolt in Hungary, and French, Israeli, and British forces invaded Egypt in the Suez Canal crisis.

In May 1957 the United Kingdom softened its embargo against Communist China; Japan and the Netherlands shortly followed suit. Repercussions spread to other members of the China Committee, with the exception of the United States. Since 1961, following a decline in trade relations between the Soviet Union and Communist China, Communist China has made substantial trade gains with Canada, Australia, West Germany, and more recently, France.

In February 1958 Communist China announced its intention to withdraw its forces from North Korea, and asked the United Nations forces to reciprocate. In August 1958 Communist China renewed large-scale shelling of Quemoy and Matsu. The United States took a firmer position than in 1954 on behalf of the Nationalist government, and the Soviet Union warned that an attack on Communist China was "an attack on the Soviet Union." The crisis of 1958 began to abate when both the United States and Communist China resumed their talks at Warsaw in September of that year. Communist China offered to negotiate a peace settlement with the Nationalists "on specific steps and conditions for the peaceful liberation of Taiwan," but was turned down on the eve of the opening of the thirteenth session of the General Assembly.[17] In March 1959 came the bloody suppression of the rebellion in Tibet by the Chinese Communists, and the question of Tibet was considered by the General Assembly. Granting political asylum to the Dalai Lama and the flare-up of border disputes between Communist China and India signified the beginning of a series of incidents which culminated in an armed conflict in October 1962.

In August 1960 Premier Chou En-lai proposed a nonaggression pact to create "a nuclear free zone" by Communist China, the United States, and all other nations confronting the Pacific.[18] The proposal, however, was not taken seriously.

Meanwhile, a significant change occurred within the United Nations. At its fifteenth session (1960–61), the United Nations admitted seventeen new states; all except Cyprus were newly independent nations of the African continent. This trend continued in subsequent sessions.

The cold war was undergoing profound changes as well. In the Communist world, the widening conflict between the Soviet Union and Communist China, first visible in late 1959, could no longer be kept under wraps. During the first decade of the existence of the Chinese Communists the assistance of the Soviet Union was indispensable to Communist China's security and economic development, but the relationship between Moscow and Peking "passed beyond the stage in which the master can guide the pupil, in which the stronger element can keep the weaker one in a state of permanent dependence through economic, political, and military superiority."[19] Their differences widened and sharpened during Khrushchev's regime.

Profoundly significant are changing relations between the United States and the Soviet Union. Recovering from the setback of the Bay of Pigs fiasco in early 1961, President Kennedy handled the Cuban missile crisis of October 1962 with great effect. Acknowledging their common interest of survival in the nuclear age and the emerging threat of Communist China, the United States and the Soviet Union began to give evidence of a new course in their mutual relations. The conclusion of the nuclear test-ban treaty on August 5, 1963, was symbolic of the new direction. While Peking's threats to the United States are largely potential, the present Russian challenge is undoubtedly real and formidable. More recently, the assassination of President Kennedy and the ouster of Khrushchev have created a period of wait-and-see on both sides. Nonetheless both the United States and the Soviet Union seem to have achieved unprecedented stability in their mutual relations—and this new stability promises to outlast future strains.

In January 1964 the French government recognized Communist China and established diplomatic relations with Peking. Communist China, on its part, successfully exploded its first atomic bomb on October 16, 1964. It is worth noting that neither France nor Communist China is party to the nuclear test-ban treaty, even though an overwhelming majority of countries have acceded to it. At the nineteenth session, the United Nations was in a state of practical "inaction" because of the fiscal and political crisis stemming from the arrears case.

The rapid multiplication of Afro-Asian nations led to an increased demand for enlarging the membership of the Security Council and the Economic and Social Council. Hence, in 1963, the Assembly resolved to submit to member states for ratification relevant Charter amendments which would increase the size of the Security Council from 11 to 15, and the Economic and Social Council from 18 to 27. Although the Communists made an initial effort to place the transfer of China's seat from the Nationalist to the Communist government as a precondition to their ratification, amendments to Articles 23, 27, and 61 of the Charter came into effect on August 31, 1965, in spite of the continued exclusion of the Peking regime from the U.N.

The "inaction" of the nineteenth session was not continued at the twentieth. But the escalation of the Vietnam war dominated the mood of the twentieth session of the Assembly. Throughout the twenty-first Assembly in 1966, the escalation of the Vietnam war continued to be uppermost in delegates' minds; meanwhile, an attentive world witnessed the upheavals on mainland China under the "great proletariat cultural revolution" waged by the Red Guards.

Bases of Power

In evaluating the bases of power at the disposal of rival participants in the past process of decision, particular attention must be given to the relative influence of the United States and the Soviet Union upon other member states; the change in the quantity and quality of U.N. membership; and the changing relation of Nationalist China and Communist China with member states.

The question of China's participation was, from its very beginning, beset by cold-war overtones. Hence the outcome of past decisions was greatly affected by the relative influence of the United States and the Soviet Union upon other member states. As a means of estimating the impact of the United States and the Soviet Union upon a member state, the total network of relations between the two major powers and the particular state must be analyzed. The most revealing single indicator is the presence or absence of an alliance.

In its efforts to "contain" the expansion of world Communism, the United States has since 1947 established a global network of mutual defense arrangements. This network includes the Organization of American States, formed in April 1948; North Atlantic Treaty Organization, formed in April 1949; Tripartite Security (ANZUS) Treaty; Mutual Defense Treaty with Philippines, 1951; U.S.-Japanese Treaty, January 1960; Southeast Asia Treaty Organization, September 1954; Mutual Defense Treaty with the Republic of China, December 1954; and the Central Treaty Organization, signed November 1955. By the end of 1955, of the 60 U.N. members, 43 nations were formally aligned with the United States. On the other hand, the bloc led by the U.S.S.R. was composed of only nine member states, including Byelorussian and Ukrainian SSR, as a result of the conclusion of the Warsaw Pact on May 14, 1955. (Albania, Bulgaria, Hungary, and Romania were not admitted to the United Nations until December 1955.) This brief comparison clearly demonstrates the relative weight of the United States and the Soviet Union in the General Assembly. With minor or negligible exceptions, the allies of the United States were the hard core of U.S. power in affecting the decisions of the United Nations, including those relating to the Chinese participation question. These nations constituted an absolute majority—the "mechanical majority"—in the General Assembly prior to 1960. So long as the "mechanical majority" was stable, United States influence was decisive.

Such stability, however, can no longer be assured as a result of the influx beginning in 1960 of African members, who generally proclaim themselves as "nonaligned" in the conduct of foreign relations. These new states have attempted in most cases to keep away from cold-war issues. They proudly identify their role as providing a bridge between the two competing blocs, as disinterested observers with an "objective" judgment in cold-war issues. It was their presence in the General Assembly that suddenly changed the balance of power in the United Nations. No longer could the United States count on the "mechanical majority" in its efforts to exclude Communist China from participation. The U.S. abandoned the "moratorium" strategy in 1961 largely as a concession to the changing pattern of bloc politics in the United Nations.

Since its founding the United Nations has undergone substantial structural changes, especially in the years marked by rapid increase of membership. The United Nations of 1967 is indeed a different organization from that conceived in 1945. Its present composition vividly reflects the emergence of the Afro-Asian nations. In 1945, 12 of the 51 original members were from the Afro-Asian continents; as of February 1967 the 66 Afro-Asian members (39 African, 27 Asian) constitute more than half of the total membership (122).

Although most of the Asian nations had been admitted to the United Nations before 1958, more than two-thirds of the African states had not achieved independence nor become members until 1960 and after. Up to 1959, when the total roster reached 82, while the African states were increasing their participation from 4 to 10 the Asian members rose from 9 to 21. In 1960—what was known to be "the African year"—all except one of the 17 newly admitted members were African nations. The impact of such an increase was felt immediately. It was most emphatically symbolized by the ending of the "moratorium period" in 1961.

The net effect of the abrupt increase of Afro-Asian nations has been amplified by the expanded role of the General Assembly, and by the shifting pattern of bloc politics within the United Nations. The changing composition of the arena has also affected the strategies employed by any participant seeking to influence decision outcomes. We shall later be concerned with the significance of these strategies for the question of Chinese participation.

The composition of formal authority in the world arena is affected by more arrangements than those explicitly involved in the structure of the U.N. We shall therefore give attention to the practices of "recognition" or "nonrecognition." While it is widely held that there is no necessary link between "recognition" of a new government or state by an individual country, and "representation" in the U.N., the consideration of "recognition" or "nonrecognition" does weigh heavily in shaping an individual member's decisions about the Chinese "participation" question. Recognition granted by a member state to either of the two competing claimants (Nationalist China and Communist China) is without question a great asset for the beneficiary. So long as the United States controlled the "mechanical majority," this element played a secondary role. With the declining influence of the United States since 1960, efforts to win support of the newly admitted members have been crucial for Nationalist China.

The year 1949 was the darkest hour for the Nationalist regime. During the winter of 1949–50, the Communist nations led by the Soviet Union extended diplomatic recognition to the Chinese Communists; and Burma, India, Pakistan, the United Kingdom, Norway, Ceylon, Denmark, Israel, Afghanistan, Finland, Sweden, Switzerland, and Indonesia shortly followed. The general assumption was that there was no future for the runaway Nationalist regime on Taiwan. The outbreak of the Korean war in June 1950, however, suddenly changed the whole picture and arrested the tide of diplomatic recognition of Communist China. From the spring of 1950 to mid-1955, not a single state extended diplomatic recognition to the Peking government, which assured Nationalist China of considerable stability in dealing with other nations. During the same period no nation was admitted into the United Nations. In 1955 the trend altered swiftly with the package entry of sixteen nations, several of whom were newly independent. The Bandung Conference of 1955 marked a victory for the diplomacy of Communist China. In 1956 a storm burst in the Middle East: Egypt, Syria, and Yemen successively broke off diplomatic relations with the Nationalist regime and extended diplomatic recognition to the Peking government. Added to this setback for the Nationalists, only 4 of 16 members admitted to the U.N. in the preceding year voted in favor of the moratorium proposal in 1956. Confronted with this new situation, the Nationalist regime has since 1957 been engaged in an unceasing diplomatic campaign to win the support of friendly nations in Latin America, the Middle East, and, recently, Africa. In 1959, 42 member states recognized Nationalist China, 34 recognized Communist China, and 5 recognized neither. As of December 1966 there were 60 member states recognizing Nationalist China, 46 recognizing Communist China, and 15 recognizing neither.

The relation of non-African nations with both Communist China and Nationalist China is on the whole stable, barring radical upheavals in the internal politics of individual nations. The relation of the two rivals with African nations is, however, comparatively precarious and temporary. Africa has become the chief arena for the pursuit of votes by the Nationalist and Communist regimes since 1960. While Communist China has maintained a relatively indifferent attitude toward winning support for U.N. participation, Nationalist China has spared no effort to promote friendly relations with African members, hoping to translate success into support on the participation question. Efforts to cultivate friendly relations with African nations of the former French territories, though somewhat adversely affected by French recognition of Peking in January 1964, was a relative success compared to Peking's recent setbacks in Africa.

Whatever short-term gains may be scored by either side, the result is more transitory than permanent, since African nations are on the whole still in a period of appraisal and reappraisal. Commitments, often inherited from the former colonial powers or dictated by expedient considerations, are relatively unstable and not immune to instant change. For example in November 1965, of the 37 African member states in the U.N., 19 had diplomatic relations with Peking, 14 with Taiwan, and 4 with neither. As of November 1966, however, 15 had diplomatic relations with Peking, 18 with Taiwan, and 6 with neither.[20]

Strategies

The Chinese participation question has passed through three stages in the General Assembly: substantive discussions in 1950; the "moratorium period" from 1951 to 1960; and substantive considerations since 1961.

In 1950 the participation question was examined by both the General Assembly and the Security Council. The General Assembly treated the question under two headings: considerations with specific reference to the Chinese participation question, and general consideration of the question of "Recognition by the United Nations of the Representation of a Member State." The substance of the question was squarely faced.

From 1951 to 1960 the issue was disposed of under the "moratorium" formula. Despite requests at each regular session, the Assembly persistently rejected any initiative to include the Chinese participation question on the agenda. The substance of the problem was not formally considered at all. The question was raised as a point of order at the opening meetings of the Assembly, or in connection with the report of the Assembly's credentials committee, or it took the form of a formal proposal for placing the item on the Assembly's agenda. These procedural maneuvers had the effect of excluding Communist China's participation year after year.

In 1961 because of changed conditions and a heightened demand, the Chinese question was included in the Assembly's agenda and received thoroughly substantive consideration. Since then—with the exception of "nonvoting" in 1964—the General Assembly has dealt squarely with the issue.

The general question of "Recognition by the United Nations of the Representation of a Member State" was referred by the Assembly in 1950 to the *ad hoc* political committee. With this general question, both Cuba and the United Kingdom submitted draft resolutions, seeking to provide guiding criteria and procedures for the United Nations to "decide on the capacity or right of a Government to represent a Member State within the Organization." The Cuban proposal suggested the following criteria: (*a*) effective authority over the national territory; (*b*) the general consent of the population; (*c*) ability and willingness to achieve the purposes of the Charter, to observe its principles, and to fulfill the international obligations of the state; and (*d*) respect for human rights and fundamental freedoms. Unlike the Cuban proposal, the British proposal emphasized the desirability and practical usefulness of attempting to employ an "objective" test. Thus it was submitted that "the right of a Government to represent the Member State concerned in the United Nations should be recognized if that Government exercises effective control and authority over all or nearly all of the national territory, and has the obedience of the bulk of the population of that territory, in such a way that this control, authority, and obedience appeared to be of a permanent character."[21]

In connection with the specific question of the Chinese participation, four draft resolutions were submitted before the General Assembly in 1950. The first was an Indian proposal calling for the representation of the Central Government of the People's Republic of China on the basis of its effective control over the territory and population. The Soviet Union submitted two draft resolutions: one would expel "the representative of the Kuomintang group"; the other would invite the participation of the representatives of the Central Government of the People's Republic of China. The fourth was a Canadian proposal to establish a special committee to study and report back subsequent to Assembly consideration on the agenda item entitled "Recognition by the United Nations of the Representation of a Member State." And pending the special committee's report, the Nationalist delegation would remain seated in the United Nations.

The content of proposals under the "moratorium" formula, as put forward by the United States during the moratorium period (1951–1960), was very different indeed. A standard formulation was as follows:

> *The General Assembly*
> 1. *Decides* to reject the request of ＿＿＿ for the inclusion in the agenda of its ＿＿＿ regular session of the item entitled 'Question of the representation of China in the United Nations,'
> 2. *Decides* not to consider, at its ＿＿＿ regular session, any proposals to exclude the representatives of the Government of the Republic of China or to seat representatives of the Central People's Government of the People's Republic of China.

It is to be noted that while the proposals of 1951 to 1953 contained the language "to postpone . . . consideration of all proposals to exclude . . . ," those of 1954 to 1960 used "not to consider . . . any proposals to exclude . . ."

In 1961, because of the changing pattern of bloc politics in the United Nations, the United States abandoned its strategy of moratorium. Responding to the growing demand for a thorough substantive discussion, the General Assembly decided to include the following items in its agenda and consider them jointly: "Question of the representation of China in the United Nations" (proposed by New Zealand); and "restoration of the lawful rights of the People's Republic of China" (proposed by the U.S.S.R.). For the first time since 1951 the substance of the question was directly argued. The U.S.S.R. submitted a draft resolution, declaring that "only representatives of the Government of the People's Republic of China are competent to occupy China's place in the United Nations and all its organs," therefore proposed to "remove immediately from all United Nations organs the representatives of the Chiang Kai-shek clique who are unlawfully occupying the place of China in the United Nations," and to "invite the Government of the People's Republic of China to send its representatives to participate in the work of the United Nations and of all its organs."[22] Cambodia, Ceylon, and Indonesia submitted an amendment to the U.S.S.R.'s draft resolution, seeking to replace the offensive language of the operative paragraphs of the Soviet text with a single provision whereby the Assembly would decide "in accordance with the above declaration (i.e., the preamble of the U.S.S.R. proposal) that the representatives of the Government of the People's Republic of China be seated in the United Nations and all its organs."[23] In the meantime another draft resolution was submitted by Australia, Colombia, Italy, Japan, and the United States—the "five-power proposal." Unlike the Soviet draft resolution, the five-power proposal urged the General Assembly to "decide" that "in accordance with Article 18 of the Charter of the United Nations, any proposal to change the representation of China is an important question." The significance of this formulation lies in the fact that according to Article 18 General Assembly decisions on an "important" question must be made by a two-thirds majority rather than a simple majority.

In 1962 and 1963 only the item "Restoration of the lawful rights of the People's Republic of China" was included in the agenda. The content of the draft resolutions, as submitted by the U.S.S.R. in 1962 and by Albania and Cambodia in 1963, was practically identical with the one submitted by the U.S.S.R. in 1961. In 1965, while the nonaligned nations submitted a "twelve-power proposal" in order to seat Peking and to oust Taiwan, pro-Nationalist nations advanced an "eleven-power proposal," which would reaffirm that "any proposal to change the representation of China is an important question."

In 1966 the two contending proposals of 1965 were reintroduced before the General Assembly. In addition, the Italian delegation, along with Belgium, Bolivia, Brazil, Chile, and Trinidad and Tobago, made a surprise move by submitting a six-power proposal, which read in part:

> *The General Assembly,* . . .
>
> *Believing* that the complexities of this question require the most searching consideration in order to pave the way to an appropriate solution, taking into account the existing situation and the political realities of the area,
>
> 1. *Decides* to establish a Committee of . . . Member States, to be appointed by the General Assembly, with the mandate of exploring and studying the situation in all its aspects in order to make the appropriate recommendations to the General Assembly at its twenty-second session for an equitable and practical solution to the question of the representation of China in the United Nations, in keeping with the principles and purposes of the Charter;
>
> 2. *Appeals* to all Governments concerned to give assistance to the Committee in its search for such a solution.[24]

With respect to the consideration of the general questions in 1950, the subcommittee established by the *ad hoc* political committee recommended that whenever more than one authority claimed the right to represent a member state in the United Nations, the question should be considered in the light of the principles and purposes of the Charter and the circumstances of each case. The following factors, among others, should be considered: the extent of effective control over the territory and the degree of general acceptance by the population; the willingness to accept responsibility for discharging Charter obligations, and the degree of "legitimacy," as measured by internal processes.

This general orientation was reflected in the course of debate on the Chinese participation question in 1950. A great deal of attention was devoted to examining and comparing the nature of the newly established Communist regime and the old Nationalist regime—the degree of "effective control" over territory and people, "legitimacy," "stability and permanency." Furthermore, despite Secretary-General Lie's effort to dispel the linkage between "recognition" by individual nation and "representation" in the United Nations, the external relations of both regimes with other nations —recognition or nonrecognition—were given significant weight. These concerns were clearly understandable in view of the brief existence of the new regime. Therefore, while the Indian delegate supported the Chinese Communist regime on the grounds of "effective control" and "recognition," the Soviet representative repudiated the Nationalist delegation as belonging to the remnants of a political regime which had been overthrown. Quoting from *The Stilwell Papers*, the Soviet spokesman described the Kuomintang group as a "gang of thugs whose sole purpose was to clutch power and maintain their machine in power." On the other hand, the representative of Nationalist China identified the Communist regime as an "illegitimate puppet" of Soviet Russia. The relevance of "consent" and "legitimacy" was echoed by the Australian delegate. The United States delegate counseled caution by pointing out that while forty-three member states of the United Nations continued to recognize the Nationalist Government, only sixteen recognized the Chinese Communist regime.

The principal issue during the "moratorium" period was whether to include the participation question in the Assembly's agendas: hence the debate centered around the "appropriateness" of considering the question in substance. Among supporters of the moratorium proposals, the principal contention was that since views regarding China's participation were fundamentally and deeply divided the discussion of this "passionate controversy" would be "untimely," and would do no good but "poison the international atmosphere." It was generally agreed that while the Chinese Communist regime was waging war against the United Nations forces in Korea from 1950–53, it would be untimely for the United Nations to decide the participation issue. The truce in Korea was followed by the Indochina conflict and the offshore islands crisis of 1953 and 1954. The allegedly improved conditions resulting from the Geneva Conference of 1954 and the Bandung Conference of 1955 were soon disrupted by the Suez and Hungarian crises of 1956. Following these another off-shore islands crisis erupted in 1958. In 1959–60 occurred the suppression by force of Tibetan protesters and the accentuation of Sino-Indian border conflicts. Those who opposed a moratorium argued that the disposition of a "passionate controversy" was one of the important functions of the Assembly. To bypass an item simply because of its controversial nature, they declared, was totally illogical and absurd. In this connection, it may be noted that no one ever suggested that the discussion be delayed indefinitely; the strategy was to proceed session by session.

While those delegates who supported the moratorium proposal were generally anxious to dispose of the item as quickly as possible by making terse and curt statements, the delegates friendly to Communist China lost no opportunity to advance substantive arguments on behalf of Communist China. Thus, technically speaking, although the General Assembly dealt only with the procedural question of inscribing agenda items, no small degree of attention was aroused by the debate, which to some extent mentioned the substantive aspects of the problem. Many of the now familiar arguments and justifications were advanced with great skill and articulateness during the debates of the moratorium period. Since 1961 these justifications have been more sharply stated and enlarged as a result of the substantive discussions.

The principal justifications in support of Peking's participation can be summarized as follows:

1] It has been asserted that the "willingness" and "ability" to discharge Charter obligations could be counted on only if a government possesses effective control over its bases of power—territory, people, and resources. Hence it is essential to ascertain which of the two rival governments does in fact exercise authority and control within state territory and habitually receives obedience from the bulk of the population. This position originated in Secretary-General Lie's circulated memorandum of 1950. When this sole test is applied, the fact of Peking's effective power over the mainland is beyond reasonable doubt.

2] It is frequently argued by political realists that mainland China is a country larger than the whole of Europe with a population approximately equivalent to one-fourth of the world population. To deny the participation of such a large and potentially powerful nation is "to ignore the existence of 700 million people" and is politically most "unrealistic." That the Peking government is in effective control of a population of more than 700 million, it is asserted, cannot be ignored in the maintenance of world public order. Only such a government would be able to carry out the obligations of the "State of China" under the United Nations Charter.

3] The principle of universality has consistently been invoked in support of Communist China's participation in the United Nations. It is argued that the United Nations is a worldwide forum in which conflicts and disputes of nations are to be solved; and if the United Nations is to perform the task of maintaining world public order, its membership should encompass all nations, including a diversity of political, economic, and social systems. The United Nations should not be considered "a league of 'good' or 'peace-loving' states organized to protect the world against the stratagems of a few 'bad' (non-peace-loving) states."[25] Although there were some expressions favoring "selectivity" in membership in the deliberations at San Francisco, the prevailing community expectations, clearly demonstrated by the rapid and large increase of membership since 1955, are in favor of the principle that the world organization should include, as nearly as possible, all the established nations on earth.

4] It has been repeatedly argued that in the absence of representatives of a government ruling almost one-fourth of the population of the entire world, the United Nations cannot perform its functions effectively. The concept of effectiveness is intertwined with the principle of universality. That is, the more comprehensive the participation, the more effectively will the United Nations articulate the common demands and expectations of the world community. Furthermore, the wider the participation, the more substantial will be the bases of power of the United Nations in discharging its tasks.

5] It is now widely held that many important problems affecting world peace and security cannot be realistically solved without the participation of Communist China, as evinced by Peking's participation in the international conferences of 1954 and 1961, which dealt with the Indochina conflict and the Laotian crisis. Particularly, no meaningful control of armaments and nuclear proliferation can be made fully effective without Communist China. And it is difficult to see how mainland China can accept and observe international control on these matters when it is not even an accredited member of the world organization.

6] It is often alleged that Communist China, belligerent as it may appear, would be more accountable to world public opinion as a member of the United Nations than as an outcast. Thus India, even in the aftermath of the Sino-Indian border conflict, continued to support Communist China on the theory that its participation would bring it under the direct discipline of world public opinion and the United Nations.[26] It is maintained that through interaction in formal bodies of the United Nations, Communist China would eventually abandon its belligerent attitudes and come to terms with other nations on a more tolerant, if not friendly, basis. Such a "mellowing influence" upon Communist China is strongly predicted from time to time.

On the other hand, in opposition to Communist China's participation, various counter-arguments have been advanced.

1] The principal argument consistently put forth by the Chinese Nationalist delegation in defense of its position in the United Nations is that of "authority," as opposed to "effective control." "The Chinese Communist regime is un-Chinese in origin and un-Chinese in nature and purpose. It, therefore, cannot represent China. . . . The present Communist regime on the mainland of China was established with the military and economic aid of the Soviet Union. It is the fruit of Soviet infiltration, subversion and military intervention in [China]."[27] In its view, the very fact that Communism is an alien ideology, fundamentally contrary to Chinese character, tradition, and values, makes the Chinese Communist regime unpopular, unstable, and precarious. Should the 700 million people on the Chinese mainland be granted a plebiscite, supervised by the United Nations, they would undoubtedly choose the "Republic of China" as their "authoritative" representative.[28]

2] The charges of "unrealism" and "deliberately ignoring" the facts of international life have frequently been directed against the United States for its persistent efforts to exclude Communist China's participation. But, it is pointed out, the channels of communication are wide open and practical interactions have taken place—such as negotiations at Panmunjom, at Geneva, and at Warsaw—even while Communist China is outside the United Nations. No one is deliberately ignoring Communist China. Peking's isolation is "self-imposed." Quite contrary to the general assertion, if there is any constant reality in the Chinese participation question, it is the belligerent and irresponsible attitudes and deeds of the Chinese Communist regime.

3] While it is desirable that the membership of the United Nations be as universal as possible—as exemplified by the rapid and large increase of total membership in recent years—this has to be qualified by the principle of responsibility. Only a nation that acts responsibly in her international conduct—that is, "peace-loving" and "willing" to assume Charter obligations—can be expected to contribute to the effective functioning of the United Nations. The principle of universality does not call for the automatic inclusion of all nations without qualification. Otherwise, Articles 4 and 6 of the Charter would be meaningless. While the coexistence of nations of differing political systems within the United Nations is perfectly feasible, the participation of a nation in the United Nations is to be judged by the relevant provisions of the Charter, particularly Article 4. Communist China's past deeds have been condemned by the United Nations as "aggression." Following the "aggression" in Korea, the Chinese Communists sponsored and supplied the communizing of North Vietnam, engaged in subversive activities in Malaya, resumed warlike threats against Taiwan, launched an armed campaign to end the autonomy of Tibet, and invaded the border of India. Furthermore, they have repeatedly preached "the inevitability of war" as an article of faith and refused to renounce the use of force in dealing with other nations. In Mao Tse-tung's phrase, "Anything can grow out of the barrel of a gun." In his new blueprint for world domination through "wars of national liberation," Marshal Lin Piao has recently advocated "encirclement of cities (North America and Western Europe) by the rural areas (Asia, Africa, and Latin America)."[29]

4] It is frequently alleged that the absence of Communist China adversely affects the ability of the United Nations to deal with major problems realistically and effectively. However, to let an irresponsible nation like Communist China participate in the United Nations would not only fail to further the effectiveness of the organization but would cause disruptive and damaging impacts on world cooperation. Peking would flout United Nations resolutions and employ obstructionist tactics to weaken and undermine the effectiveness and strength of the United Nations.

5] Apart from Communist China's nonobservance of the principle of minimum public order, the replacement of Nationalist China by Communist China would mean the issuance of a hunting license to Communist China to conquer Taiwan. Communist China's demand for the expulsion of the representatives of the Republic of China and its insistence on the "restoration of China's legitimate rights" clearly implies "that the United Nations should acquiesce in Communist China's design to conquer Taiwan and the 11 million people who live there, and thereby contribute to the overthrow and the abolition of the independent Government of the Republic of China."[30] A proposal that purports "to expel a Member which supports the Charter to make room for a regime which defies the Charter and to arm that regime with a United Nations license to make war across the Formosan Strait" is both wrong and unrealistic and would have far-reaching disruptive results.[31] Such a license would unavoidably increase tension in Asia in view of the existing hostility in the Formosa area.

6] The United Nations is not a reform school for "bad governments." The participation of an aggressive Chinese Communist regime "would vitiate, if not destroy, the United Nations as an instrument for the maintenance of international peace."[32] The U.S. representative made a sharp statement before the Assembly in 1961:

> there are ample grounds to suspect that a power given to such bitter words and ruthless actions as those of the Peking regime, far from being reformed by its experience in the United Nations, would . . . exert, all the more forcefully, by threats and maneuvers, a most disruptive and demoralizing influence on the Organization at this crucial moment in its history. . . . its admission, in circumstances in which it continues to violate

and to defy the principles of the Charter, could seriously shake public confidence in the United Nations—I can assure you it would do so among the people of the United States—and this alone would significantly weaken the Organization.[33]

The likelihood of disruptive impact can further be inferred from the absurd conditions put forth by Peking's Foreign Minister for Communist participation in the U.N. He asked the U.N., among other things, to cancel its resolution condemning Chinese aggression in Korea, to condemn the United States as the aggressor, and to expel "all imperialist puppets" from the Organization.[34]

The justifications mentioned above may supplement or overlap one another in the interrelatedness of the concepts of universality, effectiveness, maintenance of public order, and political realism. However, they do reflect differing policy considerations and degrees of emphasis; hence the preceding summary is not inappropriate to the present purpose. The emphasis put on a particular justification by the debaters was dictated by the crisis conditions at a given session. Thus, immediately following the establishment of the Chinese Communist regime in October 1949 and during the Korean war, the community expectations as to the nature of the regime—its authority, permanency, and stability—were understandably uncertain. Great emphasis was laid on the nature of the regime, the extent of recognition granted, and the happenings in Korea from 1950 to 1953. Hostilities in Korea ceased in 1953. Following the Geneva negotiations concerning Indochina in 1954, the principle of effectiveness of the Organization was invoked by the Soviet bloc, and the principle of responsibility was emphasized most in reply by opposing members. As a consequence of the "package deal" concerning the admission of members in 1955 and particularly of a large and rapid influx of member states in 1960, the principle of universality was greatly emphasized. More recently, particularly since Communist China joined the nuclear club, the effective control of armaments and nuclear diffusion has become the primary concern of the world community. And Marshal Lin Piao's theory of "encirclement" has been widely cited as a contemporary classic that discloses the Communist Chinese blueprint of world domination. Finally, while expressing disapproval of Communist China's aggressive deeds and words, no one, except the Chinese Nationalist regime, seems seriously to challenge the fact that Communist China is here to stay.

Although general attention has been centered on whether Nationalist China should continue to be seated or replaced by the Peking regime, another dimension of the problem has gradually come into view. Although no formal proposal was presented to press for a "two Chinas" or a "one China, one Formosa" solution, increasing interest along this line has been expressed since 1961. Several delegations said then that although they were in favor of Communist China's participation, they could not consent to the "expulsion" of the Chinese Nationalist government. For instance, the delegate of Sierra Leone remarked that "it would be unrealistic to ignore [the Nationalist Chinese] claims altogether and to eject them ignominiously."[35] Thus he favored negotiations with the countries on the basis of accepting the existence of the People's Republic of China, simultaneous participation of Nationalist China in the United Nations, and due regard to the position of the strong supporters of Nationalist China. Cyprus, the Federation of Malaya, and Nigeria were among those who suggested the possibility of creating appropriate machinery for this objective. This line of thought was again and again made articulate in the following years.[36]

In 1966 the Canadian delegate suggested in concrete terms a "two Chinas" solution—to seat Peking in the Security Council as well as in the General Assembly, and to seat Taiwan in the Assembly—but qualified it as an "interim solution" pending the settlement of the jurisdictional dispute between the two rival regimes. The desire to see Peking and Taiwan simultaneously seated in the U.N. was also expressed by Ireland, the Netherlands, Malaysia, and Trinidad and Tobago. In the view of the Irish delegate the question of "the representation of China" was to be rightly described as "the question of the representation of China and of Formosa in the United Nations."[37]

The preceding analysis of strategies has focused on the manipulation of symbols in the formal arena of discussion. It would present an unreal picture of the working of the political process to let it go at this. Among the other strategies used by the powers to influence outcomes, the following three merit special attention: bloc politics in the United Nations; the strategies employed by Nationalist China and Communist China to win support from African nations; and United States internal politics, with particular regard to the alignment of forces opposed to Communist China's participation.

During the period the United States had stable control over a "mechanical majority" in the General Assembly, bloc politics in the United Nations operated decisively in favor of the United States, and hence was beneficial to Nationalist China. The significance and complexity of bloc politics has greatly increased as more Asian and African members have been added. Supplementing the various formal committees of the General Assembly, the informal structures—the bloc and caucusing groups—have become an integral part of the decision process in the Assembly. The same member state may belong to more than one group; and there is in fact a complex interlocking structure.

The consolidation of the Afro-Asian caucusing group was partly a reaction to the cohesive strength of other groups. The early domination of the General Assembly by a combination of the Western European and Latin American nations made the Asian and African states aware of the necessity of effective organization among themselves in the pursuit of their common interests. Their voting pattern, however, was far from solid on many issues. While demonstrating a strong unity concerning colonial issues and economic development problems, these Afro-Asian nations have from

time to time split their votes on questions of vital importance—
some voting with the Western nations, some with the Communist
bloc, and a good many joining the abstentions. On the Chinese
participation question, there have been vast differences. In view
of the relatively fluid attitudes of the African members, it was a
task of high priority for the Nationalists to secure their support
on the participation issue.

Both Nationalist China and Communist China have employed
very much the same strategies to win the support of the newly
admitted African nations. Generally, these new nations are offered
immediate recognition by both Peking and Taipei on the day of
their independence, with the expectations of reciprocation. Other
methods include exchange of delegations, official visits by African
leaders, scholarship awards, training of African personnel, and aid
programs. In waging all these campaigns, the United States has
been solidly behind Nationalist China, which has spared no effort
to promote friendly relations with the African nations. While
Communist China has generally established official relations with
nations belonging to the Casablanca group, Nationalist China has
maintained diplomatic relations primarily with the Brazzaville
group. The former French African territories held a series of conferences beginning in late 1960 that culminated in the establishment of the African and Malagasy Union. Members of the A.M.U.,
with varying ties with France, differ from most African states on
a number of issues. The support given to the Nationalist regime
on the participation issue, though somewhat adversely affected by
French recognition of Peking in January 1964, remained invaluable
to the regime.

The need to woo these nations was illustrated by an incident
at the 1961–62 session of the General Assembly. The large influx
of new African member states in the United Nations in 1960
forced decision-makers of the United States reluctantly to conclude
that it would be increasingly difficult to prevent the Chinese Communist regime from participating in the United Nations in one

way or another. At the sixteenth session of the Assembly, an extraneous situation was presented—the question of Outer Mongolia's pending application for membership. Driving a hard bargain, the Soviet Union had deliberately chosen to link Outer Mongolia's application with that of Mauritania, a newly independent state belonging to the Brazzaville group. Initially, Nationalist China had expressed its determination to veto Outer Mongolia's pending application for membership in the Security Council. Yet should Nationalist China veto Mongolia, the Soviet Union would presumably retaliate by vetoing the parallel application of Mauritania; and the two dozen African states in the Assembly could then be expected to vote in favor of Communist China's participation as a matter of revenge against Nationalist China. Confronted with this dilemma, the delegates of the United States exerted themselves to see to it that Communist China's participation would not be facilitated by an imprudent use of the veto by the Chinese Nationalist delegation against Outer Mongolia. With great reluctance, the Nationalist regime finally yielded by absenting itself from the vote in the Security Council on Mongolia's application. Accordingly, the campaign to exclude Communist China was successfully assured at that critical session of the Assembly. The United States scored another victory.

In order to understand the strong position persistently taken by the United States, we must look into its internal politics. Various pressure groups have played a significant part in initiating and defending a firm stand against the participation of Communist China. The Korean war strengthened the determination of the United States to exclude Communist China, and in late 1953 the Committee of One Million Against the Admission of Communist China to the United Nations was created to campaign for the continuous exclusion of Communist China. Initially, the Committee consisted of two dozen U.S. senators, nearly one hundred congressmen, a number of governors, high-ranking military officers, clergymen, intellectuals and other outstanding persons. The Com-

mittee's successful campaign was clearly indicated when the plat-
forms of both Democratic and Republican parties in the presidential
campaigns of 1956, 1960, and 1964 opposed the seating of Communist China. The backing of the Committee's activities, perhaps
more Republican than Democratic, was nevertheless bipartisan
in nature, as seen by the repeated attachment of riders to foreign
aid bills in which unequivocal opposition was expressed to Communist China's participation in the United Nations. It became
unpopular for anyone to favor granting a seat to Communist
China in the United Nations. An attempt by a responsible decision-maker to explore alternatives that deviated from the status
quo invited immediate retaliation: threats to reduce the contribution to the United Nations and to curtail the annual mutual
security appropriation. Thus far these possible consequences have
been taken seriously by successive administrations. Hence the
capacity of any administration to deal flexibly with the Chinese
participation question is circumscribed by similar domestic considerations, although the Johnson administration has lately shown
signs of possible change.[38]

Outcomes

With respect to the general question of "Recognition by the
United Nations of the Representation of a Member State," the
General Assembly adopted in 1950 the resolution 396(V), as recommended by the *ad hoc* political committee. Among other things,
the resolution recommended that when controversy arose on the
question of representation, it should be "considered in the light
of the Purposes and Principles of the Charter and the circumstances of each case," by "the General Assembly, or by the Interim
Committee if the General Assembly is not in session"; and the
attitude of the General Assembly should be "taken into account
in other organs of the United Nations and in the specialized
agencies." This resolution fell short of providing useful standards
for the solution of the tangled China participation question.

As to the Chinese question, there were, as we may recall, four draft resolutions presented to the General Assembly in 1950. After rejecting a Syrian proposal to postpone a decision and the draft resolutions of India and the Soviet Union, the Assembly adopted the Canadian draft resolution with a slight amendment.[39] Accordingly, a special committee was set up to study the problem of Chinese participation. The Committee met only twice and was unable to make any recommendation to the Assembly.

From 1951 to 1960 the "moratorium proposals" sponsored by the United States were adopted by the General Assembly at each session by a "mechanical majority." These resolutions, purporting to "postpone consideration" or "not to consider" the Chinese question during the duration of each session, were not of long-term significance.

The important decisions took place in 1961. As mentioned, there were two draft resolutions (plus one amendment) before the General Assembly. After having heard from 56 speakers through twelve plenary meetings, the General Assembly on December 15, 1961, voted in accordance with the following order: (1) the five-power draft resolution declaring "any proposal to change the representation of China" as an "important question"; (2) the amendment to the Soviet draft resolution submitted by Cambodia, Ceylon, and Indonesia; and (3) the Soviet draft resolution itself. The five-power draft resolution was accorded priority in the voting. The General Assembly, while rejecting the U.S.S.R.'s draft resolution and the three-power amendment, adopted the five-power draft resolution, as proposed by Australia, Colombia, Italy, Japan, and the United States. This resolution is of such great significance that it may be well to document its content here:

The General Assembly,
Noting that a serious divergence of views exists among Member States concerning the representation of a founder Member who is named in the Charter of the United Nations,
Recalling that this matter has been described repeatedly in

the General Assembly by all segments of opinion as vital and crucial and that on numerous occasions its inclusion in the agenda has been requested under rule 15 of the Assembly's rules of procedure as an item of an important and urgent character,

Recalling further the recommendation contained in its resolution 396(V) of 14 December 1950 that, whenever more than one authority claims to be the government entitled to represent a Member State in the United Nations and this question becomes the subject of controversy in the United Nations, the question should be considered in the light of the purposes and principles of the Charter and the circumstances of each case,

Decides, in accordance with Article 18 of the Charter of the United Nations, that any proposal to change the representation of China is an important question (Resolution 1668 (XVI)).

The draft resolutions intended to seat Peking and oust Taiwan, submitted by the U.S.S.R. in 1962 and by Albania and Cambodia in 1963, were rejected by the General Assembly. No vote was taken on the issue in 1964. Similar proposals were reintroduced by pro-Peking nations in 1965 and in 1966, but were again defeated. On the other hand, the General Assembly successfully passed two resolutions in 1965 and in 1966 reaffirming the validity of the 1961 resolution that any proposal to change the "representation of China" is an important question, requiring a two-thirds majority vote in the Assembly. Meanwhile, in 1966 the six-power proposal designed to establish a study committee was overwhelmingly rejected by the Assembly.

The absolute number of member states who voted for the moratorium proposal remained relatively constant from 1952 to 1960, even though the membership rose from 60 to 99 during that period. Hence relative support for the moratorium proposal significantly declined as U.N. members increased.

From 1951 to 1959, the total number in favor of the moratorium proposal constituted an absolute majority—i.e., it exceeded the total number of opposition votes plus abstentions, including absentees. This was generally known as a "mechanical majority." The pattern coincided substantially with the overall influence of the United States on other member states during that period. Generally those nations which had the closest political or economic ties with the United States or the Soviet Union were more susceptible to influence and followed the respective positions of the United States or the Soviet Union on this issue. When deviation occurred, the relation of the particular nation with either Communist China or Nationalist China, especially in terms of recognition policy, appeared significant. For instance, Denmark, Iceland, and Norway, though allies of the United States under NATO, voted differently from the United States because these Scandinavian nations had recognized Communist China in the early part of 1950.

While the United States had control over the "mechanical majority" from 1951 to 1959, the large influx of newly independent member states which proclaimed a "nonaligned policy" led to a considerable decline of the relative influence of the United States in the General Assembly. The "mechanical majority" could no longer be maintained. Few new members were allied with the United States; hence the percentage of the Assembly vote steadily susceptible to the influence of the United States declined. In 1955 and 1960 the Assembly witnessed the largest number of admissions of new members (16 and 17, respectively). While few of the new states had close alliance or trade relations with the United States, a number of them had special ties to the Communist bloc, and the relative percentage susceptible to the Soviet bloc arose appreciably in 1956 and thereafter.

Abstentions regarding the Chinese participation question occurred even prior to 1960. During the early period abstentions were mostly among nations with no close tie with either the East or the West; or, in some special instances, the member happened to be "hard pressed" by both sides. For instance, Portugal's consistent abstentions seem to have been prompted by a desire to protect her interests in Macao by refusing to antagonize Communist China. Austria apparently wanted to maintain her "neutrality" in the midst of East-West competition. Israel, though having unilaterally granted recognition to Communist China in January 1950, did not see fit to deviate too far from the position of the United States. Actually the percentage of abstentions was small during the period.

The increase of new members in 1960 was followed by many abstentions in 1960 and 1961 (22 and 20 respectively), creating a somewhat deceptive picture of the outcome in both sessions. Because of their sudden independence and participation in the international arena, the representatives of the new nations were often uninformed or unready to take positions on United Nations issues not immediately intelligible in their experience during the recent struggles for independence. In some instances they abstained because they lacked instructions from new foreign offices with a rudimentary understanding of the issues.

A switch took place in 1962 and 1963 when member states of the Brazzaville group voted in opposition to Communist China's participation instead of abstaining again. These nations shared a past under French rule and maintained a close connection with France, particularly in the form of regular consultations on foreign policy. All but five of the seventeen members of Africa voting against Communist China's participation in 1963 were former French territories.[40]

This point was critically dramatized in 1965, as the margin of U.S. victory became thinner than ever. Whereas the proposal to seat Peking and oust Taiwan was rejected in 1963 by 57 to 41, with 12 abstentions, the vote of rejection in 1965 was 47 to 47, with 23 abstentions (including absence).

Among the allies of the United States there has been an increasing tendency since 1961 to vote against the position of the U.S. This may be construed partly as indicating the gradual decline of U.S. influence resulting from the changing nature of the cold war, and partly as a reflection of the differences in the content of specific proposals. During the moratorium period, when the issue was whether or not to postpone consideration of the question by the General Assembly, these allies saw fit to go along with the United States so as not to "poison the international atmosphere." Since 1961, however, the substance of the question has been faced directly, and their vote has expressed their support of Communist China's participation in the United Nations. The United Kingdom is a good example. The Netherlands, though having stood with the moratorium strategy, has abstained since 1961 in connection with the proposal to seat Peking and to oust the Nationalists. The French support of Communist China is another indicator of the trend.

In 1961 two important draft resolutions were voted on by the Assembly: (*a*) a five-power draft resolution characterizing any proposal to change the Chinese "representation" as "an important question"; and (*b*) a Soviet proposal to seat Communist China in place of the Nationalist delegation. On the former, a resolution supported by the U.S., the vote was 61 for, 34 against, with 9 abstentions; on the Soviet proposal, the vote was 37 for, 48 against, with 19 abstentions. Thus there was more support for identifying the Chinese representation question as an important question than there was specifically for the continued participation of Nationalist China (61 to 48). Those in support of the Soviet proposal to seat Communist China, as a rule, voted against the five-power draft resolution, seeking to settle the matter by a simple majority. On the other hand, though many nations, notably those belonging to the Brazzaville Group, abstained in regard to the Soviet proposal, they voted in favor of the five-power draft resolution. In 1965 and 1966 the margins of support for the "important question" proposal were again wider than for the continued presence of the Nationalist regime, the record being 56 for, 49 against, 12 abstaining vs. 47-47-23 in 1965; and in the next year 66-48-7 vs. 46-57-18 (i.e., 66 to 57). It is also worth noting that although a member state favoring Peking's participation automatically voted against the "important question" proposal, the United Kingdom and Indonesia took exception to this pattern. Both of them, though in favor of seating Peking, voted for the "important question" proposal.

Compared to the voting results in 1961–65, the outcome of 1966 appears to be a reversal of the developing trend toward ever increasing support for Peking's participation in the U.N. Whereas the vote in 1965 was 47-47-23 on the proposal to seat Peking and oust Taiwan, the vote in 1966 was 46-57-18. The unexpected gain for the Nationalist regime in 1966 is not to be taken at its face value, however.

The outcome was attributable partly to Peking's setbacks in external relations and continuing turmoil within, and partly to a combination of complications in 1966. Although the Canadian delegation fell short of putting forth its program of "two Chinas" in the form of a draft resolution, its effort in that direction was an indication of the growing concern among member states to find a path out of the impasse. The move headed by the Italian delegation proposing a study committee to explore alternatives and make recommendations to the Assembly caught many delegations by surprise. These new moves in the midst of the escalation of the Vietnam conflict suddenly complicated the whole picture. Not fully prepared to meet the new situation, the member states understandably took a guarded attitude not to upset, at least for the time being, the status quo, although they keenly sensed that something new was in the making, particularly in the light of the changing climate of opinion in the United States.

The six-power proposal for a study committee was overwhelmingly defeated by an ironic combination of pro-Peking and pro-Nationalist nations: whereas the former saw the move essentially as a delaying tactic, the latter suspected it to be—as the Nationalist spokesman asserted—the first step toward an eventual solution of "two Chinas" in some form. What really worried the Nationalist regime amid the "unexpected" victory was the fact that 5 of 6 sponsors of the proposal were maintaining diplomatic relations with it, and that of 34 members voting in favor of the proposal, contrary to the wishes of the regime, as many as 27 had diplomatic relations with Taipei, only 4 with Peking, and another 3 with neither.[41] In a word, the voting record in 1966 is far from conclusive in indicating a new trend favorable to the Nationalists.

Effects

Whether the Chinese participation question is a matter of "credentials" is important because of the voting requirement of either a simple or a two-thirds majority. In view of the long entanglement and its unique and complex features, coupled with all the potential values at stake, controversies regarding this question cannot be disposed of by the simple practice normally employed by the credentials committee of the General Assembly. Among the past decisions taken by the Assembly, resolution 1668 (XVI) adopted by the Assembly in 1961 had significant effect: it establishes that any proposal to change the "representation of China" is an important question requiring a two-thirds majority vote. This position was reaffirmed in 1965 and 1966.

The fact that the pro-Nationalist nations reintroduced an 11-power proposal in 1965 and a 15-power proposal in 1966 to reaffirm the validity of resolution 1668 (XVI) indicates that the authoritative effect of an Assembly resolution is confined to a particular session (unless by Rule 83 a reconsideration is granted at the request of a two-thirds majority at the same session) and is open to modification at subsequent sessions. The required vote for such a modification is a simple majority. Viewed in this light, supporters of the Nationalist regime certainly have cause for concern, bearing in mind the thin margin of 1965.

It may not be inappropriate at this juncture to examine the probable effect of the Assembly's decision regarding the Chinese question on other organs of the U.N. and its specialized agencies. So long as the status quo is maintained by the Assembly, adverse repercussions on other organs would not be set into motion. Should the Assembly decide to seat Communist China in coming years, however, what effect would its decision have on other organs of the U.N. and its specialized agencies?

It is generally accepted that each organ or agency decides its own membership as a matter of internal autonomy. Hence it is not improbable that conflicting decisions regarding Chinese participation may be reached by various agencies of the U.N., even though they may have earlier expressed their willingness to defer to Assembly decisions. With a view to minimizing such a potential risk, the General Assembly by its resolution 396(V) of December 14, 1950, recommended that "the attitude adopted by the General Assembly or its Interim Committee concerning any such question [the participation question] should be taken into account in other organs of the United Nations and in the specialized agencies." But to what extent would the decision of the Assembly be echoed?

Besides the General Assembly, the principal organs of the U.N. are the Security Council, the Economic and Social Council, the Trusteeship Council, the International Court of Justice, and the Secretariat. Because of its composition the International Court of Justice will not itself be a target in controversies over participation. It is useful to analyze the relation of the other organs with the Assembly. Taking the Charter provisions as a whole, the Economic and Social Council, the Trusteeship Council and the Secretariat are in many respects subordinate to the General Assembly. The Assembly is unique in that it is the only organ encompassing all member states of the U.N. The Charter instructs that the Economic and Social Council, the Trusteeship Council, and the Secretary-General perform their functions under the authority of the Assembly. The superior role of the Assembly is abundantly demonstrated by its comprehensive authority to elect, to approve, to regulate, to control finance, and to appraise.[42]

Should the Assembly act to seat the Peking regime in the future, its decision is likely to be followed by the Economic and Social Council, including a large number of subsidiary bodies under the Council's supervision, numerous specialized agencies, and the Trusteeship Council. In fact, faced with the participation issue in the past, these bodies were discreet enough to refrain from taking action that might deviate from an Assembly decision. Meanwhile, although the status of the Secretary-General will not be affected by the seating of Peking, he is bound to take this new fact fully into account in appointing his staff.

Unlike the Economic and Social Council and the Trusteeship Council, the Security Council stands in a unique position in relation to the Assembly. We have had occasion to comment on the relative responsibility of both the Security Council and Assembly in the maintenance of peace and security. Unlike the other two Councils, the membership of the Security Council is divided into permanent as well as nonpermanent members, reflecting the expectation of the framers that the concerted action of major powers is essential to maintaining world order. This concept is typified by the complicated voting procedure of the Council.

Article 27 of the Charter, as amended on August 31, 1965, reads:

1. Each member of the Security Council shall have one vote.

2. Decisions of the Security Council on procedural matters shall be made by an affirmative vote of nine members.

3. Decisions of the Security Council on all other matters shall be made by an affirmative vote of nine members *including the concurring votes of the permanent members*; provided that, in decisions under Chapter VI, and under paragraph 3 of Article 52, a party to a dispute shall abstain from voting (italics added).

Instead of employing the dichotomy of "important" and "non-important" questions, as in the case of the Assembly (Article 18), the Security Council distinguishes "procedural" from "substantive" matters. Whereas the Council's decisions are made by an affirmative vote of 9 members, such vote must include "the concurring votes of the permanent members" in regard to "substantive matters." (Before the amendments to Articles 23 and 27 came into effect—when the total membership of the Council was 11 instead of 15—the required vote was 7 instead of 9.) The latter requirement is the essence of "veto." Since Article 27 does not enumerate what constitutes "substantive matters," the controversy is how the Council shall determine whether a particular matter is procedural or otherwise. The answer is generally assumed to be found in the Four-Power Statement of 1945, which declares that "it will be unlikely that there will arise in the future any matters of great importance on which a decision will have to be made as to whether a procedural vote would apply. Should, however, such a matter arise, the decision regarding the preliminary question as to whether or not such a matter is procedural must be taken by a vote of seven members of the Security Council, including the concurring votes of the permanent members."[43] This statement gives rise to the problem of "double veto" by the permanent members.

It may be recalled that the General Assembly decided in 1961 —and reaffirmed in 1965 and 1966—that "any proposal to change the representation of China is an important question." Would the Security Council follow the suit of the Assembly to determine the question as "substantive"—hence subject to veto—when occasion occurs in the future?

In order to answer this question, proper attention must be directed to the past practice of the Council concerning the "double veto." In the early history of the Security Council, the Soviet delegation succeeded in invoking the application of the double veto in connection with the Spanish, Greek, and Czechoslovak questions.[44] In these three cases the President of the Council ruled a resolution "substantive" when the Soviet representative cast "no" on the preliminary question which would characterize the matter procedural. When his ruling was challenged as a point of order, the President then referred it to the Council for consideration in accord with Rule 30 of the Provisional Rules of Procedure of the Council, which provides: "If a representative raises a point of order, the President shall immediately state his ruling. If it is challenged, the President shall submit his ruling to the Security Council for immediate decision and it shall stand unless overruled." In no case were the necessary seven votes marshaled to overrule the ruling. Giving deference to Soviet invocation of double veto, other permanent members dutifully supported the presidential ruling, even though some of them had previously asserted that the matter at issue was procedural and had so voted on the preliminary question.

On subsequent occasions, however, the invocation of double veto was not honored in connection with the Formosan question of 1950 and the Laos question of 1959.

The Formosan case treated the complaint by the People's Republic of China of American aggression against China by its occupation of Formosa. An Ecuadorean proposal that purported to invite the Chinese Communist representative to attend Council meetings was introduced. Before the vote was taken Tsiang, the Nationalist representative, had requested a preliminary determination on the nature of the vote, which was dismissed by the President (British representative) to be out of order. As the vote was seven in favor, three (China, Cuba, U.S.) against, and one abstention, the President announced that the resolution was adopted. Tsiang emphatically protested it on the ground that his negative vote had the effect of double veto, thereby precluding the passage of the resolution. Whereupon the President asked the members of the Council to vote again on the question whether the Ecuadorean resolution was procedural. The response was nine votes affirmative, one negative (China); the President ruled the resolution procedural and thus adopted. Tsiang again dissented and insisted that the matter be referred to the International Court of Justice for an advisory opinion. Construing this demand as a motion of challenge, the President formally submitted the issue to the vote under Rule 30. Interestingly enough, no one voted either in favor or against, and the President declared that his ruling stood, which Tsiang continued to charge as "illegal and invalid" for violating the Four-Power Statement.[45]

The Laos question of 1959 dealt with the Laotian request for U.N. assistance, including an emergency force, to halt an alleged aggression along its northeastern frontier by North Vietnam. The United States, United Kingdom, and France jointly introduced a draft resolution which would have had the Council appoint a subcommittee to examine and receive information, to conduct necessary inquiries, and to report to the Council. While the U.S. delegate claimed the matter to be procedural under Article 29 of the Charter, the Soviet representative insisted otherwise, and requested a vote on the preliminary question. With ten votes in favor and one against (U.S.S.R.), the President, attaching no special significance to the negative vote cast by the Soviet representative, stated that the resolution was procedural in nature. The ensuing vote on the draft resolution itself showed the same result, and the resolution was thus declared to have been adopted. The Soviet delegate made no motion for a vote to overrule the presidential ruling, but concluded that "the resolution is not binding on anybody."[46]

Compared with the Czechoslovak case where a subcommittee was appointed to inquire whether the situation of Czechoslovakia endangered international peace and security, the Laotian resolution to set up a subcommittee authorized to "conduct such inquiries as it may determine necessary" in regard to the alleged aggression appears no less significant in its substantive impact. The mandate was in essence an order to investigate, "calling for reports, hearing witnesses, dispatching a commission of inquiry, or other means."[47] The presidential ruling in both cases, however, was precisely the opposite. In the Czechoslovak case as the Soviet invocation of double veto was honored, the issue was decided to be substantive—hence the Soviet veto defeated the resolution; in the case of Laos, the matter was termed procedural as a similar Soviet claim was rejected.

In sum, although the Council did on several occasions honor the claim of double veto derived from the Four-Power Statement, whose authoritative effect has consistently been repudiated by nonpermanent members, it gave no reliable guide for the future. The invocation of double veto can be rendered ineffective—hence transforming a substantive matter into a procedural one—when a shrewd manipulation by the President of the Council under Rule 30 is sustained by 7 members (5 members before the amendment to Article 27 came into effect in August 1965). The room for presidential maneuvering is far from inconsequential.[48]

In the light of the foregoing, what would be the likely response of the Security Council should the Chinese question come up before the Council after an Assembly's decision to seat Communist China?

Obviously the Nationalist delegation will insist, invoking the Four-Power Statement of 1945, that the issue is a substantive matter, which requires an affirmative vote of nine, including "the concurrent votes of the permanent members of the Council,"— hence double veto. The essential point is, will such a claim be endorsed by other members of the Council? While there may be attempts to preclude the Nationalist delegation from participating in a decision because it is "a party to a dispute," this need not be conclusive, since the proviso of Article 27 (3) which obliges a party to a dispute to abstain from voting refers specifically to "decisions under Chapter VI and under paragraph 3 of Article 52," and not otherwise. As in the Formosa and Laos cases, a President of the Council (who is assigned by rotation) hostile to the Nationalists may, by his ruling under Rule 30, shrewdly frustrate the Nationalist attempt to retain its seat by invoking "double veto." In that event, will the Nationalist delegation be able to marshal the support of at least *eight* other members to overturn an adverse ruling of the President?

No serious student of international politics can have the slightest doubt that the attitude of the U.S. will be crucial. Devoid of U.S. support, the Nationalists will fall far short of the nine votes needed to reverse the presidential ruling.[49] With its staunch support, however, the probability is high that the Nationalist claim of "double veto" will be sustained. Should the latter be the case, then, decisions of the Council and Assembly might conflict with each other regarding Chinese participation. In all likelihood, the Council will not act to substitute the Chinese Communists for the Nationalists in the foreseeable future without at least the acquiescence of the U.S. To do otherwise would precipitate a U.N. crisis of unprecedented magnitude.

Probable Future Development

BEFORE we project the probable course of future developments, it is advisable to inquire into the important factors that have conditioned past decisions and evaluate their significance for future outcomes.

It is hardly feasible to allocate precise weight to a particular variable for its contribution to past decisions. However, from the preceding analysis it appears that one decisive factor was the overwhelming influence of the United States upon other member states. Before 1960 U.S. influence in the General Assembly was so overwhelming that a "mechanical majority," contributed mainly by United States allies, was maintained, and it effectively excluded Communist China's participation. This influence, however, has considerably declined as a result of the many Afro-Asian members who proclaimed themselves "nonaligned." Furthermore, there is a new dynamism visible among United States allies, and more of them may well depart at various points from courses of action urged by the U.S. French recognition of Peking has already made its impact felt; and the Labour government of the United Kingdom has been more vigorous in urging Communist China's participation in the U.N.

During its first ten years, observers had understandable reservations about the permanency of the formal authority and effective control of the Chinese Communist regime. Genuine concern was repeatedly expressed in the course of debates as to the stability and durability of the new regime. This reserved attitude had practically disappeared, when the mainland upheavals in the summer of 1966 cast doubt on the stability of Mao's leadership. It is essential to put the current events of the Chinese mainland in perspective. Although the reports concerning the actual situation have remained fragmentary, no matter what changes in the personnel of Peking's leadership may result from the "great proletariat cultural revolution," the Communist regime on the mainland will not pass away. The world community is well advised to recognize this prospect realistically and seriously.

The condemnation by the United Nations of Communist China's aggression in Korea also appears to be a significant factor conditioning past decisions. Although the past has not been erased from the official records of the United Nations, more and more nations are increasingly reluctant to base their objection to Communist China's participation on the technical persistence of an "aggression," since actual hostilities have long ceased.

This brief account indicates that the major conditioning factors that operated in the past are decreasing their presumptive weight in future decisions on the Chinese participation question, particularly in the light of new events of current significance.

The impact of French recognition of Peking in January 1964 was acutely felt in 1965 when the division in the Assembly to seat Communist China appeared even (47 to 47, with 23 abstentions). France's new advocacy for Peking is significant because it possesses considerable influence over the African members of the French community, although the adverse effect on the Nationalist regime was not as far-reaching as expected. As France strengthens its "independent" leadership role, the tide will continue to run against the Nationalist regime.

The successful detonations of nuclear devices by Peking not only enhance Communist China's power position but also increase the concern for effective control of nuclear proliferation. This was clearly indicated when the Assembly resolved in 1965 to conduct consultations with *all* countries (presumably including Communist China) for the purpose of preparing a world disarmament conference in 1967—two weeks after the same body refused once more to seat Peking by the narrowest margin in the Assembly's history.[50] As the member states identify the halting of nuclear proliferation as a primary task, it would be difficult to dismiss the argument advanced on behalf of Peking's participation in the world organization.

It is sometimes suggested that Communist China has lost interest in U.N. membership, alluding partly to Chou En-lai's hint of forming a rival organization, and partly to Chen Yi's exaction of evidently unacceptable conditions for Peking's participation.[51] The uncertainty about Peking's genuine intention allowed some of its potential supporters to be less than enthusiastic in the past. The recent setback suffered by the Chinese Communists in Indonesia makes the threat of a rival organization more propaganda than menace. Chou En-lai's statement is probably part of his strategy of obtaining participation in the U.N. on the best terms. For while he hinted at the possibility of undertaking such a step, he was vague about what exactly he purported to do. Chen Yi's statement is to be treated in the same manner. What really matters seems to be the conditions under which Peking would be willing to participate in the United Nations.

Since the Chinese participation question has been treated as a cold-war issue, our projection into the future must be related to the probable course of future developments between East and West, particularly since the assassination of President Kennedy and the ouster of Khrushchev. These events have unquestionably created a period of wait-and-see. New and responsible elites on both sides have thus far proceeded with great caution over the course chartered by their predecessors. Even in the midst of escalation in the Vietnam conflict, both the United States and the Soviet Union seem assured—tacitly, if not expressly—of basic stability in their relation. Hence it is unlikely that the future relation between the Soviet Union and the United States will radically affect the solution of the Chinese participation question in new ways. And because of the rift between Moscow and Peking, though the Soviet Union may continue to pay lip service for Peking's participation in the U.N., its effective support is bound to decrease.

Finally, it is appropriate to locate the entire problem within the "future" framework of the United Nations in the light of the temporary paralysis and inaction demonstrated at the nineteenth session (1964–65) of the Assembly. The showdown concerning the arrears issue was finally averted. The world community—at present and for the immediate future—does not seem prepared to let the United Nations follow the League of Nations into oblivion. With all its shortcomings the advantages of a U.N. are perceived as far outweighing its failures. It is the only worldwide forum where genuine hope for practical and evolutionary "peace and security" can be kept alive through a discipline of continuous exposure, confrontation, and communication that includes the whole spectrum of world opinions on a realistic and universal basis. It is most unlikely, as we see it, that the Chinese question will come to a "happy ending" should the organization collapse. Neither, as we noted earlier, will the status quo—that is, the presence of the Nationalist regime in the U.N. to the exclusion of the Peking government—continue indefinitely simply because the voting result in 1966 turned out unexpectedly more favorable to the Nationalist regime than in 1965. A serious search among the member states for constructive alternatives already began, in a manner of speaking, in 1966. An opportune moment for solution may come when the Vietnam conflict becomes a topic of effective negotiation calling for the formal participation of Communist China.

Appraisal and Recommendation

THE CHINESE participation question means different things to different claimants and decision-makers, and despite considerable efforts, its complexities are far from being removed. Many efforts to clarify the legal questions at issue have not made solutions any easier. While there is an inclination to consider the problem a matter of "representation"—a choice between two rival governments—the "admission theory" is by no means unpopular. Secretary-General U Thant recently stated:

> Some Member States maintain that the question is one of representation, not admission. Their argument is based on the premise that China is already a Member of the United Nations —one of the founding Members, one of the five permanent Members of the Security Council. Therefore, China is already a Member of this Organization. The question, according to them, is one of representation: Who should represent China? This is the attitude held by some of the Member States. Another viewpoint is held by the vast majority of the Member States, who maintain that the question is one of admission. Of course, the General Assembly has taken up this question from year to year. The General Assembly decided by implication that it was a question of admission of a new Member, not representation. And this majority opinion prevailed.[52]

Supporters of the "representation theory," however, too often equate "representation" with "credentials" in the hope of having the matter decided by a simple majority. Concerning "admission" to membership, the Charter expressly provides that it is to be decided by the General Assembly "upon the recommendation of the Security Council." Procedurally, the Security Council's recommendation must precede the action of the General Assembly, as affirmed by the International Court of Justice in the Admission Case and United Nations practice.[53] But supporters of the "admission theory," in the course of Assembly debates, have failed to note the absence of this procedural requirement as well as the absence of application for membership from Communist China.

It appears quite hopeless to seek a rational and constructive alternative by the bland invocation of conflicting legal technicalities. As a matter of fact, decision-makers are, as a rule, more inclined to think in terms of the outcomes they seek to achieve through different alternatives. What they are ultimately interested in is not the verbal play of "credentials," "representation," or "admission," but the fundamental policies that underlie these concepts and the probable future outcomes: the continued participation of Nationalist China, the substitution of Communist China for Nationalist China, the inclusion of "two Chinas" or "one China, one Formosa." In the search for a rational and realistic alternative, it is of paramount importance to consider the potential values and community policies at stake, the contemporary community expectations and the context of world conditions, and the probable course of future development.

The overriding community goal is to maintain minimum world public order. Any solution should first of all be aimed at enhancing this goal. Hence it is essential to maximize the effective functioning of the United Nations through the application of the principle of universality and the principle of responsibility. The more comprehensive the participation, the more substantial will be the bases of power of the United Nations to perform its task and articulate the demands and expectations of the world community. And the effectiveness of the Organization can be assured only by responsible conduct on the part of member states. Furthermore, it is to be noted that a fundamental human right is at stake here —i.e., the right of self-determination for the 13 million people of Formosa.

Two claims are unworthy of serious advocacy. They are the occasional demands to exclude the participation of both National-ist China and Communist China, or to defer decision indefinitely pending adequate Charter amendment. Proposals of the kind are incompatible with the basic policies and goals of the world com-munity. These alternatives, clear-cut as they may appear, solve nothing; they postpone the whole problem. The matter cannot be left to the two parties most directly involved to decide, since the consequences are far-reaching enough to warrant a collective decision by the United Nations. It is the task of the Organization to act, not to abandon its responsibility; and it is to the credit of the U.N. that no nation has thus far seriously proposed the al-ternatives mentioned.

Our previous observations indicate that it will become increas-ingly difficult to maintain the status quo concerning the Chinese participation question. That is, it is clear that it would be un-realistic to continue to seat Nationalist China as the representative of "China" in the United Nations. It does not make sense to pretend that the Nationalist regime led by Chiang Kai-shek is still empowered with "formal authority" to speak for the millions on the Chinese mainland over whom it has had no effective control since 1949. It is irresponsible to confer the benefits of "formal authority" on a government without effective control over people, territory, or resources, and to seek to impose burdens upon a government with effective control but without the benefit of formal access to international organizations. Paradoxically enough, while the Nationalist regime is generally treated as the authori-tative spokesman for "China," reference is instantly shifted to the Chinese Communist regime when the problems affecting mini-mum world public order are raised, especially control of armaments and nuclear weapons. This double standard can no longer be maintained, if the world community is genuinely interested in public order in general and effective arms control in particular.

It has become increasingly difficult to rebut the argument that the advantages of Communist China's participation far outweigh the possible adverse effects on the United Nations as a whole. The trend toward the inclusion of Peking appears irresistible, if not inevitable, notwithstanding the voting results of the twenty-first Assembly and the current upheavals on the mainland. It would render the United Nations a disservice if the member states relax their sense of urgency—or even cherish new illusions—simply because the voting in 1966, compared to that in 1965, spells a setback for Peking in its quest for access to the world organization. The Chinese Communist regime on the mainland will not "pass away," whatever the ultimate result of the "great proletariat cultural revolution." Only a "mainland" government is "able" to employ its resources to discharge Charter obligations on behalf of "China." In the long run its participation undoubtedly would broaden the bases of power of the United Nations and enable the Organization to function more effectively.

Concerning the "willingness" of Communist China to fulfill Charter obligations, this is always a matter subject to proof; in all fairness, however, it should be granted a fair opportunity to prove itself on a normal basis within the framework of the United Nations. Dogmatic convictions on the course of conduct to be followed through all future years are unwarranted presumptions. There is good evidence to assert that a nation treated as an "outcast" behaves differently in its dealings with other nations than does an "equal member" of the world community. In the assessment of public decorum we ought not forget the conciliatory efforts of Communist China to woo the Afro-Asian nations at the Bandung Conference of 1955.

Undoubtedly Peking's participation in the United Nations would raise grave difficulties, particularly during the initial phases of transition and readjustment. It would be credulous, however, to assume that Peking's participation must inevitably paralyze the Organization. By this time the member states, particularly the newly independent nations, perceive the United Nations as an indispensable instrument of the world order in which they have so recently achieved a major stake. Under these circumstances it is improbable that any deliberate obstructionism by Peking would go unchallenged. As in the past, the Organization can be expected to survive the intransigence of any single power.

To give "China's" seats in the Security Council and in the General Assembly to Communist China acknowledges Peking's effective authority over the mainland. The undoubted effect would be to enhance its international prestige, and to enlarge the diplomatic arena available to it. However, Peking's obligations cannot, in the nature of the human condition, remain unaffected by its new opportunities. Almost imperceptibly, perhaps, intransigence is eroded by reasonableness. Peking's stature eventually will depend on tacit acceptance of the give and take of international existence.

So long as the effectiveness of the Security Council is handicapped by lack of big power unanimity, the maintenance of peace and security must depend upon the relatively active role played by the General Assembly. This, however, is a short-term view. In a longer run, the participation of a nuclear power whose authority covers one fourth the world's population is essential to the efficacy of the United Nations. Its very presence is indispensable for any lasting solution of such urgent problems as the nonproliferation of nuclear weapons or the escalation of particular conflicts.

The necessity of controlling armaments and nuclear weapons for the survival of mankind requires the inclusion of all members of the "nuclear club," even if the strategic capability of some is yet primitive. So long as Communist China is excluded, it will certainly continue to reject—as it has throughout the past seventeen years—any international agreement or decision affecting "China" taken without its participation. By bringing mainland

China into the United Nations, any responsible steps designed to elicit Peking's compliance with fundamental Charter obligations would have a better chance of support from important segments of the world community than they have today. To phrase the point with the most modest expectations, the possibility of mutual miscalculation would be greatly reduced as a by-product of Peking's joining in a steady stream of discourse.

Despite seemingly irresistible forces at work, there is neverthe-less general concern, particularly in the United States, about the possible adverse repercussions on the United Nations of seating Communist China. Such a change, no doubt, would temporarily shake U.S. public confidence, in view of its deep commitment in the whole issue. However, the argument that such a move might compel the United States to withdraw from the United Nations is subject to critical examination. A nationwide survey on the "American Public's View of U.S. Policy toward China" conducted in the late spring of 1964 by the Survey Research Center, University of Michigan, for the Council on Foreign Relations, indicates that there is almost unanimous agreement (only 5 per cent dissenting) that the United States should stay in the United Nations in the event of Communist China's par-ticipation.[54] Clearly there is a public awareness of the need to maintain and participate in the United Nations. It is also sug-gested that some segments of the population who oppose Com-munist China's participation use this issue to symbolize either their hostility to the United Nations itself or their frustration from the "no-victory" policy of the protracted cold war. Their reaction, in other words, is not directly related to the matter of Communist China's participation itself. Thus a decision to seat Communist China, perhaps a temporary setback for the United States, need not have fatal consequences for the United Nations as a whole.

If, however, a decision to seat Communist China implies a "hunting license" to Peking to "conquer" and "incorporate" Formosa, world peace and security as well as the fundamental human rights of thirteen million people would be fatally endangered. Such a course would be violently contrary to all the goals of the United Nations. As our previous analysis has shown, the participation question cannot be solved equitably without a prior or simultaneous solution of the Formosa problem. There is still time to lay the groundwork to assure the survival of Formosa as an independent entity and to safeguard the aspirations of the Formosan people to shape their own destiny. Continued adherence to a dogmatic and unrealistically inflexible policy toward the participation of Communist China without seriously exploring a rational alternative for Formosa may lead to where it is too late to save even a foothold for the legitimate claims of the people of Formosa.

To prevent the "expulsion" of the Nationalist regime from the United Nations, the so-called "two Chinas" policy has been advanced in Assembly debates. It has never formally been presented as a draft resolution in the General Assembly, although its content has gained greater clarity, articulated by the Canadian Foreign Minister at the twenty-first Assembly in 1966 and by the 1966 panel report of the United Nations Association of the United States of America. (The Canadian formula was meant to be an "interim" solution, and did not preclude self-determination for settling Formosa's controversial status.) In essence its aim is to include both Nationalist China and Communist China in the United Nations. Such a device is largely based on the theory of state succession in international law. It presupposes the formation of two successor states as a result of the Chinese civil war of 1949 —one China in Formosa and another China on the mainland. Since both are to be called "China," it inevitably raises the complex problem as to *which* China is to be considered as the *authentic* China eligible to occupy "China's" permanent seat in the Security Council. One thinks immediately of "veto" when the Security Council is mentioned; and it must be admitted that the thought of "veto" is enough to hinder many from any further thinking.

While it is generally assumed that the People's Republic of China is identical with "China," as designated by the Charter, some maintain that the "Republic of China" represents the original state of "China" and that Communist China is to be considered as a new state. Hence the seat in the Security Council would continue to be occupied by Nationalist China, even if Communist China were admitted as a new member fully authorized to participate in the General Assembly. Little documentation is required to demonstrate that the identity of "China" as a state has not changed as a result of the civil war in 1949. The government today in effective control of all the territory (except Quemoy and Matsu), resources, and people on the mainland does unmistakably represent "China" in the world community regardless of its institutional structures, its internal processes, and its external orientations. This view is in harmony with a position that has long been widely accepted in international law.

The founding fathers of the United Nations clearly had "mainland China" in mind when they granted big-power status to the state called "China" in 1945. Certainly they had not intended to have "China" understood as "Taiwan," which was then still the territory of Japan. Their expectations have been borne out through time. The five nuclear powers in the world today happen to coincide with the five permanent members of the Security Council, as designated by the Charter in 1945. It is obvious, from a realistic point of view, that the seat for "China" in the Security Council is meant to be bestowed upon whatever government happens to exercise formal authority and effective control over the mainland regardless of any change of state title from the "Republic of China" to the "People's Republic of China."[55]

The "two Chinas" formula, though similar to a "one China, one Formosa" alternative in many respects, has fundamental deficiencies, not the least of which is the perpetuation of the complex controversy over "China's" seat in the Security Council. The continuing disagreements about "one China only," "two Chinas," and "one China, one Formosa" stem not only from the

Chinese civil war of 1949 but also from the basic "uncertainty" of Formosa's status in international law after World War II. The issue is whether or not Formosa is part of "China" today. Conflicting claims and complications regarding the Chinese participation question are generated by this issue, and any attempt at a sound solution for the Chinese participation question must simultaneously consider this problem.

The "two Chinas" formula does not remove the root of the problem; on the contrary the basic issue is left unresolved. This arrangement would keep the matter as precarious as ever, with all conflicting claims left intact. As long as both mainland China and Formosa identify themselves as the state of "China," they will keep the old dilemma alive by firing salvos of hostile claims to represent "all the Chinese people." While one party propagates the myth of "recapturing mainland China," the counter-threat to "liberate" Taiwan will not die. Mutual exchanges of this sort tend to obscure the demands, aspirations, and identities of the people of two distinct bodies politic, which are physically separated by the Taiwan Straits, more than a hundred miles wide.

An essential condition of world security is the distinct separation of "Formosa" from mainland China *in name and fact*. A clear demarcation can be drawn and community expectations and demands can be stabilized realistically and rationally, based on tolerance and eventual cooperation. International recognition of the unambiguous separation of external and internal processes, coupled with renunciation of competing claims against each other by both "China" and "Formosa," would remove finally the root of a confusion that has long endangered world public order.

In 1945, when China became a member of the United Nations, Formosa was legally part of Japan. In 1949, when the Chinese Communist regime was established in Peking and the Nationalist regime sought refuge in Formosa, Formosa remained from the legal point of view a Japanese territory under Allied belligerent occupation, administered by Generalissimo Chiang

Kai-shek. Since then, while the Nationalist regime has at least retained effective control over Formosa, the Chinese Communist regime has obviously extended neither formal authority nor effective control over the island. According to the peace treaty with Japan in 1951, Formosa was expressly "detached" from Japan, though not attached to any power. Nor did the subsequent peace treaty between the "Republic of China" and Japan in 1952 stipulate any beneficiary for Japan's renunciation of Taiwan. Although both Chinese Nationalists and Communists are united in their claim that Taiwan's legal status has long been settled and that it is an integral part of China, we share the view of some major powers that the legal status of Formosa in international law remains "undetermined." The way to settle this difficulty is to apply the principle of self-determination, holding a plebiscite in Formosa under United Nations supervision, thereby allowing the people of Formosa to decide their own destiny.

Formosa has existed as a distinct political entity with its own identity and perspective outside the control of Communist China for the past seventeen years. Though Formosans in the past shared cultural and ethnic origins with mainland Chinese, they have shaped their unique political perspectives—demands, expectations, and identifications—as a result of their political experience under Japanese rule, their long period of separation from mainland China, and the special environment of Taiwan. The claim that Taiwan is part of China, as persistently put forth by both the Chinese Communist and Nationalist regimes, is based on the presumption that the popular aspirations in Formosa, today as yesterday, hold that Formosans belong to China. This presumption is unwarranted and untrue, and is given currency in the world at large solely because circumstances have denied a self-determining voice to the people of Formosa since their emancipation from Japan. Japanese colonial control passed away to be replaced by an alien "exile" government supposedly deriving its authority from "belligerent occupation" on behalf of the Allied powers.

It is time that the world respect the aspirations of the people of Formosa. The outcome of a free plebiscite would undoubtedly favor the establishing of an independent nation of "Formosa," completely separated from Communist China. We propose that this new state of Formosa be guaranteed admittance as a member of the United Nations. While all the principal factors in the context—particularly considerations of political realism and the principle of universality—are in favor of transferring China's seats in both the General Assembly and the Security Council to Communist China, an even-handed application of the fundamental principles of the Charter would also require the admission of the state of "Formosa" as a new member. Under a "one China, one Formosa" resolution, Formosa would represent the people of Formosa. Once the fiction of great-power status, as cultivated by the Nationalist regime, has been laid aside, Formosa's participation in the United Nations would be realistic, responsive, and responsible.

As an independent nation in law and fact, the leaders of the new Formosa, renouncing any claim to represent the seven hundred million people on the mainland, would no longer offer dangerous and futile provocations to mainland China. For the first time the Formosan people (eleven million native Formosans and two million mainland Chinese) would be able to identify their common future with Formosa itself. No longer split into an exile fraction cherishing delusions of faded grandeur, and a majority denied freedom of expression, a realistic commonwealth can arise from cooperative devotion and effort. Such urgent problems as 'the spectacular and formidable burden of military expenditures, the fantastic duplication and conflict of government structures, the lurking crises of economic imbalance and explosive population growth, could be tackled directly, rather than sidestepped and postponed to a mythological Utopia called the "recovery of the mainland."

The proposal of "one China, one Formosa" immediately raises the question of practicability, in view of the persisting and parallel objections of both the Chinese Communist and Nationalist regimes to such a proposal.[56] Two questions present themselves at once: First, in the light of the strong opposition unitedly voiced by Peking and Taipei, how can such a proposal be implemented? Second, if this were effected against the will of Communist China, could a new and independent Formosa survive? These are questions of fundamental importance, and we intend in later chapters to discuss the problem of implementation and viability of Formosa as an independent political entity. In the meantime, we would like to register our cautious but optimistic answers here.

The fundamental obstacle to the implementation of the "one China, one Formosa" policy or even the "two Chinas" program lies in the consistent denunciation of that policy by both Communist and Nationalist China. Such unity of objection often hinders innovative and constructive thinking and action. However, in President Kennedy's phrase, "Our problems are manmade—therefore, they can be solved by man." On the status of Formosa, as on many other issues of enormous importance to the objectives of the U.N. and the world community, we must count on persistence and fairness to aid in transforming the outlook of a new generation of Communist Chinese leaders as they come to the fore through evolutionary change.

In order to comprehend the significance of Mao and Chiang's dogmas about Taiwan being part of China, one has to go back to the history of decades of struggle between the Chinese Nationalists and Communists. The bitterness and hatred aroused were too personal to be detached from the shaping of their respective public policies. Their "seemingly uncompromising and unnegotiable" position on policies sloganized as "liberate Taiwan" or "recapture the mainland" is in no small degree a continuation of a bitter personal struggle. The Formosan problem has thus been complicated, emotionalized, and obfuscated by the persistent preachings of "lofty doctrines" utterly divorced from realities or needs of the changing world.

As of now, it seems unlikely that Communist China would

give up her claim to conquer and incorporate Taiwan, but far more surprising changes have taken place in politics. "Men do not repudiate the doctrines and dogmas to which they have sworn their loyalty," Senator J. William Fulbright has remarked, but they do "rationalize, revise, and reinterpret them to meet new needs and new circumstances, all the while protesting that their heresy is purest orthodoxy."[57] As the elder generation of politicians who were directly involved in a bitter and bloody personal struggle pass from the political stage, it can be anticipated that new elites on both sides are more likely to come to terms with the realities of life, including the separation of Formosa from mainland China, and the appropriate reappraisal and reclarification of their policies accordingly. Thus in due course it is not unreasonable to predict that community expectations can be stabilized to accept Formosa as an independent body politic, provided that Formosa's independence is genuinely sustained by the popular aspirations and collective effort of the people of Formosa. In the immediate future Formosa will continue to need defense assistance from the United States, as in the past seventeen years, but as it emerges as a viable independent nation, the United Nations would eventually become the sole shield of Formosa, as of so many small member states. Sooner or later the personnel constituting the present leadership of mainland China, or their successors, will recognize that the formation of an independent state of Formosa, whose leaders and whose people have unequivocally renounced claims to "recover" the mainland, is a bulwark protecting their own security from potential pressures from any direction.

Finally, should such a genuine effort to seek a rational solution fail to obtain immediate acceptance, it would nevertheless have the effect of broadening the bases of support, not only among the allies of the United States but also among the "nonaligned" member states. By espousing a realistic and just cause—"one China, one Formosa"—the United States cannot fail to gain broader international support in the face of Peking's continuing militancy and isolation. As indicated by recent surveys, the American public is generally receptive to the idea of Peking's participation in the United Nations, provided Formosa's security and membership are not compromised. At a time when Washington is looking beyond Mao's leadership for the eventual normalization of relations with mainland China—and when Communist China is in a position of relative weakness—it is particularly opportune to propose a rational alternative that offers some encouragement to the moderate elements in Peking. While Communist China can obstruct a rational solution, there is a limit as to what it can do: in this interdependent world no nation, large or small, can safely defy world opinion indefinitely. The "one China, one Formosa" contribution to the solution of the question of Chinese participation and Formosan independence is a viable alternate in a world where no worthwhile policy alternatives are without risk and cost, as well as benefit.

CHAPTER TWO

Self-Determination for an Independent Formosa

WHILE IT IS uncertain when and whence the first inhabitants came to Formosa, it is known that the Chinese began to migrate in substantial numbers to Formosa in the late fifteenth and early sixteenth centuries. The Portuguese were the first Europeans to reach the island, and Portuguese navigators early in the sixteenth century called the island "Ilha Formosa," "beautiful island." During the seventeenth century, foreign powers, notably the Portuguese, Spaniards, and Dutch, as well as dissident Chinese, vied for control of the island. In 1683 the Ch'ing Dynasty of China formally annexed Taiwan and kept it under very loose control for about two centuries. In 1871 the crew of an Okinawa vessel wrecked on the south coast of Formosa was murdered by the aborigines. When Japan asked for a remedy, the answer of the Chinese government was that it could not be held responsible since the outrages had been committed "outside its jurisdiction." Not until 1885 was Taiwan made into a regular province of the Ch'ing.

In 1895 Formosa and the Pescadores were ceded to Japan by the Treaty of Shimonoseki as a consequence of the Sino-Japanese war. After suppressing resistance by Formosan elites, Japan finally incorporated Formosa under the tent of its national administration.

In the latter part of World War II, Formosa became an important topic at some of the major conferences. In the Cairo Declaration of 1943, President Roosevelt, Prime Minister Churchill, and Generalissimo Chiang Kai-shek proclaimed that it was their purpose that "all the territories Japan has stolen from the Chinese, such as Manchuria, Formosa, and the Pescadores, shall be restored to the Republic of China." In the Potsdam Declaration of July 26, 1945, the three major powers—the United States, the United Kingdom, and the Soviet Union—undertook to carry out the terms of the Cairo Declaration. Subsequently, by the Instrument of Surrender, Japan accepted the terms of the Potsdam Declaration and hence the obligation embodied in the Cairo Declaration.

At the end of the war Japan surrendered Formosa and the Pescadores to Generalissimo Chiang Kai-shek, "acting in behalf of the United States, the Republic of China, the United Kingdom and the British Empire, and the Union of Soviet Socialist Republics." In October 1945 the Nationalist government established a military government under an "Administrator General and Concurrently Supreme Commander in the Taiwan Area." The Formosan people at first welcomed the new "liberators" but they soon became disillusioned when the Chinese Nationalists, assuming the role of "conquerors," proved more oppressive than the Japanese. The corruption and graft of Nationalist officials were unprecedented in the history of the island.

Reacting to the atrocities and maladministration of the Nationalist occupation authorities, the Formosans revolted. On February 27, 1947, a native woman was killed by agents of the Government Tobacco Monopoly for selling nontaxed cigarettes. The next day a large crowd of Formosans marched on the Governor-General's office after they had failed to obtain redress at the Tobacco Monopoly headquarters. The police fired upon them and at least four demonstrators were killed. The Formosans responded by attacking the Nationalist occupation authorities, first in Taipei, then throughout the island, and they formed the "Committee for the Settlement of the February 28 Incident." The Nationalist commander at first temporized, then ruthlessly crushed the mass uprising as soon as military reinforcements arrived from the mainland in March. According to conservative estimates over ten thousand Formosan leaders were massacred— a damaging blow to a territorial community that had developed few native leaders of experience and sophistication under Japanese colonial rule. A heavy proportion of the native elite was wiped out; political leaders who had survived execution were driven underground or abroad. Immediately after the revolt, the Nationalist government unilaterally proclaimed Formosa a regular "province" of China. As the civil war became more intense on the mainland the Formosan leaders sought to divorce Formosa from their unwelcome entanglement with it.

On October 1, 1949, having overthrown the Kuomintang forces, the Communists led by Mao Tse-tung established the Central People's Government of the People's Republic of China. The defeated Nationalist government fled from Nanking to Formosa in December 1949—even though Formosa was legally still part of Japan.

When the Chinese Nationalists retreated to Formosa in late 1949, most observers felt that it was simply a matter of time before the Nationalist regime would be exterminated. In early 1950 the public proclamation of U.S. dissociation from the regime was assumed to be a fatal blow. On January 5, 1950, President Truman stated: "In keeping with these declarations [Cairo and Potsdam], Formosa was surrendered to Generalissimo Chiang Kai-shek, and for the past 4 years, the United States and the other Allied powers have accepted the exercise of Chinese authority over the Island."[1] However, the outbreak of the Korean war in June 1950 changed the whole picture. President Truman, while proclaiming "the neutralization of Formosa" and dispatching the United States Seventh Fleet to prevent any attack on Formosa and any operations from Formosa against mainland China, stated in June 1950 that "the determination of the future status of Formosa must await the restoration of security in the Pacific, a peace settlement with Japan, or consideration by the United Nations."[2]

In the peace treaty with Japan, signed in San Francisco in September 1951, Japan formally renounced "all right, title, and claim to Formosa and the Pescadores." Formosa was "detached" from Japan, but was not "attached" to anyone, since no beneficiary of Japan's renunciation was specified. Similarly, the peace treaty between the "Republic of China" and Japan of April 1952 did not alter the status of Formosa. Article 2 of the treaty simply recognizes the renunciation by Japan of "all right, title, and claim to Taiwan [Formosa] and Penghu [the Pescadores]" under Article 2 of the Peace Treaty with Japan at San Francisco, without any stipulation of beneficiary.

Shortly after he took office, President Eisenhower proclaimed in 1953 that the United States Seventh Fleet would no longer be "employed to shield Communist China." Although the Nationalist forces made no attempt to mount a large-scale invasion of the mainland, in September 1954 the Chinese Communists initiated attacks against the offshore islands held by the Nationalists. In the midst of the crisis, the United States and the Republic of China signed a mutual defense treaty in December 1954 by which the United States was committed to the defense of Formosa and the Pescadores and "such other territories as may be determined by mutual agreement." Mindful of controversies over the legal status of Formosa and the Pescadores, in ratifying the mutual defense treaty the United States Senate noted that "nothing in the present treaty shall be construed as affecting or modifying the legal status or the sovereignty" of Formosa and the Pescadores.[3] The crisis led the United States Congress to pass the "Formosan resolution" even before the ratification of the mutual defense treaty. The President was authorized to employ United States armed forces "as he deems necessary for the specific purpose of securing and protecting Formosa and the Pescadores against armed attack," including "the securing and protection of such related positions and territories of that area now in friendly hands."[4]

Communist attacks on the offshore islands were renewed in August 1958 by artillery barrage against Quemoy and Matsu. The United States took a firmer position than in 1954 and in fact extended its defense to Quemoy and Matsu. Since the termination of the crisis, mainland Communists have adopted a policy of "ceremonial" shelling of Quemoy on odd days of the month, symbolizing the continued existence of the "civil war" between the Communist and Nationalist regimes.

Thus far the United States has adopted a "nonrecognition" policy toward Communist China as an integral part of its overall policy of "containment." Because the People's Republic has been excluded from formal authority, the principal official interactions between the United States and Communist China have been the ambassadorial talks commencing in 1955, first in Geneva and later in Warsaw. There have been 132 of these meetings, as of September 1966. While the United States has demanded Peking's renunciation of the use of force in the Formosan Straits, Communist China has insisted on the withdrawal of the United States armed forces from Formosa and the Formosan Straits. No progress toward a resolution of the differences is yet in sight.

As matters now stand, the Chinese Nationalists have effective control over Formosa and a seat in the United Nations, its organs and related specialized agencies. In June 1967 Communist China successfully exploded a hydrogen bomb, and is taking time to drive a hard bargain over Formosa. Although the People's Republic remains outside the framework of the United Nations, it is recognized by nearly as many nations as is Nationalist China. The overwhelming majority of Formosans abhor both the Nationalist and Communist regimes and hope to achieve independence through self-determination.

The Claimants and Types
of Claim

THE PRECEDING account of the relevant factual background, over condensed as it must of necessity be, nonetheless enables us to formulate the types of claim advanced by the rivals endeavoring to determine the future of Formosa.

In the most general terms two basic types of claim are made. On the one hand, claims are put forth that the principle of self-determination is to be applied for the establishment of an independent Formosa. The counter-claim is that the principle of self-determination is not applicable for Formosa. The former position is sponsored principally by the people of Formosa, and the governments of the United Kingdom, Ireland, and France. The latter position is voiced by both the Chinese Communist and Nationalist regimes.

While the Chinese Communists and the Nationalists have assailed one another in the most unqualified language, they have at least one contention in common concerning Formosa. They declare in unpremeditated concert that there is only "one China," not "two Chinas" or "one China, one Formosa."[5] Whatever their differences the claims of both rest on three major arguments.

The first is that the legal status of Formosa is certain and not subject to question: it is an integral part of China. It has repeatedly been alleged that to say Formosa's status is undetermined is to "make mockery of history and of realities, of human intelligence and of international agreements" and of "common sense."[6] There are differences over when Formosa was reincorporated as part of China after the outbreak of World War II. But the main thrust of the justifications advanced in support of the claim that Formosa is an integral part of China can be summarized as follows.

1] Upon the declaration of war against Japan in 1941, the Chinese government denounced all treaties between Japan and China, including the Treaty of Shimonoseki of 1895, which ceded Formosa to Japan. Hence, Formosa, a Chinese territory "stolen" by Japan, was automatically restored to China in 1941.

2] According to the Cairo Declaration of 1943, Formosa and the Pescadores were to be "restored to the Republic of China." This commitment on the part of major Allied powers, as reaffirmed by the Potsdam Declaration of July 26, 1945 and the Instrument of Surrender by Japan, have the authoritative effect of restoring Formosa as part of China.

3] The Chinese Nationalist government has had continuous and effective control over Formosa since 1945 and has represented "China" in various international organizations. The incorporation of Formosa as a "province" of China in 1947 was not objected to by any nation. Effective control being the most important element in cases of territorial change, China's claim can be justified on grounds of "occupation," "conquest," or "prescription" in international law.

4] Japan's renunciation of all "right, title, and claim" over Formosa in the peace treaty between the Republic of China and Japan implies the transfer of "sovereignty" to the Republic of China, since the latter is supposedly the beneficiary of the renunciation, even though no beneficiary is specified in the treaty. The Republic of China was a party to the treaty and at the time was in effective control of Formosa. By the same token, the conclusion of the mutual defense treaty between the United States and the Republic of China has the effect of implied recognition of Nationalist China's "sovereignty" over Formosa and the Pescadores.

5] Other justifications are based on historical, ethnic, cultural, geographical, and economic considerations. That Formosa is "an inseparable part of the territory of China" is an "irrevocable historical fact." Ethnically and culturally, the Formosan people are "a member of the great family of the Chinese nation" and "their enslavement by the United States will never be tolerated." It is also held that both economically and geographically Formosa cannot become a viable entity if separated from mainland China.

The preceding justifications are generalized for the sake of convenience. It is not trivial, however, to recall that the Chinese Communist government has never extended either effective control or formal authority over Formosa. Thus it attaches far less weight to items 3 and 4 than the Nationalist regime, and sometimes even repudiates them with qualifications.

The second argument put forth by both governments is that the question of Formosa is a domestic matter of China and outside the competence of the United Nations by Article 2(7) of the U.N. Charter, to be settled exclusively between the Nationalist government and the Communist government. Since Formosa is asserted to be part of China, the entire controversy falls essentially within the domestic jurisdiction of China. Both sides share the view that since the Chinese civil war is still in progress, the recourse to force to acquire the territory presently controlled by the other side is by no means proscribed by the United Nations Charter; it is "an internal affair of China" in which no outside powers, including the United Nations, can "intervene."

From Peking's viewpoint, if there is an international aspect to the "Formosa question," it is the perpetuation by the United States of "outright armed aggression" against the people of China by "invading and occupying" Formosa with the powerful Seventh Fleet stationed in the Formosan Straits. U.S. aggression is the sole problem connected with Formosa with which the United Nations ought to be concerned. In its view, the conclusion of the mutual defense treaty between the United States and the Republic of China in 1954 was an attempt on the part of the United States "to legalize its armed seizure of Chinese territory of Taiwan, and make Taiwan a base for further aggression against China and the preparation for a new war."[7] In the same vein, Premier Chou En-lai stated in September 1954: "[A]ll proposals to place Taiwan under United Nations trusteeship or under neutral mandate, or to 'neutralize' Taiwan or to create a so-called 'independent Taiwan state,' are attempts to carve up China's territory, enslave the Chinese people on Taiwan and legalize United States occupation of Taiwan. None of this will be tolerated by the Chinese people."[8]

The third argument shared by the Nationalists and the Communists is that the principle of self-determination is not applicable even if the question of Formosa is a matter of international concern within U.N. competence. It has been repeatedly stated on different occasions that the Chinese Nationalist government represents the public will of the people of Formosa who in turn do support the existing regime. Hence there is no room or need for the people of Formosa to exercise self-determination. It might be argued that Article 1(2) of the United Nations Charter, while recognizing the principle of self-determination, does not contain a legal definition of the principle and is meant to leave the implementation of the principle to the national governments. Moreover, the scope of application of the principle is strictly limited. The principle applies only to peoples under colonial rule and is not designed to divide territories or nations which are naturally united. The "inseparable relation" between Formosa and mainland China by reference to historical, cultural, ethnic, geographical, and economic factors leads to the statement that it is "sheer nonsense" to assert self-determination for Formosa.[9]

Spokesmen for Formosans and for some major powers, however, claim that the principle of self-determination is appropriate for use in establishing an independent Formosa.

Even prior to the conclusion of the peace treaty with Japan, President Truman and Prime Minister Attlee jointly declared on December 8, 1950:

> On the question of Formosa, we have noted that both Chinese claimants have insisted upon the validity of the Cairo Declaration and have expressed reluctance to have the matter consid-

ered by the United Nations. We agree that the issues should be settled by peaceful means and in such a way as to safeguard the interests of the people of Formosa and the maintenance of peace and security in the Pacific, and that consideration of this question by the United Nations will contribute to these ends.[10]

In recent years, in voting to seat Peking in the U.N., the British delegation has made it a practice simultaneously to reiterate its position on Formosa: ". . . sovereignty over the island of Formosa is undetermined. It therefore follows, in our view, that the question of who should represent Formosa in the United Nations is also undetermined. The vote which I shall cast in favour of the substantive draft resolution does not prejudice the position of my Government on this point."[11]

Shortly after French recognition of Communist China in January 1964 Premier Georges Pompidou made it clear in April 1964 that the act of recognition in no way implied French acquiescence to Peking's claim over Formosa. In his view, "Formosa [Taiwan] was detached from Japan, but it was not attached to anyone" under the Japanese peace treaty. This being the case, Formosa's indeterminate status "must be decided one of these days, taking the wishes of the Formosa population into consideration."[12]

Turning to the justifications formulated in support of self-determination for Formosa, these also can be conveniently summarized under three principal propositions. The first is that the legal status of Formosa remains undetermined and uncertain. Besides Formosans themselves, this view has been most consistently expressed by the British government, and to a lesser degree by the United States, France, Canada, Australia, and Ireland.[13] After the peace treaty with Japan, in 1951 Anthony Eden stated the British position regarding Formosa:

This Cairo Declaration was a statement of intention that Formosa should be retroceded to China after the war. This retrocession has, in fact, never taken place, because of the difficulties arising from the existence of two entities claiming to represent China, and the differences amongst the powers as to the status of these entities. . . . In September, 1945, the administration of Formosa was taken over from the Japanese by Chinese forces at the direction of the Supreme Commander of the Allied powers; but this was not a cession, nor did it in itself involve any change of sovereignty. The arrangements made with Chiang Kai-shek put him there on a basis of military occupation pending further arrangements and did not of themselves constitute the territory Chinese. Under the peace treaty of April, 1952, Japan formally renounced all right, title, and claim to Formosa and the Pescadores; but again this did not operate as a transfer to Chinese sovereignty, whether to the People's Republic of China or to the Chinese Nationalist authorities. Formosa and the Pescadores are therefore, in the view of Her Majesty's Government, territory the *de jure* sovereignty over which is uncertain or undetermined.[14]

The position can be elaborated:

1] The unilateral denunciation of all treaties between Japan and China by the Chinese government in 1941 did not have authoritative effect. International agreements are not to be abrogated unilaterally.

2] The basic assumption upon which the Cairo Declaration was based—that the people of Formosa desired to become part of China—has to be reappraised under the changed condition, i.e., the civil war on mainland China following the end of World War II, and the establishment of the Communist regime in 1949. The involvement of Formosa and the Pescadores in the civil war had neither been foreseen nor contemplated at the time of the Cairo Declaration. To give effect to such involvement without considering the changes in the aspirations of the people of these islands resulting from changes in circumstances would do violence to the principle of self-determination, as embodied in the United

Nations Charter, an instrument that supersedes the terms of the Cairo and Potsdam Declarations as far as the provisions of the Declarations are incompatible with Charter prescriptions (Art. 103). It is often argued, moreover, that these declarations expressly reflected the wartime expectations of no more than four participating Allied powers, and that unless these expectations were crystallized and incorporated into the peace treaty with Japan, they could have no authoritative effect on other Allied powers.

3] In both the San Francisco peace treaty with Japan and the peace treaty between Japan and the Republic of China, no express provision was made as to the beneficiary of Japan's renunciation of her "right, title, and claim" over Formosa and the Pescadores. As a rule, the formal cession of territory is effected by a peace treaty that is commonly accepted as the authoritative formulation of the shared expectations of all participants. According to these two peace treaties, Formosa was expressly "detached" from Japan; however, the island and its people have not been "attached" to anyone, evidently reflecting a general expectation that a durable settlement would be made at an opportune time in the future. Furthermore, the conclusion of a mutual defense treaty between the United States and the Republic of China in no way alters the legal status of Formosa. This was specifically recognized by the United States Senate in its approval of the mutual defense treaty.

4] The Chinese Nationalist government was asked to accept the Japanese surrender on behalf of the Allied powers in 1945 by General MacArthur. The Chinese Nationalists constituted an army of belligerent occupation, nothing more, playing a role strictly the same as that taken by the armed forces of the four powers in Germany. The nature of Chinese occupation has not been altered as a result of the conclusion of the peace treaty with Japan in 1951. The present exercise of effective control over Formosa by the Chinese Nationalist regime can, in fact, be regarded as "an exile government" that administers a former colonial territory of Japan on behalf of the Allied powers. It is sometimes assumed that

World War II is settled, but such a view overlooks the many issues that remain to be settled, among which is the status and future of Formosa. Given the tremendous influence of the United States, as one of the major Allied powers, it is not trivial to speak of U.S. responsibility to defend Formosa "as one of the aftermaths of the unsettled World War II."

5] Despite the sharing of cultural and ethnic backgrounds traceable to the late sixteenth century, the people of Formosa have undergone a unique political experience. Today they have their own identity and political outlook, clearly distinct from the perspectives held by Chinese. The past seventeen years demonstrate that Formosa can surely be a viable economic and political entity even though separated from mainland China.

The second argument in support of self-determination is that the question of Formosa is a matter of international concern whose future disposition is properly within the authoritative competence of the United Nations.

To recognize Formosa as part of China would lend substance to Communist China's claim that the employment of armed forces in the liberation of Formosa is an exclusive matter of domestic concern to China concerning which no outside powers, including international organizations, can legitimately intervene. An acquiescence in such a claim would indirectly approve Communist China's belligerent expansionism and contribute only confusion to expectations in regard to world public order. Further, the fundamental human rights of thirteen million Formosans are at stake, a matter of no small concern. In assessing the policy alternatives available, one must not lose sight of the practical certainty that if Formosa should become part of China there would be the ever present problem of minority protection for which the U.N. would be partly responsible.

The third major argument holds that the principle of self-determination is applicable and should be applied in settling the indeterminate status of Formosa. It must never be ignored, it is asserted, that the Chinese Nationalist government headed by Chiang Kai-shek does not represent the public will of the people of Formosa. Chiang Kai-shek's government was never elected by the people of Formosa. The Nationalist regime has been ruling Formosa without the openly registered "consent of the governed." Unlike the peoples who have been emancipated from colonial rule since World War II, Formosa has not been able to shape its own destiny.

Viewed in historical and contemporary perspective, the issue in the present controversy is the invocation of the principle of self-determination by the people of a former Japanese colony. The principle is invoked against the existing authority in belligerent occupation for the purpose of establishing an independent state, which implies independent participation in the world arena, coupled with full authority and control over its internal processes. The claim is made in the name of the people of a former colony; interestingly enough, not against the former colonial ruler, but the present belligerent occupation authority who is supposedly acting on behalf of the Allied powers.

The principle of self-determination, as stated in Articles 1(2) and 55 of the Charter, is more than a doctrine of "international morality"; it is a guiding principle of the whole United Nations. During its brief history, the U.N. has repeatedly affirmed the right of all peoples to "freely determine their political status and freely pursue their economic, social and cultural development."[15] This has been particularly applied to the context of colonial claims; Formosa, which was a former Japanese colonial territory, should be no exception to the application of this principle. Granting that Formosa's claim is a noncolonial one, the principle of self-determination has a universal character that includes noncolonial as well as colonial claims. Self-determination draws attention to the most rational and realistic way to decide the destiny of the people of a particular territory whose status is indeterminate. This obviously applies to the inhabitants of "the beautiful Isle."

Authoritative Decision-Makers

THERE is a divergence of views as to who are the authoritative decision-makers in determining the legal status of Formosa. Both the Chinese Communist and Nationalist regimes, in identifying the controversy as an "internal affair" of China, take the position that it is to be settled between themselves and nobody else. Some commentators maintain that the future disposition of Formosa should be effected by those Allied powers who declared war against Japan during World War II, since Formosa is an unsettled consequence of the Japanese surrender. It may also be suggested that the question be referred to the International Court of Justice. The most popular position, however, is that the United Nations is the most logical and convenient arena for solving the problem. Any future disposition of Formosa is bound to affect world public order and the human rights of Formosans and their descendants; and thus the question is a matter of international concern falling within the scope of the United Nations, and improperly left to the officials of Communist or Nationalist governments. That the member states of the United Nations today are not identical with those allied against Japan does not affect the authority of the United Nations.

In the course of finding a suitable solution for the Chinese participation issue, the future of Formosa must be brought into the open and disposed of. Policy alternatives for the solution of the question of Chinese participation are properly based in part upon the aims, projections, and strategies comprehended in an inclusive view of the future of the people of the island. A rational solution of the Chinese participation tangle hinges upon a reasonable solution of the Formosan problem. In the probable sequence of future development, the Chinese participation question will probably be raised first. The future disposition of Formosa will arise in the course of debate and negotiations having to do with participation.

As projected by the Charter, a major purpose of the United Nations is to implement the principle of self-determination, and the U.N. has already devoted substantial effort to controversies over self-determination. In fact, issues of this kind are second only to cold-war matters in significance, and the United Nations has played an impressive part in bringing these highly emotionalized problems to "peaceful settlement."

Fundamental Community Policies

HAVING formulated the basic types of claim and identified authoritative decision-makers, we seek, as in the preceding chapter, to examine the potential values and fundamental community policies at stake in the Formosan question so that the decision-makers involved can be provided with relevant guide lines for action.

The change of territory from one nation to another involves not merely a transfer of a piece of land, but of an entire community process of authority and control over people, resources, and institutions. The implications of a change of territory could be practically catastrophic for the human beings who inhabit the island, for one of the major claimants is Communist China, a power whose elite is publicly committed to the cause of world domination and to a totalitarian system of public order, whose modalities of operation are patently at odds with a public order of human dignity.

The values at stake pending a resolution of the Formosan and the participation problem go far beyond human rights, as commonly understood. World security is in the balance. Recall that the question of Formosa has been the crux of the cold-war issue in Asia for the past seventeen years. The Chinese Nationalist regime has consistently proclaimed "the recapture of mainland China" as its sacred task; and the Chinese Communist regime has never sought to conceal its policy of seeking to "liberate" Formosa by force, if necessary. Both regimes are deeply involved in hostile alignments in the world arena—if an armed conflict should arise at any point from disputes over Formosa, repercussions will extend far beyond East Asia.

Clearly, the basic community policy to be identified and recommended for dealing with the Formosan question is the maintaining of at least minimum public order. Implied is the minimalization of coercion, particularly of military force. Since territorial disputes too often occasion "public disorder," the international community had sought to proscribe the use of force in the acquisition of territory. These efforts began well before the establishment of the United Nations, when the use of force was still a permissible means of change. The Stimson doctrine, intended to deny the fruits of territorial expansion by violence, was typical of this attempt. Crystallized and refined, this policy has been incorporated into the United Nations Charter, so that today's world community is obligated to insist on "peaceful procedure" in cases of territorial change.

As we indicated before, what is at stake in territorial change is the entire community process of authority and control over people, institutions, and resources as well as boundaries. In the final analysis, what counts most is people. While value impacts on other participants or communities are not to be overlooked, it is after all the inhabitants in a given territory who are most directly and keenly affected by any territorial change. In deciding the future destiny of a given territory, it is understood that the ultimately effective decision-makers should be the people directly implicated. This assumption is accepted with added intensity in an age of "rising nationalism" and of "rising expectations for democracy." If the conception of human rights means anything at all, it includes the prescription that when territorial changes occur the basic freedom of people to choose their community and pattern of political life must be assured. If community expectations are to be effectively stabilized, therefore, the settlement of any territorial disputes must take into account the genuine perspectives—the demands, identifications, and expectations—of the people most directly involved. This is also the surest way to insure optimum utilization of human and natural resources in a society where at least the minimum value goals and institutions of civilization prevail. Deviation from this policy leads to "permanent instability" of public order as well as to an endless series of troublesome issues in the field of human rights. In a state of "permanent instability" the goal of optimum value production and enjoyment can hardly be expected.

In the dispute regarding the status of Formosa diversities of view are generated by different perspectives about which basic community policies are relevant to international agreements. As in all other fields of human affairs, a delicate process of balancing "stability" and "change" is ever present in the field of treaty-making. Our fundamental viewpoint has been formulated elsewhere in these words:

> If principles of authority are to control the flow of decision, it is ultimately essential that they be embodied in the expectations of the effective participants in the world community. At no time can it be taken for granted that human expectations, or the demands and identifications with which they interlock, are unchanging. Nor can it be validly asserted, without appropriate verification, that the words of treaties or other written documents, mirror community expectations. Since viewpoints are in flux, today's structure of expectation is open to change, and in fact is bound to change, as new conditions arise and new suggestions are put forward and assimilated.[16]

The social process of the world community is composed of nations of varying size, structure, and function; hence a world organization must play a very active and integrating role in maintaining world public order. The critical task is to assist in clarifying the common interests of effective decision-makers, distinguishing by appropriate procedures between inclusive and exclusive interests among the common interests, as well as drawing lines between common and special interests.[17] As an aid to the exercise of judgment, legal doctrines formulate paired opposites of policy that indicate the range of choice open in the examination of particular and general questions. Among the most salient doctrinal pairs is the broad claim to "domestic jurisdiction" versus claims of central authority. No doubt the doctrine of "domestic jurisdiction" will continue to be invoked by national elites in support of particular claims to limit the authority to act of the U.N. and similar organizations, as the Chinese Communists and Nationalists have done in attempting to preclude the consideration of a "one China, one Formosa" policy alternative. In view of the overriding commitment of the U.N. to peaceful settlement and human rights, it is intolerable that the doctrine of domestic jurisdiction should be applied to a situation in which inclusive consequences are so gravely involved as in the Formosan problem. The proper decision-makers for the future of Formosa are both the U.N. and the people of Formosa.

Trends in Past Decisions and Conditioning Factors

TO PUT the contending claims over Formosa into proper perspective, we shall examine the flow of past decisions (and the conditioning factors) relating to the acquisition of territory, domestic jurisdiction, and the principle of self-determination, and discuss these in order.

Claims Relating to the Acquisition of Territory

The customary international law governing the acquisition of territory developed at a time when the European powers were the dominating participants in the world arena. The acquisition of territory was part of the "empire-building" process of the competing colonial powers. While acquiring vast areas of overseas territory, resources, and markets, the rivals proudly proclaimed themselves as carrying the "white man's burden" on a "civilizing mission" around the world.

These nations, sharing the heritage of Christianity and a strong sense of national unity, acquired substantial military strength as a result of the growth of science, technology, and industry. Their immediate targets of expansion were the "uninhabited regions" or "regions inhabited by savages or semi-civilized peoples." Areas suitable for immigration, such as the land masses of North and South America, Australia, New Zealand, and parts of Africa, were occupied through full settlement. The next target was Asia. In these populous areas European migration for permanent settlement was relatively unimportant. The immediate objectives were physical resources and markets, linked in various ways to cultural expansion in religion, education, health, and certain other sectors. In one form or another, weak nations or territorial communities of the Asian continent became the prey of European colonial powers. The next major target was most of the African continent; though not fully suitable for settlement, it was valuable as a resource base and as a potential market. Finally, the polar areas and rather isolated islands, though practically uninhabitable or with scarce resources, were sought primarily for their potential significance in modern strategy.

In the course of expansion all instruments of policy were mobilized—with the military force a decisive one. Among the colonial powers, there were early starters and late comers. And their relative power position was by no means static in the world balancing of power. The world has been mapped and remapped in accord with the shifting weight of competing powers. Within loose restrictions the use of military force was accepted as a permissible mode of change, including the acquisition of territories. Understandably, the damaging repercussions of the use of force were by no means as far-reaching as in today's world, given the low degree of interdependence and the rudimentary weapon technology at that time. Moreover, in the nineteenth century in particular, the concept of "the survival of the fittest" was at its height in both international and domestic arenas. Since the expansionist powers identified their role as a "civilizing mission," concern for the aspirations of the local inhabitants of a newly acquired territory were given little heed in the formulation of customary international law regarding the acquisition of territory. Rather, the basic concern of decision-makers—the big powers—at that stage of history was how, in a power-balancing world, to stabilize community expectations in favor of perpetuating the fruits of expansion.

As they eventually developed, the modalities of acquiring territory under traditional international law are generally classified into five categories: accretion, occupation, prescription, conquest (or subjugation), and cession.

"Accretion" is the result of natural or artificial land formations. It presents little problem. "Occupation" applies only to "unappropriated territory" (*terra nullius*). And "prescription" is defined as "the acquisition of sovereignty over a territory through continuous and undisturbed exercise of sovereignty over it during such a period as is necessary to create under the influence of historical development the general conviction that the present condition of things is in conformity with international order."[18] Jennings elaborates the difference between "occupation" and "prescription" in the following terms:

> Occupation can only apply to territory that is *res nullius*; it is in all cases lawful in origin, and the mere passage of time has no place in it, provided only that the apprehension of the territorial sovereignty be effective. Prescription, on the other hand, is a portmanteau concept that comprehends both a possession of which the origin is unclear or disputed, and an adverse possession which is in origin demonstrably unlawful. For

prescription, therefore, the possession must be long-continued, undisturbed, and it must be unambiguously attributable to a claim to act as sovereign. It depends as much on the quiescence of the former sovereignty as on the consolidation through time of the new.[19]

One element common to all acquisition of territories is "effective control," regardless of modalities. The literature arguing over what constitutes "effective control" is abundant. Quite evidently the underlying policy consideration is to maximize resource utilization, since only an effective occupant is in a position to exploit resources to his best advantage.

The profound changes since World War II are sensitively reflected in the flow of decisions dealing with former colonies. In consequence of the rapid multiplication of nation states the older European powers no longer take the initiatives that lead to territorial change. Instead, the emerging nations of the Afro-Asian continents are the dynamic participants in redrawing the map of the world. The primary objective in the acquisition of territory is no longer proclaimed to be a "civilizing mission" or called "empire building." New objectives enter the political process and stimulate the crystallizing of new justifications for permissible alterations of territory. Foremost among these innovations is a greatly intensified demand that the boundaries of bodies politic conform to popular aspirations, thereby insuring both the protection of human rights and the acceptance of world public order.

Tremendous discrepancies continue to characterize the bases of power among nations. There has, however, been a pronounced change in the patterns of disputes over territory. In the imperial era the predominant controversies were between great powers and small powers, or among great powers; and these confrontations were accompanied by high expectations of violence. To an increasing extent the contemporary scene witnesses territorial clashes between small powers who generate a climate of threat, punctuated by overt acts of violence. In former times the lesser powers were rather quickly policed by a major power, or their cause turned into a clash between empires. The territorial problems that arise from the disintegration of formal colonial empires and the emergence of newly independent states are far too complicated and different to be met by customary international law. And as the "unappropriated land masses" on the planet have practically disappeared, the traditional community prescriptions originally designed to deal with territorial changes concerning such land masses have become of limited relevance. (They may, however, have a new lease of life in an age of astropolitics.)

While all instruments of policy continue to be employed by claimant states in support of territorial claims, the use of military force as a means of change, particularly of territorial change, is expressly proscribed by the United Nations Charter. Before the establishment of the United Nations, the use of military force to acquire territories or other valued assets was not regarded as impermissible—even in the form of large-scale "war." The "subjugation" (or "conquest") of a territory or a nation as a result of armed attack was an acceptable mode of effecting transfers of territory from one nation state to another. While the Covenant of the League of Nations made "resort to war" unlawful under certain circumstances, it refrained from outlawing "war" altogether.[20] Understandably, in the nineteenth and early twentieth centuries, there was less common interest in restraining violence. Hence the policy that guided traditional international law was an attempt to localize coercion by giving community approval to the quick settling of disputes obtained by mobilizing superior strength.

However, since territorial expansion and acquisition often disrupted world public order, there were some initiatives even during that period to deny the fruits of expansion to aggressors through collective "nonrecognition." The Stimson doctrine was typical of this line of effort. The traditional international law in regard to conquest, however, has been most profoundly affected by the expectations incorporated in and crystallized by the United Nations Charter. The fundamental community policy projected by the Charter embodies both a negative policy of minimalizing the deliberate use of coercion as a means of value change and a positive policy of promoting the shaping and sharing of values by persuasion. In its negative formulation, the principle seeks to prohibit any unilateral use of coercion by one state against another as an instrument of value change. Article 2(4) provides that "All Members shall refrain in their international relations from the threat or use of force against the territorial integrity or political independence of any state, or in any other manner inconsistent with the Purposes of the United Nations." In its positive formulation, it seeks to promote the stability in the expectation of freedom from unauthorized coercion that is indispensable to the optimum production and distribution of values. Article 2(3) of the Charter states that "All Members shall settle their international disputes by peaceful means in such a manner that international peace and security, and justice, are not endangered." Taking the Charter as a whole, it is commonly accepted that force is in general prohibited save for self-defense and community police action. Though there is a minority that dissents from this expectation, it is increasingly conceded that there is no permissible place for the acquisition of territory through "conquest" (or "subjugation") in the contemporary world.

Nonetheless it may be asserted that the acquisition of territory resulting from self-defense against an aggressor state is still feasible. Self-defense being permissible, acquisition of the aggressor's territory would hence be permissible. This argument misconceives the scope of self-defense. In contemporary expectation self-defense is considered permissible insofar as it is necessary and proportionate to the task of repelling aggression. As soon as aggression is effectively repelled, the state acting in self-defense must immediately discontinue its defensive operations. Otherwise, it may itself become a new aggressor. In order to undertake "necessary and proportionate" self-defense to repel aggression there is no need to "acquire" the aggressor's territory. To attempt to make a fine distinction between the acquisition of territory by permissible and impermissible coercion would most certainly open a pandora's box of far-reaching consequences that would defeat the basic community policy of seeking to maintain world public order. There is an obvious and ever present danger in licensing "acquisition by permissible coercion" in this decentralized world of ours, where the maintenance of minimum public order depends so heavily upon the reciprocity and mutual restraint of nation states in their intercourse with one another.

In the traditional conception of "cession," there are two kinds: noncoercive and coercive. For cession made free from coercion, as in the case of the U.S. purchase of Alaska, there is little ground for objection if the necessary internal processes of decision conform to appropriate standards. It is "cessions" resulting from major coercion that have to be reappraised in the light of the community policies projected by the Charter. Since the Charter makes it impermissible to acquire territory by "conquest," it is evident that a cession designed to formalize the fruits of unlawful coercion cannot be accepted. Note that this change of basic community policy cannot be applied retroactively to the acquisition of territory by conquest or coercive cession in the past; otherwise, established usages would suddenly dissolve, and we would find ourselves living in a yet more insecure world.

At present the world community still confronts a number of territorial problems that were inadequately settled or left unsettled after World War II. It has been a long-sustained practice to effect cession in the aftermath of a large-scale armed conflict through the conclusion of a peace treaty. A "peace treaty" is generally considered to be an authoritative prescription that expresses the shared expectations of both victorious and defeated states subsequent to the termination of a state of "hostility." Even when conquest was fully permissible, traditional international law gave deference to peace treaties as superseding initial arrangements made during the period of hostility. The underlying policy consideration is profound. Expectations expressed in the midst of hostility are more often than not dictated by military expediency and necessity—"victory and nothing but victory." Other relevant policy considerations are apt to disappear altogether or to receive cursory attention. Hence the commitments made under the emergency conditions of wartime are at best a precarious and unstable foundation for future order. Sooner or later they lead almost inevitably to the disruption of public order—usually sooner than expected. Hence a cooling-off period for noncoercive negotiation after the cessation of hostilities is imperative. Only in an atmosphere of relative nonviolence and nonemergency can both victorious and defeated states be expected to appraise all the relevant factors and interests at stake in shaping a durable policy. This is why under traditional international law emphasis was put on the importance of the "peace treaty." One of the primary functions of such an instrument was to clarify the mutual expectations of the parties, and especially the defeated powers, in regard to any change of territory. The "territorial clauses" have been particularly well-drafted for the purpose of preventing subsequent claims of ambiguity. Hence, traditionally any transfer of territory is prescribed in no uncertain terms.

The creation of the United Nations does not alter the significance of peace treaties as authoritative formulations of the common policy of both victorious and defeated states at the close of hostilities. But the Charter does inject a new community policy into the situation insofar as territorial changes are concerned—the principle of self-determination. Even in the nineteenth century, efforts were made to mitigate deprivations imposed upon inhabitants in cases of cession by requiring a "plebiscite" in which the populations most concerned could express their preferences. Several treaties concluded during that period provide that cession would not become authoritative and effective without the consent of the inhabitants as ascertained by plebiscite. President Wilson's advocacy of the principle of self-determination, though it re-echoed grandly throughout the globe, had very limited success in the territorial settlements after World War I. Not until the United Nations Charter did a great multilateral treaty clearly proclaim the principle of self-determination as a basic policy of the world community. The practice of the United Nations thus far has made it crystal clear that a "decent respect" for the genuine aspirations of the people concerned is the ultimate guide for effecting territorial change. This principle will be further elaborated later. Here it suffices to note the significance of this principle in the context of territorial transfer. The cardinal point to grasp is that it is at last perceived that much more is involved in changing the status of a territory than acres. We re-emphasize that the entire community process of authority and control over people, resources, and institutions is at stake. Changes are also brought about in the external as well as the internal process of a given domain. If territorial changes are to occasion the least peril to world public order the settlement must defer fully to two interdependent considerations, the minimalization of coercion, and self-determination. Any imposition of territorial change in contravention of these basic community policies carries the seeds of its own destruction, and hence resembles a time bomb that threatens the security of the whole world order.

Claims Relating to Domestic Jurisdiction

Decisions affecting the future of Formosans will also be influenced by the deference accorded past trends of response in the world community to claims of "domestic jurisdiction."

Article 2(7) of the United Nations Charter provides that: "Nothing contained in the present Charter shall authorize the United Nations to intervene in matters which are essentially within the domestic jurisdiction of any state or shall require the Members to submit such matters to settlement under the present Charter;

but this principle shall not prejudice the application of enforcement measures under Chapter VII." This is the well-known "domestic jurisdiction clause," frequently invoked to reject United Nations competence to deal with a particular dispute. There are, of course, matching counterclaims, as is to be expected from our knowledge of the doctrinal polarities that characterize a legal system. But the "domestic jurisdiction" formula is so acceptable to the elites and masses of a nationalistic era that it is little wonder that it has figured prominently in the debates of the U.N.

Article 2(7) of the Charter is traceable to Article 15(8) of the Covenant of the League of Nations, which provides that: "If the dispute between the parties is claimed by one of them, and is found by the Council, to arise out of a matter which *by international law is solely within the domestic jurisdiction of that party,* the Council shall so report, and shall make no recommendation as to its settlement" (italics added). During the era of the League, the Permanent Court of International Justice made a significant contribution in the Tunis-Morocco Nationality Decrees case. At issue was whether the dispute between France and Great Britain on the Nationality Decrees promulgated in Tunis and Morocco (French zone) on November 8, 1921, and their application to British subjects fell solely within the domestic jurisdiction of France. Rejecting the French claim, the Court declared: "The question whether a certain matter is or is not solely within the domestic jurisdiction of a state is an essentially relative question: it depends upon the development of international relations."[21] This passage is frequently quoted by commentators. In other words, the concept of "domestic jurisdiction" can be made meaningful only by reference to the context of world conditions at a given time.

Time and again recourse has been had by competing claimants to the legislative history of Article 2(7). The records of the San Francisco Conference, however, offer no conclusive answer one way or another. The founding fathers of the Charter neither saw fit to deprive or curtail the United Nations of the necessary authoritative competence essential to the effective performance of its tasks, nor wanted the Organization to "pry into" matters generally considered to be the exclusive concern of individual nation states. As no one need be reminded, the line to draw is indeed far from obvious.

Concepts in international law are definite to the extent that they are uniformly understood in content and procedure. Expectations about content are necessarily somewhat vague, since the contingent circumstances to which they refer are alluded to in general terms. Hence the importance of procedure—of who is authorized to act how to apply the content to concrete situations. As commentators, we can discover the structure of assumptions in the world community about "domestic jurisdiction" by exploring the record of the U.N.

Whenever a dispute comes to the notice of the Organization, Article 2(7) of the Charter necessarily receives initial attention, save in certain cases that are regarded as clear-cut. Claims and counterclaims regarding U.N. authority are generally juxtaposed.

No single power has a monopoly on invoking the concept of domestic jurisdiction. It has been asserted by many nations—large and small, authoritarian and nonauthoritarian. Partly as a result of the pride of the new nations in their recently won "independence," its invocation is not an uncommon practice.

While it appears simple to ascertain the immediate objectives sought by competing claimants who repudiate or accept U.N. authority in a given dispute, it is by no means easy to detect and demonstrate the underlying policy considerations of these claimants. Even the attitudes of a single power are far from consistent. Its position is more often than not dictated by the degree of "involvement" and "interest" perceived in a given dispute; and it often appears to fluctuate independently of the level of crisis at a given time.

Aside from questions of human rights, of the form of government of a state, of the non-self-governing territories, and of community police actions, the domestic jurisdiction claim is most frequently advanced in contexts where "the right of all peoples to self-determination" and "territorial disputes" are involved. Notably, the domestic jurisdiction question was raised in controversies involving Morocco, Tunisia, Algeria, and Cyprus, where the principle of self-determination was at issue. In opposing claims on the part of colonial peoples to exercise self-determination, the colonial powers have often resorted to Article 2(7) of the Charter as a shield for the perpetuation of their rule in the dependent territories. In the cases that concerned Tibet, Cyprus, and West Irian, territorial disputes were involved. As to Tibet, the effectiveness of the claim of domestic jurisdiction depended in no small measure on whether Tibet was part of Chinese territory. In Cyprus and West Irian, claims to independence that were advanced by a third state were bluntly repudiated by the administering states.

In spite of the persistent objections voiced by a few states, such as Portugal and South Africa, it has been well established that the United Nations has the authoritative competence to deal with disputes relating to self-determination. In cases relating to "colonial territories," it is obvious enough. Not only has the United Nations hastened the political independence of the non-self-governing territories by dramatizing the cause of colonial peoples to the world, it has also made significant contribution to the economic, educational, and social welfare of non-self-governing peoples. On the other hand, with minor exceptions, the United Nations has not been seriously involved in the questions of self-determination for peoples who do not reside in "colonies or trust territories." The limited success of the United Nations does not imply a lack of formal authority, but reflects a sense of realism about the base values actually at its disposal.

However, when a territorial dispute involving the demands for self-determination is current, the decision-makers as a rule are able to link the seriousness of the dispute with maintaining world public order. And when world public order is perceived to be threatened, the United Nations is usually able to make a move.

Taking the practice of the United Nations as a whole, the final response to claims of domestic jurisdiction has not been simple. The outcome seems to have been shaped by reference to the major purposes of the Organization in the light of the contextual factors perceived as relevant to a given dispute. Such an approach is the only rational way of operating in an inordinately complicated world situation. Claims to domestic jurisdiction are turned aside whenever an important territorial dispute involves genuine demands for self-determination and a significant degree of potential threat to world public order.

Claims Relating to the Principle of Self-Determination

If we are to understand the long evolution of decisions in reply to the third kind of claim, that of self-determination, it is necessary to review the historical sequence and to give some attention to the combination of factors that conditioned the sequence. The principle of self-determination had its origin in the seventeenth century when nation states first emerged. The principle was deeply rooted in the concept of "nationality," at the time divorced from considerations of human rights or democracy. Prolonged religious wars made acute the position of many minorities—often "national minorities." In the beginning the problem was regarded as a matter that solely concerned a sovereign and his subjects. As the degree of interdependence grew, the problem of minority protection began to assume an international dimension, since a third state might on occasion demand self-determination on behalf of minority groups lying within the jurisdiction of other nation states. Gradually, therefore, self-determination came to be seen as a manifestation of "collective" rather than individual will. Following the French revolution, the concepts of "democracy" and "the sovereignty of the people" were introduced. As a practical procedure for relating these principles of content to concrete circumstances, the "plebiscite" came into use to determine the "public will" of the people in territorial disputes.

The principle of "national self-determination" was crystallized at the end of World War I under the strong championship of President Woodrow Wilson. In his language: "No peace can last, or ought to last, which does not recognize and accept the principle that governments derive all their just powers from the consent of the governed, and that no right anywhere exists to hand people about from sovereignty to sovereignty as if they were property."[22] Self-determination guided the settlement of territorial disputes between nations as well as within states. There was, however, the tacit expectation that self-determination was applicable only to European contexts, and the colonial possessions of European powers in Asia and Africa were excluded from its application. Although the Covenant provided that "the wishes of the populations" were to be the principal consideration in selecting the mandatory power for class A mandates, the provision was virtually ignored in practice, to say nothing of classes B and C. The network of the new mandates system was not deliberately applied to the task of preparing dependent peoples for ultimate self-government. And from the first the mandates system was crippled as a universal set of arrangements by the fact that it applied only to the territories of the *defeated* powers. As a result, the application of the principle of self-determination at the end of World War I was confined to the "unsettled areas of Eastern Europe and the Near East."

During World War II, the principle of self-determination was proclaimed in the Atlantic Charter. Whatever reluctance there was among old colonial powers to apply it to themselves, self-determination possessed a universal appeal deeply rooted in the concept of human dignity and closely related to the maintenance of world public order.

In 1945, at San Francisco, at the end of a long and delicate negotiation the world community finally recognized this principle as essential to peace and security as well as to human rights, and upheld its application to all "peoples," regardless of geographical or racial factors. Aside from Article 55 and the relevant provisions concerning the "Non-Self-Governing Territories," the Charter identifies one of its major purposes as to "develop friendly relations among nations based on respect for . . . self-determination of peoples."

While the basic community policy of self-determination is projected in unequivocal language by the Charter, its application in concrete circumstances is not unchallenged. The question is raised whether this is a "political" or "legal" right; in other words, do the Charter provisions have any authoritative effect whatever? In the light of United Nations practice, such a doubt can no longer be entertained. The principle of self-determination has been affirmed and reaffirmed, applied and reapplied. It is beyond any reasonable doubt that this principle "had exercised and would continue to exercise a profound influence upon the creation and existence of States and upon the relations between them."[23] Aside from actions in concrete cases, the United Nations has taken the initiative to further the realization of self-determination through various studies and resolutions, climaxed by the 1960 resolution for immediate decolonization. As a matter of fact, practice regarding the right of "every people to determine . . . by whom they will be governed" has become a cornerstone of world public policy in the brief history of the United Nations. No principle of the Charter is ever given "unlimited application," however.

The meaningful question to ask in examining the exercise of self-determination is "who gets what, when, and how." If we can contextualize the trend of past decisions in these terms we shall have a helpful aid to the rational application of the principle in the future. On the whole, the United Nations has considered general community policy, the relative merits of claims and counter claims, and other relevant contextual factors. Even in the absence of a systematic or general statement trends can be generalized from the actual operations of the U.N.

Claims to self-determination fall in two broad categories: claims in the "colonial contexts," invoked by a colonial people against a colonial power; and claims in the noncolonial contexts. The former category is generally grounded on the relevant provisions of Chapters XI–XIII of the Charter. As to the latter, in addition to Article 1(2) "respect for self-determination of peoples," other grounds such as "maintenance of international peace and security" (Article 1(1)), "sovereign equality of states" (Article 2(1)) and "nonintervention in the domestic affairs" (Article 2(7)) are also invoked. At times, however, the interplay of "colonial" and "noncolonial" elements is by no means clear. While the colonial claims resort to this principle primarily to justify "decolonization," the noncolonial claims seek such outcomes as readjustment of boundaries. In the final analysis, the claimants are seeking to effect territorial changes one way or another, and the decisions are to be analyzed accordingly.

At the very beginning of the United Nations' existence, the Indonesian question dramatized the issue of self-determination. Despite Dutch opposition, the Security Council took charge of the case and facilitated the final settlement by reference to the principle of self-determination. Claims to self-determination often arose in contexts where the charge of infringement of "sovereignty" and "independence" was made by one state against another, notably the Greek question in 1946, the Czechoslovakian question in 1946, the Iranian complaint against the U.S.S.R. in 1946, the Hyderabad issue in 1948, the Yugoslavian complaints in 1951, and the Hungarian question of 1956. Sometimes the claims to self-determination were put forth by a third state against other states, notably the Pakistan claim against India about Kashmir, the Greek claim against the United Kingdom about Cyprus, the competing claims of Indonesia and the Netherlands against each other with respect to Dutch New Guinea (West Irian), and the Moroccan claim against France about Mauritania. Other claims generally arose in contexts where colonial and dependent peoples were demanding the exercise of self-determination. Among others, these were the issues raised in the disposition of former Italian colonies, the Palestine question, the Togoland question, Cameroons, Ruanda-Urundi, and Southwest Africa.

Generally speaking, while the United Nations has played a significant part in facilitating the application of this principle to the non-self-governing peoples, it has not shown equal zeal in dealing with noncolonial contexts. In cases involving colonies, the basic community policy of self-determination has been applied not only to hasten the negative function of "decolonization," but also to perform the positive function of enhancing the welfare of the peoples concerned. However, noncolonial issues that involve self-determination will be of greater significance in the years to come, as the United Nations becomes less fearful of objections based on domestic jurisdiction. The intensified demand in many noncolonial configurations will doubtless contribute to this development. If colonial peoples, many of whom have a relatively thin command of modern science and technology, are receiving the benefits of self-determination, why should these advantages be withheld from more advanced entities?

The Charter stipulates "self-determination of 'peoples'," and hence leaves the door wide open to arguments over "who" is entitled to self-determination, constituting an eligible "national unit." In ascertaining the basic unit of "nation" or "peoples" to exercise self-determination, the sociological, geographical, historical, psychological, and political factors of a social context have been recognized as relevant. Thus there is generally reference to the distinct features of the population concerned in terms of race, language, religion, or cultural heritage. It is also considered pertinent to discuss whether the territory involved is an identifiable territory or sufficiently contiguous to constitute one geographic unit.[24] The United Nations Charter provides that in the administration of colonies "due account should be taken of the political aspirations of the people" (Art. 73(b)), and the United

Nations has endorsed the "freely expressed views of the people concerned" (Art. 76(b)) as an important factor. Since the concept of democracy as "government with the consent of the governed" is deeply rooted, a "plebiscite" has come to be identified as a procedure inseparable from the practical exercise of self-determination. The wishes (perspectives) of the people—their demands, expectations, and identifications—are commonly conceded to have great weight. In practice, the exhibited willingness of the population concerned "to consider themselves as one people" is given special attention.

While no single test is considered to be "conclusive," the United Nations has been notably cautious in ascribing weight to assertions based on historical considerations. The general view seems to be that attempts to modify the status quo on the ground of past historical connections tend to ignore the existing political realities, including the contemporary community expectations of a people. When historical issues are introduced, however, the most perplexing problem is how far back to trace the history. Although a colonial power may base its present claim on the history of colonial rule, the competing claimant may base his claim on the centuries prior to colonial control. This question was squarely raised in the cases of the Franco-Moroccan dispute over Mauritania and the Dutch-Indonesian dispute over Dutch New Guinea (West Irian). The overwhelming majority of delegates were inclined to address themselves to existing political realities and to attach more weight to recent historical considerations. Clearly the underlying policy consideration is to stabilize community expectations on the basis of "current history." The decision-makers of the U.N. seem firmly disposed toward the view that a genuine exercise of self-determination is best achieved by deference to the genuine shared demands and expectations of the people within an identifiable territory, whose sense of distinctive identity is based on a common and hence relatively unique political experience.

Before proceeding further, the significant fact ought to be

noted that in practice the United Nations has shown great deference to "the established boundaries" of existing nation states. In no instance has the United Nations taken the position that any component part of a nation state is entitled to break off by the direct exercise of self-determination. Hence the general consensus holds that the principle of self-determination is not a unilateral "right of secession." So far as dissatisfied segments of the population within an established state are concerned, the pronounced view is that their best protection lies not in separation but in arrangements for minority protection, coupled with guarantees of effective participation in the decision process.

Having arrived at a provisional identification of "who" is entitled to self-determination, decision-makers then face the problem of when and under what conditions self-determination is to be realized. While the spokesmen of a "colonial people" typically demand the immediate realization of unconditional self-determination, the colonial or administering powers no less typically call for the fulfillment of certain requirements as a precondition. By reference to Charter provisions, the colonial powers assert that the development of self-government in the dependent or trusted territories is to be effected "according to the particular circumstances of each territory and its peoples and their varying stages of development" (Art. 73(b)). They often make lofty statements to the effect that their presence or administration was at the invitation or with the consent of the colonial people in the first place, and they simply cannot betray their sacred trust by abandoning these people before they are able as well as willing to manage their own affairs. To do otherwise, in their view, would contravene Charter policy.

Before 1960 the United Nations at no time characterized the exercise of self-determination as "unqualified" or "unconditional." In an exploratory, developing approach, not all colonial peoples were granted self-determination at the same time or to the same extent. But in 1960 a sweeping policy statement was made, and it is important to assess its bearing on U.N. decisions. In a resolution, the "Declaration on the Granting of Independence to Colonial Countries and Peoples" (passed on December 14, 1960 almost unanimously), the General Assembly, emphasizing the "necessity of bringing to a speedy and unconditional end colonialism in all its forms and manifestations," declared that "[i]nadequacy of political, economic, social or educational preparedness should never serve as a pretext for delaying independence," and urged that "[i]mmediate steps shall be taken, in . . . all . . . territories which have not yet attained independence, to transfer all powers to the peoples of those territories, without any conditions or reservations, in accordance with their freely expressed will and desire."[25] While the practical application of this sweeping formulation of policy must still be related to the special conditions surrounding any case, the declaration reaffirms basic community policy in unmistakable language.

Taking the provisions of the Charter as a whole, it appears that the world community has as much interest as the people directly concerned in seeing that a solution to problems of self-determination are beneficial to all. Hence, when examining a claim to self-determination, the Organization usually makes inquiry as to: (*a*) the prospect of the territory or people concerned of becoming a viable state; (*b*) the present stage of advancement; and (*c*) the effect of granting or refusing the exercise of self-determination. It is considered beneficial to the welfare of the people directly concerned that they have a reasonable prospect of becoming a viable entity—politically and economically—in this increasingly interdependent world. The concern of the U.N. for a viable and self-sustained economy is amply demonstrated by the emphasis on "economic sovereignty," as symbolized by the Declaration on "Permanent Sovereignty over Natural Resources."[26] It is also expected that they should be capable of managing their own affairs so as eventually to become a responsible member of the world community. While it may be too much to hope that the new nation can contribute substantially to world public order in the near future, it is not unreasonable to insist that it have enough political unity and strength to prevent it from becoming an immediate source of world insecurity. In estimating the degree of advancement of the people concerned, reference is generally made to the educational and political institutions of a given territory. Some minimum standard in these fields is regarded as essential to a sensible and meaningful exercise of self-determination.

No major value consequences of self-determination are regarded as irrelevant by U.N. decision-makers who are faced with concrete problems of application. In regard to Cyprus, for example, since a Turkish minority was involved, the U.N. did not see fit to grant full self-determination to the people of Cyprus, since this would have led to a merger of the island with Greece. It is significant that both colonial and noncolonial powers tend to link their cases with the concept of "minimum public order," though from different perspectives. Whereas the colonial powers argue that the weakness displayed by a chaotic internal situation is apt to tempt big or neighboring powers, the anticolonial powers insist that the continuation of a dependency relation perpetuates an inherent instability that invites third party "intervention." The United Nations has shown readiness to consider potential security implications in the course of shaping its response to claims of self-determination. Hence, while the United Nations has neither "endorsed" nor "condoned" colonialism in any form, it has been fully aware that a premature and inadequate application of self-determination will probably have adverse effects on the maintenance of world public order. This concern was prominently displayed in the cases of Libya and Eritrea. The final decision not to partition Libya or to form Eritrea as a separate entity was prompted in no small part by precautionary considerations relating to minimum order. Similar criteria led to the different treatment given to Togoland and Cameroons.

Assuming that the conditions to be met in order to exercise

self-determination are understood, an intriguing question is whether a blank timetable ought to be set for all territories or for some specific territories, or whether all problems of timing should be determined by the contextual consideration of each case. The suggestion is sometimes made that to set a timetable may have an encouraging effect on the perspectives and operational exertions of the people concerned. However, although the majority of member states favor self-determination for all people with minimum delay, they seem to agree that cases differ too much from one another to warrant the adoption of "blanket" timing.

Another question of decision strategy is the procedure to implement an exercise of self-determination. Shall implementation of the principle be left to the discretion of the powers in effective control, to such international organizations as the United Nations, to consultation between ruling authorities and the people—or simply left to armed revolt? Understandably, while claimants for self-determination generally advocate international participation, the colonial powers tend to insist on exclusive implementation procedures. Thus far the United Nations has acted against any claim that the administering authorities have exclusive competence. With respect to trust territories, since the United Nations bears direct responsibility, it naturally performs the necessary tasks in a process of self-determination. In the case of non-trust territories, if genuine demands for self-determination are believed to be at stake, the United Nations does not hesitate to play an active part in the controversy.

While there is a general impression that claims to self-determination in the postwar world have arisen only in a context of extreme controversy, in which security is threatened by general expectations of violence, this has not always been so. Not a few controversies have been worked out harmoniously and quietly between the administering authorities and the people concerned. When the participants directly involved appear able to work out their mutual differences in a satisfactory manner, the United

Nations is prudent enough not to step in. A direct noncoercive settlement is most conducive to reconciliation between the participants concerned with relations after independence. The United Nations has been careful to insist on being satisfied that such a direct consultative procedure is not being used as a pretext, but is effective and genuine. We can therefore conclude that the U.N. does not as a rule shrink from its responsibility whenever it appears that no just settlement can reasonably be expected from negotiation between the immediate parties.

No serious champion of world public order denies that self-determination ought to be given effect without violence. At times, however, recourse to violence may be the only alternative open to a suppressed people. In a world preoccupied for the most part with national and regional affairs, we sadly concede that on occasion the use of violence is the only practical strategy for dramatizing the cause of a people struggling for self-determination. Claimants who resort to violence never fail to express their preference for a nonviolent solution, arguing that local censorship and world inattention have left them with no other choice. In Algeria, Indonesia, Hungary, and Angola the violence flared on a substantial scale. The United Nations, while expressing regret for the fact of violence, seems to have made no condemnation of its use by the suppressed peoples. In Katanga, however, the United Nations took a different position. Evidently such a difference must be attributed to the basic judgment of the U.N. regarding the soundness of the particular claim to self-determination. Although the interpretation remains controverted, we cannot resist the conclusion that the United Nations does not disavow self-determination by revolution under all circumstances, notably when a people who are capable and genuinely identified with one another are blocked from access to the channels of world attention.

Finally, while the exercise of self-determination is generally equated with "independence," it is not always the case. The United Nations has demonstrated its flexibility by allowing a variety of different arrangements to give effect to a demand for self-determination. Self-determination, fully analyzed in the context of world politics, can be shown to envisage a wide range of alternatives ranging from considerable self-government inside an existing state through an autonomous status within the frame of an established state, to complete independence. The differences in these outcomes are obviously classifiable according to the degree of participation in external as well as internal processes. "Self-government" (the first category mentioned above) takes two forms: "assimilation of people" and "integration of territory." The former is accomplished on an individual and nonterritorial basis: the people concerned become full citizens of the state to which they choose to give allegiance. As a result of "integration of territory," the people of the territory concerned participate in the internal processes of the larger state, giving and receiving varying degree of benefits and burdens, as agreed. "Autonomy" moves a step further. No distinction is made between "assimilation" and "integration." The people exercise more comprehensive control over their internal decision processes, without, however, having independent competence to participate in the external processes. As for the significance of "independence," people form themselves into a new body politic with complete authority and control over its people, resources, territory, and institutional practices; they have an independent authority to participate in the international arena of formal authority.

In the postwar cases in which self-determination was granted, the overwhelming majority have chosen to become independent, hardly surprising in this age of nationalism and decolonization. It is often suggested that a new association based on "self-government" or "autonomy," involving less than full and independent participation in the world arena, is objectionable. This position is unnecessarily restrictive of choice, and overlooks the point that in many situations the scope of effective influence is larger within the frame of a large state than in the formalistic grandeur of a microstate. In many circumstances, however, a small state is the only practicable outcome, since the conformist pressures operating within a totalitarian or traditionally absolute set-up may be plausibly identified as a conclusive threat to any nominal arrangements of an "autonomous" character. In any case, the fundamental requirement conveyed by the language of self-determination is a *procedure*, not a pre-set result. Whether the outcome in a particular case is "independence" or otherwise is less important than whether a choice is genuinely and freely made in the course of a proper plebiscite. If the freedom of choice of the people is sustained, the policy aim of self-determination is adequately achieved, and the decisions of the world organization exhibit the flexibility that is realistically adapted to the contextual complexities of world affairs.

Probable Future Development

SINCE ANY policy recommendation is open to change in the light of future contingencies, we shall consider the present question in the light of estimates of the probable course of future development. We must, of course, base our estimation of the future on knowledge of trends and conditions to date.

Traditional international law on the acquisition of territories, developed to answer problems arising from "unappropriated territories," loses its significance as "unappropriated" land masses on this planet are exhausted. But this does not mean the end of territorial issues around the globe. Future problems are most likely to arise in areas inadequately settled or left unsettled after World War II because of the postwar development of the cold war. Boundary issues caused by the disintegration of former colonial empires and the rapid multiplication of newly independent nations also signify troubles ahead. While the acquisition of territory through naked use of military force will probably decrease, nation states are bound to press competing territorial claims by alleging a wide range of justifications, whether acceptable to others or not. The world community will continue to expect that territorial disputes will be settled by noncoercive procedures; mankind's primary task is to maintain world public order by minimizing coercion. No rational man can deny that man's survival depends upon the consolidation of at least minimum public order on a world scale.

As "decolonization" gradually comes to an end, the significance of the principle of self-determination in the colonial context will decline. This does not, however, signify an end to questions of self-determination, since these also arise when peoples who do not think of themselves as "colonials" nevertheless assert a political identity separate from the dominant element in the nation state in which they are incorporated. While we anticipate increasing cooperation among nations through global and regional functional organizations, nationalism will probably remain highly appealing as a means of registering dissatisfaction with a disadvantaged territorial position. Hence the principle of self-determination will be of continuing significance in future territorial controversies. The reaffirmation of basic community policies in the context of decolonization has organized a set of perspectives that render it distasteful to deny a voice to more advanced participants in the universalizing culture of science and technology. The spread of this common civilization, despite inner conflicts of view, has also spread the democratic theory of the consent of the governed as essential to human dignity.

Our estimate of the future includes the assumption that the United Nations will continue to play a decisive role in settling territorial disputes. The same factors that have strengthened the disposition of the U.N. to restrict the role of claims of "domestic jurisdiction" will continue to operate, probably with more effect, as the world grows more interdependent.

Finally, as we have linked the solution of the Formosan question closely with Chinese participation in the United Nations, our projection of the probable course of events must include the Chinese participation question. We have, however, dealt with this dimension of the problem before, and no repetition is needed at this juncture. The Vietnam war will eventually become a topic of effective negotiation, and in connection with a Vietnam settlement serious community concern will focus on the Formosan and the Chinese participation question.

Appraisal and Recommendation

HAVING canvassed the goals of public policy in world politics and dealt with the claims and decisions in a common set of international problems, we are better able to reappraise the situation, and to propose recommendations to the various decision-makers.

No tissue of doctrinal argument, however imposing, can be properly evaluated unless the relevant decision-makers recognize whose values and institutions are at stake, in what degree and form. When a transfer of territory is claimed, the primary point is that far more is involved than a piece of land. At stake is the entire decision process of a territorial community—formal authority and control over people, resources, and institutional practices as well as territorial space. What most immediately counts in the Formosan matter is the destiny of thirteen million people whose way of life will be irreparably affected for generations. In dealing with so vital and complicated a problem, decision-makers must take all contextual factors into account, including recent history and present conditions, as they affect the application of the basic policies of the world community.

As indicated in the analysis of trend, the basic community policies applicable to a territorial dispute are clear. The principal aims are to lessen the use of coercion to insure public order, and to sustain free choices made on the basis of genuine popular aspirations of the people in the disputed territory; in a word, the principle of self-determination, supplementing the principle of least coercion. Such fundamental community policies are clearly projected in the United Nations Charter and have been consistently upheld in U.N. practice.

It has been well established in international law that an international agreement, particularly a treaty of cession, cannot be abrogated unilaterally. The Chinese claim that Formosa automatically became part of China in 1941 cannot be taken seriously. If honored, such a proposition would disrupt the existing stability of community expectations in regard to national boundaries anywhere on the globe. Clearly, a unilateral denunciation has no authoritative effect whatever on the existing status of Formosa.

The initial desire of the four major Allied powers (China, U.S., U.K., U.S.S.R.) to "restore Formosa and the Pescadores to China," expressed in the Cairo Declaration of 1943, the Potsdam Declaration of 1945, and the Japanese Term of Surrender of 1945, was made at a time when a full-scale war was in progress and Formosa was ruled by Japan. It is surely too much to expect decision-makers acting in such circumstances to take a balanced view of all relevant contextual factors, particularly long-term considerations. To be authoritative and effective, a preliminary commitment of this kind would have to be crystallized and incorporated into the peace treaty that terminates hostilities.[27] Here the pertinent agreement is the peace treaty with Japan of 1951, which authoritatively formulates the common policies of Japan and the Allied powers regarding their mutual relations after the termination of "war." International law has long recognized the fundamental importance of peace treaties to delimit the state of affairs between victorious and defeated powers. Only commitments made in an atmosphere free of active violence can consider other than military necessities and hence provide a reasonable basis for peace and stability. Despite the numerous declarations made by the major Allied powers in the heat of war, the adjustment of the new structure of relations must be based on the relevant provisions in peace treaties in which both defeated and victorious nations participated.[28] In a peace treaty the "territorial clauses" are drafted with particular care to prevent subsequent allegations of ambiguity. Since territorial claims are among the principal sources of conflict in world affairs, it is well recognized that "who renounces what, to whom, and when" is to be stated in unequivocal terms.

When the U.S., U.K., and China expressed their initial desire to return Formosa to China in 1943, a basic presumption was that it was compatible with—or at least not offensive to—the general aspirations of the people of Formosa. The Chinese Nationalists soon succeeded in alienating whatever sanguine expectations had initially been present, and drove the Formosans into revolt. The massacres by the Nationalist occupation authorities in 1947 sent the surviving leaders underground or abroad. As the Chinese civil war intensified, most Formosans tried to dissociate themselves from the entanglement that had been thrust on them. They wanted no part in the civil strife on the mainland. The establishment of a Communist regime in Peking in October 1949 was totally unexpected by the world at large, including the major Allied powers who had joined in the various wartime declarations. The people of Formosa became more apprehensive than ever of a "China" under a Communist system. The outbreak of the Korean war in 1950 radically heightened both the "cold" and "hot" war in Asia and elsewhere. As a result, the strategic importance of Formosa for the security of the west Pacific was suddenly dramatized. The occurrence of these events—before the conclusion of the peace treaty with Japan—completely changed general community expectations about the future disposition of Formosa on the eve of the San Francisco Peace Conference with Japan in September 1951.

As a consequence, the initial wartime program of the four Allied powers to "restore Formosa and the Pescadores to China" was neither put into effect nor endorsed at the 1951 peace conference with Japan in which 51 Allied powers participated.[29] (Neither Communist China nor Nationalist China was invited to attend.) In the peace negotiations there was, to be sure, basic disagreement as to which regime, Nationalist or Communist, represented China. Above all, there was widespread concern that to transfer Formosa, a Japanese colony, from Japan to China without giving deference to the voice of the population on the island would violate the principle of self-determination of the United Nations Charter. Hence while Japan's renunciation of her "right, title, and claim" over Formosa was made unmistakably clear in the territorial clause of the peace treaty, the beneficiary of the renunciation was not specified.

This omission was neither negligence nor oversight; nor was it intended to imply that Formosa belonged either to Communist or Nationalist China. The parties to the treaty agreed that a rapid restoration of peaceful relations between the Allied powers and Japan must not be hindered or delayed by such highly controversial issues as the ultimate disposition of Formosa. The prevailing expectation was that the legal status of Formosa, though temporarily left undetermined, would be decided by appropriate decision-makers at an opportune time in the light of the purposes and principles of the United Nations Charter. In this connection, a statement made by the British delegate to the Peace Conference was instructive:

> The treaty also provides for Japan to renounce its sovereignty over Formosa and the Pescadores Islands. The treaty itself does not determine the future of these islands. The future of Formosa was referred to in the Cairo Declaration but that Declaration also contained provisions in respect to Korea, together with the basic principles of non-aggression and no territorial ambitions. Until China shows by her action that she accepts those provisions and principles, it will be difficult to reach a final settlement of the problem of Formosa. In due course a solution must be found, in accord with the pur-

poses and principles of the Charter of the United Nations. In the meantime, however, it would be wrong to postpone making peace with Japan. We therefore came to the conclusion that the proper treatment of Formosa in the context of the Japanese peace treaty was for the treaty to provide only for renunciation of Japanese sovereignty.[30]

Since not all nations declaring war against Japan participated in the San Francisco Conference, the peace treaty obliged Japan to "conclude with any State which signed or adhered to the United Nations Declarations of January 1, 1942, and which is at war with Japan" and not a signatory of the treaty, "a bilateral Treaty of Peace on the same or substantially the same terms as are provided for in the present Treaty" (Article 26). Thus, following the patterns of the San Francisco Treaty, a bilateral peace treaty was concluded between Japan and the "Republic of China" in 1952. With respect to the disposition of Formosa and the Pescadores, Article 2 states:

It is recognized that under Article 2 of the Treaty of Peace with Japan signed at the city of San Francisco in the United States of America on September 8, 1951 (hereinafter referred to as the San Francisco Treaty), Japan has renounced all right, title and claim to Taiwan (Formosa) and Penghu (the Pescadores).

The choice of language is significant in that it conveys exactly the same expectation previously incorporated into the San Francisco Treaty. Much to the chagrin of the Chinese Nationalist regime, it failed, despite insistent attempts, to have the Sino-Japanese peace treaty specify "China" as the beneficiary of Japan's renunciation of her right, title, and claim to Formosa and the Pescadores.

Nor did the conclusion of the mutual defense treaty between the United States and the Republic of China constitute an implied recognition of "Chinese sovereignty" over Formosa. Article VI of the mutual defense treaty stipulates that "the terms 'territorial' and 'territories' (in Article II and V) shall mean in respect of the Republic of China, Taiwan and Pescadores" and "such other territories as may be determined by mutual agreement." In order to avoid creating the misconception that this defense treaty constituted in any way an implied recognition of China's sovereignty over Formosa and the Pescadores, the United States Senate in the course of ratification stated that "it is the understanding of the Senate that nothing in the present treaty shall be construed as affecting or modifying the legal status or the sovereignty of the territories referred in Article VI (i.e., Formosa and the Pescadores)."[31] The legal status of Formosa, as understood by the Senate, had on a previous occasion been clarified by Secretary of State John Foster Dulles at a press conference when the defense treaty was signed amid the first offshore islands crisis. In his words,

> technical sovereignty over Formosa and the Pescadores has never been settled. That is because the Japanese peace treaty merely involves a renunciation by Japan of its right and title to these islands. But the future title is not determined by the Japanese peace treaty, nor is it determined by the peace treaty which was concluded between the Republic of China and Japan. Therefore, the juridical status of these islands, Formosa and the Pescadores, is different from the juridical status of the offshore islands (Quemoy and Matsu) which have always been Chinese territory.[32]

While both the peace treaty with Japan and the peace treaty between Japan and the Republic of China were not specific about the beneficiary of Formosa and the Pescadores, the fact remains that since 1945 the Chinese Nationalist regime has not only exercised effective control over Formosa but enjoyed membership in numerous international organizations. Hence it is asserted that, if not through "cession" via peace treaties, at least through other modes of acquisition such as "occupation," "prescription," and "conquest," Formosa has become Chinese territory.

But clearly the deliberate omission of a beneficiary for Japan's renunciation was not designed to render Formosa an "unappropriated territory" in favor of an effective occupant. It was temporarily left undetermined because of the intricate surrounding factors and a prevailing expectation that the matter would be settled at an opportune time by the appropriate decision-makers. Continued administration of Formosa by the Nationalist regime has not transformed its "effective control" into "authoritative acquisition." Similarly, neither "prescription" nor "conquest" fits. The question of Formosa's status under the Nationalist administration has been at issue all these years. And the prohibition of force as a means of territorial change in the United Nations Charter has left no doubt that "conquest" has no place in contemporary international law.[33]

The indeterminacy of Formosa's status has continued as the world moves from crisis to crisis and the United Nations fails to find a proper solution regarding China's participation. Since the extemporized emergency arrangements that originated in belligerent occupation are not yet regularized, the Nationalist regime continues to exercise control over Formosa. Yet the voting arrangements under the Nationalist rule have in effect excluded the people of Formosa from managing their own affairs. The Constitution of "the Republic of China," as currently applied in Formosa, went into effect in December 1947 while the Nationalist government was still in power on the mainland. According to the Constitution, the national administration is divided into three levels: the central government, the provincial governments, and the county (city) governments.

The central government consists of the following organs:

1] The National Assembly: its prime responsibility is to elect (and recall) the President and Vice President, and to amend the Constitution;

2] The President: the head of the state and the commander-in-chief of the armed forces;

3] The Five Yuans: (a) the Executive Yuan is "the highest administrative organ"; (b) the Legislative Yuan has responsibility for legislation, including appropriation; (c) the Judicial Yuan is "the highest judicial organ"; (d) the Examination Yuan, as "the highest examination organ," deals with matters pertinent to public functionaries, ranging from examination and employment to promotion and protection; (e) the Control Yuan, whose authority is to censure and impeach high government officials (including the President and Vice President), audit, and give consent to certain key presidential appointments.

Viewed in terms of their aggregate functions, the National Assembly, the Legislative Yuan, and the Control Yuan together constitute a "Congress," as commonly understood in other political systems. The members of these organs are directly or indirectly elected. The President and Vice President are, as indicated, chosen by the National Assembly. The highest officials of the Executive, Judicial, and Examination Yuan are appointed by the President with the consent of either the Legislative or Control Yuan.

When the Nationalist regime unilaterally declared Formosa a province of the Republic of China, Formosa joined in the "congressional" elections held by the Nationalists under the new Constitution in late 1947 and early 1948. According to the election laws then in existence, the quota of Taiwan's representation was 19 of 3045 members of the National Assembly, 8 of 773 members of the Legislative Yuan, and 5 of 223 members of the Control Yuan.[34]

In 1949 the effective domain of the Nationalist regime was reduced from a land of 3,800,000 square miles and of 500 million people to an "occupied territory" (Formosa) of 13,885 square miles and 8 million people (plus the tiny offshore islands Quemoy and Matsu). Under the circumstances one would expect that presently the Nationalist regime would modify the mainland government structures, simultaneously obtaining a new mandate from its actual population on Formosa.

This is not, however, what the Nationalist regime has seen fit to do. Perpetuating the political myth that the Nationalist government remains "the only legitimate government of China" and that Taiwan is "only one of the thirty-five provinces of China," the constitutional structures of 1947 have continued to operate in Formosa without change. Notwithstanding the duplication of structures and the conflict of jurisdictions, on top of the "provincial government of Taiwan" sits the "central government" of "the Republic of China," recognizing the same "congressional" representatives who were elected on the mainland, as if the Nationalist regime were the actual rulers of the mainland.

There were altogether 2296 "congressional" representatives— 1643 in the National Assembly, 551 in the Legislative Yuan, and 102 in the Control Yuan—who reported for duty to the Nationalist regime during the first years of its exile in Formosa (excluding mainly those who stayed behind on the mainland).[35] These representatives who were elected in 1947 or 1948 for a term of three or six years by the constituencies on the mainland (except the handful of Formosan representatives) found themselves without constituencies as a result of the Nationalist exile to Formosa. Nevertheless, the "central government" in Taipei remains as it was in Nanking in 1949; they have continued to hold their official positions and exercise authority in Formosa, though neither re-elected by, nor responsible to, any constituency whatsoever.

The key fact of political life in Formosa today is clear: the "Republic of China" has under its effective control only Formosa, with a population of thirteen million, of which eleven million are native Formosans and two million are mainland Chinese. The public will of these thirteen million people has supposedly been reflected during the past seventeen years by the "congressional" representatives elected almost two decades ago by the electorate on the mainland. The eleven million native Formosans are not represented by eleven of every thirteen members of these "congressional" bodies; on the contrary, the actual figure in 1964 was 18 of 1521 in the National Assembly, 6 of 473 in the Legislative Yuan, and 5 of 82 in the Control Yuan. (Since the Nationalist exile to Formosa in 1949 the actual personnel of these bodies has decreased from year to year in the absence of elections to fill seats vacated by death or otherwise.)

Spokesmen for the native Formosans have demanded that this anomalous situation be righted, that the population of Formosa receive realistic representation at "every" level of political decision. These demands have time and again been dismissed by the Nationalist regime on the ground that the existing constitutional situation, though indeed extraordinary, is no more than temporary. The position is that as soon as the Nationalist government "recovers" the lost territory on the other side of the Formosa Straits, there will at once be a nationwide election and Taiwan, of course, will be included. Hence, the government argues, the proper solution lies not in modifying existing constitutional structures to elect representatives according to Formosa's present population, but rather in marshaling every effort to achieve the purportedly common goal, a "return to the mainland." Once the mainland is "recovered," it is said, all problems will be settled. Meanwhile, the people of Formosa ought to be grateful that they are given limited voting rights authorizing them to elect local officers such as county or city councilmen, magistrates and mayors, and members of the "Provincial Assembly" of Taiwan. (The people of Taiwan do not enjoy the right to elect their own governor. The governor has been appointed as a rule from among top Nationalist generals by President Chiang Kai-shek.)

This "grand scheme" is both brash and subtle. The obvious result is to perpetuate the monopoly of power by the Nationalist regime, and to block native Formosans from effective participation in top-level policy-making and execution. To demand a realistic and reasonable modification of the obsolete constitutional structure is to engage in nothing less than sedition, a crime subject to court-martial and a maximum penalty of death.[36]

In an epoch of accelerating decolonization, the denial of self-determination to the Formosan people has aroused little world concern. Primarily we can explain this by the efficiency with which the Nationalist regime has exploited its monopoly of diplomatic and communication channels, and the rigor with which any attempt by native Formosans to make their grievances known has been suppressed. The massacre of Formosan leaders from all walks of life by the Nationalist occupation authorities in 1947 has been followed by a systematic and totalitarian police control. There has been no freedom of speech, association, and assembly in Formosa; in fact the island has been living in a formally declared state of "martial law" since 1949.

Externally, the Chinese Nationalist regime has monopolized all diplomatic channels that purport to speak for the people of Formosa as well as the true mainland government through a wide network of diplomatic missions around the globe. No Nationalist ambassador is a native Formosan. Even in the low echelons of the diplomatic service, only a handful are Formosan, and these have no part in policy-making. Supplementing official channels, the regime has conducted successful propaganda campaigns around the world by projecting a distorted image to the audience, particularly its staunchest ally, the United States. The extent and scope of the intensive "publicity campaigns" waged by the Chinese Nationalist regime—campaigns in the final analysis financed out of the United States aid—were recently disclosed in hearings by the Senate Foreign Relations Committee on the activities of foreign agents in the United States.

The effectiveness of the Nationalist regime in suppressing the Formosan people who are attempting to communicate even outside Formosa is demonstrated by an incident in 1961. Dr. Thomas Liao, then President of the Formosan exile government established in Japan in 1955, had applied to enter the United States to present the cause of the Formosan people to the United Nations and to the general public of the United States. Presumably because of Nationalist influence his application for a U.S. visa continued to be rejected. When the Kennedy administration assumed office the State Department was reported ready to admit Liao; in the end, however, its position was reversed, presumably as part of the "Outer Mongolia deal." During the 1961 session of the General Assembly, the Nationalist regime initially displayed a strong determination to veto Outer Mongolia's application for membership, but finally did not. The *New York Times* reported that an important concession of the United States to obtain Chiang's nonexercise of the veto was official assurance that Liao would continue to be excluded from the United States.[37]

The anomalous political situation in Formosa today not only constitutes a deprivation of the right of self-determination of the people of Formosa, but also presents a continuing threat to world security. The situation points eventually to an explosive catastrophe.

Although its effective domain has been confined to Formosa in the past seventeen years, the Nationalist regime continues to assert that there is only one China, and that it is the only legitimate government representing all the Chinese people. Hence its fundamental policy is to "recover" (invade) the mainland, by force or any other means. Confronted with unceasing provocations by the Nationalist regime, Peking is no less militant in claiming that since Taiwan is an integral part of China, it is at liberty to use force to "liberate" (conquer) Taiwan. Both sides share the view that since the Chinese civil war is still in progress, the use of force to acquire the territory presently controlled by the other side is not proscribed by the United Nations Charter; it is "an internal affair of China" over which no outside powers, including the United Nations, can "intervene." This festering menace has twice brought the world to the brink of a catastrophic armed conflict: during the offshore islands crisis of 1954–55, and again of 1958.

Up to now the Formosan question has been considered in a context dominated by a handful of "exile" Nationalists who continue to rule the great majority contrary to their will. This may be expedient as a short-term policy, bred of crisis confusion. In a longer perspective, however, the policy cannot be defended. Assuming that the United Nations, incorporating the principal members of the world community, is genuinely concerned with the maintenance of public order and the general welfare of the thirteen million people of Formosa, any future decision regarding Formosa must be based on deference to the freely expressed will of all the people so deeply and immediately concerned.

The most informed participants in the San Francisco Peace Conference knew only too well that the Formosan problem had not been settled. As early as 1950, at the request of the United States, the question of Formosa was formally discussed by the United Nations; but the time for settlement was not considered ripe. There is little prospect today that an international conference could be convened specially for this purpose. In all likelihood the problem will move to solution in connection with the Chinese participation question in the United Nations. A basic difficulty, we noted, in any attempt to solve the Chinese question is the uncertain nature of Formosa's status in international law. As the issue of Chinese representation presses for early solution, "the opportune time for disposing Formosa's future," as anticipated by the peace treaty with Japan, is at last approaching.

To seat Communist China in place of the Nationalist delegation in both the General Assembly and the Security Council without guaranteeing a just status for Formosa would amount to a license for Peking's armed conquest of Formosa. The disposition of an indeterminate territory implicating world peace and security is definitely beyond the domestic jurisdiction of China. It is, on the contrary, a problem of such international concern that it comes within the purview of the United Nations. It is imperative that the world community put an end to a situation that condones the use of Formosa as a drill ground for the Nationalist militia openly designed to mount an attack against the mainland.

The solution most appropriate to the United Nations—and one well-established in international practice—is to apply the principle of self-determination and to hold a U.N. supervised plebiscite in Formosa. To give effect to self-determination, all contextual factors of a historical, geographical, sociological, and political character are relevant; but, above all, paramount deference goes to the genuine demands and aspirations of a people possessing a distinct sense of identity.

After Formosa was ceded by Japan in 1895, Japan effectively cut Formosa off from the modern Chinese Nationalist movements that gained headway about the turn of this century. The broken ties between Formosa and mainland China have not been restored by the Nationalist occupation. On the contrary, the massacres of 1947 shattered finally any lingering illusion held by Formosan leaders that their aspirations could be realized within a Chinese political framework. The establishment of a Communist regime on the mainland heightened popular apprehensions about "China" at the same time that the authoritarian police control of the Nationalists reinforced Formosan demands for independence. Since their ancestors migrated from mainland China to Formosa nearly three centuries ago, the people of the island have acquired a distinct identity by virtue of their unique political experience and isolated special environment. Beyond their separate identity, a factor preparing the people of Formosa for responsible self-management in the modern world is their relatively advanced standard of education and living.

An independent Formosa will enhance the common interest of the world community as well as contribute to the general welfare of the Formosan people. A new independent state would cut down the provocative if impotent threat that the Nationalists persist in when they insist upon preparing for a future attack on Communist China under the pretext of "liberating 700 million compatriots." A new Formosan government would promptly drop this absurdity and deprive mainland China of its most plausible justification for any attempt to use military force against Formosa. Granted that the Peking regime would continue for some time to press historical claims to Formosa as part of Chinese territory, the present-day relevance of such rhetoric would be properly discounted by a world community acquainted with and hence immunized against these empty assertions. Further, if there is doubt as to the viability of Formosa as an independent state located at the periphery of Communist China, the history of the past seventeen years can be cited to dispel this view.

It is entirely in harmony with United Nations policy to grant self-determination to the Formosan people—a decision that in no sense condones haphazard secession. It is one thing to apply the principle of self-determination to the disposition of a territory like Formosa, and quite another to talk about self-determination as a propagandistic pretext for secession. There are no grounds to assert that self-determination is to be denied the members of a body politic on the theory that they neglected in the first place to submit to masters whose racial characteristics differed conspicuously from their own.

We should finally like to emphasize that the position that the people of Formosa are entitled to self-determination in no way depends on accepting the argument that the status of Formosa remains undetermined. Even if it should be decided that the various acts and statements that have accompanied General Chiang's occupation of Formosa amount to an execution of the commitments to return the island to the "Republic of China," the right of self-determination must override such execution. The very purpose for which the peoples of the world have in recent years created the right of self-determination is to accord oppressed groups the opportunity to break the bonds of establishment. In applying the right to give peoples in Africa and Asia their freedom, it has not been suggested that prior establishment could not be abrogated in the cause of freedom.

An Emerging Nation

CHAPTER THREE

The Transition to Independence

H AVING RECOMMENDED THE "one China, one Formosa" policy as a solution for Chinese participation in the U.N. and Formosa's status, we deem it essential to consider the world social process as a whole, and to orient ourselves in a continuum embracing the past, the present, and the future. Since any policy alternative is primarily future-oriented, we must anticipate how things will eventually turn out, who will undertake what measures, under what conditions, and with what probable consequences. We make statements not only about the probable course of future development, but also of anticipatory evaluation of the costs and gains in carrying out the recommendations. We provide a disciplined analysis based on available knowledge of relevant conditions and trends to date, rather than arbitrary speculations at random. This is in essence what we call a "developmental construct."

"One China, One Formosa"

IN THE preceding two chapters, we have taken the position that the legal status of Formosa in international law has been undetermined since its emancipation from Japanese colonial rule and that the principle of self-determination should be applied to settle this indeterminacy. After becoming an independent nation through a plebiscite under U.N. supervision, Formosa would be admitted as a new member of the United Nations. Meanwhile, Communist China would occupy China's seats in both the General Assembly and the Security Council, in place of the Nationalist delegation.

The continued pursuance of the "one China" policy, repeatedly advocated by both Chiang and Mao, keeps alive the dogged determination of both regimes to "liberate" the other. It perpetuates threat and tension in the Formosan Straits area, with the potential of embroiling the U.S. and U.S.S.R. in a massive armed conflict triggered by either Chiang or Mao. Should the "civil war" continue, the discrepancy between the bases of power of Taiwan and of the mainland suggests that Peking will prevail over Taiwan. Under the logic of the "one China" policy, the outcome would be an eventual takeover of Formosa by Communist China. In this light, the danger of an ambiguous "one China" policy is more than clear.

The "two Chinas" formula presupposes the existence of two "Chinas," one in Formosa and one on the mainland, resulting from the civil war of 1949. If this formulation were to be accepted, the Nationalists' renunciation of claims to invade the mainland presumably should be coupled with Communist China's renunciation (express or implied) of claims to conquer Formosa. The outdated constitutional structures of 1947 would have to be replaced by a new constitution related to the constituencies and the conditions of Formosa. Such a transition, welcoming anyone of mainland origin who remained in Formosa, would be supported by most Formosans, with the possible exception of a few "super-nationalists" who demand that Formosa be exclusively for native Formosans. This development would be an evolutionary step in the common interest of the population, since it necessitates the cooperation of native Formosans and mainland Chinese in living and working together with a sense of shared identity, totally separated from Communist China. Its implementation, however, requires the acceptance and cooperation of the ruling Nationalist elite, even if Peking's opposition can be disregarded for the moment.

Indeed, if the Nationalist regime were willing to cast away an obsolete ideology and reorient its political structure and national policy on a realistic basis, it would proclaim Formosa an independent nation (regardless of official title) *completely separated from mainland China*—and the entire Formosa problem would be less complicated and less insecure. Proponents of the "two Chinas" policy somehow base their theory on the assumption that sooner or later the ruling Nationalist group would accept this policy, tacitly if not expressly, notwithstanding its present intransigency.

This expectation may in due course turn out to be the crux of a gigantic miscalculation. There has been no indication whatever of a self-generated change of the kind postulated on the part of the Nationalist ruling group. Proponents of the "two Chinas" policy generally recognize that two steps are essential, both depending on the exercise of strong U.S. influence on Chiang's regime: to withdraw from Quemoy and Matsu; and to facilitate the "democratization" of Formosa's internal political process. Despite her repeated public and private hints, the United States has thus far failed to move the Nationalist regime in either direction. In the historical perspectives of Chiang Kai-shek or his likely successors, it is less offensive to be labeled "dictators of Formosa" than "Han traitors" (who "lost part of China" to "aliens"). They have been and will be strongly opposed to any attempt to separate Formosa from mainland China, a position held by both Chinese Nationalists and Communists. Accepting this formula would mean the immediate disintegration of the Nationalists' monopoly of power in Formosa.

While both the advocates of the "two Chinas" and the "one

China, one Formosa" programs share the ultimate objective of keeping Formosa an independent nation and a member of the United Nations, free from Chinese Communist control, the "two Chinas" policy, given the present conditions, can have disastrous consequences.

A "two Chinas" plan would implicitly, if not explicitly, sanctify the authority of the Nationalist regime to rule the people of Formosa, even though the regime has never obtained a mandate from them and continues to exclude the overwhelming majority of the population from managing their own affairs. To prolong this anomaly would aggravate tensions to an unbearable degree. Should the Nationalist regime no longer be able to suppress a unified popular opposition, a new development is by no means out of the question. Desperate Nationalist leaders, some of whom are near the top and who have a long background of equivocal relations with the Communist world, may very well negotiate with Peking for assistance.

Confronted with the contingency of a conspirative arrangement by a few Nationalist rulers, the community of nations, including the United States, would perhaps be as inactive as they were with Tibet. Thus a well-intentioned plan ("two Chinas"), originally designed to keep Formosa from Communist control, may well make Formosa a second Tibet.

We ought to cherish no illusions about the Nationalist regime. It is more "Chinese" than "anti-Communist." The underlying problem is not merely to terminate the Nationalist power monopoly, but to prevent Formosa from eventually falling into the hands of the Chinese Communists. The future of Formosa is not a private matter between Chinese Communists and Nationalists, but a question of freedom or slavery for thirteen million people.

Proponents of the "two Chinas" policy suggest that whereas the "two Chinas" policy is the surest way to retain Formosa's membership in the U.N., the "one China, one Formosa" alternative may unintendedly forfeit Formosa's membership—since the latter would necessitate a separate application for membership by the new Formosan republic, presumably after Peking's occupancy of "China's" seats in the Security Council and the General Assembly. Although this possibility cannot be ruled out, it is not to be taken for granted.

According to the proponents of "two Chinas," as long as Communist China is unwilling to accept a "two Chinas" solution, the Nationalist delegation would continue to occupy "China's" seat in the Security Council, excluding Peking. The immediate effect of passing a "two Chinas" resolution would probably be to prolong the *status quo* by continuing to seat the Nationalist delegation as the representative of China pending Peking's acceptance.[1] The defense of the *status quo* would, however, compromise Formosa's future by failing to resolve Formosa's indeterminate legal status and by continuing to ignore the wishes of most of the population. While the international status of Formosa remains obscure and precarious, the world community may in the not too distant future be faced with a delicate situation in which the member states become so anxious to have the *immediate* benefit of Peking's participation in the work of the U.N. as to be willing to seat Peking in place of the Nationalist delegation and to condone Peking's claim over Formosa.

The "one China, one Formosa" alternative goes to the heart of the problem, even at the risk of sacrificing Formosa's membership for a short time (if Peking exercises the veto). If the right of self-determination by the people of Formosa were firmly recognized by the world community, there is ground for believing that Formosans would eventually eradicate the existing political anomaly through self-help and create a viable and responsible body politic. Given the intricate cross-pressures characteristic of the world politics of our time, it is not unthinkable that such a development might in due course reconcile Peking to Formosa's membership in the U.N. Recall that in 1961 the Nationalist regime found it useful to bow to the expediency of not opposing the membership application of Outer Mongolia. Moreover, in the event of a "conditional" resolution endorsing "one China, one Formosa," Peking may decide not to occupy "China's" seat in the U.N. immediately. In that contingency Formosa might conceivably complete its self-determining procedure and apply for U.N. membership even before Peking actually takes part in the Organization.

The United Nations can undertake the "one China, one Formosa" policy only if the major powers, particularly the United States, endorse it—or at least show no objection to it—and stand firm in the face of strong opposition by Chinese Nationalists and Communists. Judging from the tradition and character of the United States and from all specific policy statements and measures, the continuing "national interest" as conceived by U.S. decision-makers seems *not* to use Formosa as a base to mount an invasion of Communist China. The aim is rather to strengthen the defenses of Formosa sufficiently to prevent it from falling into the hands of Communist China. Such an adverse development as the amalgamation of Formosa with the mainland would rupture the integrated defense line that stretches from Japan to the Philippines. While the policy of "containment" of Communist China may continue for some time, deliberate provocation against the mainland is an unlikely objective of the United States. The cost is perceived as too high, not in the immediate military sense, but in the longer range perspective of world accommodation by agreement in the nuclear age. In other words, the United States interest lies in keeping Formosa from falling into Communist hands, rather than in using it as a takeoff point for invading Communist China. This fundamental security interest is shared by Japan, the Philippines, and other nations to the south that are apprehensive of Chinese Communist expansionism.

In the past seventeen years, this basic U.S. goal of keeping Formosa out of Communist hands has led to giving full support to the Nationalists as "the only legitimate government" of "China." On a short-term basis, this policy seemed to be successful. The balance of advantage and disadvantage is changing, however. The relation between the United States and the Nationalist regime is inherently precarious: as long as the Nationalists get their way, all is calm on the surface. During World War II, any hint of declining U.S. support was met by the counter threat of concluding a separate peace with Japan. More recently the Nationalists have hinted at the possible necessity of making a deal with the Chinese Communists; and the option continues to be open. Thus far Chiang has quite successfully executed the tactic of blackmailing the United States.

In their fundamental objectives and interests in Formosa, there are irreconcilable differences between the United States and the Nationalists. While the existence of the regime in Formosa has been assured by U.S. military assistance, the leadership has not and evidently will not content itself with the status of the "government of Formosa." The articulate immediate objective is to retain its international status as "the only legitimate government" of "all the Chinese people"; the ultimate aim is to recapture the mainland. The United States is aware of the danger in giving currency to so provocative and unrealistic a goal. Hence while Washington continues to recognize the regime as the only legitimate government of China, the U.S. seeks to restrain the Nationalists from unilateral military action against the mainland. This dilemma is well exploited by Peking when it propagates the assertion that the "Chiang Kai-shek clique" is the "tool" used by "U.S. imperialism" to engage in "armed aggression and occupation of Taiwan."

In the face of the current upheavals resulting from the "great proletariat cultural revolution" on the mainland, Chiang Kai-shek has once again told the world that the promised land is just around the corner and the Nationalist regime is ready to "pick up the pieces left by Mao's collapse."[2] With all deference to President Chiang, it would appear to any knowledgeable student of China affairs that the future of mainland China will be shaped by the people on the mainland, rather than by the Nationalist cohorts driven off the mainland almost two decades ago.

There may come a point when submitting to the Nationalists' blackmail will compromise the essential interests of the United States. The pursuit of an inflexible policy on behalf of the *status quo* will alienate most Formosans. There are, in fact, many indications in the U.S. of growing dissatisfaction with the established policy. By switching its support from the Nationalist ruling minority to the people of Formosa, the United States would demonstrate that it has no intention of using Formosa as a base for attacking mainland China. Such a policy benefits all who are concerned with security and cooperation, including Communist China itself.

A Plebiscite in Formosa

THE OBVIOUS step in implementing the "one China, one Formosa" policy is to grant self-determination to the people of Formosa. The exercise of self-determination commonly takes the form of a plebiscite by the population concerned. Because of the intricate interplay between Formosa's internal and external processes, it is imperative that the United Nations supervise this plebiscite in Formosa, considering several things.

ELIGIBLE VOTERS   All people with permanent residence in Formosa today, mainland Chinese as well as native Formosans, over twenty should be eligible to participate in the plebiscite. This would include those who are temporarily abroad for study or other purposes.

AVAILABLE OPTIONS   A plebiscite should sustain freedom of choice. The range may include (*a*) establishing an independent nation, separated from mainland China, with authority to participate in international affairs; (*b*) union with mainland China, without independent authority to engage in international affairs, but with a guaranteed degree of "internal autonomy"; (*c*) U.N. trusteeship, as an interim measure pending ultimate disposition by the inhabitants of the island;[3] and (*d*) maintaining the *status quo* by continuing Nationalist rule.

VOTING PROCEDURE AND MACHINERY   Voting procedure and machinery can be based on the existing administrative set-up in Formosa, provided direct United Nations supervision is assured. It is of paramount importance in contemplating a plebiscite that the actual distribution of assets in Formosa be realistically considered. The Nationalist regime has organized bases of power throughout Formosa through its control over the armed forces, the regular and secret police, the government machinery, the national treasury and enterprises, the mass media, the party organization, and the youth movement. In contrast to this display of effective power, the Formosan people, though they have a relatively high standard of education and substantial private wealth, are basically unorganized and divided. The obvious discrepancy between the ruling minority and the people calls for an effective supervision by the United Nations, particularly in view of the "security measures" traditionally employed by the Kuomintang to intimidate and deceive the voters in the brief history of Formosa's local elections.[4] The United Nations must be empowered with sufficient assets, including formal authority, to provide the necessary safeguards for a free and genuine choice.

TIME TABLE   The first point to be settled is whether Formosa's plebiscite should take place before or after Communist China's participation in the United Nations. If it could be arranged to precede Peking's participation, Communist China would presumably be less likely to try to upset the plebiscite process and to veto Fomosa's application for U.N. membership. It is doubtful, however, that such an arrangement would be acceptable to Peking. The implementation of a plebiscite does take time, probably a minimum of one year's preparation. Accordingly, should Communist China be seated in the United Nations within the next few sessions of the General Assembly, Formosa's plebiscite and its membership application would, at the earliest, come a year later.

The essential point is to obtain a prior commitment from the major participants, as was done in the "packaged admission" of member states to the U.N. even in the heat of the cold war in 1955. Agreement is necessary if Formosa's self-determination and ensuing application for U.N. membership are to be successful in spite of Peking's possible occupation of China's seats in the Security Council and the General Assembly.

Another consideration has to do with the time needed for initial campaigns of enlightenment and for other preparatory measures. Some time must be allowed to make sure that points of view other than the Nationalist line are properly heard.

OTHER SAFEGUARDS   Formosa is separated from mainland China by the Straits of Formosa, which is about 100 miles wide. Although any Communist armed attack across the Straits can be covered, infiltration and subversion is something else again. In order to forestall Communist China from upsetting by armed attack Formosa's search for self-determination the United States must continue to safeguard Formosa, as she has done for more than seventeen years, during the transitional phase. In preparing a plebiscite, the United Nations should also deter Communist infiltration and subversion. Since one of the principal choices open to voters is to be part of Communist China, the problem is to permit persuasion while preventing subversion.

Meanwhile, tension inside Formosa may be explosively high. The general public, though largely unorganized, may be expected to grow more actively resentful of the authoritarian machinery to which they have been subordinated. Hence it is absolutely necessary that adequate U.N. personnel perform the policing function in the interest of genuine freedom of choice. A great free forum of debate, not an arena of overt or covert violence, is the object.

OUTCOMES AND EFFECTS   The passage of a U.N. resolution authorizing and outlining concrete measures for a plebiscite would be the first of several difficult steps. It might provoke the Chinese Nationalist regime into withdrawing from the United Nations and attempting to resist U.N. involvement in Formosa's internal process. The Nationalist resistance, stubborn as it might be, would be short-lived, especially since both leaders and rank and file members of the Nationalist minority would come to recognize that they had a far brighter future in the new Formosa than in blind opposition or in desperate overtures to the mainland. If, as is likely, U.N. personnel were prevented from entering Formosa, the strong support of the world organization would inaugurate a series of chain reactions, both within and outside Formosa, that would most probably culminate in the disintegration of the Nationalist regime and in the establishment of a new Republic of Formosa.

In view of the ineffectiveness of U.N. resolutions with such problems as apartheid in South Africa and the unilateral declaration of independence by a racist minority regime in Southern Rhodesia our summary assessment of Formosa's future development may be called too credulous. The United Nations being what it is, it is said, what impact can a resolution endorsing Formosa's self-determination actually have? The question of implementation is undoubtedly crucial. Hence in the following pages we give more detailed consideration to the probable sequence of transition and development. It is not beside the point, however, to underline at this juncture some fundamental differences between the situation in Formosa and either South Africa or Southern Rhodesia.

Of a total population of 18 million in South Africa, about 3.5 million are white and the rest are nonwhite, including Africans, "coloreds," and Asians. In Southern Rhodesia, the white population numbers only 220,000 (less than 6 per cent), of a total population of 4.2 million. Since the wall between white and nonwhite communities in these two areas is built along the racial (color) line, the possibility in the foreseeable future of genuine fusion of both sides is extremely limited. This is not the case in Formosa, however. Although the present population of the island can be approximately divided into 2 million mainland Chinese and

11 million native Formosans, there is no race (color) line as such in existence. Generally speaking, although their perspectives are not identical on many issues of crucial importance, they are not by the nature of things two inherently hostile groups. The overwhelming majority of the mainland Chinese, along with the native Formosans, are joint victims of the degenerate Nationalist machine. In fact, the liberal elements of both communities have time and again made efforts to bridge the gulf between the two groups and to clarify and act for the realization of their common interests. Thus far they have made little headway—explained partly by the KMT's tactic of divide-and-rule, designed to prevent the formation of an alliance between the two that might threaten the existing elite, and partly by the KMT's commitment to a political myth that precludes them from identifying themselves fully with Formosa. Thus when the U.N. endorses "one China, one Formosa," the resulting crisis will alert liberal elements on both sides to the fact that their common future lies in working as partners to build a new Formosa. They can be expected to turn away from the dream world of a "recovered" mainland, and to join in repudiating a handful of irresponsible politicians whose sense of public interest has been overwhelmed by the pursuit of private advantage.

In terms of education, skill, wealth, political sophistication, and other value assets, the white and nonwhite communities in South Africa and Southern Rhodesia represent two different epochs. The situation in Formosa is totally different. Native Formosans are denied the effective access to the top level of policy-making and execution in both the civilian and military arenas. In terms of all other value assets, however, native Formosans are at least as well off as the mainland Chinese. The masses, though under continuing political deprivation, are endowed with acute political awareness and a great potential for political organization and skill.

With a view to maintaining "white supremacy," both South Africa and Southern Rhodesia have systematically practiced racial discrimination in military recruitment: while military training is compulsory for all physically able white males, nonwhite males, with minor exceptions, are excluded from training in skills of violence (and hence of control). Modern weaponry, military organizations, and specialized skills of violence are the virtual monopoly of the white in these two territorial communities. The masses have little choice but to reconcile themselves to perpetual deprivation so long as powerful outside assistance is unavailable. Here again the situation in Formosa is fundamentally different. Although native Formosans have not been consulted in the shaping of defense policy or programs oriented toward realizing the goal of "mainland recovery," their manpower has been mobilized. Contrary to their general predisposition, native Formosans as well as mainland Chinese are subject to an extensive program of compulsory military training and service. More than 80 per cent of the rank and file of the Nationalist armed forces are native Formosans, though the officer corps is predominantly mainland Chinese. As we will show later, this might become a decisive factor in shaping Formosa's future.

Finally, the racist policies pursued by the ruling regimes of South Africa and Southern Rhodesia, reprehensible as they are, do not depend on international approval. Though the continuation of these policies does drive them into greater international isolation, if international isolation is unaccompanied by effective collective sanctions there is little adverse effect on the political myths or the power practices on which the ruling elites depend. In the case of the Nationalist regime, survival and stability depend fundamentally on continuing international recognition of its status as "the government of China." Deprived of its existing though fictitious international status, the political myths in terms of which the elite justifies its monopoly of power in Formosa would altogether lose credibility. As its political fictions are liquidated, the foundations of the present power structure will suffer erosion.

Communist China's Reactions

CONFRONTED with a U.N. resolution sustaining the "one China, one Formosa" policy, Communist China can be expected to respond vehemently. It might refuse to participate in the United Nations if bound by "preconditions."[5] Since the takeover of 1949, Peking has been fundamentally uncompromising on the question of Formosa for four reasons.

Chinese Communists want to put an end to the prolonged Chinese civil war by eliminating the last vestige of all reactionary elements, notably "Chiang Kai-shek's clique." As long as the Nationalist regime remains, the socialist revolution is perceived as incomplete.

Highly sensitive to security interests (particularly at the periphery), Communist China seeks to control the widest possible sphere of influence around all national borders. So long as Formosa is in the hands of an independent power, any attempt by Communist China to expand to the western Pacific will be curtailed.

Chinese Communist elites, possessing a sense of historical mission, seek to restore the "grandeur" of the Chinese empire. The reincorporation of all territories that have ever been under China's control is regarded as essential to such grandeur.

In the past seventeen years, the United States has been identified as Communist China's prime enemy. Communist leaders used the United States' constant threat to consolidate their internal order and reconstruct the nation. The Nationalists who rule Formosa have been stigmatized as puppets of the United States, and the U.S. has been accused of engaging in armed aggression and illegal occupation of Formosa. As the mutual hostility of the United States and Communist China has not diminished through time, "Formosa" and "American imperialism" are often mentioned in the same breath. In the liturgy of its propaganda Peking has used Formosa as a constant reminder of "American imperialism," hence as an enduring provocation to the tightening of internal solidarity. The separation of Formosa from the mainland signifies perpetual threat and insecurity, which is obviously much more than a matter of "face."[6]

Since its inception the Chinese Communist regime has changed the details of its policy toward Formosa several times. Initially, Peking's plan to "liberate" Formosa was primarily military. The grand military design, however, was blocked by the U.S. presence in the Formosan area as a consequence of the Korean war and the subsequent mutual defense treaty between the United States and the "Republic of China." After the Bandung Conference of 1955, Communist China's program was suddenly shifted to a "political offensive" in which direct negotiations were urged with the United States and the Nationalist regime respectively. The 1958 offshore islands crisis was a test of the seriousness of U.S. commitment in the Formosa area. When the United States stood firm in support of the Nationalist regime, Premier Khrushchev was widely reported to have exerted a significant restraining influence upon Peking. The crisis focused world attention on Quemoy and Matsu and heightened the widespread concern for possible escalation.

In order to avoid a major calamity in the train of adventurist actions by either Peking or Taipei, the government of the United States, among other powers, began seriously to ponder over some form of a "two Chinas" policy as a practical means out of the impasse. Both the Communist and Nationalist regimes seem suddenly to have realized the symbolic value of maintaining a "perpetual status of hostility and tension" in the offshore islands area. Even after the crisis was over Communist China began a "ceremonial" shelling of Quemoy in October 1958 to show the world that the Chinese civil war was still on and "there is only one China." She became more sensitive than ever about any proposal of "two Chinas" or of "one China, one Formosa." On various occasions Communist elites have stated that the question of "Taiwan" is unnegotiable. In the ambassadorial talks between mainland China and the United States in the past twelve years,

"Taiwan" has been regarded as "the primary issue" by Chinese Communists. They assert that unless the United States is willing to make concessions on this account, no other business can be broached. Hence officially the ambassadorial talks have so far had little tangible result, though both sides consider it useful to keep the channel of communication open.

As their power position has consolidated and their economy has developed, the Chinese Communist elites have been disposed to believe that time is in their favor—particularly so after mainland China "paid the initiation fee" for membership in the "nuclear club." This is true despite the current upheavals under the "great proletariat cultural revolution." Presently the Chinese Communists seem to be taking a longer perspective toward Formosa without, however, showing any sign of compromising their ultimate position. Evidently they believe that they can afford the luxury of waiting for many years to see the Formosan problem settled.[7] Moreover, since the 1958 offshore islands crisis, Communist leaders may have been counting on the fact that the Nationalist regime would eventually come to terms with them at the expense of the "weak," "suppressed," and "unorganized" Formosans. It is not farfetched to suggest that the Nationalists and the Communist Chinese have at least a tacit understanding that to perpetuate the "one China" doctrine is to perform a great historical service for the motherland. In this perspective any transfer of power to the native Formosans is tantamount to betraying the historic and mystic unity of "China."

Finally, from all available indications, Communist China seems little interested in participating in the United Nations. In the early years of its existence the present regime, still weak internally, was very much concerned to enhance its weight in the worldwide arena of formal authority. As its bases of power increase, its interest in U.N. participation decreases. It welcomed the withdrawal of Indonesia and even hinted at the establishment of a rival organization to compete with the United Nations.[8] More recently, it has put forth some obviously unacceptable conditions for its participation, including cancellation of a U.N. resolution condemning Chinese aggression in Korea, U.N. condemnation of the U.S. as an aggressor, revision of the Charter, and inclusion of "all independent States" in, and expulsion of "all imperialist puppets" from, the Organization.

Nevertheless, should the U.N. resolution provide that Formosa's plebiscite and application for U.N. membership come after Communist China's occupancy of seats both in the General Assembly and the Security Council, the leaders of Communist China would probably not be so foolish as to lose an opportunity to have her voice magnified in the world arena. The Chinese Nationalist delegation may very well withdraw from the United Nations before or on passage of the U.N. resolution; and Communist China, seizing the first opportunity to occupy the seats vacated by the Nationalist delegation, may then obstruct Formosa's self-determination and veto her application for U.N. membership, while claiming to "liberate" (or to "represent") Formosa.

Chinese Nationalist Reactions

CONFRONTED with a U.N. proposal to include Communist China's participation and to grant self-determination to the people of Formosa, the Nationalist delegation will undoubtedly try to prevent action by the Organization. However, should it become clear that the Nationalist delegation cannot withstand the overwhelming pressure of member states, the delegation might choose to withdraw even before a showdown, even though such a drastic act would render the Nationalist regime more isolated internationally.[9]

According to this scenario of future developments, while Communist China would be in the United Nations, the Nationalist delegation would be out. Thus isolated externally, what course of action would the Nationalist regime pursue internally? Many hope

—and expect—that the regime would at long last come to terms with the realities and show willingness to facilitate an eleventh-hour fusion movement by modifying the constitutional structures in order to insure equal participation for all the people of Formosa in national political decision-making.

This expectation, however, may be illusory. Instead of a genuine fusion movement, a highhanded attempt to suppress mounting opposition may be more probable. To do otherwise would mean the immediate collapse of Chiang's present "monopoly of power" and the total disavowal of the myths upon which the Nationalist regime has been based. Indeed, the top figures of the Nationalist elite, too long accustomed to the use of power for their private advantage, seem determined to hold on to their present dominance at all costs.

In order to "consolidate" and "perpetuate" its power monopoly in Formosa, Chiang's regime has invented and clung to many doctrines and formulas. Aware that survival depends in no small measure on the credibility of these myths, the regime is highly sensitive to dissent and never hesitates to suppress any slight sign of challenge to them. Notable among their doctrines are:

1] Formosa is an integral part of China. There is only "one" China, and the "Republic of China" (now in Formosa) led by the Nationalists is the "authoritative" spokesman of all China, whose mission is to "recover" the mainland now temporarily ruled by the Chinese Communists.

2] It is absurd to make a distinction between the native Formosans (85 per cent of Formosa's population) and the mainland Chinese (15 per cent). For they are all Chinese; and if there is any difference between them, it is simply the "timing of settlement" in Formosa (early comers and late comers) and nothing else.[10]

3] The Nationalist government in Formosa is a popular government, supported by the general public and committed to the ideal and practice of "democracy." There is no ground for alleging that the Nationalist government has either discriminated against the so-called Formosan Chinese or has excluded them from effective participation in political decision-making.

4] Chiang Kai-shek is the "savior" of China, whose leadership is indispensable to China and will be everlasting.

As for the claim that Formosa is part of China, and that "only one China" exists today, we have provided the pertinent facts in the preceding two chapters. Here we note that the continued occupation of Quemoy and Matsu has served as the symbolic link for the Nationalist claim to "represent" the whole of China. To repudiate either the "two Chinas" or the "one China, one Formosa" proposal, spokesmen for the regime have frequently pointed to the fact that it occupies these offshore islands. In Formosa (an island of 13,885 square miles), the Nationalist armed forces total 600,000 with 85-90 per cent of the "national budget" diverted to defense expenditures—which incidentally is strictly in confidence and not subject to legislative control.[11] The massive military build-up, out of all proportion to the economic capacities of Formosa, is justified on grounds of the existence of the civil war with Chinese Communists and of the Nationalists' sacred mission to "liberate" compatriots under the torture of the Communist government. The following statement, selected at random, typifies the KMT's propaganda theme: "To us recovery of the mainland is a sacred mission and to end Communist aggression in Asia is to remove the danger of a nuclear war. It is our duty to launch a punitive expedition against the rebels, to deliver our compatriots from under tyranny, and to recover the mainland."[12]

As a matter of propaganda, the Nationalist regime has gone all the way to play down or ignore the actual differences and tensions between native Formosans and mainland Chinese in the hope of preventing a distinct sense of identity and political awareness, and of fostering an apparent "solidarity." Recently the regime has gone so far as to stigmatize the Formosan independence movement as a conspiracy initiated, exploited, and supported by the

Chinese Communists.[13] This is an extreme use of "smear tactics" for the purposes of generating "fear" among the Formosan people and of forestalling external support and sympathy for their cause.

The appearance of internal solidarity that results from consistent evasion of sensitive though vital issues tends to widen the gap between the native Formosans and the mainland Chinese. The unfortunate effect is to bring about a virtual breakdown of the mutual communication so essential to the future viability of Formosa. In time the rank and file members of both groups are likely to discover that they are victims of a "curtain of ignorance" and of "deliberate deception." They may respond irrationally in the midst of emergency. We shall elaborate further on this deep-rooted problem in the section that immediately follows.

To claim that the Nationalist government today is a democratic government ruling with the consent and support of the governed is to make mockery of "democracy." While opinions may differ in detail, it needs little documentation to realize that the Nationalist regime is essentially a garrison-police state. The continued existence of a state of emergency (the proclamation of martial law) in Formosa since 1949 has virtually suspended civil rights and deprived the individual of their protection. All this is allegedly done in accordance with what is called the Constitution of the "Republic of China." Under one pretext or another, a civilian can easily be court-martialed without due process of law. The people are prohibited the freedom of assembly as well as of association. A newspaper or magazine can be instantaneously suspended by executive order if it is critical of the regime's policies. Opposition is not tolerated; only echoes of the official line are allowed. A reign of terror runs throughout the island, testifying to a comprehensive and seemingly effective network of secret police.

Chiang Kai-shek is a man stubbornly convinced of his historical mission; there is no reason to doubt that he believes himself to be indispensable to China. As he grows older, he has revived the "family dynasty," so characteristic of centuries of Chinese politics. The defection of many of his top and trusted aides in 1949 moved Chiang closer to his own family members, particularly his older son Ching-kuo. Although his sphere of effective control has been greatly curtailed and is presently confined to the tiny island of Formosa, he seems to enjoy wielding power within this limited domain more than ever before. In the selection and utilization of human resources, what primarily counts is "loyalty" to the Gimo, not ability. Actively concerned with his own family fortune he has come to assume that what is good for the Chiangs is good for the general welfare, including the long-term interests of millions of Formosans. He seems to perceive his enduring role in Chinese history as one who would never yield to the Communists, even in extreme adversity. In the pursuit of his "glorious mission," Chiang has led the people of Formosa to live in dream and illusion. Practically all the day-to-day problems of the masses have been promised a solution the day Chiang Kai-shek recovers the lost territory, the mainland of China. For example, a continuous theme has been that Formosa's pressing problems of population explosion and unemployment can easily be solved once Chiang Kai-shek is back on the mainland.

The leadership gap is widening dangerously, since Chiang has himself dominated the political scene for far too many years, consciously acting to prevent the growth of a leadership that might conceivably threaten his unique position. When Chiang passes away, the people of Formosa will suddenly find themselves living in a totally different world, one they are not equipped to meet realistically and rationally. As a measure of the peculiar atmosphere of prison and mental hospital that characterizes the regime of Chiang, it is taboo in Formosa to mention or explore constructive alternatives to Chiang's proclaimed slogan of the "recovery of the mainland of China."

No matter how unreal yet provocatively damaging they may appear, these myths have been projected to the outer world as well, by massive propaganda campaigns. The established doctrines have been dogmatically reiterated in the United Nations, notably when the question of China's participation was in debate. On the internal front any challenge is quieted by the garrison-state police techniques. Any proposal to abandon the slogans of "one China" or of "recovery of the mainland" is tantamount to sedition. We must re-emphasize in this connection that U.S. support of Chiang's regime has been a decisive factor in perpetuating the whole system.

Recall that in 1947, while acting on behalf of the Allied powers in occupying Formosa—then legally still Japanese territory—the Nationalist government unilaterally declared Formosa to be "one of the 35 Provinces" of China. When a nationwide election was held in late 1947 and early 1948, Formosa was allowed to participate in the process by electing its own proportion of representatives. These representatives, elected in 1947 or 1948 for three- or six-year terms by the constituencies on the mainland, found themselves no longer with constituencies as a result of the Nationalist exile to Formosa. Notwithstanding the expiration of terms and the total loss of their mainland constituencies, they have since 1949 continued to hold their positions and to exercise authority in Formosa. They have assumed *de facto* "life tenure" as "representatives of the people," an act made possible by the "authoritative interpretation" of a rubber stamp "Council of Grand Justices." These representatives still profess to exist, despite their lack of responsibility to any constituent at all; to be exact, despite their lack of any constituency whatever. The key fact of political life in Formosa today is clear: the "Republic of China" has under its effective control only Formosa. The national will of these thirteen million people has supposedly been reflected during the past seventeen years by representatives elected in 1947 or 1948 by 500 million people of mainland China.

Such an absurdity is the crux of the political process in Formosa. The issue is far more fundamental than liberalizing somewhat the police control presently exercised by the Nationalist regime. Even in West Germany, South Korea, or South Vietnam, there are nationwide elections by a nationwide electorate. Elections in Formosa, often called "democratic" by spokesmen of the KMT, are confined to the election of local officers, such as mayors, magistrates, councilmen, and provincial assemblymen.

In the event Formosa should be confronted with a crisis resulting from international support of the Formosans' cause, a more highhanded police control of the under-represented Formosans is the first probable response, rather than a genuine fusion movement designed to enhance the cooperation of native Formosans and mainland Chinese.

The Response of the
Formosan People

A RUTHLESS display of Nationalist force to hold on to its power would further alienate the Formosan people and convince the waverers that the Nationalist regime is determined to exclude them from access to power at all cost and for all time. Indignation and disenchantment among the Formosans would inspire a common surge toward action. Dissatisfied and potentially explosive elements would thus come into the open.

A distinctive history and location have given to the people of Formosa a set of predispositions that set them apart from mainland Chinese. Except for a tiny remnant of aboriginal tribes, the ancestors of today's eleven million native Formosans come from the Chinese mainland, notably Fukien province across the Straits of Formosa, and their migration to Formosa dates back to the seventeenth century or earlier. Fifty years of Japanese rule had a great impact upon the sense of identity among Formosans, modifying earlier legacies from Fukien. At the close of World War II, the disintegration of former colonial empires was hardly in sight, since the decolonialization inspired by nationalism did not strongly assert itself until the emergence of the cold war. Thus in October 1945, when the Nationalist forces acting on behalf of the Allied powers came to occupy Formosa, the Formosan people greeted them with mixed feelings. Emancipation from Japan had come so suddenly and unexpectedly that the Formosans were not sure what they wanted. Nevertheless they somehow cherished the hope that they would be better off under Nationalist rule than they had been under Japanese colonial rule.

This frame of mind, however, was short-lived. After less than a year and a half of Nationalist rule, the Formosans rose in revolt against the Nationalist authorities. The retaliatory massacre and persecution of Formosan leaders has led to a bitter hatred of their Nationalist oppressors so deeply ingrained that it would be naïve to think that the Formosans have forgotten the past "bloody debt." Rather they have learned a hard lesson well under the tutelage of a continuous reign of terror—"to be cautious, and never act prematurely." Their hatred and contempt for the *regime* has unfortunately often been broadened to include *mainland Chinese in general*, and the innocent and equally miserable mainland Chinese of low rank become scapegoats of the Formosans' bitter resentment against the regime. It is, after all, the day-to-day frictions of "little men" that cause immediate concern.

The lot of the mainland Chinese in Formosa is by no means a happy one. According to their composition, interests, and perspectives, they can be classified approximately into three groups: the top layer of the KMT's power structure, including top military officials; educators and bureaucrats at all levels on government payrolls; and the lowest stratum, including the rank and file in the armed forces, veterans and their families, and other workers. In the top stratum of the KMT's power structure are those who, having identified their career with the ups and downs of Chiang's family or the fortunes of the KMT, enjoy the highest degree of comfort in Formosa today. They are a very small group. Naturally, in order to consolidate their "vested interests," they have gone all the way with the Nationalists.

The people in the second group are comparatively well educated and hence equipped with various skills. They had not possessed vast wealth when they first sought refuge in Formosa in 1949; for the most part they have been in government services, including educational institutions and public enterprises. While they might have been qualified for their jobs in 1949, the competence of many of them is questionable today because of their advanced age and a lack of modern knowledge and skill. Undesirable as they may be, they have been kept in their positions as a means of providing them with a livelihood. As most of the higher positions of the government bureaucratic system are held by "unproductive people" who ought to have retired long ago, the government administration generally lacks new blood. "Senior citizens" block the path of promotion, as long as an office is a form of relief. Far from being deeply satisfied with the regime, Formosa's bureaucrats nevertheless depend on it for an income, and see little assurance of holding their present posts should power be transferred from the KMT to native Formosans. Hence their resentment against the regime is tempered by personal considerations. "Don't rock the boat," is the essential philosophy. If constrained to choose between the "Nationalist regime" and "Formosans," they would, though reluctantly, support the regime that keeps their rice bowls reasonably full.

The third group, the least educated, consists primarily of lower-class workers and retired servicemen and their families. In general, they are no better off than most native Formosans. Having no share of the KMT's spoils, they live precariously as beneficiaries of the government's meager welfare programs. The luckiest ones have married native Formosan girls; as a consequence, a growing sense of belonging to the Formosan community (a gradual process of "Taiwanization") is visible among them. Some of them—an extreme minority—still sincerely believe that someday their "savior" Chiang Kai-shek will lead them back home and reward them with land on the mainland; this has in fact been promised them "by statute" once the lost territory "on the other side of the Formosan Straits" should be recovered. Most lower-class mainlanders, however, cherish little hope for a better life. They have outgrown any illusion about the Nationalists' recovery of the mainland. Neither do they have any long-range plans for what is left of their lives. Miserable as they are under Nationalist rule, they could hardly care less should Formosa be turned over to Communist China—many of them would no doubt welcome a change. Because these people have the least to lose, they may well act irrationally and impulsively during crisis. The potential danger, however, is lessened because this group consists, comparatively speaking, of a large number of the elderly.

As there are basic differences among the mainlanders in terms of "vested interests" and perspective, it is little wonder that there is an inherent tension among them. Native Formosans, however, tend to put all mainland Chinese under the same category, and to overlook the inner cleavages that tend to separate them from one another. The few who are firmly embedded at the pinnacle of the KMT's power structure have denied effective participation in the power process to the mainland Chinese as well as the rank and file of native Formosans.

Both groups are fellow victims of historical tragedies and of the KMT's totalitarian and fictional modalities of control. It is evident—particularly from the purges carried out in the name of the "great proletariat cultural revolution"—that the Chinese in Formosa can expect no proper place within the framework of Communist China; they have been "poisoned" by years of exposure to, and compromise with, the reactionary KMT. Though overpopulated, Formosa has room enough to accommodate mainland Chinese as well as native Formosans, provided that basic national policies are realistic and rational. It is not a matter of impulsive generosity, but of common interest that native Formosans and mainland Chinese learn how to live and work together. By sensibly clarifying and recognizing common interests, native Formosans and mainland Chinese can in time establish genuine communication.

Up to the present, as we have emphasized earlier, the fiction of recovering the Chinese mainland has been more or less successful in keeping the Formosan populace living in dream and illusion. It is asked to make sacrifices every day; and the reward is remote and vague promises. The center of daily life is Formosa, yet everyone is constrained or misled into publicly identifying his future with a land most of them have never seen. The irony of the situation is increasingly perplexing and frustrating to generations of young people. Indeed, time may have run out for genuine communication between native Formosans and mainland Chinese. The widening communication gap generates mutual misgiving, deception, and withdrawal, which are cumulatively detrimental to the stability and welfare of Formosan society and politics.

Moreover, the Nationalist regime has skillfully adopted a strategy of "divide-and-rule" in Formosa—encouraging not only a grand division between mainland Chinese and native Formosans, but fostering divisions among native Formosans themselves.

Being the last survivors of one side in a vast struggle for power, Chiang and his machine are well seasoned in ways and means of preventing organized and effective opposition. From the very first the Nationalists have resembled conquerors more than liberators in Formosa. In the tradition of colonial powers, native Formosans have been rewarded as tools of the KMT—particularly if they inform on, or otherwise act against, fellow Formosans. Since the native population is an overwhelming majority, the perpetuation of monopoly power by a Nationalist minority requires some ingenuity. For example, the regime has tried to erect a façade of fairness concerning native Formosans. It has found it advantageous to have "token" participation at the top level of government by Formosans of the older provenance. At present, the native Formosans who occupy key decision-making positions can be named: the Minister of Internal Affairs, one Minister without portfolio (there are altogether seventeen cabinet members, including ministers without portfolio), the President of the Legislative Yuan (equivalent of the speakership in Congress), the Speaker of the

Provincial Assembly of Taiwan, and two permanent members of the Central Committee of the Kuomintang (there are altogether 19 members).

We now come to the "ingenious" trick. Offices open for the "token participation" of Formosans are as a rule filled by a very special kind of Formosan—the *pan-san* ("half-hillbilly"), those lucky enough to be associated with the Nationalist regime back on the Chinese mainland long before the regime sought refuge in Formosa. While Formosan by place of birth, they have incorporated the perspectives of the Nationalist elite and identify their interests largely with the regime. Initially they were a bridge between the mainland Chinese and the masses of native Formosans. However, they have been edged into a squeeze play. They are often compelled to carry out unpleasant tasks, such as lavishly praising the fairness and honesty of KMT elections, which every educated citizen in Formosa knows to be tricky and illegal. No one has the slightest doubt about how long the *pan-san* Formosan would hold his job if he ever allowed his conscience to be his guide and obviously he is only too aware that his career lies in absolute loyalty to the regime, rather than in conveying the genuine feeling entertained by the relatively awed and inarticulate masses of native Formosans. Yet ironically, no matter how loyal he may be to his master, the loyalty will never be reciprocated by the regime's wholehearted trust.

This special category of Formosans has doubtless cultivated an interesting philosophy to rationalize its existence; otherwise, life would be a nightmare. While the Nationalist regime utilizes these people with reservations, appointing them the spokesmen of native Formosans, the native Formosans look down upon them as creatures not of their own kind. There is unquestionably a cleavage between the *pan-san* Formosans and the native community.

Though "national elections" are out of the question in Formosa today, "local elections" are held to elect such officers as magistrates, mayors, and members of county or city councils. The Provincial Assembly of Taiwan has also become a battleground for native politicians. (Recall that the "governor" of the "province of Taiwan" has always been handpicked by Chiang, never elected by the citizens of "Taiwan province," voting under the banner of KMT's version of democracy.) The Nationalists have made deliberate efforts to create a factional division among native Formosans, hoping to prevent them from becoming either a unified or an effective force. As long as Formosan politicians remain fragmented, the Nationalists are reasonably secure in their monopoly of power.

The KMT's basic strategy of rule in Formosa goes deeper than divide-and-rule. In order to block demands for participation in the key decision-making process, the regime has deliberately attempted to discredit the Formosans' ability to rule themselves. The Nationalists frequently advance as a reason to bar Formosans from key positions that no adequate talent is available among native Formosans. To some extent this charge is true; and it is true because the Nationalist regime made it so. This is one of the self-fulfilling prophecies most common to a colonial elite. The massacre in 1947 of Formosan leaders was a fatal blow to the prompt emergence of Formosan leadership, since under the colonial rule of Japan only a limited number of Formosans enjoyed both political sophistication and experience.

The immediate shortage of talent among native Formosans became more acute when the official language was changed from Japanese to Mandarin Chinese. The generation of Formosan leaders who were in the prime of their political life when the Nationalists took over had been educated in the Japanese language in the Japanese educational system. Key government positions were now dominated by "carpetbaggers," the mainland Chinese.

Though the language handicap of Formosan elites might have been easily remedied, the regime deliberately attempted to prevent the growth of trained Formosans. Of the sixty ambassadors sent abroad by the regime, there is not a single native Formosan, indicating a lack of confidence in Formosans' loyalty to the regime. As political and bureaucratic sophistication and ability come not only from classroom instruction but from practical training, the continuous denial of Formosans' participation in the important decision-making process tends to create a vicious circle. Pressed for wider sharing of power, the regime responds that there is no adequate talent among native Formosans.

Even in local politics, the KMT regime has not hesitated to strike down influential native politicians under one pretext or another. It has sought to create the impression that native politicians, once given a chance, are as corrupt as the mainland Chinese, if not worse. Once the regime is determined to terminate the political life of a prominent figure, there is no shortage of ammunition, partly because the regime has itself fully exploited the weaknesses of local politicians. Given KMT machine control, a political figure of integrity, independent of the party line, rarely gets anywhere. The entire political operation under the grand design of the KMT has the net effect of indulging "mediocrity" and of depriving "excellence." No wonder after seventeen years of "democracy" under the Nationalists, the quality of democratic practice in Formosa has deteriorated. In the face of the KMT's all-pervasive control many able men have shunned "dirty politics."

In any event, the situation is plainly discouraging to promising young men with a sense of dedication and devotion to the public interest. The low quality of Formosa's local politics that results from the resignation and withdrawal of potentially able individuals provides the regime with additional ammunition to support the allegation that Formosans' chances of access to key positions are limited by their "inferior" qualifications rather than by the discrimination by the KMT.

Not surprisingly, native politicians have become almost wholly occupied with petty squabbles with one another, and remain ignorant of or indifferent to the fundamental problems that compromise the future. Although the confusion and corruption among native Formosans is so emphatically a result of the regime's deliberate manipulation and intimidation, native Formosans share some responsibility. From what is known of human responsibility we can say that important changes in outlook can begin with candid self-understanding, especially among potential leaders. The Formosan national character does at present have serious limitations; once recognized, much can be done to master the handicaps.

Years of subordination to colonial rule in the past and present seem to have injected into Formosans' character the so-called "slave" disposition, that is, willingness to be contented with second-class citizenship. The tragic outcome of past resistance against alien rule has left a widespread sense of the futility of self-assertion against alien forces. Having lived in a state of constant "uncertainty," they tend to take a short-term outlook, and their perspectives, conditioned by the harshness of life and the limited opportunities offered by a small island, are strongly oriented to the opportunism of the immediate.

They tend passively to endure exploitation, taking some comfort in the belief that since the native Formosans constitute the overwhelming majority of Formosa's present population, a gradual transfer of power from the Nationalists to the native Formosans is "inevitable." Ultimately, they think, the KMT is doomed in Formosa. This view entirely overlooks the constant threat of Communist China's intention to "liberate" Formosa, and the ever-present contingency of a Communist-Nationalist deal, should the Nationalist control over Formosa become shaken and its blackmail against the United States backfire.

Nevertheless the generally high level of education, despite its dogmatic character, provides hope for the nation. It is by no means out of the question to speed up the process of national enlightenment among Formosans. They share a remarkable number of grievance-producing experiences. For example, discrimination against the native Formosans is nowhere more conspicuous than in the armed forces. Practically every Formosan enlisted man is treated as a second-rate citizen, and this remains a vivid memory that can hardly be forgotten during one's lifetime. His sense of identity as Formosan becomes stronger, and a sense of indignation emerges.

Thousands of young men with adequate military training and experience, cherishing a single-minded resentment against the Chinese Nationalists, will in due course prove to be a valuable asset for Formosa's independence and development. They will not move prematurely; this lesson they have learned. They know that as long as the United States is solidly behind the Nationalists, an armed revolt has little chance of success; and the cost would be unbearably high. One must recall that they have been waiting for an opportune time to act since 1947. But should the international community in general and the United States in particular demonstrate their support for a genuine exercise of self-determination in Formosa, the Formosan people would respond to the call.

A Nationalist-Communist Deal

WHEN THE demand for self-determination becomes a popular movement, the Nationalist regime would find itself no longer in the comfortable position of an unchallenged ruler. A critical point can be expected when Formosans' opposition, crystallized around a common goal, cannot be suppressed. This internal opposition to the Nationalist ruling group would rapidly escalate, culminating in acute crisis as a consequence of any serious U.N. effort to resolve the China impasse, whether in the form of "one China, one Formosa" or "two Chinas."

The principal choices open to the regime at that time are two: to seek genuine fusion and conciliation with native Formosans by permitting them to participate effectively in political decision-making at all levels; and to pursue a more highhanded policy by soliciting external aid, particularly that of Communist China. For the reasons elaborated before, we are pessimistic about the prospect of a genuine fusion movement between the Nationalists and the native Formosans even at this juncture. A more thinkable step would be a deal between Chinese Nationalists and Communists —another in the series of past arrangements. From the perspectives of top Nationalist rulers, to ask help from "brothers" on the mainland in order to hold fast a territory allegedly "belonging to the motherland" is a noble thing to do. On the other hand, to yield Formosa to Formosans under pressure is tantamount to a surrender to "aliens," which is nothing less than "treachery" in Chinese eyes.[14]

The Chinese Communists have long sought to exploit cleavages within the KMT, the fears of mainland refugees that they will be absorbed by the Formosans, and the frustration and desperation of refugees whose dream of "returning to mainland China" has vanished. At the height of the Chinese civil war, the Communists at one point did try to organize some native Formosans sympathetic with Communism as a front for the eventual takeover of Formosa. However, it soon appeared that Formosans were "more Formosan than Chinese," and any symbols based on close identification with the mainland had little appeal to them.

By 1958, in the midst of the second offshore islands crisis, it had become abundantly clear that Formosans wanted Formosa for Formosans, and were uninspired by the prospect of sharing the "illusory grandeur" of a Chinese empire at some distant point in time. Perceiving these perspectives, the Chinese Communists began to shift strategies. They greatly intensified their direct appeal to the mainland refugees, seeking to capture their nostalgia and attempting to alarm them with the gloomy prospect of being overtaken by native Formosans. This new strategy has taken a variety of forms, including a "letter offensive," direct correspondence with the Nationalists by their relatives, close friends, and former colleagues on the mainland.

Since inaugurating this campaign the Chinese Communists

have counted on their "brothers" to hold Formosa steadfast as part of the "motherland." For their part, they say that they would be glad to help out their brothers in need—even those condemned by them—in preserving their "family fortunes." The "war criminals"—Chiang and his top aides—would be pardoned and rewarded for their commendable deeds in defending the "interests" of the Chinese empire, without yielding an inch to "aliens," which cover Formosans as well as "U.S. imperialists."[15]

It appears probable that a deal between Chinese Nationalists and Communists, of the kind foreshadowed in the London *Observer* in 1962, would be made known to the world at that crucial moment in Formosa's history. Dennis Bloodworth reported from Singapore that the "Chiang Kai-shek family, which controls Nationalist Formosa, has reached a secret agreement with China's Communist leaders in Peking."[16] The principal terms, as agreed upon, were reported as follows:

1] No "serious attack" against each other during Chiang Kai-shek's lifetime;

2] The implementation by Chiang's family, after his death, of an accord, whereby Formosa would become an "autonomous region" of Communist China, enjoying a status similar to that held by "Tibet," though still under Kuomintang control;

3] To hold a "referendum," ten to twenty years later, to decide whether Formosa should be independent or part of Communist China; and

4] The establishment of a buffer administrative district, with free movement for all, in the areas of Quemoy and the Communist-held port of Amoy, preceded by substantial reductions of garrisons in the off-shore islands.

That agreement was reportedly the outcome of "seven years of tenuous contact and tentative negotiations," which began shortly after the 1955 Bandung Conference when Premier Chou En-lai made "peace gestures" to Formosa. Through direct negotiations with the Nationalists of an "exclusively Chinese understanding," the Communists seek to lay the groundwork for forestalling an ultimate transfer of power to native Formosans (whom they actually regard as "aliens") and for facilitating the ultimate takeover of Formosa. This move would also serve the purpose of deflecting Chiang Kai-shek from any commitment to the United States.

While vehemently denied by Kuomintang spokesmen, the terms of the alleged agreement are in general conformity with those reported by the Hong Kong *Standard* on October 26, 1958, when the second offshore islands crisis was subsiding. Bloodworth's article came shortly after President Kennedy publicly rebuffed Chiang Kai-shek for his threat to invade the mainland and when both Chen Cheng, late Vice President, and Chiang Ching-kuo, the Generalissimo's son, were immersed in a power struggle for the eventual succession to Chiang Kai-shek. Hence it was suggested that Chiang Ching-kuo "wanted to reach an understanding with Peking which could be utilized in case the USA [sic] withdrew its protection and backed Chen Cheng as the Generalissimo's successor."[17] This might be so. As of now, however, Chiang Ching-kuo has marshaled and consolidated overwhelming effective power, with no formidable rival in sight. (Chen Cheng died in March 1965, but even before his death, Chiang Ching-kuo appeared to have won decisively.) But this fact has not materially affected the significance of the report. There are grounds for believing that political exchanges between Chinese Nationalists and Communists, through one agent or another, are no novelty.

While there is no conclusive proof of the existence of the deal alleged by Bloodworth, its materialization is a distinct probability in the contingency outlined earlier. As during World War II, when massive U.S. aid was slow in coming, Chiang's government blackmailed the United States by threatening to conclude a separate peace treaty with Japan. It was done in a most subtle way, amounting to blackmail in substance but something else in form.[18] This tactic has paid off handsomely in the past; and there are ample provocations for its continued use in the future. As long as the United States is solidly behind the regime, there is no point in initiating a play of this sort. But once the United States is no longer willing to go along with the regime, they would not hesitate to resort to it. Clearly there will come a time when the United States, acting out of its enlightened self-interest, will no longer tie its fortunes with the Nationalist regime. Certainly the present cordial relations between the United States and the Nationalists are at best full of latent conflict. Come a crisis, the Nationalists can be expected to act as "Chinese first, anti-Communists second." The recent defection of Li Tsung-jen, once Acting President of the "Republic of China," to Communist China after a sixteen-year exile in the United States is a vivid reminder.

The individual most likely to play the part of Li in such a deal is Chiang Ching-kuo,[19] the so-called "Little Chiang" and the most feared man in Formosa today. Ching-kuo passed his formative years in Soviet Russia studying and working, and his wife is Russian. Though he returned to China in 1937, while in Russia he had denounced his father as a "public enemy" of the Chinese people, an exploiter of the masses. He was reported to have been at odds with Madame Chiang for some time (probably because Chiang Kai-shek divorced Ching-kuo's mother to marry Madame Chiang). Any such cleavage has apparently been remedied to consolidate the family fortune.

As he grows older, the Generalissimo becomes more and more concerned with his family fortune. The widespread defection of many of his most trusted aides and generals in the midst of the civil war with the Communists has evidently convinced Chiang that he can trust nobody but his own family. His older son appears to be picked for the task of consolidating the family fortune. It is worth noting that before the expiration of his second term as President, Chiang Kai-shek said he would not seek re-election for a third term (a third term was expressly forbidden by the Constitution). Shortly after, however, the Generalissimo reversed his position, urging the reluctant delegates composing the National Assembly to suspend the applicability of "the limitation clause" (Article 47) in his case, and promising to raise their salaries.

What made Chiang change his mind is still a matter of speculation. One of the principal considerations was that, if Ching-kuo was to succeed him, it seemed in 1960 that his son needed all the help he could get. At that time, Vice President Chen Cheng was too strong and popular to be challenged by Chiang Ching-kuo. There was a general consensus that Chen Cheng was the Number Two man, the heir apparent to Chiang Kai-shek. This did not discourage Chiang Ching-kuo, however. His grand design for the ultimate acquisition of leadership was systematically and intensively initiated as soon as his father was inaugurated for the third term. "Little Chiang" seized every opportunity to develop his own bases of power under the shield of his father's authority and control, and he scored handsomely within an astonishingly short time. While many observers have reservations about the transferability of loyalty from father to son, he has undoubtedly emerged as the heir apparent, as of now. There is no challenge comparable to Chen Cheng on the horizon.

As Secretary-General of the National Defense Council, Minister of Defense, the ranking member of the Standing Committee of the KMT, Chiang Ching-kuo has effective control over the police and intelligence services, key military and civilian appointments, the political department of the armed forces, the administration of ex-servicemen, and a militant youth movement. In 1966 Chiang Kai-shek started his fourth term as President, with Yen Chia-kan the new Vice President. The deliberate choice of Yen, a colorless administrative technician, coupled with the expanded emergency power of the President newly authorized by constitutional amendment, is interpreted as an interim move toward "Prince" Ching-kuo's eventual succession to his father's leadership status.

Of all the top KMT officials, Chiang Ching-kuo is said to be the only one exempt from taking an anti-Communist oath.[20] If this is an indication of his close tie with the Chinese Communists —bound even by a pledge of loyalty—the possibility that he is to play an active part in any deal with the Communists is not farfetched. He may well have spent a lifetime as a frontier guards-man for the Chinese Communists.

Even if there is no ground for the preceding interpretation, Ching-kuo is still the most likely choice to make a deal with Communists. Chiang Kai-shek himself cannot come to terms with his long-time foes without suffering a devastating loss of self-respect, of "face." He does not want to be remembered by future generations as yielding to the Communists in desperation late in life. His son, however, is in a different position. Apart from what has been said above, other fundamental power relations are involved.

Some people might think it likely that native Formosans rather than Chinese Nationalists would solicit Communist assistance. Presumably while Chinese Nationalists are apprehensive of a Communist purge, native Formosans may act impulsively out of despair and revenge. At an earlier stage, when the civil war between Communists and Nationalists was still indecisive and the Nationalists had only just sought refuge in Formosa, the Chinese Communists did try to appeal to native Formosans by using Formosan leaders who resided on the mainland as spokesmen for Formosans in the hope of forming a "united front" to overthrow the Nationalists. But the effort was in vain. As a consequence, the Chinese Communists purged a one-time comrade, Shieh Shey-hon (Miss Snow Red), the symbolic Formosan leader who had been entrusted with the task of liberating Formosa. She was condemned for being "reactionary," which meant that she had envisioned a future of Formosa as independent, separated from Chinese Communist control. In their bones, the Chinese Communists know only too well that Formosans would want no mainland Chinese sitting on their backs.

In the midst of the 1958 offshore islands crisis, when proponents of the "two Chinas" policy were gaining influence, the Chinese Communists suddenly realized the significance for their purposes of the continued existence of the Nationalist regime, with its claim to be "the only legitimate government" of "the only China." As long as Formosa is in the hands of the Nationalists it is assured of being part of the "motherland." The Communists thereupon appealed to the mainland Chinese in Formosa, admonishing, "Brothers, don't let Formosans or American imperialists bury you in the Pacific."

It is worth reiterating that this theme was directed to the mainland Chinese. The Communists have no illusions about Formosans. Neither do Formosans have illusions about Communists. Though they are highly dissatisfied with the Nationalist rule, they are fully aware of the probable consequences of seeking help from Chinese Communists. To start with, they see that they have no effective bargaining power vis-à-vis Chinese Communists. There is no emotional basis or past tie for establishing trustworthy communication between them. Above all, native Formosans are apprehensive of a Communist system, which is understood to be even more intolerable than Nationalist rule. To get rid of the Nationalists with the help of the Communists is inviting a wolf into the house to fight a dog.

As thoughtful Formosans see it, if they receive any genuinely constructive help, it will come from the United States and Japan. They are still confident in the United States, even though they are disappointed and critical of the U.S. for having found it expedient to back the Nationalist regime for so many years. Hence, unless extreme irrational elements come to the top in a time of absolute desperation, there is no chance that Formosans will make a deal with Chinese Communists, thereby jeopardizing their security and their survival.

Should Chiang Ching-kuo become the successor to his father's "dynasty," he would find it more gratifying to be "first" in Formosa, rather than second or third man in the Chinese Communist hierarchy, which would put him at the mercy of the Communists. Grown to maturity in a long series of intense and vicious power struggles, he cannot be so naïve as to trust Communist good will to make a deal favorable to him in a situation where relative bargaining power is only too discrepant. "Little Chiang" certainly could not feel at all secure unless he has had an understanding with Chinese Communists all these years. The analysis does not end here, however.

After his father's death or retirement, Chiang Ching-kuo's number one position in Formosa can be made stable only with the full backing of native Formosans. The price of such backing is their full and effective participation in political decision-making at all levels. From all indications he is unwilling to pay this price. He seems to believe that as his police control has been effective in the past, so it will be effective in the future. Perhaps this is the crux of his miscalculation, as it so often is with tyrants. Confronted with a situation in which he could no longer suppress popular opposition—for example, when the United States seemed no longer willing to arm a Chiang tyranny—the obvious move would be to solicit Communist assistance by way of a deal with Peking, in the hope of prolonging his power and protecting his family fortune.

The immediate impact of a Nationalist-Communist deal, if allowed to materialize, is obvious. Formosa would then become a second Tibet. Initially the Chinese Communists would make lavish promises of a high degree of "autonomy" for the Formosan people, but the deception would soon be exposed. Once Formosa is generally accepted as part of China, the international community could do as little to defend the fundamental human rights of the Formosan people as they have done in Tibet. If no effort is made to forestall or nullify a transfer of power to the Communists, Formosa would be doomed to remain in the Communist orbit.

The crucial factor in the contingency of a Nationalist-Communist deal, however, is the United States. To the United States, such a deal would be shocking indeed, even if not totally unanticipated. Most of the American friends of the KMT have been more devoted to the values and institutions of the non-Communist world, and hence to the traditional orientation of the United States, than they have been charmed by Chiang. If they, like the Formosans, are betrayed by Chiang or his successor they would be in an embarrassing and traumatic position. They would want an explanation, an illuminating map of reality, both to comprehend a shocking development and to chart another course of action.

It is easy to guess that a strong current in U.S. public life would seize the occasion to seek to restore an isolationist withdrawal from world affairs; more specifically, to abandon Asia and the Far East to the "Asians," even if they are also "Communists." They would urge that the Seventh Fleet cease to operate to deter the mainland, and U.S. interests in Formosa and elsewhere would be redefined in such a way that U.S. diplomatic, economic, informational, or military backing could not be counted on, no matter what restrictions were imposed. Presumably the U.S. shield would be withdrawn from the Philippines, Southeastern Asia, and India.

The advocates of petulant isolationism would be supported in part on very different grounds by another element in U.S. politics. The deal between the KMT and the Communists would be interpreted by some as an opportune moment to seek what they believe to be a long overdue accommodation with Communist China. Hence the Formosan people would be left to their fate, with their denial of self-determination ignored or treated as a *quid pro quo* for the normalization of relations between the United States and Communist China. That is to say, if the future gives the appearance, as in the past, that the whole Formosan problem is merely a problem of power politics between the major powers, and not a matter of "life or death" and "freedom or slavery" for the

Formosan population, the United States may find a gracious way out by saying that after all the Formosan problem is an internal affair of the Chinese people—a matter between Chinese Communists and Nationalists, and no one else. The line could be that since Nationalists and Communists have peacefully settled their disputes, it is certainly no business of the U.S. to meddle in Formosa. With such a rationalization the United States might be able to get out of the Formosan impasse with little if any sense of guilt.

That this thinking may eventually affect the policy of the U.S. government cannot be ruled out. But it is not a tradition of the American public to remain indifferent to human rights. Nor is it an American tradition to retreat in the face of difficulty. Communist sedition and KMT duplicity are not necessarily decisive when weighed against the many security interests that the U.S. has acquired in the Far East as well as in the world as a whole. American national character is sufficiently self-confident to meet duplicity with counter assertion. The United States would most likely continue her defense of Formosa, should Formosa be sold out to Chinese Communists by the Nationalists.[21]

As long as the United States is firmly committed to the defense of Formosa by the continued presence of the Seventh Fleet in the Taiwan Straits, Communist China would not be in a position to take direct military action across the Straits to come to the rescue of the Nationalists even if a Communist-Nationalist deal were in existence, and Communist subversive and infiltrative activities within Formosa are intensified.

Confronted with a conspirative arrangement between the Communists and the Nationalists in defiance of the public will of the people concerned, the implication of the vital difference between "one China, one Formosa" or "two Chinas" is painfully obvious. A "two-China" resolution presumably acknowledges the authority of the Nationalist regime to make decisions for the Formosan people. The international community, especially the United States, would have difficulty in finding legal justification for taking counter measures. This difficulty would not arise under a "one China, one Formosa" resolution. Neither the United States nor the world community would be legally inhibited from rendering assistance to the people of Formosa in frustrating an unlawful (unconstitutional) act by a handful of the Nationalists. In this way, the legitimate interests of the Formosan people would be preserved, and the ends of peace and security in the Far East served.

Self-Help

UNLESS Formosans are for themselves, who will be for them? To obtain international support they will have to show the world that they can be helped to help themselves, and provide a promising alternative for the future of Formosa. If the overthrow of the Nationalist regime would lead only to a series of chaotic emergencies, as in South Vietnam after the death of Ngo Dinh Diem, even the most generous and sympathetic friends would hesitate to embroil themselves in another impasse.

At that critical hour when Formosa is in imminent danger of being bargained away, the only hope for the cause of self-determination is for the Formosan people to demonstrate their common aspirations unmistakably to the world. A settlement that disposes of the destiny of thirteen million people as though they were rocks and sand cannot be tolerated.

In order to appraise their effort at self-help in realistic terms, it is useful to classify Formosans into two main categories: Formosans inside Formosa, and Formosans abroad. This breakdown is necessary, as they are confronted with different situations.

Internally, as a result of the ideologies cultivated by the Nationalist regime, the Formosan people have been psychologically "disarmed." Their sense of identity is obscured, and they are uncertain what strategies to use in struggling for status. The police control of the KMT has deprived them of organized military strength and political organization. Under the terms of the "emergency order" in force since 1949, there is no freedom of speech, assembly, association or peaceful petition. A potential opposition party that promised to reflect the demands and interests of native Formosans was crushed even before it was organized, and a principal initiator, Lei Chen, sentenced to ten years' imprisonment for sedition. The only influential Formosan newspaper, headed by Li Wan-chiu, was taken over by the government when Li also played a part in the attempt to organize a constructive opposition party.[22]

In order to prevent organized armed revolt, a substantial percentage of Formosan draftees are sent to Quemoy and Matsu—a hundred miles away from Formosa. Formosan soldiers stationed inside Formosa are denied access to ammunition. By preventing the Formosan people from becoming effectively organized and armed, the KMT has been able to keep them in subjection. As every political analyst knows, it is extremely difficult in the contemporary world to initiate a successful popular revolution without the support of armed forces. In Formosa key military positions are occupied exclusively by Nationalist generals. Native Formosans, on the other hand, account for more than 80 per cent of the rank and file of the Nationalist armed forces. Hence it is not altogether certain where the balance of military strength would be during a crisis.

As for wealth, the regime has amassed substantial resources by their economic policies and by managing the national treasury, public enterprises, and party enterprises. Compared with the assets of the Nationalist regime, Formosans' private wealth is limited. In spite of the rosy picture of a Formosa that has graduated from dependence on U.S. aid, some economists believe—and some Nationalist elites cautiously suspect—that official American echoes of the Nationalist economic achievement could be a calculated tactic to draw American attention away from Chiang's slogan of "the recovery of mainland China," and to insure continuing congressional support for selective aid programs. Why, if Formosa's economic progress is as great as alleged, are the problems of unemployment and underemployment becoming worse than ever? Why does inflation continue steadily? Why are more business firms going bankrupt?[23]

In talk about Formosa's economic progress, the land reform program quickly occupies the focus of attention. Reform can claim its success because the landlords who were exposed to deprivation happened to be law-abiding native Formosans. (Aside from benefits to tenant farmers, one direct consequence of the land reform is to consolidate the Nationalists' power by weakening the only Formosan elite having substantial local influence.) Had the landlords been mainland Chinese, there would have been no successful land reform. Some offset must be recognized, moreover, against the alleged gain for farmers resulting from land reform by the combined effect of the imposition of manifold taxes, the low-price policy imposed on farm products, and the unfair rice-fertilizer exchange ratio. The burden of taxes borne by the people is reflected by a popular saying in the Formosan community, "Taiwan Wan-swei," meaning both "long live Taiwan!" and "Taiwan, the island of ten thousand taxes." The main farm product in Formosa is rice purchased in large quantity by the government to feed 600,000 soldiers and hundreds of thousands of government employees. Although the relative price index of nonfarm products rises sharply every year, the regime has consistently held very tight control over rice prices to assure a supply of staple food at minimum cost—an operation executed at the expense of the relative purchasing power of the farmers. As to the unfair rice-fertilizer exchange ratio, it is a unique phenomenon in Formosa. The government monopolizes the fertilizer market; hence the farmers, in order to get the fertilizer needed for farming, must trade rice for government-controlled fertilizer. The ratio of exchange is not a result of the market operation of supply and demand, but one of administratively determined prices set by the government, and obviously disadvantageous to farmers.

Businessmen, laborers, and civil servants are hardly better off. In the "thriving" economy, businessmen would seem to be the chosen beneficiaries of "economic progress." But this is not so. Far from being a "free economy" in any responsible sense, Formosa's economy is peculiarly "politicized." The success or failure of a business firm depends not upon its management according to economic and technological considerations, but upon its "political connections," which enable it to evade disproportionately heavy taxes and to obtain government loans and favors. Often a business concern survives primarily because of its ability to "evade taxes" by the use of bribery or fraudulent bookkeeping. In these undercover matters mainland Chinese businessmen are relatively well off, since the key government positions are dominated by mainland Chinese. Profit-making through collusion between governmental officials and businessmen is in no sense an uncommon practice in Formosa. In 1966 there were five corruption cases involving many top government officials—cabinet members as well as members of the Legislative and Control Yuans and the delegates to the National Assembly. The total loss to the public in these cases, it was estimated, amounted to 75 million dollars. In a case concerning illegal policy loans to a textile company, the Control Yuan initiated an impeachment proceeding against the Minister of Economic Affairs and the Minister of Finance. In a case of collusive theft of soybeans, a number of top legislators were indicted.[24]

For the lower-income class, life is made harsh by the imposition of a heavy tax. According to the present tax structure, about 80 per cent of the government revenue comes from "indirect taxes," primarily in the form of a sales tax or other commodity tax. While there is no lack of relatively rich people, these people usually can get out of paying taxes through skillful manipulation of their wealth, and the regime has refrained from resorting to a direct tax as a principal source of revenue. As for the poor, they have no money to buy or influence power-wielders—though they are "skinny" they are taxpayers. Hence the standard of living of lower-income people is made lower because of the basically unjust tax system.

Turning to the younger generations, while they may manage to earn a living one way or another, they are generally underemployed or inadequately employed. As many Formosans see it, their job opportunities have been blocked by thousands of "unproductive Chinese" from the mainland who ought to have been retired long ago. Dissatisfaction among college graduates is most serious and prevalent. Many of them have been compelled to accept jobs far beneath their capabilities. For thousands of college graduates, their last hope is to study abroad—notably in the United States, Japan, Canada, and more recently in Western Europe. Many of them leave Formosa with a sense of desertion, but though they have few illusions about the hardships that may be encountered in foreign lands, they simply cannot conceive that their exile abroad could be more miserable than life in Formosa under KMT control. The regime has wisely left this door open as a safety valve for the dissatisfied.

In any event, there are substantial grounds for believing that many dissatisfied elements are generating in Formosa today. On the one hand, as a consequence of monopoly control over the armed forces, police, party organization, national treasury and national enterprises, government machinery, and the youth movement, the Chinese Nationalists have created a misleading appearance of calm. On the other hand, as a consequence of accumulating political inequality, discrimination, and economic deprivations, a keen sense of "intolerable deprivation" has spread among the Formosan people. Denied access to power, the Formosan people have no minimum assurance of "life, liberty, and the pursuit of happiness." Their indignation is most strikingly aroused in their military service, where the division between mainland Chinese and native Formosans is so clear-cut.

As practically every family has someone who has served in the armed forces at one time or another, the political awareness deriving from personal experience is general. In due course the military skill acquired from practical training and experience may prove invaluable. The real strength of Formosans, however, remains more potential than apparent. Under the effective operations of the complex network of the Nationalist secret police, any attempt at revolt unaccompanied by outside assistance is likely to fail. Rather than being incited to act prematurely at great cost and risk, it is more realistic that Formosans be alerted and psychologically prepared for forthcoming crises in which outside cooperation can provide a reasonable chance of success. Their ideal role is to respond, not to initiate. Once their children, brothers, and sisters abroad have formed a unified and effective front for the struggle of Formosa's self-determination, those in Formosa will respond, particularly if international support, including that of the United States, is forthcoming.

Of thousands of young Formosans studying abroad, about 80 per cent come to the United States, 15 per cent to Japan, and another 5 per cent to Canada and Western Europe. Less than 7 per cent of them have returned to Formosa on completing their graduate study. In the United States today, there are perhaps more mainland Chinese studying than native Formosans, although the number of the latter recently has increased substantially.[25] Their perspectives about the future of Formosa are strikingly distinct.

Mainland Chinese students do not identify Formosa as their home, even though for the most part they have been brought up and educated in Formosa. When they leave Formosa for the United States, they generally have a longer term plan. What the future holds for China (or Formosa) is uncertain and they take the view that any one person can do little to change the course of China's future. As the future will take care of itself, there is little rational ground for an individual to pursue an uncertain path full of hazards. What counts is to live today, with a decent income and an assurance of permanent residence in the United States (or even better, with U.S. citizenship). Engineers and scientists are best off among the aliens who live in the United States. Many who formerly were specializing in the social sciences and the humanities have out of necessity changed their specialization to library science, computer science, mathematics and engineering, and so on, in order to obtain a dependable job and sponsorship for permanent residence in the United States. They study, work, and prepare for the future with increasing experience and skill and with some personal wealth accumulated by conscious saving.

Should Sino-U.S. relations become normalized and mainland China once again become a desirable place in which even those Chinese from "reactionary elements" or with "capitalist indoctrination" can feel secure, they probably would go back to the mainland. They have been patiently waiting for the day they can join their brothers on the mainland in building up a "new China" and share in the grandeur of a rejuvenated "fatherland." They tend to think that nobody can prevent China from reasserting its proud and rightful place under the sun. While at the moment the regime "on the other side of the Straits" happens to be Communist and totalitarian in every sense of the word, they expect this phase to pass away as China eventually evolves into a community more tolerable than it appears to be now. Hence their immediate concern, while in the United States, is to equip themselves without getting frustrated by the tide of world events that are beyond the immediate comprehension or control of any single individual. As for the future, it belongs to those who prepare for it.

The native Formosans are in a somewhat different position. Impressionable as they are, they get highly stirred up by what they see, read, and experience in the foreign lands. It does not take them long to realize they have been victims of the KMT's systematic and "hypnotic" rule. They suddenly become skeptical of practically all the KMT's dogmatic indoctrinations. For them, Formosa is indeed their home and their affection for it grows stronger. Their families are there and they hope that what they learn abroad can make a contribution to the island. The division between mainland Chinese and native Formosans appears much wider than they had realized. During their stay in foreign lands, their association with mainland Chinese, if any, is generally confined to a handful of those who happened to be friends and classmates back in Formosa. With an awakening sense of identity and of grievance at the hands of mainland Chinese, they are aware of hazards ahead should they choose to return while Formosa remains under the totalitarian control of the Nationalists. They have a home, but one to which they do not feel secure to return, and they become reconciled to the idea of staying in foreign lands for the time being at least.

Of thousands of young Formosans abroad, some are highly apprehensive of political involvement—a predisposition molded by the Nationalist reign of terror. They were taught to regard any political involvement as a risky business, endangering not only the safety of their family in Formosa under Nationalist control, but also their continued stay in a given nation. Should they be put on the KMT's blacklist because of utterances and behavior repugnant to the party line, they could not be assured of the annual extension of the passport that allows them to stay in the host country. Their withdrawal from political involvement can be clearly seen from their evasion of issues both in public and private.

Political passivity is sustained by "naïve optimism." In this view, since the overwhelming majority of Formosa's population today is native Formosan, power will naturally shift from Chinese Nationalists to native Formosans. This being the case, why make premature sacrifies simply from impatience?

Some also cherish a "pan-China" ideal, favoring reunification with mainland China so as to share the grandeur of a "great China." The formation of such a mentality may result partly from alleged "farsightedness," and partly from frustration abroad. Some, like many mainland Chinese, become convinced more than ever before that in twenty or thirty years China will "inevitably" emerge as a first-rate power, if not *the* dominant power, on the earth. Others, because of the frustrations that result from personal failures abroad in the pursuit of respect, skill, wealth, and affection, reason that if only they were proud citizens of a "great China," their place anywhere would be universally acknowledged by aliens —whites and nonwhites alike. Their failures abroad, as they see it, come in no small measure from their lowly status as citizens of a small nation dominated by a corrupt regime.

There are some, as might be expected, whose sense of futility has led to the view that Formosa is doomed to be ruled by aliens —Japanese yesterday, Nationalists today, and Chinese Communists tomorrow. Their cynical view is fortified by their reading of history: Formosans' past resistance against alien rulers has invariably led to tragedy. As Communist China appears to be far more formidable than the Japanese empire or the Nationalist regime, out of a cynical sense of "realism" these Formosans believe that it is only rational to come to terms with their lot. They feel strongly that even if Formosa could be independent for the time being with external assistance, notably from the U.S., it would in the long run be at the mercy of Communist China. China's takeover being "inevitable," Formosans cannot afford to be so foolish as to "offend" the Communists by proclaiming an independence that can be made possible only under the dominating, and temporary, influence of the United States.

A large segment of overseas Formosans do not fall into the categories mentioned above, however. These people do care a great deal for the future of Formosa, and intuitively hope that an independent Formosa may someday come into being. They would like to do something about it, but have only vague notions about how to proceed. Their personal enthusiasm, weakened through limited contact and discouraging communication with others, gradually fades away. They tend to have a sense of limitation, and severely discount the significance of an individual's contribution to such an overall cause. Moreover, in the stress of a repressive environment, they find that their personal enthusiasm not only sparks no fire, but also adversely affects the efficiency of their daily work, which intensifies the dissatisfactions of their life. It is too much for an ordinary human being to make life intolerable for himself by vague, though absorbing, ideals. After all, happiness seems to mean that one lives today, and devotes time and energy to study, work, courtship, marriage, and family. Concern for the future of Formosa tends to grow weaker and weaker, rather than to stabilize in forms of collective action.

There are, however, a number of Formosans who have not lost faith in the future of the island and its people, and have dedicated themselves to furthering the cause of Formosa's self-determination. In the contemporary context 1947 can be regarded as the beginning of Formosa's independence movement. After the 1947 massacres, the surviving leaders realized that Formosa's only hope of a distinctive evolution lies in its own independence outside the framework of Chinese rule in any form. The survivors went underground and abroad. Many of them fled to Hong Kong and established the League for the Reliberation of Formosa in the summer of 1948. On September 1, 1948, they petitioned to the United Nations on behalf of the Formosan people to place Formosa under U.N. trusteeship, with an expectation of eventual independence. Following the swift Communist takeover of mainland China, the group led by Thomas Liao sought exile in Japan and created the Formosa Democratic Independence Party in February 1950. In 1955 a provisional government of the Republic of Formosa was organized in Tokyo, with Liao as its President. Under systematic harassment by both Chinese Communists and Nationalists, Liao's influence was greatly curtailed. The organization succeeded neither in broadening its bases of support among Formosans (particularly the younger generation) nor in obtaining United States or Japanese assistance. Eventually internal friction virtually incapacitated it as a revolutionary organization; and these feuds culminated in the defection of Liao to the Nationalists in

May 1965. While Liao's real motives for returning to Formosa are still a matter of speculation, his frustrations, caused by marginal support in the previous eighteen years, must have played no small part in his decision.

Formosan students in Japan created the Formosan Association, initially called Taiwan Chinglian (Youth) Associates and presently also known as United Young Formosans for Independence, in February 1960 with substantial, though often secret, support from some 25,000 businessmen residing in Japan. Through its publication of *Taiwan Chinglian* in Japanese and *Independent Formosa* in English, the Association won support among Formosans in Japan. Its approach to the whole problem, as seen from its publication, demonstrates a balanced emphasis on moderation and reason. While its influence in the United States is still negligible, its promotional activities in Japan have made headway. Because of geographical nearness, past relations, and present economic ties, Japan remains the headquarters of the independence movement.

In 1963, Formosans in Canada created a Committee for Human Rights in Formosa, a group said to have played a significant part in ultimately obtaining Nationalist clemency for Professor Ming-min Peng by appealing to the Canadian government and other channels. And in Europe an organization known as United Formosans in Europe for Independence has recently come into being.

Because the United Nations headquarters are situated in New York and the United States is the key nation whose decision is most likely to affect the future of Formosa, the success or failure of Formosa's independence movement in the United States will probably be decisive for the future. Formosans studying in the United States organized the United Formosans for Independence in 1960, and published *Ilha Formosa*, but independence activities in the United States so far are less than impressive. Aside from a lack of numbers, there is no strong financial backing similar to that in Japan. Nor is the support that the U.S. has given to the Nationalist regime in the past a trivial obstacle. Nevertheless, the wide circulation of the *Declaration of Formosans*, for whose authorship Professor Peng and Messrs. Shieh and Wei were convicted of "sedition" by the Nationalists, has most recently evoked a spontaneous grass roots response among the Formosan student groups in the U.S. If the Formosan youth on the island—under the tight supervision of the KMT police control—dare speak up at great risk, Formosans abroad must respond to the call. Through persistent efforts the fragmented local organizations scattered in Philadelphia, New York, Wisconsin, Los Angeles, Kansas, Baltimore, Boston, Houston, and Oklahoma were in 1966 channeled into a centralized organization that encompasses the entire United States. This new organizaton, United Formosans in America for Independence, has improved financing and wider circulation of its monthly *Formosagram*.

Nevertheless, the difficulties common to the entire independence movement are many. The "leadership gap" comes immediately to mind. Generally speaking, leadership of a body politic is provided by the generation in its forties or fifties. This, however, is not the case for the native Formosans. Of that generation, Thomas Liao was the best known internationally, yet not only had he never rallied general support among the native Formosans, but he ultimately yielded to the Nationalists. The surrender of Liao seems to symbolize the end of the leadership of the older Formosans—whose sense of bitterness toward the past handicaps their creative concern for the future—in the struggle for independence. Younger generations are left without a visible and respected leader, and with no program to follow. They will have to chart their own course rather than follow and broaden a path outlined by their predecessors. From a generation of Formosans born after World War I, tempered by World War II, awakened by colonial and totalitarian rules in this age of mass communication and technological development, a new leadership may well soon appear.

As to general apathy of Formosans abroad, it stems in no small measure from fears of possible deprivations imposed by the Nationalists on families in Formosa. The Nationalist regime has succeeded in its reign of terror by deliberately leaving obscure its standard for evaluating an individual's activities. In undertaking a political activity, one has no rational way of estimating the probable consequences in terms of indulgence or deprivation. As long as the prospect of self-determination is remote, few people are likely to risk their necks. Unless positive activities of a preparatory and interim nature are engaged in, the attitude of postponement can freeze into resignation. Common action that gains limited objectives, even if it produces some retaliation, prevents a national movement from atrophy. If a collective movement is even in a rudimentary stage of expression, it can influence the power situation by spontaneous, general, and costly responses to suppressive measures. For instance, deprivations aimed by the KMT against students abroad, such as denying passport renewal on a massive scale, would backfire in disorders in Formosa.

It is important for the independence movement to undermine the view that Formosans will win by default, that the Nationalists will fail to renew themselves. After fifty years of rule by Japan and twenty years of rule by Nationalists what follows will not necessarily be self-rule by Formosans. Should Formosa come under the Chinese Communists, the families of Formosan students abroad would be the first victims of Communist China's "class struggle," since their families typically belong to the upper or upper middle class. What they conscientiously seek to preserve by refraining from political involvement may be irreparably lost. When this is realistically clarified, it is hard to believe that the student group will remain indifferent to the significance of the independence movement.

The independence movement has been confused and dispersed in part from lack of a realistic "blueprint" of action. Often a sense of futility is generated by a lack of knowledge as to how, under what conditions, the goals of self-determination can be achieved. Or how changes can be effected. What measures are essential to transition? How can a viable and independent Formosa be established? What is the constructive alternative to the Nationalist rule?

At the initial stage of a movement, divergent views of what is the best approach are inevitable. Against an organized and formidable enemy such as the KMT, diversity may become a fatal liability. Because there are eleven million native Formosans and two million mainland Chinese in Formosa today, it is important for any responsible organization to make clear its position on the future status of mainland Chinese in the framework of a "Republic of Formosa." Should they be treated equally as Formosans, or differently? Should they be granted citizenship in the new Republic automatically? Will their participation in the political decision-making process be guaranteed?

We shall explore these questions further in ensuing chapters, but we submit here that the overwhelming majority of the mainland Chinese residing in Formosa today, like native Formosans, are victims of tragic historical developments and of the Nationalist reign of terror. There is a basic common interest between native Formosans and mainland Chinese to live and work together, who have much to gain by working together and cooperating, and a great deal to lose by splitting apart. A realistic independence movement rejects the power structure of KMT domination, not mainland Chinese in general. Unless native Formosans and mainland Chinese learn to live, and work, and communicate in a shared destiny, they will continue to be at the mercy of a tiny KMT elite. It is in their enlightened self-interest for native Formosans to grant equal status to the mainland Chinese, not simply a humanitarian matter. Mainland Chinese should bear in mind that Formosa, small as it is, is big enough for people of good will to live and prosper. Such a position has to be made clear to internal as well as external audiences.

The analysis does not imply that at this stage independence

organizations are advised to be fusion organizations, composed of native Formosans and mainland Chinese. As Formosans' bases of power are, at this stage, weak vis-à-vis the Nationalists, the Formosans cannot afford the luxury of taking a "security risk." To include mainland Chinese in an organization for Formosa's independence would give the KMT a good chance to infiltrate and destroy the organizations. Unlike the KMT, Formosa's independence organizations are in their infancy and have little ability to resist infiltration or to survive crises. It is desirable that they make clear their moderate position and programs for the mainland Chinese in a new Republic of Formosa, but it is no less important that they cherish no illusions, and try to consolidate their own organizations first with native Formosan members. This basic principle is essential to the effectiveness of the organization and to their appeal to the Formosan public. At a later stage, when independence organizations have reasonable expectations of permanency, it will be feasible to permit the participation of the mainland Chinese in the task of superseding the Nationalist regime.

These organizations are presently limited by a shortage of funds and of full-time devotees of the task. While the organizations in Japan are substantially financed by Formosan businessmen in Japan, the financial backing here in the United States is relatively weak, though contributions are said to be on the increase. Here too active members are typically graduate students working for their Ph.D. or individuals who are otherwise employed; hence working for Formosa is a part-time operation.

Unlike the KMT, the Formosan independence organizations have practically no armed forces, no strong staff, no substantial economic assets, and no access to diplomatic arenas. But one thing is clear: the Nationalist regime has no monopoly of the "ideological instrument." Hence the strategy available to the independence movement is a massive and intensive "enlightenment" process. Formosans abroad are relatively well educated; to change their indifference into active support, there is no more effective weapon than a resort to "communication." To gain sympathetic support of governments and nations concerned, the indispensable weapon again is communication. In the United States, despite its official support of the Nationalist regime and the influence of the "China lobby," there are channels and predispositions open to the champions of Formosa.

The China Lobby

THAT THE "China lobby" continues to influence the foreign policy of Washington is generally recognized in the United States, and any activity on the part of Formosans or their friends will encounter overt and covert opposition in many quarters. A remarkable fact about the pro-Chiang elements in American politics is that they have been successful in preventing the public from hearing about Formosa in full and scholarly detail. Few books are suppressed in the United States, yet the pro-Chiang interests, it appears, have been able to accomplish one of these feats of suppression. A comprehensive study entitled "The China Lobby in American Politics," written by Dr. Ross Koen and published by Macmillan in 1960, has been officially withdrawn for unexplained reasons. Although announced, and evidently distributed immediately on publication, this book has not subsequently been made available.

The operations of the China lobby in the United States can be traced to the days before the United States entered World War II, when assistance was tendered to potential allies in the form of lend-lease. In 1940 a team headed by T. V. Soong, ex-finance minister and Madame Chiang's brother, launched a massive campaign in the U.S. to obtain more aid for the Nationalist government. The campaign was a success because, as one writer put it, Soong was able to "collect influential friends who could circumvent or overwhelm opposition."[26] We shall not dwell here on the story of U.S. aid to China during the war, except to say that many outstanding and responsible leaders of the American war effort came through this experience thoroughly disillusioned with the public and private policies of Chiang Kai-shek, and especially with the personal enrichment of the Soongs and Kungs (both in-laws of the Generalissimo). They came reluctantly to the conclusion that the rigidity and corruptness of the Kuomintang leadership would sooner or later contribute to a political and social catastrophe of the first magnitude.

The catastrophe came much more quickly than had been anticipated, even by some of the most pessimistic observers. As Kuomintang misrule provoked ever more alarming difficulties, the regime redoubled its efforts to obtain more and more millions from the United States. In 1947, following the unsuccessful truce mission of General Marshall and a substantial aid cut, the China lobby's activities in the U.S. were redoubled. In the wake of a succession of Communist victories in North China, Madame Chiang came to the United States in December 1948 to appeal for support in defeating Chinese Communists. The intensified campaigns did not go unnoticed. Thus on August 25, 1949, then Congressman Mike Mansfield, charging gross misuse of U.S. aid funds by Chinese officials, requested the investigation of "the activities of the lobby now brazenly being conducted in this country in behalf of the National Government of China and certain personalities connected with it."[27]

The Communist takeover of the mainland in October 1949 did not end the activities of the China lobby in the United States. At the outbreak of the Korean war, as Formosa became the focal point of power politics in the Far East, the exiled Nationalists sought to consolidate their position in Formosa as a matter of survival.

Besides Chiang's own followers and his paid agents, many Americans of good will were and are sympathetic to the cause of the Nationalist regime, especially Christian missionaries and busi-

nessmen who had been active on the mainland. These Americans
are generally nostalgic for the "good old days" before the Communist seizure of power cut their ties with China. Generations
of Americans, recruited particularly from the farming communities of the nation, have sent missionaries and mission dollars
to China; and many missionary children found a livelihood in
missionary, educational, medical, and business activities in changing China. The thin veneer of Christianity—the result of a century
or more of effort—nevertheless counted heavily among the modernizers of China's ancestral society. Much of the American support of Chiang Kai-shek is to be ascribed to his symbolic
significance as at least a nominal Christian married to a Christian
—an American-educated wife. Given the cumulative stake of so
many Americans in the pre-Communist mainland, it is not surprising to find that it was possible for the China lobby to mobilize
substantial support for a policy that was not only anti-mainland
Communists, but readily assumed that this policy was furthered by
endorsing Chiang's regime on Taiwan, and Taiwan's occupancy
of "China's" seat in the U.N. After the Korean truce the Committee of One Million Against the Admission of Communist
China to the United Nations came into being and actively es-
poused the Nationalist cause.

The supporters of Chiang in the United States took advantage
of the almost unparalleled period of national bewilderment, frustration, and mutual recrimination that followed the seizure of
the mainland by the Communists. The rebuff in China was so
shocking and utterly unexpected to the public as a whole that the
American "self" was plunged into crisis. The demand by Americans on the national government is for continuing success in
pursuing the inclusive and exclusive interests of the country. The
demand for success—measured by every value—is as intense at
the national level as it is in private careers. Indeed, the demand
can quickly become more intense when the frustrations of private
life are suddenly displaced onto a public symbol of the self at a

time when national value deprivations have been unexpectedly experienced. The individual American did not feel that anything he intended or did could account for America's expulsion from the mainland. Hence he was open to the suggestion—a suggestion supported by deep unconscious predispositions—that America had been betrayed. But by whom? Chiang was in retreat; hence he did not seem to be the betrayer. Certainly the "Communists" were obvious candidates. But how could the Americans be so weak or misled unless some Americans were misleading other Americans? Thus the plausibility of a conspirative, scapegoat theory: "Communists in the State Department." Here was the national mood and theme that sustained McCarthyism in the early fifties; and McCarthyism was fed by information much of which came from the China interests close to Chiang.

Nor did the demise of McCarthyism slow down Chiang's efforts to influence American officials or the general public. Nationalist propaganda has not been handicapped by a shortage of funds. Although it is difficult to estimate what fraction of U.S. aid to the Nationalists was diverted for propaganda use, it is obvious that American dollars had a curious way of flowing back to the United States. As Senator Morse put it, "It is probably reasonable to assume that some of this money is being used to finance propaganda . . . chiefly to promote more money being given to Chiang and the Chiang forces. This suggests to some a closed circuit of American dollars flowing from Congress to the Nationalists and back again in the form of lobbying activities for still more money for Chiang."[28] Aside from monopolizing the diplomatic channel to speak "on behalf of the Chinese people," the Nationalists also have influential friends in the sphere of mass media.

The fact that Communist China has been in stable control over the mainland for the past seventeen years and has emerged as a nuclear power has provoked little change of orientation among the friends of Chiang. On the contrary, in the wake of the successful detonations of nuclear devices by the Communists, Madame Chiang once again came on a propaganda mission to the United States. While the status of her visit remained ambiguous, it appeared that she was campaigning hard to persuade the United States to initiate a pre-emptive strike against the nuclear installations of the Chinese Communists.[29]

Despite the formidable advantages of the Chiang forces in the United States, time is redressing the balance. The initial effectiveness of the China lobby depended in no small degree on the emotional shock of the Communist takeover on the mainland and its participation in the Korean war. Not only have the shock effects worn off, but the ensuing years have produced a gradual sense that all is not as represented about the Nationalist regime in Formosa. Nevertheless, the older perspectives have been sustained by the assumption that the Nationalists are "the only alternative" to adding a "Communist Formosa" to Communist China.

A favorable recounting of the accomplishments of Chiang's government emphasizes the economic development of the island. The common inference is that economic development spells political development, a proposition that has attained the status of a new "iron law" of society. In recent years the iron has begun to rust as the facts of discrepant political growth become more accessible in many new nations. The situation in Formosa is far from conforming to the shallow optimism of the early economic developers or the calculated projections of Nationalist propaganda.

That the unimaginative and rigid policies of the United States toward China and Formosa have begun to change is evident. A new element of flexibility is reflected in the recent hearings of the Senate Foreign Relations Committee. Sensing the mood of the nation, the Johnson administration has responded by clarifying the policy of "containment but not isolation" of Peking, adopting such concrete measures as exchanges of physicians and scholars. The current turmoil of the "cultural revolution" on the mainland is being closely observed by the China watchers. The U.S. government is looking beyond the present leadership of Mao Tse-tung's generation, even though it is prepared for negative responses presently. Even if the Communists continue to freeze their intransigent posture toward Americans, the U.S. will eventually be able to reverse the present situation by leaving new alternatives open to the emerging leadership in Peking. The onus for their "self-imposed isolation" will rest squarely on the mainland Chinese.

The new flexibility displayed by the Johnson administration reflects the changing mood of the public. Actually a recent survey suggests that the public at large is ahead of the government in open-minded readiness toward dealing with Chinese Communists.

The calendar is catching up with Chiang as well as Mao, affording the populace of Formosa, as well as the mainland, opportunities for a new dynamism. Chiang is eighty years old now. No student of politics can fail to grasp the point that a viable U.S. policy toward Formosa during the coming years must take into account the genuine demands and aspirations of the Formosan people. The Formosans can themselves expedite this process by telling the truth about Formosa, until now unavailable or unknown to the American public.

Uprisings in Formosa

THE PASSAGE of a U.N. resolution supporting Formosa's self-determination would not automatically see its implementation. On the contrary, it would presumably harden the determination of the Nationalist regime to exert every resource at its command to resist U.N. participation in holding a plebiscite in Formosa. But even if the Nationalist regime should succeed in excluding U.N. personnel from Formosa, the moral support of the world organization is sufficient to initiate a sequence of important changes within Formosa. Inspired by international support, the

Formosans' independence movement will gain momentum. As their demands mount for immediate and effective participation in decision-making, internal tensions will reach a point of no return if these are countered by Nationalist suppression. The regime will probably attempt a deal with the Chinese Communists to suppress mounting opposition. Communist assistance to the Nationalists will be intercepted by the United States, who will then be on the side of the Formosan people; and the internal tension within Formosa will erupt into an uprising in which the masses of the people seek to overthrow the Nationalist regime.

In a violent uprising, the relative strength of the armed forces of the major participants determines the outcome. The Nationalist regime is most likely to count on its armored divisions, plus the protection of the air force. The armored divisions, with immense power and mobility, are well designed to cope with internal uprisings. They consist primarily of mainland Chinese, so that in the event of a Formosan revolt, they can be counted on to be loyal. The air force is similar, with a substantial number of the pilots being mainland Chinese. As for the ground forces, the situation is sharply different. Native Formosans constitute more than 80 per cent of the rank and file of the Nationalist armed forces. In an uprising, given proper direction, they would gallantly perform the task of protecting Formosan civilians.

The priority task therefore is to take necessary measures to incapacitate the crushing operations by the Nationalist armored divisions and air forces. This requires close cooperation between the United States and the Formosan people. Although United States military groups are present in Formosa in an advisory capacity, they have a fairly thorough knowledge of the real strength of the Nationalist forces, including its armored divisions, air force, and key military installations. It may not be too difficult to para-lyze the effectiveness of Chiang's "special divisions" if realistic precautions are taken. Moreover, the United States, through a tight control of ammunition supply to the Nationalist forces, can compel the regime to surrender within a reasonably short time. The geographical configuration of Formosa, we believe, is not suitable for waging prolonged guerrilla warfare. The battle has to be won decisively and promptly.

To minimize bloodshed in an uprising, great efforts have to be made to avoid the mutual killing of native Formosans and mainland Chinese. Their common enemy is a handful of the Nationalist power-wielders. These two groups of people should be enlightened before hand that they have a shared destiny in building Formosa as a democratic and viable political entity in the world community; and every effort should be directed to minimize irrational elements in the shaping of crucial decisions. The task of clarifying the common interests of native Formosans and mainland Chinese becomes more urgent in the context of crisis. The hour is late, but with conscious purpose that task is not out of the question. The belated task of establishing genuine communication between native Formosans and mainland Chinese and of arousing a sense of common interest can be initiated by a large-scale radio broadcasting program emanating from Japan or Okinawa, if sympathetic cooperation can be obtained from Japan and the United States. Under the present conditions, such a task cannot be done within Formosa under the eyes of the KMT's secret police.

Meanwhile, in a mass uprising within Formosa, the United States ought to be prepared to come to Formosans' aid by returning soldiers stationed in Quemoy and Matsu to Formosa, lest they should be seized and detained by Chinese Communists as hostages and as a means of blackmail against the newly independent Formosan Republic.

Unlike the tragic ending of the "228 incident" of 1947, a popular uprising in Formosa today is most likely to succeed, for the changed conditions are profoundly significant. In 1947, shortly after the Nationalist occupation of Formosa on behalf of the Allied powers, the Formosan people were not quite sure what they wanted—indeed their sense of identity was still very weak. When the "incident" took place, the general public was caught unprepared to organize a long and decisive battle. Not fully aware of the nature of the Nationalist rule, Formosan elites were deceived by the temporizing attitudes of the Nationalists' governor general of Taiwan. Their naïveté was shortly answered by the massacres performed by the reinforcements sent by Chiang Kai-shek from the mainland. Worldwide attention at the moment was directed to the deteriorating developments on the Chinese mainland for the Chinese civil war was at its height, and Formosa was an isolated and forgotten island in 1947.

This, however, is not the case in 1967. Generally speaking, the Formosan people have a high degree of political awareness, resulting from a high level of education and from experience with the systematic and intolerable deprivations of the Nationalist regime. Their overriding aspirations are unambiguous—to be independent and separate from Communist China. Formosa today has become a focal point of international politics in the Far East as a result of the protracted cold war. Since the welfare of thirteen million people is at stake, it is better understood that the future of Formosa is not simply a matter between Chinese Communists and Nationalists. Any revolt on the scale of the 1947 "incident" can not go unheeded by the world. Constituting an important link in the anti-Communist defense line stretching from Japan to the Philippines, Formosa can count on the United States to continue the present commitment to defend her in the event that Communist China should attempt to come to the Nationalists' rescue by sending armed forces across the Formosan Straits. Above all, the native Formosans have been taught and trained to fight.

Violence is by nature an objectionable and disagreeable policy alternative for any responsible decision-makers. It is often argued that once violence is set into motion, the final outcome may be unpredictable as well as unmanageable. If a "one China, one Formosa" resolution does not rule out the possibility of a mass uprising, it is said a "two Chinas" formula would seem more acceptable to decision-makers in that it is a peaceful and evolutionary move. In another twenty or thirty years, practically all high-ranking Nationalist rulers, including the top representatives elected by the mainland constituencies in 1947 or 1948, will pass away, and it will be inevitable that Formosans emerge as masters of their own political destiny on the island.

This line of argument, at first seemingly persuasive and agreeable, is not to be taken for granted. Since the Nationalist regime will be as opposed to "two Chinas" as "one China, one Formosa," to acknowledge its authority to rule Formosa (which is implied in a well-meaning plan of "two Chinas") could be exploited by the regime to intensify its police control rather than to move in the direction to which the plan points. A plan ("two Chinas") that tends to ignore the real source of an explosive situation—the perpetual monopoly of power by a few to the exclusion of the majority—and to sidestep the fundamental issue—the future of thirteen million people rather than that of a small minority of Nationalist rulers—can claim neither realism nor moderation. Despite good intentions, it may actually precipitate an explosive crisis that might have been averted were the festering menace squarely faced.

Since a policy alternative is future-oriented, there is little assurance that a "two Chinas" policy would encounter any less incalculable variables than the "one China, one Formosa" policy. While no violent uprising within Formosa is suggested by the proponents of a "two Chinas" proposal, this does not imply that there would be no violence under a "two Chinas" plan. It is simply that no analysis comparable to the present study has been undertaken that attempts to face the problem of implementation and transition in applying the "two Chinas" policy. If advocates of a "two Chinas" program were to execute a similar undertaking, the possibility of a mass uprising in Formosa could not be ruled out as long as the majority of the people—relatively sophisticated political animals of the twentieth century—are excluded from managing their own affairs. Though economic growth under the Nationalist regime has not spelled a comparable political development, yet the rising standards of education and living are likely to accelerate a rising demand for immediate participation in important decisions at all levels.

In stressing the virtue of moderation and evolution, the advocates of "two Chinas" are prone to counsel the Formosan people to be "patient." We would be among the first to accede to this prescription if only Formosa were in an isolated world, or in a world free of the threat of Communist China. But as long as the existing political anomaly and injustice of Formosa are condoned in the form of continuing Nationalist rule, time is emphatically in favor of Communist China rather than the people of the island. A weak Formosa, ridden by accumulated wrongs and internal dissensions under the protracted rule of an exile "clique," would be prey to Communist China. By the time the present generation of Nationalist rulers passes away—when power would, in the view of "two Chinas" proponents, supposedly transfer from the Nationalists to the Formosans—Communist China may be so powerfully armed with modern weapons that decision-makers, national as well as international, could be obsessed by the idea of seeking a "long overdue" accommodation with Peking at the expense of the Formosan people. It is our strong expectation that only a Formosa made viable by emancipation can prevent itself from being bargained away in a world where "power politics" is often equated with "realism." Formosans need a government that is able to muster the genuine support of its citizens.

Finally, once again we say that in projecting the sequence of probable future developments, we are in no way claiming to be prophets. What we have done is to utilize available knowledge of relevant trends and conditions as an aid for tentatively projecting the future. The Formosa situation, in common with all significant situations, is essentially fluid. Any ultimate stabilization depends to a large extent upon what the Formosan people and the world community together can and will do at moments of crisis. The usefulness of disciplined projections of this kind to decision-makers is in anticipation of contingencies, including the anticipatory evaluation of policy alternatives.

Independence—And After

CHAPTER FOUR

Goals and Strategies

Attaining independence does not mean an end to the search for Formosa's nationhood in the contemporary world community. Rather it signifies the beginning of a new task; the objective is not only to terminate Nationalist rule but also to foster Formosa's progress and development. Too often the task of nation-building is conceived as finished when independence is achieved. But unless a new nation can cope with the hazards in its path, its life may be very short indeed.

In the struggle for independence, there is an identifiable common enemy, usually the colonial ruler, against whom the masses can easily be mobilized. Once the common enemy is gone, however, the internal solidarity of pre-independence days is replaced by factions reflecting diverse interests and demands. The "demogogic" elite can no longer hold the people together by mere appeal to emotion, and in the face of ever emerging problems, the "rising expectations" of the people easily become "rising frustrations."

Nation-building is a multi-dimensional task involving all aspects of national life, all principal value-institutions of a body politic, and external as well as internal relations. It can be considered as progress toward a self-sustaining process of value accumulation; and it is gradually mobilizing the talents of the policy scientists of our time. The goals of development are gaining clarity; historical perspectives deepen; the interdependence among conditioning factors is better understood; probable lines of future growth are more fully projected; and invention and evaluation of policies designed to maximize, or at least to achieve minimum, results are forging ahead.

Five Fundamental Goals

THE MOVEMENT toward a self-sustaining process of power accumulation and structural change is of paramount importance. Unlike the measurement of capital aggregates in the accumulation of wealth, the technique of power measurement is rather new. As far as an internal process of decision is concerned, power accumulation means potential support of the constitution; more explicitly, all changes in the predisposition to employ or defend basic allocations of authority and control in the state. An essential trait of development is innovativeness; changes are structural, not merely cyclical. Formosa's political development will necessarily involve all changes in authority and control that alter the basic features of the decision process. Structural changes may take the form of shifts in the degree of participation in power shaping and sharing; or in the allocation of power among decision-making organizations. Transformations from autocracy to oligarchy to democracy (in practical operations) are changes in degree of participation. Substantial shifts in the balance between central and noncentral units, or among organs at a given level of competence, are examples of changes in the allocation of power.

A self-sustaining level of power accumulation is reached when the nation is able to furnish its own trained personnel, to achieve structural innovation with minimum resort to coercion, and to mobilize resources for national goals.

A long-run goal is to establish an ideology of progress and commitment to power sharing. One of the most important policy conflicts in the contemporary world continues to turn on the pattern of power distribution. In manifest content the ruling elites of the globe are substantially united in supporting democracy as an ideal of government. They differ, however, in the stringency with which they apply the conception to themselves and others. Totalitarian states diverge in practical operation from popular government, and we need not hesitate to say so. Similarly, many nontotalitarian states diverge in degree from effective power sharing; and there need be no tactical unwillingness to be equally outspoken about these discrepancies. The overriding goal of human dignity presupposes effective general participation in the decision process. Such a position means, for example, that the connection between economic and political growth is candidly accepted as problematic. Today it is impossible to demonstrate that industrialization necessarily achieves the preconditions of popular government. Commitment to widely distributed power as a value-goal does not carry with it any necessary attachment to socialistic or capitalistic institutions.

A third goal is sufficient power to maintain national independence, hence effective political demand for economic development and for growth in all value-institution sectors of the body politic. Effective independence is a collective demand to function as a nation state, which carries with it control over the base values upon which power depends. Obviously political development calls for economic growth, and lagging economic growth is at least a partial consequence of political underdevelopment. If past decision processes had been more realistic in planning for the future, many states would not have lagged behind states that eventually infringed their independence after achieving economic superiority. Looking back at the expansion of Europe, a fascinating question is why the elites of the extra-European world failed to estimate the significance for their future of the changing present. Equally impressive are the examples of acceleration that power elites have often been able to give economic growth. The record draws attention to the reality-orienting task of the decision process of every political unit in world politics, and underlines the significance for political realism of social development.

A fourth goal in Formosa's nation-building is a willingness and capability to play a responsible role in world politics. The unrestricted pursuit of power is not an acceptable component of a developed national state.

It is not unusual in the study of development to insufficiently emphasize external power relations. The theory of economic growth might seem to furnish a precedent for neglecting the external dimension of acts of accumulation. The impression that economic development deals exclusively with the internal evolution of an economy is largely illusory, however. Early capital accumulation depends in most cases on active participation in foreign trade, investment, and aid; and modern strategies of production must be imported from a few centers of conspicuous creativity. True, the history of Soviet development shows that at various phases rapid accumulation can be largely divorced from active engagement in world markets.

Political modernization, however, is not to be achieved by progressive withdrawal from world politics. A nation state has a self-sustaining power position when it plays a responsible role in foreign affairs, and has achieved an internal process of decision which is stably innovative. A developed nation state expects, and is expected by other members of the world arena, to conform to an inclusive body of authoritative prescription; and this expectation implies an internal system of public order both able and willing to comply.

In a political sense every nation state must remain somewhat underdeveloped so long as the arena of world politics falls short of an inclusive public order in which transnational responsibilities are effectively defined in terms of human dignity. There are, of course, great differences among nations in the levels of political growth attained during a given epoch. No one seriously doubts that Great Britain currently sustains a high level of responsible participation in world affairs, or maintains an internal public order that affirms and approximates many ideal norms. On the other hand, the states of the Soviet bloc that have been dependent on the Kremlin are only beginning to move toward a sufficient breadth of contact with other states to gain the cumulative experience and discipline needed for full acceptance as internationally responsible.

It may be pertinent to give some examples of the indices which show the accumulation (or disaccumulation) of predispositions to act responsibly in external affairs: universality of recognition; exchange of diplomatic officials; membership in transnational organizations; acceptance of third-party assistance in the persuasive settlement of disputes; the obligation to aid in the sanctioning activities of transnational bodies; maintenance of impartial legal protection of aliens in harmony with transnational norms.

A final goal for Formosa is an internal process of decision whose structures—both formal and informal, organized and unorganized—constitute a system of public order capable of creative, realistic problem-solving in pursuit of a rising level of participation in all values. There are seven distinct phases in a process of decision: intelligence, promotion, prescription, invocation, application, appraisal, and termination.

The *intelligence* phase functions appropriately when it supplies realistic information about trends, conditions, and projections that clarify overriding goals and the invention and evaluation of policy alternatives. As technology advances it becomes both necessary and possible to rely heavily on mass media and research agencies to supply current intelligence and, in conjunction with schools, to shape the socialization process.

The *promotional* phase of decision is perhaps the most distinguishing mark of advanced polities. Promotions include diverse demands and operations that are noncoercively pursued to affect the course of decision. In caste-bound societies the political process operates on the authoritative and controlling expectation that nonpower castes have nothing to say about what goes on. Under conditions of vast distress they may erupt into the arena of politics; but this is a sign of chaos, not of orderly participation. Political party systems (not one-party dictatorships), pressure groups, and public commentary are fundamental features of power sharing in big-scale states; and they are substantially missing from "village plus oligarchy" or "village plus democracy" at the inclusive level.

Prescribing is the act of formulating perspectives relating to authority and control; in a word, it is a fundamental aspect of law-making. It is often hinted that the discipline of rule-writing, resented and evaded as it may be, spreads the expectation the controversies will be impartially resolved and that traditional loyalties of family, neighborhood, and tribe will be undermined for the ultimate benefit of officials who live up to the Weberian model of rationality. There is little empirical knowledge, for instance, of the volume and impact, if any, of the attempt to stabilize expectations by codification.

Administrative structures are heavily though not exclusively specialized to the *invocation* and *application* of prescriptions. In bureaucracies structures become more specialized to functions. Our knowledge is particularly deficient in detailed accounts of the interplay of police, magistrates, and citizens.

Under the prod of foreign sources of aid, many developing countries have acquired personnel and facilities for conducting *appraisals* of their own performance.

One of the most neglected and potentially rewarding features of the study of decision in developing nations is *termination*. Modernization unavoidably accelerates obsolescence. It is not impossible to arrive at quantitative estimates of many traditional claims, or to inquire into the policies of compensation, if any, which have been adopted in reference to them.

Eight Guiding Strategies

HAVING clarified the fundamental goals for Formosa's national development, we shall articulate guiding principles for devising strategies that can maximize these goals. The invention, evaluation, and selection of development policy presupposes that goal values are clarified and that factors facilitating or blocking progress are identified.

Strategic timing of the component elements in the sequence of development is vital. Strategies are likely to be most realistic when the problems of a particular nation can be seen in the global context of change, which includes estimates of the future no less than description of the past and present.

One identifiable component of the social process is the predispositions that affect development in various cultural configurations. The Japanese, for instance, perceive much of their civilization as derived from China, and presumably find it easier to acquire foreign traits than the Chinese. Folk societies are self-absorbed, hence predisposed to regard the stranger and his works as inimical or irrelevant. Although peasant villages may be drawn to some extent into a general political and market system by the demand to supply recruits and taxes (or tribute in kind), there may be no image of the self that extends far beyond the village, and especially no expectation of capability or demand to affect the mysterious decision process of larger units.

The class structure of a nation provides a set of social environments that affects the predisposition of each class group in ways that condition political development. At any given moment the significant question is whether and to what extent the active elite perceives itself as threatened from within or without by novelties that in principle can be incorporated into established myth and technique. If indigenous elites have already been subordinated (though permitted to continue) by foreign empires, predispositions are deeply affected by the strategies of the imperial rule to which they are subjected. If progressive patterns have been partially incorporated by some members of the indigenous elites, dissenting elements will probably break away from accommodation with the colonial master and join a coalition of middle and lower class elements who strive to secede from the empire. Generally political elites have resorted to the principle of minimum power loss or risk, seeking to make the fewest changes in power they expect to be able to get away with.

Contemporary research is particularly impressive in the study of interest groups, that is, groups that are less inclusive than class distinctions or cut across class lines. Important results also come from studies of communication. It is pointed out that totalitarian rulers have been more alert to the use of communication instruments than democracies.

Communication studies also lead to discussion of the personality factors in development. The underlying motivations and incentives for individual achievement certainly cannot be overlooked in the analysis of nation-building.

The relevance of crisis level is well demonstrated by the process of nation-building of Turkey. Turkey was so positioned that it was an object of active power strivings by the elites of other nations and empires. Top elites in Turkey became adept at postponing internal changes that would modify the traditional bases of authority and control. Postponement was achieved by playing one external rival against another, and by introducing promised rather than consummated innovations.

As strategies of political development are greatly affected by the timing and placing of conditioning factors, it is important to depict as accurately as possible the worldwide centers of the origin, diffusion, and restriction of political, economic, and social changes. Generally speaking, the completed map of inclusive change can lay the foundation for providing an understanding of the dynamics of accelerated or retarded diffusion. The circumstances can be identified in which innovations come to the attention of individuals situated at various geographical and social distances from where the innovations appear. Who perceives himself better off by directing anyone's attention to changes? By ignoring them? Among those who hear of change who sees himself better off (in terms of all values) by facilitating or blocking diffusion? As a result what patterns of route and zone are followed as innovations spread?

A second guiding principle is to think contextually, keeping policy questions related to the goal values of all whose effective support is required for success. The challenging task is to invent policies, and to devise programs of presenting policy, that elicit the coalitions needed to put forward effective demands to innovate.

Individual perspectives are always involved; but individuals are also members of organizations whose collective activities must be adapted to the requirements of development. An organization is to be understood as a pattern of situations which are interconnected by communication and collaboration. An official agency exists when a stable routine of formal and informal messages comes to the attention of officials (and other significant participants) and when these messages are interpreted by common criteria. The message flow must be managed in a way that permits the overt collaborative operations of the organization to be stabilized. The personnel, equipment, and other facilities available to the total enterprise are assembled, processed, and eventually released as a stream of outputs. Each component situation within the organization is appropriately structured when it mobilizes the value expectations, demands, and identifications that leave the participants better off than they were before.

This analysis of an organization shows why it is necessary to apply to organizational analysis all the categories pertinent to any social process, whether organized or unorganized. Patterns require specification in terms of values at stake and of institutional routines. The contextual approach to the strategy of development provides guidance as to the procedures to be used in thinking about their application.

A third guiding principle is decisiveness. It affirms the importance of avoiding confusion or paralysis during nation-building by maintaining a decision process that produces realistic and timely commitments. Communication networks may be overloaded; but indecisiveness may be a result of poor collaborative as well as poor communicative synchronizations. It is impressive that for a long time the Japanese people moved smoothly toward political development.

The principle of decisiveness is not applicable to all circumstances and must sometimes be disregarded. When the effective elite is hostile to political innovation, the strategy of development calls for measures that increase the strength of whatever factors make for indecisiveness in the official process of decision, and the simultaneous cultivation of a revolutionary alternative. A similar strategy is indicated if the established elite is oriented toward a totalitarian or reactionary bloc in the world arena (unless there are solid grounds for predicting that further development will change the alignment of the state).

Strategies of national development require simultaneous emphasis on a universal minimum of literacy and education, and on the rapid preparation of highly expert personnel. This is a warning against unbalanced skill and enlightenment policies; more concretely, a warning against the neglect of universal education (as in Turkey) or the overproduction of university-trained students without a future (as in several countries, particularly Formosa).

Strategies of nation-building must realistically encourage administrative merit without undermining or precluding the growth of responsible legislatures, parties, and other plural associations. In his contextual analysis about "the conditions under which non-bureaucratic power centers capable of subjecting bureaucrats to political control flourish or decline," Riggs acutely pointed out that "when the political arena is shifted to bureaucracies—a shift marked by the growing power of military officers in conflict with civilian officials—the consequences are usually ominous for political stability, economic growth, administrative effectiveness, and democratic values."[1]

Under various circumstances selling public offices has strengthened the position of a monarch in his struggle to obtain revenues and loyalty, outweighing such rivals as the great landlords or the ecclesiastical authorities. As Marx points out: "the chief effect of the emerging merit bureaucracy may be said to have been in the direction of vastly increasing the viability of constitutional government. Popular rule, easily distorted by volatile partisanship, cries out for the counterweight of considered assessment of issues. . . . The political spokesman and the practitioner of administration, though often at odds with each other, learned to appreciate their separate yet mutually dependent contributions."[2]

Sound strategy also requires the ideological incorporation of the entire nation into the challenging task of popular development, and encourages self-awareness of the process. The role of leaders to whom charismatic eminence is imputed has often been a conspicuous feature of national consolidation. The personal image of the hero is a common experience that contributes to the popular components of an all-embracing myth. Such miranda must be supplemented by more generalized and explicit doctrines and formulas; but they are indispensable to a system of national identification.

Miranda, doctrine, and formula gain impact, elaboration, and stability as a by-product of collective problem solving. Popular government needs to be part of national programs of action; and the same point applies to the acceptance of international responsibility, or any other objective of comprehensive political growth.

We also recommend a national strategy of induced initiative, fostering growth with minimal use of coercion. In many countries an important element in the national elite is committed to the goal of transforming a traditional society. They are, however, fully aware of elite elements firmly committed to the established order, opposing innovations that will weaken their ascendance. In desperation the modernizers are sometimes disposed to adopt coercive strategies for seizing power, liquidating reactionary elements, and mobilizing the manpower required for accelerated change. Strategies of desperation are not always necessary to get things moving, even in a state whose territory includes folk societies that have never been assimilated to the nation or to the science and technology of today.

A strategy of induced initiative, however, is directly appropriate to the task of activating suppressed peasant societies. It has been demonstrated that the peasants were victims, not of bad blood, but of social deprivation, and that properly encouraged they could become a national resource at all levels of creativity.[3] It is our concern to devise strategies whereby the consequences of past deprivation can be overcome among the suppressed peasantry, and overcome at the least human cost to all concerned. More particularly the challenge is to improve strategies of induced innovation.

No matter how ambitious the goals of development may be, changes are usually a step-by-step process. The overall problem is to persuade specific persons at particular places and times that they will be better off by adopting new rather than repeating old social practices. Thus the aim is to change perspectives and operations, and eventually to consolidate the perspectives and operations conforming to the innovation sought. Put in simple terms, recurring ideas and sentiments (subjective events) constitute "perspectives," and recurring ways of doing things (nonsubjective events) are "operations." We speak of a relatively stable pattern of perspectives and operations as a "practice."

The strategy calls for several choices to be made by the innovators. What practices shall be introduced? What role shall the innovators play as value sources in the community? What role shall they play as models of proper practice? What participants in the community structure shall be chosen to expedite innovation? What timing shall be adopted for all acts of strategy?

A final principle is that of priority. Nation-building involves immense tasks of all kinds, and will always reveal more problems than can humanly be absorbed by the resources available at a given time. Confronted with competing program demands, decision-makers have to establish some priorities depending on the development goals and cost-benefit relations. It is inadvisable to seek quick returns on the surface at the expense of long-term development. Nor is it realistic to expect "patient" cooperation from the public by focusing on long-term goals without more immediate achievements that are essential to continuing popular support. In projecting long-term goals for national development, an enlightenment campaign must not be allowed to deteriorate into a stream of remote promises designed to distract attention from the endless sacrifices of today. If the ruling elite cannot improve the lot of living generations, grand promises to generations yet unborn are cruel hoaxes. From time to time, development goals have to be given specification viewed from long-term, mid-term, and short-term perspective. For this purpose, an integrated and contextual approach for programming is vitally needed. It can best be done by a fairly independent institution specializing in the functions of planning and appraisal on a stable and continuing basis.

It is unfortunately necessary to leave many principles of strategy in an ambiguous state, for remarkably few guidelines are available on the details of organizational structure. There is agreement that development means substituting specialized for generalized organs. Yet all is indefinite when we search for criteria of judging the degree and timing of specialization. That a balance is required between centralization and decentralization is admitted, yet we have few suggestions to apply when confronting concrete circumstances. Other problems of organization, such as the concentration or deconcentration of power in organs at the same level of competence, face the same ambiguity.

It is appropriate, therefore, to underline once again the contextual principle as it relates to planning, and to suggest that all relevant events be kept at the focus of attention of advisors and final decision makers.

CHAPTER FIVE

The External Process
of Decision

Having clarified the basic goals and strategic guiding principles, we shall relate them to the trends, conditions, and projections for Formosa's development with a view to making fundamental proposals. In the contemporary context of world conditions, the task of nation-building involves the external as well as the internal processes of a nation. Hence we shall submit our proposals under two principal categories: nation-building as participation in an external process of decision; and nation-building as an internal process of decision. The former is our concern in this chapter.

Independence and Security

OF ALL THE urgent tasks of national development nothing is more fundamental than the problem of national security. In order to become a viable body politic, in order to play a responsible role in world affairs, a nation large or small must be assured of its national security before any grand design can be pressed forward.

With the rise of Japanese militarism, Formosa was incorporated into the defense complex of the Japanese empire. During World

War II, Formosa was a base for advancing toward the South Pacific and Southeast Asia. As Japan collapsed, Formosa suffered considerable wartime damages. Since the Allied command decided against landing in Formosa at the end of the war it was occupied solely by Nationalist forces acting on behalf of the Allied powers in the Far East.

Because of the full-fledged civil war going on in the mainland, Formosa was neglected early in the Nationalist occupation. In 1949, when Chinese Communists took over the mainland and the Nationalists sought exile in Formosa with some one-and-one-half million military and civilian refugees, observers noted that it was only a matter of time before Communists would try to realize their goal of "liberating" Formosa. At that juncture, the United States government published "White Papers" declaring the policy of "let-dust-settle" regarding Formosa.[1] This dark hour of the Nationalist regime was brightened by the outbreak of the Korean war in June 1950. President Truman immediately proclaimed the "neutralization" of Taiwan by dispatching the U.S. Seventh Fleet to the Formosan Straits. It was intended both to prevent Communist China from attacking Formosa and to restrain Nationalist forces from invading the mainland.

When the first offshore islands crisis took place in 1954, the United States and the Nationalist government concluded a mutual defense treaty, thereby forging a missing link in the anti-Communist defense line stretching from the Aleutian Islands to the Philippines. The treaty, formalizing U.S. defense commitment to Formosa, provides a strict limitation on the freedom of action of the Nationalists to undertake any military action against mainland China.[2] The applicability of the treaty to Quemoy and Matsu was tested during the second offshore islands crisis in 1958. On finding a link between the defense of Formosa and the defense of Quemoy and Matsu, President Eisenhower was prepared to extend U.S. defense to both Quemoy and Matsu.

The Nationalist government has taken great pains to declare

that any attempt to "recover" (not "invade") mainland China by military action is an inherent right in the discharge of a sacred mission, and is not "offensive" at all. Hence there was considerable concern in 1962 when the Nationalist government was reportedly planning an imminent military action against the mainland while Communist China was plagued by an acute food crisis. President Kennedy in a press conference and the U.S. ambassador to Poland privately to the Chinese ambassador assured Communist China of the defensive purposes of the United States in her commitment to the Nationalists regarding Formosa.[3] Recently, in the wake of Communist China's successful atomic tests, a pre-emptive destruction of Chinese atomic installations has been suggested. Advanced when the Vietnam war is escalating, this proposal seems once to have had significant though never decisive support in the United States. In any event, in accounting for the basic stability of Formosa today, one must be ever mindful that it is the United States' presence in the Formosan Straits, not the 600,000 "first-rate" armed forces of the Nationalists, that has deterred Communist China from undertaking military adventures against Formosa and the Pescadores.

After Formosa attains its independence, what kind of arrangement is needed to provide for its maximum security? It may be suggested that a status of "neutrality" is a feasible alternative, with the United States and Communist China the principal sharers of the responsibility of implementation. Granting that a strong case can be made that it is in Communist China's interest to let Formosa remain independent and neutral, there is little indication that the ruling Communist elites can be prevailed on to accept this alternative. Confronted with the new reality of Formosa's independence, Communist China is most likely to exhaust all the bases of power at her command in pressing her claim to incorporate Formosa, covertly if not overtly. Hence any attempt to establish a neutral status for Formosa appears to be unrealistic. With certain exceptions, such as Switzerland and

Austria, genuine neutrality seems extremely untenable in the contemporary world. A paper guarantee may disarm the guaranteed state and make it a prey of those who seek expansion.

As in the past 12 years, Formosa's security interest in the foreseeable future can best be assured by continuing the close alliance relation with the United States. Pressed by both Communist China and Chiang's ruling elites, a continuation of alliance relations with the United States, based on the current community expectations and existing arrangements, can be assured of continuing popular support.

In its continuous efforts to contain Chinese Communist expansion, the United States seems to have considered it strategically vital to engage in "holding operations" in areas vulnerable to Communist Chinese expansion, with a concurrent hope that a better relation would ultimately evolve when the new generation of Chinese Communist elites—with less revolutionary zeal than the present leadership, "baptized" by the Long March of the 1930's—come into power. This basic thinking is apparently shared and feared by Mao and his immediate supporters, and accounts in part for the savage power struggle waged in the name of the "great proletariat cultural revolution." What was once considered to be the unparalleled asset of Peking's leadership—the "absolute" unity and cohesiveness of the "Yenan generation"—is a thing of the past. Viewed in this light, the significance of the present struggle in Vietnam can be understood more properly. Should Formosa survive the trying period when the Communists show no sign of compromise toward her new status, and the old rivals headed by Mao and Chiang in the Chinese civil war pass away from the political scene, the new elites of mainland China can be expected to attach less personal sentiment to the traditional policy of opposing an independent Formosa. Through gradual resymbolization, they can reconcile themselves with the facts of Formosa's political life.

A new alliance between the United States and the "Republic

of Formosa" will have distinctly different implications from the existing relationship between the United States and the "Republic of China." When the alliance concerns a nation whose sole territorial claim is over Formosa (not over mainland China), the "defensive purpose" of assistance from the United States is beyond doubt or reproach. Communist China can be assured that at no time would Formosa be used as a base for initiating military action against the mainland. The practical effect may be to relieve Communist China's fear of attack from Formosa, an apprehension insistently played up by the Communists for at least domestic consumption. Should the new expectation stabilize through the years, tension will be released in the Formosan Straits, with the consequent solution of the present triangular entanglement of Communist China, the United States, and Formosa. The key to the whole problem, it is clear, lies in self-help by the Formosans. Only when they can be sufficiently helped to help themselves will Formosa stand a chance of survival.

It may be asked whether a continuation of a close alliance with the United States means that Formosa will be nothing more than a puppet of the United States. In view of Communist China's ever present threat, can it not be prophesied that Formosa is doomed to fall under the domination of Communist China if the United States withdraws her present commitment? Why go through the agony of short-lived independence, only to be dominated by the United States, which in turn may abandon Formosa to mainland China?

These questions are more hypothetical than real. As will be elaborated shortly below, it is not inevitable that Formosa must cease to exist. Extinction as an independent power is inevitable only if the Formosan people fail to control their own destiny through self-help; and to equate assistance from the United States with U.S. domination is misleading. Given the present context of world conditions and the changing concept of defense, which nation can claim to be independent in some absolutistic sense?

The concept of "collective security" holds the key to the answer. It is necessary to look only at Japan and the nations of Western Europe to grasp the essential point involved. Emerging from the disasters of World War II, they were heavily dependent on U.S. economic and military support to achieve the high levels of prosperity that they have come to enjoy. No one who is acquainted with the facts and willing to recognize them would dream of treating these resurgent nations as puppets of the United States. A far more realistic description is to call them partners in a joint enterprise; they surely are not master and servants. The practice of maintaining close coordination and consultation over key decisions in the fields of military and foreign policy vividly reflects the accelerating interdependence of all peoples. Within the limits of the objective situation, each nation preserves authority and control over its process of decision. So far as Formosa is concerned, the record shows that the United States has sought neither territorial expansion nor special commercial interests.

Finally, a comment is needed to clarify future arrangements with regard to Quemoy and Matsu. Geographically, historically, and militarily, Quemoy and Matsu are inseparable from mainland China. As distinguished from Formosa, Quemoy and Matsu are beyond dispute accepted as Chinese territory.[4] The Nationalist regime retains them for their propaganda significance as symbols of the continuous existence of the Chinese civil war and Chiang's alleged authority over all China. As indicated earlier, in 1958 President Eisenhower found himself trapped in a position that afforded little choice but to link the defense of Quemoy and Matsu with Formosa's. To have withdrawn under pressure could have been interpreted as a setback with some disastrous implications. However, should withdrawal result because Formosa achieves independence and because the U.S. deliberately confines its commitment to Formosa and the Pescadores, no negative implication is involved. Once Formosa becomes independent, it is fitting and proper that the islands should be returned to mainland China.[5]

Participation in
Transnational Organizations

BACK IN THE nineteenth century Japan's process of modernization was accomplished in a relatively calm setting where she was
allowed to concentrate fully on her internal process, without being
upset by the tide of world events. In today's world, however, a new
nation, no matter how small, cannot escape from playing a role
in world affairs, even though it may not be quite ready for it.
More and more the United Nations has become the center of
attention for newly independent nations in their first exposure to
the outside world.

As a founding member of the U.N., China was accorded big-
power status as a permanent member of the Security Council.
Initially the Nationalist regime represented China in fact as well
as in name; after 1949, however, its representation of "China" has
become more fiction than fact. Its effective control over population
was reduced from five hundred million to eight million (in 1949);
its territory was sharply confined to an island whose legal status
is yet to be settled. Nevertheless, the Nationalist delegation continues to represent "China" in the United Nations, occupying both
seats in the Security Council and the General Assembly. This
peculiar phenomenon was a result of Communist China's aggressive action in Korea and the cold war. Aside from maintaining
close relations with the United States and Japan, the Nationalist
government has persistently sought to deny Communist China
access to international organizations in the past seventeen years.

With symbolic status as a big power legally, the "Republic
of China" (Formosa) has been assessed to pay U.N. dues disproportionate to Formosa's size and resources, which impose a
considerable drain on Formosa's limited assets. In order not to
be excluded from voting in the United Nations, the Nationalist
government has managed to comply with Article 19 of the Charter,
no matter how painful that burden may be.[6] While for some

time, with the blessings of the United States, the Nationalist government was accorded the deference due a big power of election to the Economic and Social Council and other key committees, this is no longer the case. China, as represented by the Nationalist delegation, has not been re-elected to the Economic and Social Council since 1960. The newly established committees on disarmament and peace-keeping operations do not include the Nationalist delegation. In other words, its legally symbolic status of a big power is being eroded. Fewer and fewer member states wish to buy the fiction that the Nationalist delegation represents 700 million Chinese in the United Nations—a myth kept alive by the overwhelming influence of the United States upon other member states at an earlier time.

If Formosa were admitted to the United Nations as representing only Formosa and all the Formosan people this fiction would cease to exist. Though not a permanent member of the Security Council, Formosa's loss of big-power status in name does not imply the curtailment of its possible role in the United Nations affairs. Freed from dogmatically preconceived and unrealistic myths, the Formosan delegation would be in a position to contribute responsibly toward problem solving in a rational and balanced way, rather than a narrow, premeditated frame of reference. The Formosan delegation would have no need to "double talk," as did the Nationalist delegation in its obsession to justify its position as the "representative of China."

An independent Formosa, even as a viable and responsible member of the world community, would in the long run rely heavily on the collective security measures of the United Nations. It is the manifest destiny of intermediate powers to speak in the name of humanity and "peace on earth." As in the past, the intermediate powers will continue to contribute to the enrichment of international life and world civilization. From this active role a viable Formosa would not shrink.

In this day of ascendant nationalism, while nation states continue to assert their "sovereignty" and "independence," the scope of transnational organizations has greatly expanded, in response to the interdependence of international life. It is not unreasonable to expect that the expanding functions of the transnational organizations in the sphere of human welfare, with their pervasive and far-reaching impacts, may in time prove to be an essential stabilizing factor, thereby contributing to public order in much the same way that France's bureaucracy has nurtured the political stability of that nation. The new transnational structures will serve as constant reminders of common interest in increasing the effectiveness of the United Nations as a whole. Emancipated from the fantastic and provocative role that it has had to play in recent years, the new leadership of Formosa will be free to play a constructive part in the new frontier of human welfare.

While the world community remains underdeveloped in that an inclusive public order is absent, the members of this generation contain elements attempting to do what is humanly possible and practical toward achieving an order in which the concept of human dignity finds concrete expression. Aside from participating actively in transnational organizations and cultivating wide and friendly relations with other nations, Formosa can play a responsible part by accepting third-party assistance in the persuasive settlement of disputes, accepting obligations to aid in the sanctioning activities of transnational bodies, and maintaining impartial legal protection of aliens in harmony with transnational norms.

Sharing in the Evolution of the Pacific Community

AS A MEMBER of the contemporary world community, a new Formosa will find it necessary to play a responsible role not only in the United Nations, but in regional structures of cooperation.

Formosa is not at present advantageously positioned to maintain close relations with neighboring nations in the Pacific area.

The dogmatic orientation of the Nationalist regime in international affairs has erected barriers of many kinds. Adhering to the myth of "one China," the Nationalists have made it a policy not to establish relations with any nation that maintains diplomatic relations with Communist China. The Peking government reciprocates in the same fashion. Each side refuses to participate in an international conference or organization in the presence of the other. As the diplomatic sphere of Communist China expands, Nationalist China grows more isolated from other Asian nations, and even from other developing countries. Except for a few strong anti-Communist nations, Formosa finds herself very much isolated in Asia; and in the opinions of specialists on bloc politics in the United Nations, Nationalist China is not considered a member of either the broad Asian or the Afro-Asian group. This is largely a result of Nationalist China's obsession in claiming to represent all China.

The recent creation of the Asia Bank is a step forward in the regional cooperation of Asian nations. The major concern of the governments involved is economic development. Having achieved impressive economic growth, an independent Formosa can be useful in assisting the development of its sister states in Asian (and African) continents. As Formosa's stage of development is not too far apart from its sister states in Asia, these nations would find its recent experience especially relevant to their efforts. Formosa's transforming of much of the agricultural sector into an industrial sector and in giving balanced emphasis to both can be of great significance for other nations originally in similar circumstances.

Unlike the experience of Japan, Formosa's experience has been accumulated in the contemporary context in which newly developing nations generally find themselves, that is, hard pressed by the tide of world events in general and of cold-war politics in particular. Today's nations cannot shut themselves away from the outside world: they must deal with external relations and domestic development at the same time, under the stress of many competing pressures and counter pressures. Japan's economic takeoff occurred when many of today's new nations were still under colonial control, when there was no cold war, and when there was far less interdependence in international life. Japan's experience, while valuable, is more historical than current.

In Formosa's search for a meaningful role in regional cooperation, it would seem strategic to cultivate "Pacific consciousness" and to establish a "Pacific Community." The Pacific Community would be the counterpart of the Atlantic Community in name, but fundamentally different in emphasis. It would also be different in its basic orientation from the Asian and Pacific Council (ASPAC) recently created in 1966. Rather than basing itself on military alliances, the Pacific Community would be primarily concerned with the development of communication and tourism, to take advantage of the cultural distinctiveness and ecological diversity of the region and the opportunities that abound for the joint exploration of the Pacific ocean. This community, at the initial stage, could embrace all nations and territorial communities bordering the Pacific that share common goals, including Japan, Korea, Formosa, the Philippines, Vietnam, Malaysia, Indonesia, Hawaii, the Pacific islands, Australia, and New Zealand. Understandably, the very diversity of language and culture may be a barrier to communication; but this is where the attraction lies. Through the enrichment and development of cultural distinctiveness, a solid foundation can be laid for the tourist industry in this space-shrinking age. The joint exploration of the oceans, beneficial to the fishing industry and mining, would expand the frontier of economic life and provide food and other resources for the Pacific nations. In this area cooperative efforts are more efficient than separate programs.

Formosa can fit into this new pattern of regional development magnificently. Like many other nations, Formosa spares no effort to promote the tourist industry. As we shall elaborate later, we consider it of utmost importance that Formosa recognize and fulfil its uniqueness by selective renewal and conservation of its ancient and authentic Chinese cultural heritage. As the nation becomes more widely engaged in new activities in the Pacific, the Formosan people would not only find it exciting and challenging, they would unobtrusively emancipate themselves from much of the narrow-mindedness nurtured by the traditional outlook of a small island.

Relations with Mainland China

SINCE ITS establishment in 1949 Communist China has persistently declared its ultimate goal to "liberate" Formosa, by force if necessary. Strategies have changed through time as conditions dictate, but the basically offensive goal remains unchanged. Communist China is vehemently opposed to the idea of Formosa's permanent separation from the mainland by the route of "independence." Should Formosa become independent in the near future, Chinese Communists are bound to exploit potentially discontented elements within the new body politic and to intensify infiltration and subversion, assuming that overt armed attack is deterred by the continued presence of the U.S. Seventh Fleet in the Formosan Straits. As long as Communist China's hostility persists, Formosa has no choice but to defend her national security by close alliance with the United States; only in this way is it possible to deter or repel any military action by Communist China across the Formosan Straits. Meanwhile, outlawing the Communist party will remain an essential precaution to insure the internal order of the new Formosa as long as it is not an instrument to suppress legitimate dissents as it has been under the KMT's reign of terror.

It is precisely during the period of transition that Formosa will be particularly vulnerable to Communist subversion and internal chaos. If a new Formosa, without Chiang Kai-shek as its head, can marshal popular support to the task of national development and survive the crucial years of transition, the future of the nation will be much better assured than it is today. The present hostility between Peking and Taipei is, it is true, a conflict of ideology; but it is more. Specifically, it is a continuation of the personal struggles (and hatreds)—disguised in the symbols of public interest —between Mao & Co. on the one hand, and Chiang & Co. on the other. Their struggle dates back at least to the Long March of the 1930s. Their struggle for power was highly personalized; the scars of the past are too deep to be overlooked in their lifetime. As long as the Mao and Chiang generation of veteran leaders remain in power, any attempt to change the *status quo* seems hopelessly complicated. As the second echelon of leadership emerges on the mainland, however, it may eventually be feasible for the elites to come to terms with the fact of Formosa's independence and separation from mainland China.

It is to be underlined afresh in this connection that the self-help of the Formosan people, their willingness and capability to take destiny in their own hands, is the key to any hopeful future change. Only when the Formosan people can demonstrate to the world that Formosa's independence is neither a personal affair of Chiang's nor an artificial outcome of U.S. strategy, but a crystallized expression of popular aspirations and efforts, more elements of the world community will be favorably disposed to acknowledge Formosa's new status in the world arena. As the new status becomes viable and stabilized, lingering Communist claims to incorporate Formosa would gradually fade away. The claim to include in one grandiose Chinese empire every acre of territory that had ever been part of its domain would linger as a fossil in the textbooks, but as a practical matter of policy it would no longer exacerbate transnational relations.

As we have said, it is sometimes questioned whether an independent Formosa, given its limited resources, is merely a transitory phase to eventual "reunification" with mainland China. If so, why should the Formosan people pay the price required to define a new role practically certain to antagonize Communist China and hence prejudice Formosa's future status in the framework of a glorious Chinese empire? The underlying assumption is that Communist China is destined to be a very powerful nation toward which neighboring nations, including Formosa, would gravitate. The basic configuration of world politics is assumed to be toward concentrating power in a few centers (Washington, Moscow, Peking, and probably Paris) at the expense of intermediate and small states.

Granted the strength of the tendencies that found expression in the emergence of a few superpowers, we must not lose sight of the counterforces that modify the rate of movement in this direction, and typically call an eventual halt to the swallowing up of intermediate and small powers in the process. Ours is an epoch of nationalism. Many newly independent nations, emerged from centuries of oblivion, have only recently found their collective identity. The people of these nations cherish too dearly their new status of independence, and their leaders are therefore able to take advantage of the opportunities of a marginal position in relation to the superpowers to veer toward alignments that can defend a newfound position in the community of nations. Formosa occupies a geographical position at the periphery of mainland China, a location that provides a focus of identity and a base of alignment with countervailing powers in the Pacific region, and, more inclusively, among the members of the United Nations. Smaller nations contribute to world security by modulating the confrontations of the principal states with one another.

We are accustomed to organized groups of contrasting size and potency establishing a balance of power that is stable for long periods. In the economic sector, for example, the rise of giant corporations in many markets does not destroy all the competing units. On the contrary, a familiar pattern includes a few super units, several intermediate units, and a multitude of lesser entities. Common interests are discovered in defending the essential integrity of a system in which the tendencies toward a single imperial organization or a completely bi- or tri-polarized pattern are successfully resisted within the new equilibrium of forces. It is by no means impossible that the public order of the future will be worked out in the framework of the present international system. A public order capable of maintaining at least minimum security can come about in gradual fashion. The peace-keeping forces and procedures of the U.N. can be strengthened and taken for granted. As hyperdestructive weapons are more generally accessible, the strategic dangers involved in their deployment will be more widely understood in military, diplomatic, and lay circles throughout the world community. If major coercions are avoided for years, and minor coercions are successfully dealt with, a growing sense of security can add to the frequencies of pluralizing and decentralizing modes of collective action. The superpowers themselves may be gradually modified as the perpetual alert generated by the arms race is superseded. *The overcentralizing tendencies of superpowers themselves can be modulated or reversed not by the use of force, but through the stimulation and cultural distinctiveness of intermediate powers.*

It is increasingly apparent that Communist China's bid to represent the wave of the future is a failure. The serious setbacks suffered by Peking extending from Indonesia to Cuba are of more than momentary significance. They are remarkable reminders of the fundamental limitations on the strategies and the assumptions with which China approaches the outside world. The political tradition of China is nonegalitarian. The classical assumption of Chinese rulers was that the entire civilized world was ruled from the capital of the empire. Those barbarians who were not fully assimilated were allowed to pay tribute to the court. It will be recalled how the rulers in the last Dynasty, the Ch'ing, took it for granted that Queen Victoria was prepared to pay tribute to China. The traditional arrogance of the political tradition has reemerged with Mao and the Communist regime. Not only is the distasteful tie to the big brother in Moscow in jeopardy, but the highhanded approach to the new nations has aroused vigorous counter assertions of independence. Formosans have only to recall the advent of Chiang and his defeated army and party to understand the inbuilt limitation of mainland China for success in the more equalitarian world system of today. A dramatic rebuff to Communist China occurred when the leaders of the Afro-Asian world refused to go along with the Chinese attempt to convene a top-level conference that would exclude Soviet participation and denounce United States action in Vietnam. The Vietnam crisis itself was precipitated by the attempt of the Chinese Communists to exclude U.S. influence from Asia. The drive led to massive concentrations of U.S. forces near the borders of China in an effort to protect the interests of the U.S. in free Asian peoples rather than in an aggrandized Peking. Peking's overall setbacks in the international arena have recently been accentuated by the internal turmoils of the "great proletariat cultural revolution."

The new Formosa can play a creative role in these developments. Traditionally there was hardly any room for large-scale freedom in China: the Chinese people were subordinated to the absolute authority of the emperor at the apex and to the immediate pressures of magistrates and gentry. This long tradition of centralization and regimentation has not only been perpetuated but reinforced by the totalitarian Communists on the mainland. The challenge confronting a new Formosa is to demonstrate that the Chinese culture is adaptable to the modern context, and is capable of achieving collective pluralism and individual freedom. If it can be shown that even in a highly centralized tradition there are great potentials for diversity and freedom, Formosa's experience will be a stimulating model to other nations.

It must be distinctly understood that a diverging policy on behalf of pluralism and personal freedom does not imply a persisting hostility to mainland China. As long as Communist China persists in adopting a hostile attitude toward Formosa, it is unlikely that Formosans will be lulled into believing that Communist China will immediately yield her ambition to "liberate" Formosa, ambitions forcefully and consistently stated in the past seventeen years. However, the geographical proximity, the shared cultural heritage and ethnic backgrounds, do strongly suggest that a "good neighbor policy" is in the common interest of Formosa and mainland China. Even if Communist hostility continues, Formosa can show openmindedness and flexibility. Once Communist China is ready to "let Formosa alone" by respecting her political independence and territorial integrity in deeds as well as words, then a mutually beneficial relation can be established. Formosa's independence does not imply the arbitrary rejection of everything Chinese. Our position on this issue will be made abundantly clear later in our recommendation that "Mandarin Chinese" be adopted as the official language of the new Formosa.

Finally, it may be suggested that the current aspiration of the Formosan people to be independent of mainland China is perhaps principally prompted by the deeprooted apprehension of the extremism of Peking's present leadership. Once, it is said, a more moderate leadership emerges on the mainland—say, in twenty or thirty years—the people of Formosa may voluntarily desire to unite with the mainland. The short answer to this hypothetical question is "yes" and "no." The answer is "yes" if the people of Formosa continue to be excluded from managing their own affairs for twenty or thirty years under the continuing Nationalist rule. On the other hand, the answer is a definite "no" if—as we expect to be the case—the people of Formosa will become the masters of their own political destiny during the next twenty or thirty years. They will, like any other people, cherish too dearly their newly won pride of being first-class citizens to surrender it gladly.

Policies toward Overseas Chinese

THERE ARE about seventeen million Chinese living outside the boundaries of mainland China and Formosa, and approximately 96 per cent of them are concentrated in Southeast Asia, particularly in Thailand, Malaysia, Indonesia, and Singapore.[7] The migration of Chinese to Southeast Asia dates back to the fourteenth century (the Ming Dynasty), and primarily attracted people from the coastal provinces of Fukien and Kwangtung (Canton). At that time, the new areas were ruled by native princes and Chinese settlements were limited. As the British, Dutch, and French extended their colonial empires and their sphere of trade over these areas, the Chinese began to emigrate on a large scale to supply badly needed manpower, especially late in the nineteenth century and since.

Through hard work, generations of overseas Chinese have established themselves in their host nations as a key commercial class, their business operations ranging from small retail establishments to large commercial firms. Preoccupied with the accumulation of wealth, overseas Chinese have a tradition of avoiding serious involvement in local politics. Instead of identifying with the host communities, overseas Chinese maintained close ties with kinsmen in the motherland by regular remittances and correspondence. Proud of Chinese cultural superiority, overseas Chinese have continued to teach the Chinese language from generation to generation. The prevalence of Islamism and Hinduism in Southeastern Asia has been a further significant barrier to the assimilation of the Chinese minorities.

Before World War II the overseas Chinese relied mainly upon the colonial authorities for protection, and in turn they were utilized as middlemen between the colonial government and the native population. At the turn of this century, Chinese nationalism began to spread among the overseas Chinese. In marked contrast to the general practice of noninvolvement in local politics, they became highly engaged in the politics of the motherland. Witness the strong financial support given to Dr. Sun Yat-sen in establishing the Republic in 1912 and to the Nationalist government during the Sino-Japanese war. Even today, overseas Chinese as a whole are still praised as "the mother of revolution." When the Nationalist government consolidated authority and control on the mainland in 1927, it began to set up a comprehensive network of consulates throughout Southeast Asia, determined to be the protector of all overseas Chinese. Inheriting the traditional view that China was "the center of the world," the Nationalist government claimed that "where there are Chinese, there is China"; hence all persons of Chinese origin were considered to be Chinese. This perspective has found concrete expression in the law of nationality, which incorporates the principle of *jus sanguinis*, whereby all persons of Chinese blood are regarded as Chinese nationals, irrespective of place of birth or possible conflict of nationalities. The result is a serious problem of dual nationality among overseas Chinese.

The establishment of the Chinese Communist regime on the mainland coincided with the emergence of newly independent nations as the colonial empires disintegrated. For overseas Chinese, the termination of colonial rule meant an end to the special protection hitherto provided by the colonial governments. Kindled by a strong sentiment of nationalism, the local population, elites and nonelites alike, have shown widespread resentment against the overseas Chinese who so often dominate the local economy yet remain isolated from local political and social life. Acting in the name of the common good, the ruling elites of these ex-colonies do not hesitate to impose highly nationalistic and discriminatory measures upon "nonassimilated" (or more properly "unassimilable") aliens. These policies range from economic to educational activities. No longer can the Chinese be assured of their economic position without pledging allegiance to the new order. They not unnaturally look for help from their motherland, whether they conceive the leaders to be in Peking or Taipei.

Accepting the protection of the legitimate interests of overseas Chinese as a constitutional responsibility, both National and Communist regimes have understandably expressed deep concern about the difficulties that face overseas Chinese.[8] In effect, the campaign to win the support of overseas Chinese has become an extension of the Chinese civil war, with Southeast Asia as a new arena. While the Communist regime considers the support they give a symbolic validation of its formal authority and control, the Nationalist regime continues to pose as the authoritative government of China. Their campaigns are further complicated by other considerations. On the one hand, there is a strong desire to protect overseas Chinese, and on the other, a serious intent to cultivate good relations with the new governments. The choices open to them require a delicate balance since problems that arise in the protection of overseas Chinese, particularly "dual nationality" questions, often are significant barriers to friendly relations. Confronted with the dilemma, both Nationalist and Communist regimes have made great efforts and changed strategies often; however, their positions are less than consistent.

Under the myth of "one China" shared by both Chiang and Mao, the Nationalist and Communist regimes have made it a policy not to establish diplomatic relations with a nation that recognizes the rival regime. As a result, their degree of influence over overseas Chinese in Southeastern Asia depends primarily upon their diplomatic ties with each nation. So far neither side has scored a decisive victory in winning the minds of overseas Chinese; moreover, given present conditions neither can expect to do so in the near future. Generally speaking, while their long-term perspective is likely to be oriented toward mainland China, as demonstrated by their common pride in Communist China's atomic detonations, overseas Chinese are presently more concerned with immediate problems. Dictated by the paramount consideration of preserving their present economic position, overseas Chinese have been sufficiently realistic to make their preferred choice in the light of the basic policy ("pro-Peking" or "pro-Taipei") and distinctive circumstances of the nations in which they reside. More often than not, they would prefer to keep a "neutral" posture, at least for the time being.

In attempting to win the minds of overseas Chinese, the Nationalist regime has employed two basic strategies in recent years. One is to attract investment, through incentive plans, by overseas Chinese in Formosa's economic growth. Another is to help educate overseas Chinese by general scholarships (with considerable U.S. aid) for college study in Formosa. The significance of overseas Chinese investment in Formosa tends to be exaggerated. From 1950 to 1965, it totaled only $122,500,000. As of 1965 there were 114 firms in actual operation, employing 16,113 persons. In 1965 their total exports amounted to $9,733,269.[9] As to the educational program through extensive scholarship offers, it remains more or less a publicity contest. By urging close and articulate identification with the "Republic of China," the regime has added a complicated dimension in the already harsh life of overseas Chinese. An overseas Chinese must decide whether or not to become a national of a given host nation. The competing claim of the Nationalist regime to represent his interests adds a complication to this crucial choice.

A new Formosa can and should adopt an enlightened and progressive policy toward overseas Chinese. It is in the common interest of the overseas Chinese and the various host nations to foster the assimilation of overseas Chinese into the mainstream of the political life of the local communities. Overseas Chinese ought to be encouraged to identify with the local community, since this is where their activities center. By now it should be apparent to them that it is hardly possible for them to preserve their economic interests without minimum access to power. Together with the native people, they can contribute usefully in the building of new nations. The new government in Formosa can help facilitate this process of assimilation and integration in Southeast Asian nations by avoiding ambivalent policies that tend to aggravate their hesitation in the making of difficult choices. Such a policy will also improve Formosa's relations with each nation, since mutual understanding and good will are concretely exemplified. A progressive policy on the part of the new Republic does not mean that Formosa would turn its back on overseas Chinese. On the contrary, Formosa will continue to encourage cultural as well as economic cooperation with overseas Chinese.

CHAPTER SIX

The Internal Decision Process: Constitutional Structures and Functions

IN DEALING with the internal aspect of nation-building, we shall focus our attention on two principal categories, the constitutional process, and the other institutional processes. We shall deal with constitutional structures and functions in the present chapter.

The Allocation of Authority and Control

THE INDISPENSABLE task in formulating a new constitutive order is the adequate allocation of authority and control among various government organizations. Fifty years of Japanese rule left colonial, not self-ruling, legacies for Formosa. The constitutional practices under the Nationalist regime, abnormal as they are, are likely to have considerable and in many ways beneficial impact upon the future course of Formosa's constitutive process.

The constitution of the "Republic of China," as currently applied in Formosa, went into effect in December 1947 while the Nationalist government was still in power on the mainland. In the early part of 1947, while acting in the capacity of military occupier on behalf of the Allies, and although from the legal point of view Formosa remained a Japanese territory, the Nationalist regime unilaterally declared Formosa one of the thirty-five provinces of the Republic of China. This move made it possible for Formosa to participate formally in the constitutive process—the election of a small assigned number of representatives—when the constitution came into effect in December 1947. As a result of the Communist takeover in October 1949, the viability of the Constitution has never been tested on the mainland.

The Nationalist regime sought exile in Formosa in December 1949 and proclaimed Taipei the new capital of the Republic of China. The authoritative and partly effective domain of the Nationalist regime was reduced suddenly from 3,800,000 square miles and of 500 million people to an island of 13,885 square miles and 8 million people. Because of this loss of nearly 98.4 per cent of its constituents, the obvious suggestion was made that necessary modifications and adjustments be introduced into the basic pattern of the allocation of authority and control, and that a new mandate be obtained from the existing constituents in Formosa, since the effective control of the Nationalist regime was now confined to Formosa.

Unfortunately, while the Nationalists have seen fit to declare martial law and to suspend civil liberties since 1949—a period of "Communist rebellion"—they have not seen fit to accept any proposal for structural change, no matter how moderate it may be. As mentioned before, the underlying policy is to deny effective participation in the power process to native Formosans. Since the flight from the mainland, the entire constitutional framework of 1947 has been kept intact; on top of the provincial government of Taiwan sits the central government of the Republic of China, with huge skeleton staffs, as if it were exercising authority over a land of 700 million people.

The allocation of authority and control among various organizations embodied in the 1947 constitution has thus been applied to the wrong people, the wrong place, and at the wrong time. Understandably, when a constitution designed to chart the political process of a land of 3,800,000 square miles and of 500 million people is imposed, without the slightest adjustment to changed conditions, upon an island of 13,885 square miles and 8 million people, its workability is extremely doubtful. This doubt is reinforced when it is recalled that the elected representatives, who derived their mandate from constituencies on the mainland nearly twenty years ago, have assumed *de facto* "permanent tenure" without re-election, and purport to represent 13 million people in Formosa. These "elected representatives" of the people, who include members of the Legislative Yuan and the Control Yuan and delegates to the National Assembly, all of whom claim to be counterparts of congressmen, total around 2200 in Formosa today. They are not responsible to those most affected by their decisions, Formosans who have never elected them and have no power to remove them. They do not hesitate to take advantage of their privileged positions in the pursuit of personal interests. For instance, the members of the Legislative Yuan have kept a statute to the effect that those who have been in that body for more than three years (regardless of their legal education and experience) can practice law, even though it is otherwise necessary to pass a stringent national bar examination in order to qualify.[1]

With no fear of failing re-election, the representatives could have become a tyrannical and dominant oligarchy. The towering figure of Chiang prevented them from incapacitating the executive. Chiang considers himself entrusted with a mandate from "Heaven," indispensable to China. When he was barred from re-election for a third term in 1960 by constitutional limitation, he appealed to the delegates to the National Assembly (whose prime responsibility is to amend the constitution and to elect the President and the Vice President) to make him eligible for re-election "during the period of Communist rebellion." Chiang's continuous holding of the office of the Presidency and his unchallengeable position have made the Legislative Yuan a rubber stamp at his disposal. The representatives echo Chiang's policies, without questioning the desirability or feasibility of particular courses of action; Chiang's overwhelming leadership and the myths he symbolizes enable them to live in perpetuity at public expense.

Despite detailed provisions in the constitution that carefully provide for a genuine division of authoritative competence between the national government and provincial governments, the super-imposition of the central government on the province of Taiwan has deprived the Formosans of even minimal autonomy. Even the chief executive (governor) of the "Taiwan province" has been handpicked by Chiang Kai-shek, not elected by the people of Formosa. The functions and jurisdictions of the central govern-ment and of the provincial government of Taiwan are largely overlapping. This has not only led to confusion, waste, and in-efficiency; it has sharply curtailed the role of Taiwan's government.

As far as the judiciary is concerned, it cannot liberate itself from the KMT, regardless of elegantly written constitutional pro-visions for judicial independence. Together with the secret police and the KMT, the judiciary has often been condemned as one of the three biggest public enemies in Formosa today. The people generally do not expect the court to vindicate justice; they wish only to be let alone and therefore immune from the "administra-tion of injustice."

These are consequences of the extraordinary circumstances in which the constitutive process of the Republic of China operates in Formosa. Formosa's experience cannot of course serve as a sound and sufficient basis for judging its viability were it applied to the mainland. As the constitutional charter of 1947 operates in a set-ting totally different from the one originally envisaged, definitive judgments grounded solely on analysis of the practices of the rulers of Formosa are unjustified. Nevertheless it may be relevant and useful to comment in theoretical terms on the constitutive prescriptions considered as a whole.

The basic pattern for the allocation of authority and control, as provided by the present constitution of the Republic of China, is supposedly based on Dr. Sun Yat-sen's political theory of a "five-power constitution." This theory is acclaimed by his followers as a crystallization of wise and selective incorporation of Western political wisdom, Chinese tradition, and Dr. Sun's innovation. The five-power constitution is alleged to be an improvement of Montesquieu's theory of separation of powers. In comparing the major political systems of the West with the traditional Chinese system under centuries of dynastic rule, Dr. Sun observed that long before the invention of Montesquieu's theory China had had a well-established constitutional practice of separating three powers. Unlike the trichotomy of legislative, executive, and judicial authority, the Chinese version was said to be: powers of the Emperor (including legislative, executive, and judicial powers), power of examination, and power of impeachment (or censorial power). Dr. Sun asserted that fusing two powers peculiar to China (examination and impeachment) with the three powers of the Western world would cure the evils frequently seen in the representative governments of the West, notably the "spoils system" and "partisan politics." Hence his grand design was to break down the traditional imperial authority into three independent branches of government—legislative, executive, judicial; to slice out of the legislative the authority of impeachment and censorship; and to take away from the executive the authority of examining for civil service. On an equal footing, these are the five powers—execution, legislation, adjudication, examination, and control.

Another of Dr. Sun's innovations was a fine distinction between the "political power" (Cheng Chuan) of the people and the "functional authority" (Chih Chuan) of the government delegated by the people. Viewing the operation of a constitution as a gigantic machine, he compared the former to a generator and the latter to a machine. His aim was "to give the people that kind of machine they can drive at will." A favorite analogy of Dr. Sun's to illustrate this division was the relation between master (the people) and chauffeur (the government). He said that the chauffeur must be carefully chosen from those who were competent, but it was the master (the backseat driver) who was to decide where to go.[2]

Dr. Sun's five-power constitutional theory found concrete expression in the constitution of 1947.[3] According to its stipulations, the "political power" (Cheng Chuan) is vested in the National Assembly composed of delegates directly elected by the people (one delegate from each county or municipality), and the "functional authority" (Chih Chuan) is shared by the President and five branches of the government—the Executive Yuan, the Legislative Yuan, the Judicial Yuan, the Examination Yuan, and the Control Yuan.

The authoritative competence of the National Assembly is as follows: to elect the President and Vice President; to recall the President and Vice President; to amend the constitution; to vote on proposed constitutional amendments submitted by the Legislative Yuan by way of referendum; and to exercise the authority of "initiative" and "referendum" concerning general legislation on behalf of the people when more than one half of the counties (Hsiens) and municipalities of the entire nation have exercised the said authority in their local communities. (At a special session in February 1966 the National Assembly voted to exempt itself from this limitation. Without waiting for the recovery of at least one half of the territory in the mainland, they can now exercise the authority of initiative and referendum regarding general legislation during the period of so-called "Communist rebellion."[4]) Except for special meetings, delegates meet *once every six years,* on the eve of the presidential election.

The President is declared the head and commander-in-chief of the state. The Executive Yuan is stipulated as "the highest administrative organ," the Legislative Yuan "the highest legislative organ," the Judicial Yuan "the highest judicial organ," the Examination Yuan "the highest examination organ," and the Control Yuan "the highest control organ" of the state. In order to settle disputes that may involve more than two Yuans, the President is entrusted to act as arbiter.

The problem immediately arises as to who is the real chief executive of the state, the President or the President of the Executive Yuan (commonly called the "Premier"). While the President is elected by the National Assembly, the Premier is appointed by the President with the consent of the Legislative Yuan. The Vice President of the Executive Yuan and all ministers, with or without portfolio, are appointed by the President upon the recommendation of the Premier. The President is authorized to promulgate laws and issue ordinances, but these must be countersigned by the Premier or by both the Premier and the ministers or chairman of the commissions concerned. During the recess of the Legislative Yuan, the President may issue emergency orders and undertake necessary measures under certain conditions, subject to the requirement that they must accord with resolutions of the Executive Yuan Council. Being elected by the National Assembly, the President is presumably responsible to it. The Premier, Vice Premier and all ministers of the Executive Yuan, though appointed by the President, are responsible to the Legislative Yuan. As long as Chiang Kai-shek is the President, there is no mistake as to who is the boss. (Incidentally, all credit goes to Chiang, and blame is passed on to the Premier and his cabinet.) Given a lesser figure as President, the story may be quite different. It is both obvious and dangerous that the constitution is fundamentally unclear about the location of executive responsibility.

The relationship between the Executive Yuan and the Legislative Yuan is outlined in Article 57. The Executive Yuan is responsible to the Legislative Yuan in three major ways: It is obligated to make policy reports to the Legislative Yuan, and the members of the Legislative Yuan are entitled to interrogate the

Premier and his cabinet members. The Legislative Yuan may, by resolution, request the Executive Yuan to alter an important policy. In that case, the Executive Yuan may, with presidential approval, ask the Legislative Yuan for reconsideration. Should the Legislative Yuan reaffirm the original resolution by a two-thirds majority the Premier shall either comply with the resolution or resign from office. With respect to a resolution on a statute, the budget, or a treaty, the Executive Yuan may, with presidential approval, request the Legislative Yuan for reconsideration. Should the Legislative Yuan uphold its original act, the Premier shall either abide by the resolution or resign from office. Also, while the Premier is appointed by the President with the consent of the Legislative Yuan, no member of the Legislative Yuan may hold concurrent office in other branches of the government.

From the preceding summary it appears that the pattern of allocating authority between the executive and the legislative, as provided by the Chinese constitution, is in a way unique: some features resemble the parliamentary system, while others are similar to the presidential plan of government. The appointment by the President of the Premier is contingent upon the consent of the Legislative Yuan. The President promulgates laws and issues Executive orders that are countersigned by the Premier and occasionally by the relevant ministers as well, as a matter of joint responsibility. The Executive Yuan is responsible to the Legislative Yuan. By a two-thirds majority, the Legislative Yuan can compel the Premier to effect an important policy change or to accept certain legislation that is opposed by both the President and the Premier. These are among the devices borrowed from the parliamentary system of government.

The presidential system is the obvious model for some other features of the Chinese constitution. With presidential approval, the Executive Yuan may send a statute back to the Legislative Yuan for reconsideration. Members of the Legislative Yuan are barred from concurrently holding executive posts. The Legislative

Yuan cannot compel the resignation of the Premier and his cabinet by a vote of nonconfidence, nor is the Executive Yuan empowered to dissolve the Legislative Yuan.

These arrangements are often said to have fused the merits of the presidential and parliamentary forms of government into a new system. The fact of the matter is otherwise. The partial and piecemeal incorporation of patterns from both have missed the essence of either system. It is elementary political wisdom that the effective operation of authority must be coupled with responsibility. In the parliamentary system, the central concern is to insure close collaboration between the legislative and the executive, leaving the ultimate source of authority in the parliament. In the presidential system, the distinctive emphasis is on checks and balances, although it is perfectly clear that both the executive and the legislative branches derive their authority directly from the people. Many institutional devices are invented for this purpose. By incorporating checks and balances into a system whose principal emphasis is on collaboration, the Chinese system creates no little confusion and complication. It achieves neither "checks and balances" nor "close collaboration." We have pointed out earlier how elusive is the task of identifying the actual chief executive. Because of this ambiguity, the position of the Premier (the President of the Executive Yuan) is extremely awkward. While the Premier is appointed by the President with the consent of the Legislative Yuan, can he be removed by the President without the consent of the Legislative Yuan? (Unlike the consent of the U.S. Senate for cabinet members, the consent of the Legislative Yuan seems to imply responsibility on the parliamentary model.) In the event that the Legislative Yuan compels the Premier to effect an important policy change or to accept a piece of legislation by a two-thirds majority, the Premier can hold onto his office, even though the Legislature has clearly demonstrated its nonconfidence in him. Under such circumstances, what meaningful relationship can be maintained between the executive and the legislative?

The Control Yuan is said to be a unique Chinese political institution, originally known as the Yu Shih. A Yu Shih was charged with the responsibility to investigate corruption and to maintain law and discipline in government. As "the highest control organ of the state," it exercises "the powers of consent, impeachment, censure, and auditing." The Control Yuan's competence to consent is confined to presidential nominations of the President and Vice President of the Judicial Yuan and of the Examination Yuan, the "Grand Justices" of the Judicial Yuan and members of the Examination Yuan. This function is obviously similar to the consent of the U.S. Senate to presidential nominations. To supervise government administration, the Control Yuan is endowed with comprehensive investigative authority. Its supervisory functions range from personnel to administrative measures and to public expenditures. The Control Yuan may censure (without prior investigation) or impeach (after investigation) a particular government employee who was found guilty of a violation of law or dereliction of duty. It may even initiate impeachment proceedings against the President and Vice President, the ultimate decision to be made by the National Assembly. When the administrative measures of the Executive Yuan are found inappropriate, the Control Yuan may urge correction and revision. Although the annual appropriation is made by the Legislative Yuan, actual spending is subject to the Control Yuan's auditing process. Even this brief description indicates that some of its competence parallels the sphere of the U.S. Senate, some the House of Representatives, while the remaining authority pertains to administration. The Control Yuan, whose members are elected on the basis of each province (or its equivalent), is sometimes called the Chinese senate. This is extremely misleading, for it has no share at all in the legislative function.

The Control Yuan seems to exercise a sniping function at the expense of the other branches of government without itself being responsible for clarifying and promoting public policy; nor is the

Control Yuan collectively responsible for its participation in administrative arrangements. It does not present the electorate with a comprehensive appraisal of the degree to which the government has given effect to public policy. If it did so, some means would be required to hold it accountable for partisan or special interest assertions. On the whole it must be concluded that the designers of the Control Yuan failed to distinguish between the functions of invocation and application and of appraisal. Hence responsibility has been dispersed with no corresponding gain.

The Examination Yuan is another unique Chinese institution. As "the highest examination organ of the state," it is in charge of matters pertinent to "examination, employment, registration, service rating, scale of salaries, promotion and transfer, security of tenure, commendation, pecuniary aid in case of death, retirement, and old age pension" for public functionaries. The recruitment for civil service is said to be based on a long tradition of "open competitive examination," designed primarily to prevent the executive from appointing unqualified persons. While the objective is commendable, it tends to create a gap between the examination process and the actual needs of the executive: what the Examination Yuan considers as qualified, established by written tests (with minor exceptions), does not necessarily meet the needs of the executive. Furthermore, by partially depriving the executive branch of authority to promote or transfer, the Examination Yuan has had a disruptive effect on administrative efficiency.

It is also worth noting that while the Nationalist regime boasts that "the open competitive examination" is a time-honored tradition of the Chinese society, it has not measured up to this tradition in Formosa. According to the official report of the Examination Yuan, of a total of 220,000 civil servants in Formosa today only 17.3 per cent are recruited by competitive examination, whereas in Great Britain and the United States the percentages are 85 and 80 respectively.[5]

Under the Chinese monarchy the emperor wielded ultimate

authority of legislation, execution, and adjudication. Hence an "independent" organ specialized to examination or impeachment was primarily designed to mitigate the hardships of despotism and to reduce the abuses of bureaucracy. The ministers were appointed by and responsible to the emperor; they did not stand on an equal footing with the emperor, nor were they free to act as a "check and balance" against imperial authority. From dynasty to dynasty, the emperor, endowed with ultimate and absolute authority, was responsible only to "the Heaven," not to the people. In the absence of public opinion implemented through the press, political parties, and pluralistic associations, the traditional limitation on arbitrary government was to complicate the administrative system, especially at the level of personnel administration and supervision.

In working out the pattern of allocation of authority and control, the founding fathers of the Chinese republican constitution seem to have been unaware of the implications of the popular form of government which they alleged they were introducing. The principal task, as we now see it, is to establish a decision process that can act effectively while remaining responsible to the people. A republican form of government must generate a political class that is selected by the competitive processes of elections and debate. The politicians must take the principal burden of mediating between the huge electorates of a large-scale state and the agencies of official action. If the level of corruption rises, a political means must be available to "kick the rascals out." Standards of efficiency and honesty may rise as the body politic comes to accept the wisdom of higher qualification and greater personal integrity. The experience of the Chinese republic suggests that it is a mistake to use the administrative devices appropriate to a monarchy as a substitute for focusing responsibility squarely on the shoulders of elected officials whose offices are authorized to exercise great power. The role of politicians was confused with that of administrators to such an extent that "examinations" were also relied on to determine the qualification of candidates running for some elective offices. Lifting agencies of examination and control to an equal footing with the other three powers—legislative, executive, and judicial—seems to contradict the basic principles of effectiveness and responsibility required by modern governments.

As far as the judiciary is concerned, there has been no discernible tradition of judicial independence in Chinese history. Nevertheless as "the highest judicial organ of the state" the Judicial Yuan was given jurisdiction over the council of grand justices for the interpretation of the constitution, statutes, and orders; the supreme court for dealing with civil and criminal cases; the administrative court for adjudicating administrative suits; and the committee on the discipline of public functionaries for handling disciplinary matters referred to it by either competent administrative authorities or the Control Yuan. The interpretation of the constitution is done on an abstract basis, rather than in the thick of "controversies or cases." In the process of litigation, attorneys seldom argue their case by challenging the constitutionality of a particular statute or order. Judicial independence, though a resounding goal, is adversely affected by various institutional arrangements. The present judicial system has three levels: district courts, high courts, and the supreme court. While the supreme court is under the Judicial Yuan, the appointment, promotion, and transfer of judges of both district and high courts are under the jurisdiction of the ministry of justice of the Executive Yuan. Being highly involved in politics, the ministry of justice tends to show little restraint in exerting political influence upon the judges under its supervision. (As far as criminal prosecution and execution is concerned, procurators at all levels—district, high, supreme—are under the command of the ministry of justice.)

In his eminent treatise translated as "The Constitution of the Republic of China," Yin-Chou Shieh, Vice President of the Judicial Yuan (former Chief Justice of the Supreme Court), sums up the present system as a "hodgepodge" and a "total confusion," since it is constituted of forms taken out of context, and unfused to the requirements of a viable system.[6]

It is not our intention to adopt a purely negative attitude toward the institutions now prevailing, or partially established, in Formosa. Nor do we regard it useful to adopt a passive view of the problems facing the new order. Our immediate concern is the question of Formosa's future, and this cannot be satisfactorily dealt with unless we are convinced that the nation can achieve a decision process adequate to the challenges of independence. We shall therefore move back and forth between the general principles of popular government and the potentialities of the Formosan people in the circumstances in which they are likely to find themselves.

In an age of continuing crisis and heavy government involvement, a nation state cannot operate effectively at home or abroad unless it can institute and maintain a decision process that can mobilize the whole body politic. The redesigners of the organs of government will find it necessary to give consideration to the system as a whole, including the various functions that must be performed in different degree by every structure. Some institutions will serve as a focus for particular tasks—prescription, for example —but no organ can be viable that does not provide for an internal process in which every function appropriate to decision is articulated with all the others. Hence, although it will not be practicable for us to deal in detail with every major structure, it is important to keep the total problem in mind for future reflection.

The principal choice to be made in designing a popularly governed body politic is the role of the chief executive in relation to the nation as a whole and to the organs that mediate between the two. The present ambiguity of the chief executive is not tolerable in a responsible system of popular rule. The constitution has survived only by betraying its ostensible devotion to the rule of the people, and operating as something else—"a one-party oligarchy," "a despotic garrison-police state," "a one-man tyranny." These phrases specify particular features of an obvious deviation from an authoritative and controlling democratic system.

Formosa will need a chief executive who can act decisively; hence it is probable that the presidential form of government is best adapted to the exigencies of the situation. The uncertainty as to the location of top executive authority must be settled. Equally evident is that decision implies responsibility. In some contexts the parliamentary system seems particularly fitting, as in Great Britain, where the complex expectations on which the system is based have slowly evolved. In Great Britain the monarchy is the ceremonial executive, providing at once a unifying symbol and a convenient instrument for managing transitions between the holders of effective control. As developed in the United States the president is both the chief of state and the wielder of executive power. The presidency is directly linked to the electorate, and it is taken for granted that he is the leader of one of two or more freely competing political parties. Many of these connotations are understood in Formosa, even though Chiang Kai-shek has operated a one-party monopoly and the presidential office is poorly designed to combine strength with responsibility.

Instead of having a Legislative Yuan, a Control Yuan, and a National Assembly all claiming to be the Congress, we propose a one-house Congress. In a unitary state with no special historical tradition, the existence of two houses only complicates the legislative process. It might be suggested that the two-house system is ideal for Formosa immediately after its independence; if the lower house were based on popular representation, the upper house could be elected exclusively from among the present members of the Legislative Yuan, the Control Yuan, and the delegates to the National Assembly. Such an arrangement would be congenial to the privileged political class of the present state and aid in accommodating them to the new order. The suggested upper house would unquestionably contribute political experience; it would also represent a minority, the remaining two million mainland Chinese. While there is considerable merit in this proposal, it would have many negative consequences. An independent Formosa will need to chart a new course. By allowing the hard core of the Nationalist elite to continue to occupy a privileged position in the Congress, the upper chamber proposal would tend to perpetuate an obsolescent ideology. It might well become the rallying point of a "second revolution." So far as wisdom and experience are concerned, the more able and flexible members of the older elite can find opportunities to contribute in other channels.

While the functions and responsibility of the executive and the legislative are reasonably distinct, problems arise in coordinating the President and the Congress. The presidential system has a built-in danger: stalemates may occur between the executive and the legislature. In the history of the United States, this danger, though by no means insignificant, has not led to serious consequences, primarily because of the strength of the political and civic culture of American society. Formosa can benefit from a comparative knowledge of the working of the presidential system in successful and unsuccessful cases, and adopt institutional practices that promise to mitigate unproductive conflict and contribute to a sound political culture. Aside from the usual coordination devices, such as submission of bills and budgets by the executive, legislative consultation and inquiry, it is desirable that the sphere of joint action between the President and Congress should be reasonably broad, particularly in key appointments. The simultaneous election of the President and congressmen is also conducive to a more harmonious working relationship between the two branches. In this connection, a term of four years seems reasonable for both the President and congressmen. A referendum can be a means of resolving stalemates between the President and Congress in a land of Formosa's size and standard of literacy. The President further needs to have authoritative competence to decree a state of emergency to cope with crises without being paralyzed by prolonged debates in the legislature.

It is convenient to consider the other organs of government besides the legislature that stand between the chief executive and the electorate, or occupy an approximately coordinate position with the President and the Congress, before we examine the electorate itself. One way to introduce the other possible structures is to analyze in more detail the role of the chief executive as a participant, and sometimes the principal participant, in all seven of the decision functions that we distinguish.

To start with the *intelligence* or *planning* function. This is concerned with the clarification of the goals of the body politic, and with the evaluation of policy alternatives in the light of probable future developments, and of historical trends and scientifically ascertainable conditioning factors. The chief executive has ready access to the focus of attention of the entire community. As a means of emphasizing his influence on the intelligence process, the written constitution of Formosa will do well to make explicit the President's obligation to appear on regular occasions, such as the opening of a legislative year, to deliver a "State of the Nation" message outlining national goals and alternatives. Such a message will not be exclusively devoted to the intelligence function, but it is important to mention this part of the operation explicitly, since it directs attention to the common objectives of national life and to the shared uncertainties of estimating the future.

Part of the chief executive functions are *promotional*, obligating him to give active endorsement and support to issues and men. His task is complicated by the multiple identities in whose name he is entitled to speak, and whose interests he is expected to support. At one level the President is the leader of the nation as a whole, particularly in the external arena; at another level he is the leader of a party or coalition of parties who are attempting to persuade the electorate to back them up. As a recommender of legislation the promotional function of the chief executive is fully evident.

We have covered the prescribing function by emphasizing the veto power of the presidency on matters of legislation. It is obvious that the chief executive must be authorized to play a very large part in the *invocation* function, since this refers to the first steps of law enforcement or the initiation of official action in concrete circumstances. The same point is relevant to the later or final phases of *application*.

The chief executive must have a recognized part to play in the *appraising* function, which strives to assess the degree to which policy objectives have been reached by official action, and to locate responsibility for success and failure. If anything is an obvious necessity in democratic government, it is that no monopoly can be tolerated in the appraisal function, and that every participant has a double role, since he appraises his own performance and that of others. The final appraisal rests with the electorate; so too does the authority to act on the basis of appraisal and to hold elected officials responsible for what happened, either by continuing them in office, or turning them out. It is necessary to proceed on a doctrine of collective responsibility if the electorate is to find a practicable way of making its judgments of responsibility effective. Hence whoever has power must also have a degree of responsibility commensurate with the scope, range, and domain of his power. The chief executive must be able to appraise his aggregate success and failure, and also locate specific officials subject to his direction who have contributed to the result. The identifying of particular participants is part of the application function; so, too, are measures taken to administer sanctions (positive or negative) to them. The "State of the Nation" message is an occasion on which the chief executive reaches the ear of the electorate: and the constitution can help to make explicit his obligation to deal with success or failure in achieving national goals and prescribed policies, including an assessment of the executive's own role in the result. We know that sweeping appraisal statements occur in the usual characteristic rhetoric of politics. We take it for granted that officials will claim credit for successes and attempt to shift responsibility for failure. The important point is that this rhetorical form expresses the fundamental judgmental problem in the political process, and that it is to be taken with full seriousness.

The chief executive, finally, must participate in the *terminating* function. It should be clear that one of his obligations is to propose that obsolete prescriptions be ended and that just compensation be given to those who have built up legitimate expectations of advantage under the old prescriptions. In this connection we allude once more to the changed position that mainland Chinese will occupy in the new Formosa, and the importance of statesman-like leadership in the termination of their privileges.

The foregoing recapitulation of the presidential role in all seven decision functions underlines the enormous importance of this office. No argument is needed to justify the statement that the President must be empowered to obtain and use ample man-power and facilities to assist in carrying his burden. At the same time reflection suggests that the new Formosa, in common with popularly governed states anywhere, must avoid putting so many assets under the control of the President that he comes to exercise monopoly power and overrides the freedom of the electorate to make a genuine choice. In recent history a complex structure of government was exploited for antidemocracy. Under changed cir-cumstances the unambiguous responsibility of the President and the Congress must be clear. This does not, however, imply that complicated arrangements are not necessary if the new Formosa is to achieve its high potential.

In regard to some decision functions, notably intelligence, For-mosan constitution-makers would have an unusual opportunity to arrive at solutions that take advantage of the rapidly accumulating experience of modern governments. An outstanding trend has been the emergence of planning, of systematic and comprehensive ex-amination of the potential impact of government on society and of society on government. In some states the planning function is crippled by too close association with other functions, notably prescription and application. Estimations of the future, and cre-ative inquiry into objectives and strategies, need some exemption from total immediate commitment to action programs. At the same time the intelligence function must be closely linked with those who make immediate as well as long range commitments. We therefore conclude that the intelligence function requires a high degree of independence from the President or the Congress, while performing tasks that tie them to the flow of decision. We think that organs of intelligence are needed whose position is coordinate with the principal branches of government as conceived under the five-power constitution, shorn of the damaging uncertainties about responsibility. We propose to link intelligence and appraisal in the same structures.

For the effective performance of intelligence and appraisal functions, we suggest the creation of independent institutions, including tentatively a council of national security, council of governmental organization, council of economic development, council of science, education and culture, and council of health and welfare. These ought to be composed of well-rounded experts of high caliber in their respective spheres, and to be independent of presidential as well as of congressional direction. The initial appointment of key positions on these councils would be made by joint action of the President and Congress (the consent of Congress signifying more than courtesy, as in the case of most cabinet appointments). The terms of key officers must be long enough to assure their independent exercise of authority—say, nine years— with removal only in extraordinary cases. In this way the pressures of immediate partisanship would be reduced. But the councils would presently reflect any stable shift in direction on the part of the electorate.

While the executive does not dispense altogether with the functions of intelligence and appraisal within its own framework of decision, administrative departments are swamped by day-to-day duties. Each department tends to project its horizon narrowly from the perspective of its immediate worries. Innovation is largely inhibited by a cynical, short-range sense of "realism." As a defensive mechanism against encroachments by others, each department is reluctant to concern itself with affairs of other departments. Hence it is difficult if not impossible to achieve long-term and integrated planning on an interdepartmental basis. Even if a staff planning agency is established whose members are freed from the departmental ladder, the defensiveness of the presidency in relation to the Congress manifests its pervasive influence.

Absolved from bureaucratic routine, the proposed councils will be able to look beyond currently exciting events to consider the future in a longer perspective. Their obligation, as prescribed in the new charter, would include regular reports to the President, the Congress, and the nation at large on national goals, proposed national plans in their separate fields, and summaries of success or failures to date, together with an appraisal of the effect of factors external or internal to government. Statements of national goal are likely to be sufficiently general to carry most Formosans with them. Proposed plans, on the other hand, involve cost and benefit estimates that may influence the allocation of resources among national and subnational governments and among the several components of government. Hence the councils must have unquestioned access to information in order to make independent yet well-grounded proposals, and to avoid multiplication of staff.

The appraisal of success and failure to date is the hottest political obligation of the councils. Whatever can be taken as endorsement will be repeated in the Congress, in party campaigns and in the press. Similarly, any statement that can be interpreted as an adverse comment on the office-holders will be seized on by their opponents. Hence the councils are bound to be involved in political controversy; and this is essential if they are to be a serious factor in the decision process. By injecting a more long-range and multi-partisan, if not nonpartisan, view into political life, the councils can contribute to the rationality and realism of collective judgment. Since they are not authorized to prescribe particular programs, or to initiate the prosecution or impeachment of specific officials, their reports give prominence to aggregate goals and strategies.

It will be essential to the successful operation of the councils that they win public confidence in their capability and integrity of purpose; and this will depend on the caliber of the first councils. In every sector of society with which a council will be concerned, modern research and training provides a substantial body of knowledge, with particular emphasis on data-gathering and processing methods. This is most obvious, perhaps, in the fields of economic development, education, and public health. The councils will need to keep close contact with the universities at home and abroad, and to be sensitive to the hopes and needs of all components of Formosan society.

The intelligence and appraisal functions can begin in an unofficial status long before independence. Now is the time for persons dedicated to the cause of Formosa's self-determination to begin, particularly for Formosans abroad. The process can take the form of a series of decision seminars. A concentrated and continuing effort can crystallize common demands and expectations having to do with nation-building into concrete programs for the future. The experience of collective participation in working out common programs would also contribute to the sophistication and the leadership ability of the potential elites of Formosa.

The intelligence function in a truly democratic body politic must be shared between government and private individuals and organizations. Although the source of information, official or unofficial, is justified in withholding specific messages for various periods of time, and may also spread the messages in limited circles for similar periods, a presumption exists in favor of public access to knowledge and to estimates of the future.

Limited space constrains us to omit comment on agencies of government that deal primarily with functions other than intelligence, appraisal, and prescription. One agency is too important, however, not to emphasize its independence of presidential or congressional pressure. The reference is to the judiciary. Judicial organs are principally devoted to invocation and application. They differ from other agencies concerned with these functions in that they focus on controversies about the exercise of power, or controversies among private parties arising from alleged deviation from the standards established in the prescriptive codes of the system of public order. Controversies over power are constitutional (*constitutive*) questions. Litigation between parties over contractual agreements or over alleged wrongs involves the supervisory role of government, since the government is not authorized to step in unless an initiative is taken by a party to the dispute. The comprehensive code also includes controversies that arise in connection with government *regulation* of the limits within which the social process can flow. If the prescription is to preserve a competitive as against a monopolistic market, for example, the action may be initiated by a public prosecutor to dissolve a monopolistic combine. Controversies are also generated between those who operate government *enterprises*, like the post office, and other parties. Every prescription involves sanction; but some sanctions are not able to modify conduct because the individual or group involved cannot be influenced by ordinary measures. Hence many modern codes provide *corrective* means of coping with deviation that results from incapacity or lack of opportunity, for instance.

For the administration of all codes the body politic must rely on the judiciary. It is to be taken for granted that judicial independence is indispensable to justice in a community committed to the goal values of human dignity. No nation can achieve justice when its judiciary is perceived by the public as "one of the three biggest public enemies." The makers of the government structure in Formosa will have an opportunity to contribute to the formation of a genuinely independent judiciary. At the apex of the judicial system would stand a constitutional court, charged with the interpretation of the constitution in general and the protection of fundamental human rights in particular. Besides the constitutional court provision must be made for tribunals authorized to deal with broad areas of controversy where some degree of specialization will expedite the disposition of cases and the probability of informed justice. Hence it is reasonable *to provide for civil and criminal courts, finance courts, and administrative courts.*

The present system of West Germany suggests the composition of the judiciary. For instance, in regard to the constitutional court, former judges of the Supreme Court may have permanent tenure, while other justices may serve nine-year terms. Tax enforcement is a complex and expanding sector where special courts are needed. Administrative courts are appropriate for administrative issues involving government employees. But matters of bureaucratic discipline ought in the first instance to be handled within the framework of the administrative hierarchy, since administrative efficiency calls for a distinct line of authority.

If special interests are to be kept at a minimum the role of the ministry of justice and the executive cannot be adjudication. The ministry is properly authorized to *invoke* action by an arrest or by initiating a claim, and by conducting preliminary investigations. The adjudication of civil and criminal cases—from district, high to supreme court—comes within the sphere of the judiciary. In unusual instances, however, it is appropriate to authorize the chief executive to moderate the final application of severe sanctions by exercising the pardoning power.

If justice is to be done in the new Formosa the judges themselves must be deeply dedicated to the conception of the equality of all men before the law. It is obviously impossible to legislate professional convictions. Nonetheless the practices authorized by the constitutional charter and the goals of public order articulated in its clauses can have a permeating impact on attitudes. Ruling elites too often view the law as prescribed only for the common citizens, priding themselves on being above the law. This mentality of "the privileged class," popular as it is, is harmful to the consolidation of the rule of law. Despite their special "sacred mission" in the community, it must be acknowledged that as a group judges cherish predispositions not too far apart from ordinary bureaucrats. They are very susceptible to outside influencing by means of power or wealth. If the self-respect of judges is to be fostered their security of tenure should not be rendered ineffective by allowing tenure judges to be transferred from one post to another without their consent. Aside from a generous increase in salary, reforms in legal education and in judicial recruitment and training would be helpful in elevating the status of judges in the nation.

A note is needed to clarify the place of "examination" and "control" functions within the framework of the new constitutive order. Whereas the functions of planning and appraisal in regard to the civil service can be dealt with by the proposed council of government organization, matters pertinent to examination, recruitment, promotion, and assignment are properly left to the executive in the interest of administrative efficiency. There will be no need for an independent institution of "control" on equal footing with the executive, legislature, and judiciary. The function of auditing can be better performed by the legislature, because of its control over appropriations. So can the impeachment of high elected officers such as the President and Vice President—an action that will presumably be quite rare. Bureaucratic discipline comes within the domain of the executive. Issues of criminal responsibility should be handled through judicial institutions.

The foregoing has dealt almost entirely with the structures that mediate between the chief executive and the national electorate. Hence the emphasis has been on the horizontal allocation of authority. We have favored a separation of power among a small number of organs that specialize in different functions within the total decision process at the national level. The five-power model provides a precedent in Chinese and Formosan experience for this relatively "deconcentrated" pattern in preference to a highly "concentrated" or "pyramidal" form in which a hierarchy would spread downward from the chief executive. Not hierarchical subservience but approximately coordinate functioning is the objective of all systems in which the "separation of powers" is followed. We are advising the makers of the new constitutional structure of Formosa to adopt a different set of criteria for the detailed application of the principle. It is, however, an advantage to have had exposure to the theory, if not the practice, of deconcentrated power.

We do not ignore the subnational allocation of authority. To what extent would it be wise to centralize power in the hands of national organs, or to decentralize power at the level of more local units? Many considerations point to the conclusion that Formosa will need to continue a relatively centralized plan of government. Formosa's existing administrative districts—Hsien (county) and city—are designed for the convenience of national administration without any special reason of traditions, federalism, or localism. As the island is small and the network of transportation and communication is well developed, the pattern of demands and expectations exhibits striking uniformity: it is highly desirable that an effective centralized government be maintained. So long as a centralized government can be held responsive and responsible to the people, effective participation in the national power process is the key to decisions that meet the rising needs of the people.

Despite the trend toward uniformity of demand, however, many affairs are local and can most fruitfully be carried out in small units. Under Nationalist rule citizens' participation in the election process has been confined to local affairs, hence the people have a much firmer grasp of local affairs than of national affairs in which they have had no voice at all. The present level of local autonomy should be cherished and made even more effective in the future.

Wide and Equal Participation

WE HAVE focused on the chief executive and the other structures that perform specialized functions as agents of the community. We concern ourselves at this point with the degree of participation appropriate to the people themselves, acting principally as an electorate.

During the fifty years of Japanese rule, the Formosan people had very limited access to power shaping and sharing. Formosans' first taste of the general exercise of voting rights came in 1951 when the Nationalist government launched the program of "local self-government." Although the level of "national" decision-making is not involved, local elections provide an invaluable opportunity for citizens to participate in local affairs. At present an active share in local self-government is mainly at two levels: the provincial affairs of Taiwan; and county (Hsien) and municipal affairs.

First, participation in the decision-making process of their own "province" is presently confined to the election of members to the Provincial Assembly, whose resolutions are largely advisory. The governor of the "province of Taiwan" is appointed by President Chiang Kai-shek, not elected by the residents of Taiwan. In recent years practically all the governors of Taiwan have been Nationalist generals who enjoyed Chiang Kai-shek's confidence. (The incumbent governor, Hwang Chieh, was the former chief of Taiwan Garrison Headquarters, the principal secret police headquarters.)

Second, magistrates and mayors are elected, as are members of the county and city councils. County or municipal councils are advisory. Magistrates or mayors find it necessary to appoint a ranking KMT member as their "chief secretary." A chief secretary exerts effective control and is the liaison between the county (or city) and the ruling Kuomintang. This marginal degree of local self-government was further diminished when at the end of 1966 President Chiang decreed an immediate change in the formal status of the city of Taipei, whose present population is over one million. By this act, Taipei has been made a "special city" under the direct control and jurisdiction of the "central" government rather than the "provincial" government of Taiwan. Although the real motivations underlying this move are still a matter of speculation, it appears clear that this would serve at least two major purposes for the Nationalist regime. First, since the mayoralty is changed henceforth from an "elective" to an "appointive" office, hereinafter the mayor of the city will be closely identified with the party line of the ruling KMT. (Not unaware of this implication, Mayor Henry Kao—a non-KMT member elected in 1964 by popular vote and "appointed," before the expiration of his "elective" term by President Chiang, first mayor of this new "special city"— said: "Don't congratulate me yet. I have no fixed term of office. I may be fired tomorrow.") Second, since Taipei is the nerve center of Formosa's finance, commerce, and industry, this move would enable the Nationalist regime to exert a tighter financial control and enjoy a larger share of island revenues.

In addition to the sharply limited authority granted to local governments, the KMT's unfair election practices (its "security measures"), coercion, and a policy of divide-and-rule, have characterized local politics with factionalism, general apathy, mediocrity, and corruption. Notwithstanding the KMT's concentrated and systematic efforts to coerce voters into supporting its nominees, Formosans do not altogether capitulate under intimidation, particularly voters in metropolitan areas. Thus in the mayoral election of 1964, independent candidates were elected in three out of five cities (Taipei, Tainan, and Keelung) against the heavy odds of the KMT machine. It is not irrelevant to note that even this degree of participation in local government was never achieved by the Nationalists on the mainland.

Within the framework of an independent and democratic Formosa, not only would the present degree of citizens' participation be preserved; it would be greatly extended. The exercise of voting rights would no longer be confined to local governments, since popular government calls for participation in the election of the President and of congressmen. Probably the basic unit of local self-government in the future will be the existing administrative districts—16 counties, 5 cities (whose population ranges from

110,000 to 1,200,000) and 1 special district. The election of congressmen could be patterned on the existing practices of electing
members to the Taiwan provincial assembly.

"One man, one vote" is fundamental to the whole election
process. No matter how multiple the interests of the individual
voter, he is enabled to choose among them in the context of national, subnational, and transnational policy. Experience has shown
that popular government is fostered by direct and universal suf-
frage and the secret ballot.

The simplest and most satisfactory way to choose the President
would be to give a voice to all citizens aged twenty or over. It may
be suggested that the President ought to be elected indirectly—
continuing in effect the present system of electing delegates to the
National Assembly which in turn elects the President—presumably
on the grounds that the people are not quite ready to make a
sound choice. Such a position is not persuasive since Formosa is
substantially different even from the mainland China of 1947. In
1947 mainland China—a land of 500 million people spread over
a vast territory divided by many physical barriers—had an underdeveloped economy, widespread illiteracy, poor networks of communication and transportation, and a rudimentary level of civic
participation. There were tenable grounds for counseling against
direct, popular election of the President. In contrast, Formosa is
small, blessed with relatively high standards of living and literacy,
widely dispersed urban centers, highly developed networks of modern communication and transportation, and considerable experience in political participation. Indirect systems are not likely to
survive the growth of modern institutions of popular government
—notably competing political parties, pressure associations, and
channels of communication. This has been the story of the American republic, for example, which also provides a precedent for
well-instructed Formosans. The choices are likely to give currency
to public leaders who learn how to achieve and defend public
rather than special interests. Put the point in the crudest terms,

it is definitely more difficult to bribe thirteen million people than the delegates of an assembly. The principal consideration in favor of direct election is the enormous contribution it is bound to make to the political education of the nation. When people can see the bearing of their ballots on major national decisions, apathetic attitudes toward politics are drastically reduced. And this, in the final analysis, is the real strength of a workable democracy.

The makers of the new frame of government for Formosa will be able to draw on established practices when they devise the new pattern of congressional elections. They can profit from the arrangements for electing members to the Taiwan Provincial Assembly. It is reasonable to propose the following: (1) *Congressional districts should be based on the existing districts for the election of members to the Provincial Assembly*; as indicated before, sixteen counties, five cities and one special district. (2) *The total number of congressmen can be set as 130, about one representative for every 100,000 constituents, with a minimum of two for each county.* At present, the members of the Taiwan Provincial Assembly number 74, with one member representing about 150,000 constituents. A Congress with a membership of 130 is a workable legislative body, with enough members to staff several committees. (3) *The "multi-member constituency" system is preferable to the "single-member constituency" system.* At the ratio of one congressman for every 100,000 persons, each district would have two to twelve representatives. (4) *Each voter under the multi-member constituency system makes a single choice among candidates on a single list. He does not vote on any party list as such, although the party identifications of each candidate are marked.* (5) *Votes for one candidate are not transferable to others.* (6) *The winners are the candidates equal to the number of seats assigned to each district who obtain the most votes.* (7) *Special guarantees should be provided for women candidates and aborigines.* Under the present election laws, women candidates are granted a quota of 20 per cent in a district having more than four representatives.

(This special protection for women candidates is equally applied to some other elective offices.) The underlying policy is to foster women's active participation in a society where the disparity in the traditional position of men and women is only too apparent. Also, because of the special conditions confronting the aborigines (about 1.5 per cent of the total population), they have been given 3 out of 74 seats in the Provincial Assembly. These special protective measures, widely accepted by the Formosan people, should be continued.

We must give further consideration to the recommendation for a multi-membered district system. Political scientists generally recognize that popular government thrives best where the chief executive acts decisively and responsibly. This result is most often achieved where the two-party system is the dominant pattern of party rule; and this, in turn, is favored by the "single-member constituency" system. If the two-party system were our sole concern, we would be strongly inclined to recommend the single-member plan, notwithstanding the inherent difficulty of redistricting in order to avoid gerrymandering. But we feel obliged to take other policy considerations into account as well.

Uppermost is to design ways and means of insuring equal and effective participation by two million mainland Chinese in the congressional elections. It is not advisable to assure their representation by fixing a quota (a 2-to-13 ratio) by formally institutionalizing two separate groups—mainland Chinese as opposed to native Formosans—in the new constitutive order. Such an arrangement would perpetuate the existing cleavage and impede integrated development of the new nation. Under the circumstances some form of proportional representation seems to offer a sound alternative. The present system of electing provincial assemblymen (which is a form of proportional representation), upon which we base our proposed system of congressional elections, has been sustained by general community expectation and practice to date. Not only are Formosans accustomed to it, but they also find it simple and clear. The procedure has had no disruptive effects, such as factional rivalry among multiple parties (in large measure because of the predominant position of the KMT and its suppression of effective opposition parties). The prevailing system allows some representation of "independent candidates" who are not affiliated with one-party rule. A radical change from the existing system to the "single-member constituency" plan would not only have a disruptive impact on established perspectives and operations, but would be viewed with apprehension by mainland Chinese as a deliberately discriminatory measure aimed at curtailing their representation. Understandably they cannot feel secure under a constitutive order in which they are likely to be grossly underrepresented.

Although multi-member constituencies present some problems in the sphere of effective and responsible representation, when compared with single-member constituencies, several means can be used to moderate these difficulties. *A provision must be made to identify the party affiliation of each candidate.* In the immediate future, independent candidates may continue to be elected. In the long run, however, their role will be rendered negligible as a sound party system takes shape.

We strongly advise against any attempt to mix corporate or functional elements with the proportional system. Representatives of designated groups within a constituency are apt to be absorbed with the promotion of special interests. The obligation of a representative, however, is to find a way to integrate particular interests with the common interests of the community. This exacting task is handicapped when the candidate is labeled with a nonparty identification, since he is expected to be bound by group perspectives as they are conceived at the moment. If the candidate is less tied to a particular group he is better able to appeal to a coalition of interests, and to propose policies that may win gradual acceptance by elements at first opposed. A political party—conceived in fundamental terms—is a group that puts forward candidates in its own name and takes a position on major issues confronting the public as a whole. Some parties, it is true, fall far short of this definition in the sense that they tie themselves closely with a single interest which they seek to further above all others. The give and take of a completely competitive electoral process usually erodes such special parties for the benefit of more comprehensive programs.

It is essential to underline the importance in the new Formosa of taking precautions to insure the integrity of the electoral process at all levels. Years of experience under the KMT has created a highly distrustful attitude about the "impartiality" and "fairness" of the local elections. Fully aware of the KMT's obsession with total victory in every election, the voters often find themselves double-crossed, since the function of supervising the election process is in the partisan hands of KMT members. In the future, the impartiality of election at all phases has to be assured as a first significant step toward the restoration of public confidence in the meaning of their participation.

Guarantees of Civil Liberty

ANY CONSTITUTIVE process that deals seriously with establishing a public order whose goal is power shaping and sharing on a democratic basis will *provide effective guarantees of civil liberty, including unambiguous safeguards for the two million Chinese of mainland origin.*

The universal acceptance of the Declaration of Human Rights evinces a strong desire on the part of the articulate spokesmen for mankind to realize the goal of human dignity. Few nations declare themselves in favor of "human indignity" characterized by the supremacy of a self-perpetuating caste, even if the caste is in the majority. One important strategy for the consolidation of a regime that defends human and civil rights is to incorporate appropriately worded clauses into the constitution. The constitutional provisions emphasize general norms of content coupled with operational procedures. While there is frequently a discrepancy between words and deeds, the statements in the fundamental code serve as a focal point through time for crystallizing community expectations and demands.

A fundamental human right is to be a member of a nation state. For the overwhelming fraction of mankind this affiliation is automatic, resulting from birth and residence in a body politic that looks upon one as a member. Other situations, however, have stressed the opportunity to choose one's national identity. This occurs when the great majority of people in a territory proclaim their identity as a new nation state. This move almost invariably poses complications for those who are uncertain of their future in the new land. Formosa is no exception. In fact, the entire problem is confused by conflicting and unsettled claims put forward at the end of World War II. While in military occupation on behalf of the Allies after World War II, the Nationalist regime unilaterally proclaimed Formosa one of the 35 provinces of the "Republic of China" and declared all the native Formosans formerly under Japanese rule nationals of the Republic of China. Will all present-day nationals of the "Republic of China" with a permanent residence in Formosa (excluding overseas Chinese), automatically be granted the nationality of "the Republic of Formosa"?

It has been suggested by some advocates of Formosa's independence that this depends upon whether they are native Formosans or mainland Chinese. According to their view, all native Formosans will automatically become nationals of the new Formosan state, while mainland Chinese must be required to apply for "naturalization" on an individual basis, with freedom to leave Formosa if they choose. In that case, the new government would solicit international cooperation in accommodating these people to nations of their choice, including Communist China. By drawing a distinct line between native Formosans and mainland Chinese, this proposed policy would build in a barrier to a speedy and full integration of all the people in Formosa in the new order. If a newly independent Formosa were to wrestle with the problem of naturalizing two million people, it would practically exhaust all available administrative talent for this single task during the crucial period of transition.

Nationality is the very embodiment of one's identity and allegiance. In order to forge an integrated nation dedicated to the common goals of a free society, we propose that *all the Formosan people be automatically granted the nationality of the new Formosan state, but in deference to the individual's freedom of choice, everyone—native Formosan and mainland Chinese alike—is entitled to choose otherwise.* In the latter event, the new regime would cooperate to the fullest in facilitating the realization of the individual's aspirations. By "all the Formosan people," note that we include mainland Chinese as well as native Formosans permanently residing in Formosa. The new nation would be unwise to overlook the importance of taking special precautions to aid in forging a common collective identity. The present difference between mainland Chinese and native Formosans in their perspectives and "vested interests" should be realistically faced. Under the new order, as native Formosans assume overwhelming authority and control, the problem of guaranteeing equal protection to two million mainland Chinese will become a matter of grave concern. For no one can be sure that the new Formosan elite, given a free hand, would not act impulsively out of a shortsighted sense of grievance, seeking to retaliate against the deprivations imposed by the KMT in the past. Unless adequate measures are taken to insure effective and equal participation by mainland Chinese in the mainstream of political life they will not be able to identify fully with the new order. As a potential guardian, a hostile Communist China will not hesitate to seize every available excuse to intervene in Formosan politics. No clairvoyance is required on the part of native Formosans or mainland Chinese to understand that a divided Formosa is a peril to both.

As we have emphatically indicated, while the protection of minority rights is of utmost importance, it must not be allowed to paralyze the decision process. In a new nation, the capacity of the government to act with promptitude and effectiveness is absolutely necessary. The civil war in Cyprus after its independence is indeed a reminder. To protect the rights of the minority group—the Turkish community, about three-tenths of the population of Cyprus—very complicated and rigid provisions were embodied in the Cyprus constitution. The President is required to be a citizen of the Greek community, the Vice President of the Turkish community, elected by the Greek and Turkish communities respectively; and authoritative competence is distributed between them by explicit enumeration. The House of Representatives is constituted on a 7:3 ratio (35 Greeks and 15 Turks). And the amendment to certain constitutional provisions must be approved by a two-thirds majority of the representatives of *both communities* in the House. This means it is practically impossible to amend the constitution to meet the changing needs of the nation. The simultaneous existence of the Greek community and the Turkish community is formalized by the constitution, so that any one born to each community belongs henceforth to that community. A special constitutional court is established to deal with cases involving the fundamental rights of the people. The court consists of three judges, one from the Greek community, one from the Turkish community, the third is a "neutral" president. These complicated arrangements, reflecting a compromise settlement amid international crisis and pressure, bred government paralysis and general frustration from the beginning, and culminated in the bloody and tragic civil war shortly after the attainment of nationhood.

The lessons are vivid. Unlike Cyprus, the ratio between mainland Chinese and native Formosans is 2 to 11. Native Formosans and mainland Chinese are not grouped in two separate regions of

the island, but are mingled together and widely dispersed throughout the island. This makes it extremely difficult for Formosa to
adopt a "quota system" for elective offices according to the existing population ratio. Moreover, any measure that formally institu-
tionalizes the separate existence of two groups by drawing a line
between them tends to perpetuate a division that is vitally detrimental to integration and unity. There is no distinct difference
in appearance or in other physical features between native Formosans and mainland Chinese; whatever differences there are lie
in their perspectives. Under the Nationalists the gap has not been
narrowed because of the regime's peculiar mythology of mainland
recovery. While they have little illusion about mainland recovery,
the mainland Chinese, harassed by the KMT's intense internal
propaganda, have thus far found it hard to perceive themselves as
citizens of "Formosa." Once the basic goal is oriented toward
building Formosa as an independent member of the world community, however, the perspectives of all can be effectively reshaped
accordingly. The process would be deferred and endangered if two
groups—native Formosans and mainland Chinese—were perpetuated in the constitution. We have already proposed a series of
institutional arrangements for the purpose of protecting individual
and minority rights, such as the "multi-member constituency"
system, an adaptation of proportional representation, for congressional elections.

   If the significance of these innovations is to be fully comprehended and accepted by all concerned in the new public order of
Formosa, a comprehensive campaign of enlightenment is indispensable. Native Formosans must be alerted to the fact that
genuine integration and cooperation with mainland Chinese is a
matter of their enlightened self-interest, since nothing less is at
stake than the survival of Formosa as an independent state. At
the same time mainland Chinese can and are to be assured that
their skills and experience will be welcome in building the new
commonwealth and that their permanent identification with it is

greatly to be desired. Divided, little can be done; together, a viable and independent nation can be brought into the world arena.

The central problem of civil liberties goes much further than such special tasks as affording protection to a minority group. If a body politic cannot insure freedom for all, it will not succeed in providing protection to its minorities. By insuring fundamental liberties for all people—who are, after all, common victims of the totalitarian control of the KMT—the protection of human rights can become a living reality. The most important civil liberties are, of course, freedom from unauthorized custody, freedom of expression, freedom of assembly and association, freedom of religion, freedom from intrusion into privacy, and protection of property and of the rights of labor.

The problem in realizing fundamental civil rights in many of our communities is not the lack of elaborate constitutional provisions, but a wide discrepancy between constitutional prescriptions and effective practice. Ours is an epoch of continuing crises of national security. As the tensions that lead toward garrison-police states continue, national security becomes the prime concern of practically all bodies politic, including free societies.[7] In continuing crisis the role of the investigative services is bound to grow. The function of the political police is to gather information on the basis of which determinations can be made as to whether or not a person serves an established public order. A vitally necessary function in any continuing crisis of national security is carried on under conditions that readily lend themselves to the abuses described often and deplored. The procedures of political police the world over exhibit marked similarity, for the job is basically the same and proceeds under the cover of secrecy.

Contemporary Formosa provides an extreme example of a garrison-police state. Inheriting a long tradition of oriental despotism, the Nationalist ruling elites do not hesitate to rely on ruthless power and coercion. Despite an impressive inventory of civil liberties in the constitution, the perspectives of civil liberty are utterly alien to the KMT. To them, overwhelming predominance of power is the prime value; and hence respect for the individual is irrelevant. The political expediency of the ruling class is the only standard actually in use. To carry out its reign of terror in Formosa, the Nationalist regime has officially put the country in "a state of national emergency" (Communist rebellion) since 1949, with the resulting suspension of civil liberties under martial law. A complex and efficient network of secret police is operating —the Bureau of National Security (under the Ministry of Defense), the Taiwan Garrison Headquarters, and the Bureau of Investigation (under the Ministry of Justice) headed by Chiang Ching-kuo. It was recently estimated that in 1964 Chiang Ching-kuo had under his control about fifty thousand regular police agents, and that paid informants throughout Formosa might number as many as ten times that figure; together they constitute nearly 5 per cent of the population.[8] Under one pretext or another a civilian can easily be made subject to court-martial. Using the convenient cover of coping with Communist subversion, the secret political police operating in Formosa today are primarily concerned with eliminating elements considered dangerous simply because they espouse Formosa's independence. While Formosa's independence and separation from Communist China for the past 17 years is an obvious reality, any attempt to stabilize this state of affairs formally or to call attention to the situation is treated as sedition (see ch. 3).

Should Formosa become *legally* independent in the near future, she will find herself in a continuing crisis of national security, resulting largely from the intransigent hostility of Communist China. No doubt the political police will continue to be as indispensable to the new as to the present system of public order. The central challenge to the emerging elites, since they cannot do away with the political police altogether, will be *to maintain a proper balance between national security and individual freedom.*

We take for granted the point that maintaining national security is closely related to and integrated with the other value processes in the national context. While the function of the political police by its very nature requires secrecy, abuses can be reduced by dealing with the function candidly as part of the necessary activity of any government, popular or totalitarian. An open attitude can modify the sinister and mysterious atmosphere that generates fear and suspicion. The political police should be put under supreme civilian control and precautions taken to keep the operation in the hands of freedom-minded elites. A systematic and conscious program of recruitment and training is needed if the police are to commit themselves strongly to the goal values of a free society. Effort should also be made to elevate the police to a respectable role in the community, and to overcome the gap that often stigmatizes the police in the perspective of most civilians.

Civil liberties are most effective when the broad canons of freedom are explicitly joined with procedural practices. Hence the crucial importance of due process in executive and judicial administration. Not unmindful of the limitation of mechanical devices, we nevertheless consider it vital to build in procedural safeguards based on due process. They are clarifiers of who is responsible for doing what to whom how.

Finally, it is to be emphasized that an enlightened and responsive public holds the key to the realization of civil liberties on a large scale. The press—meaning all media of communication—bears a heavy responsibility in this regard. Its most subtle contribution is a sense of common identity by the coverage that it provides for events that reveal the thoughts and feelings of others. Most directly, of course, the media must call attention to encroachments on human rights and rally the forces of resistance. Newspapers, radio and television, supplementing the schools, are the principal expositors of the goal values of a free society.

Protection of Political Parties

IN THE OVERALL decision process, political parties are indispensable agencies to promote public policy. This role is particularly critical when a network of pluralistic associations is still in its infancy. Political parties are the institutions developed by large-scale modern democracies to channel individual and group demand into workable programs for community-wide action.

Under the colonial rule of Japan, while some Formosan elites formed organizations such as the Formosan Cultural Association, they were given no chance of organizing a political party in any functional sense.

Under the Nationalist rule, the Kuomintang has been dominant, monopolizing both formal authority and effective power. The Young China party and the China Democratic and Socialist party are in "token" existence only, serving the KMT's propaganda purpose of seeming to show that more than one party exists in Formosa. These parties occasionally rely on the KMT for financial assistance, and often for the mediation of their internal feuds.[9] Their nominal position is generally understood: in Formosa's local elections, "independent" candidates without a party identification have had a better chance of winning than the candidates put forward by these parties. The role of the Nationalists has in effect been a one-party (KMT) rule, and remains so today. And it is an open secret that the Kuomintang is substantially financed by the national treasury.[10]

As the founding party of the Republic of China in 1912, the Kuomintang has played a unique role in "tutoring" the people. With long experience in the ruthless power struggle in Chinese politics, the KMT is well seasoned in the tactics of totalitarian control. As a result of the purge or death of liberals such as K. C. Wu, Sun Li-jen, C. J. Yin, and Chen Cheng, the KMT is dominated by a hard core group that preaches "rule by naked power," and skillfully imitates the rule of terror and the organizational methods prevalent in Soviet Russia under Stalin and in Communist China today.

Although native Formosans are widely recruited into the KMT's apparatus at different levels, they have so far been denied effective access to key decision posts. The movement to form a constructive opposition party with primary orientation toward the goal of Formosa's development, based on the genuine cooperation of Formosan and mainland elites, was crushed in 1960 before it had achieved public expression. Had that movement been allowed to materialize, the proposed party (the Chinese Democratic Party) would have recruited Formosan elites into effective organization and political action, probably culminating in an overall reorientation of fundamental national policy (a gradual shift from offensive toward defensive purposes vis-à-vis mainland China) and a gradual erosion of the KMT's monopoly power. Indeed, it would have constituted a formidable rival to the KMT. This explains why the KMT seized that particular juncture to imprison Lei Chen, the principal organizer, under the charge of sedition, and why other prominent figures involved in the movement were disbanded by KMT's "carrot and stick" technique.

It seems appropriate that the KMT be legally dissolved, for it has long since become a reactionary element retarding the achievement of progress and the general welfare of the people.

There is a distinct possibility of a sudden and rapid multiplication of political parties, in revulsion against the KMT's one-party rule, once the people achieve genuine freedom of association and expression. The sudden growth of too many political parties may disrupt the very stability that is badly needed by a new nation during its initial period of transition. An effective means of curbing this probable development, it is widely assumed, is the "single-member constituency" system. In the preceding sections, however, we have proposed the "multi-member constituency" system instead, principally as a means of giving the two million mainland Chinese representation without adopting measures that block national integration. This being the case, two preventive measures are needed: an intensified campaign of civic education to bring home to everyone the close relation between party politics and the decision process as a whole; and a conscious effort to create a powerful party on behalf of Formosan independence that welcomes all who are willing to devote themselves to this goal.

There is an obvious danger involved in seeking to substitute, in effect, a Formosan National Party for the KMT. The chief advantage of the move is to provide a united goal, a unified leadership, and a disciplined organization when it is most necessary. Basic precautions can be taken to reduce the risks involved. In terms of membership, the party ought to be inclusive, embracing the main segments of the population—the different classes and professions—thus reflecting the entire spectrum of perspectives and interests in the body politic. It ought to enlist intellectuals who have engaged in the independence movement abroad, as well as leaders who are seasoned in practical experience at home under the trying conditions of KMT rule. It should not fail to enlist the services of former KMT personnel on a merit basis. If former KMT members—who incidentally will be in great numbers—are indiscriminately treated as "political outcasts" in the emerging power process, they will make desperate attempts, in one form or another, to regain lost ground. The sure way to prevent "disbanded" KMT elites from disrupting the new order is to grant them a proper place within the framework of the new power process. People join the KMT for a variety of motives. Opportunism is one; but frequently a decision to become a KMT member is out of a sheer necessity for survival. In terms of ideology, the party that leads the independence movement is most likely to gain popular support, with a balanced emphasis upon democracy, national independence, and a free economy tempered by government participation and by comprehensive welfare guarantees and programs. A less inclusive ideology will be unable to mobilize support for the task in hand.

As to the place of the Communist party in the new order, there must be an unambiguous solution. Whereas the new republic should endeavor to provide as much freedom as possible, the exercise of freedom must be kept within limits compatible with national development, particularly when stability is a vital need during the period of transition. At present, the Communist party is outlawed; any affiliation with a Communist party is an act of treason, subject to court martial and a maximum penalty of death. The basic national policy of opposing Communism in general and Chinese Communism in particular has become an article of faith. This expectation is widely shared and crystallized in Formosa today. Given the context, a decision to outlaw the Communist party in a new Formosa could scarcely be regarded as an undue imposition on freedom of expression and association. To consolidate the expectation of being anti-Communist will be a source of strength and stability for the new republic, rather than a sign of weakness. After all, one of the principal grounds for Formosa's search for independence is the determination to forestall Chinese Communist control. As Communist China is bound to intensify her threat to "liberate" Formosa even after Formosa's independence, outlawing the Communist party is indeed a matter of survival for the newly independent nation. Even if direct military action remains less than practicable in the near future—assuming that the United States continues to commit herself firmly to the defense of Formosa—Chinese Communists are likely to resort increasingly to the tactics of infiltration and subversion. Formosa's security depends, in the final analysis, upon its ability to cope effectively with this potential threat. The act of outlawing the Communist party is an indispensable measure for national security.

We cannot conclude our proposal regarding the constitutive process for Formosa without paying some attention to the problem of amending the constitution. As the future cannot be foreseen and the structure of expectations of the new body politic as a whole will be in constant flux, there is always need for amendment so as to permit constitutional growth. The Constitution, in Chief Justice Marshall's words, is "intended to endure for ages to come, and, consequently, to be adapted to the various crises in human affairs."[11]

Under the present system, a proposed constitutional amendment may be submitted by either the National Assembly or the Legislative Yuan. The competence of the Legislative Yuan is confined only to the submission of proposals; the ultimate authority to decide rests solely with the National Assembly. Article 174(1) of the 1947 Constitution requires an amendment to be decided by "three-fourths of the delegates present at a meeting having a quorum of two-thirds of the *entire* Assembly." Although the "quorum" of the National Assembly in Formosa remains dubious—as the present membership of the Assembly in Formosa falls short of "two-thirds of the entire Assembly"[12]—it has adopted several important amendments operative for the duration of the "Communist rebellion." Notable among these are votes: (1) to remove the procedural requirements of Articles 39 and 43 regarding the limits on the exercise of the presidential emergency power; (2) to suspend the application of the limitation clause (Article 47) which forbids anyone to be elected as President or Vice President for more than two terms; (3) to expand the presidential power by authorizing him to readjust administrative and personnel organs; (4) to authorize the President to arrange, where feasible, elections of members to central representative bodies to replace dead members and to take account of any population increase (not to be confused with general re-elections); and (5) to allow the National Assembly to exercise the authority of initiative and referendum in regard to national legislation by removing the restrictions of Article 27.

Although these provisions have no less authoritative effect than other provisions of the constitution, they are, it is asserted, not "constitutional amendments" as such, but "temporary provisions effective during the period of communist rebellion." The Nationalist regime goes on to allege that "the constitution of the Republic of China of 1947" is an important weapon to reestablish constitutional authority on the mainland, and hence has been kept wholly intact even while the government is confined to the limited domain of Formosa, engaged in the preparation of "the sacred mission." To make these provisions operative "during the period of Communist rebellion" is to perpetuate the monopoly and absurdity of Nationalists' power at the expense of the Formosans.

Since our proposed constitutional framework for Formosa provides no comparable place for the National Assembly, the amending practice used to the present time affords little guidance for the future. However, framers of the new Formosan constitution can benefit from knowledge of comparative constitutional theory and practice. In their endeavor to maintain a proper balance between stability and flexibility, they should see to it that the amending process is neither exploited by the native majority as an instrument of tyranny and discrimination, nor manipulated by the mainland minority as an instrument of obstruction and inaction.

As a matter of procedure, we propose that the President and members of the Congress (e.g., one-fifth of the total membership) be given the competence to initiate proposals for constitutional amendments, which are to be approved by the Congress by a two-thirds majority. The Congress shall then transmit proposed amendments to the county (city) councils for ratification; when ratified by more than three-fourths of the county (city) councils, amendments to the constitution shall become effective. An alternative method, we suggest, would be a popular referendum (by a decision of three-fourths majority of the national electorate). This is feasible in view of the compact size of the island, the high standard of general education, the development of communication and transportation, and the likelihood of active civic participation.

CHAPTER SEVEN

The Internal Decision Process: Selected Problems

Having dealt with the constitutional process, we shall now be concerned with other internal structures and functions of nation-building.

Economic Planning and Development

WHILE WE DO NOT subscribe to the idea that the problem of nation-building is simply a matter of economic development, we cannot overemphasize the key role played by economic development in the overall process. The rising expectations of the people, full of pride derived from newly acquired independence, can easily be translated into rising frustrations if a new regime fails to produce results in economic development at an early stage.

When Japan first took control, she undertook to create an economy in Formosa that was both dependent and complementary in nature. It was dependent in the sense that while in Japan proper a great effort was under way to achieve self-sustaining industrialization, the plan for the island of Formosa was to develop agriculture. In order to complement the needs of Japan proper, Formosa's economy was geared to produce items previously purchased from world markets for home consumption in Japan. Hence, while exporting sugar and rice to Japan in large quantity, Formosa imported manufactured goods such as textiles and fertilizers from Japan. Also, in order to mobilize Formosa's economic resources effectively, the Japanese government took monopoly control over the production and distribution of camphor, salt, opium, tobacco, and liquor. These government monopolies, except opium, were subsequently inherited by the Nationalist regime.

A serious effort was made to construct an extensive irrigation network, to introduce scientific methods, and to create farmers' associations. As the standard of literacy rose, the Formosan farmers became more receptive to technological change. As part of the program of agricultural development, industrial investment was initially centered on sugar refining. However, as World War II approached, the Japanese government began to hasten its efforts to industrialize Formosa with a view to meeting the empire's wartime needs. Besides establishing an efficient network of communication and transportation, the capacity for producing hydroelectric power was sharply increased, with the development of chemical, oil refining, and aluminum industries in mind. While Formosa's industrialization came into being less than voluntarily during Japanese rule, it nevertheless did provide a solid foundation for Formosa's economic growth under the Nationalist regime.

At the end of World War II, Formosa's economy was nearly in ruins from the extensive American bombing during the war. The wartime deterioration of physical equipment, however, was insignificant compared to the destruction and undermining of the economy soon after the war. As soon as Chen Yi, the governor general appointed by Chiang Kai-shek, occupied Formosa "on behalf of the Allied powers," he lost no time in converting all of the former Japanese enterprises into a network of government monopolies. According to conservative estimates, 90 per cent of all economic enterprises then in existence in Formosa were placed under exclusive government control.[1] While more than 20,000 Japanese technicians had gone back to Japan, practically all Formosan employees, regardless of their experience and ability, were replaced by "carpetbaggers" from mainland China who had had no experience in the management and operation of Formosa's enterprises. Business enterprises were either divested of all movable capital assets or compelled to close down because of incompetent and reckless management. Machinery and equipment were shipped to the mainland till 1949. Under the imposition of a compulsory licensing system, all private enterprises were subject to arbitrary exactions that virtually wiped out private enterprise in Formosa. The mainland "carpetbaggers" (or "new conquerors") were concerned with the quick accumulation of personal wealth, and cared little about the problems of Formosa's rehabilitation and reconstruction. Consequently, agricultural production declined precipitously and prices rose astronomically. A fatally disruptive inflation sent Formosa's economy back practically to the barter system.[2]

When the Nationalist regime retreated to Formosa, the island's role became vital. No longer was Formosa treated simply as a conquered territory but as a base from which to launch preparations for the recovery of the mainland, a base on whose stability and prosperity depended the survival and the future of the exile regime. For the first time there was serious concern on the part of Nationalist elites for Formosa's economic growth. While the "refuge" in Formosa was still viewed as "temporary," the ruling elites began to make genuine efforts to develop Formosa's economy to consolidate a base for survival, if not for the eventual recovery of the mainland.

The Korean war facilitated the task of reconstruction with the increase in U.S. aid. The normal operation of the hydroelectric power and transportation network was quickly restored. With the collaboration of the Joint Commission on Rural Reconstruction, the regime initiated a comprehensive land reform in 1949, reducing farm rent to 37.5 per cent of the crop yield, selling public lands, and initiating a land-to-the-tiller program.[3] As a result, by 1952 the national output was restored to the prewar level.

Having assured the basic stability of Formosa's economy, the regime launched a series of four-year economic plans in 1953. The first four-year plan (1953–56) gave balanced emphasis to the agricultural and industrial sectors. To enhance agricultural productivity, new farming techniques were introduced, the effective use of chemical fertilizers was stressed, and the irrigation network was improved. In industry high priority was given to the production of consumer goods for internal consumption, the expansion of hydroelectric power, transportation, and communication. The textile industry was sharply expanded. While balanced emphasis on agricultural and industrial sectors continued during the second plan (1957–60), special effort was made to diversify industrial production and promote export trade to meet the balance of payments. From 1953 to 1960 revenue fell far short of the outlay required by the plans; the deficit financing that was increasingly employed led to disruptive inflation. As a result, bank advances to the government more than tripled and the internal price level doubled; the depreciation of Formosa's currency was largely disguised by a complex system of multiple exchange rates. Before the beginning of the third four-year plan (1961–64), measures were taken to stabilize the currency by substituting a uniform single exchange rate (U.S. $1 = 40 new Taiwan dollars) for the previous multiple exchange rates. The underlying emphasis of the third plan was on the industrial sector. In a continuous effort to broaden Formosa's industrial base and to promote export trade, energy-producing industries (plastics, glass, and cement), heavy industries (steel, machinery, shipbuilding, automobiles), and the refining of natural gas and petroleum received attention. The fourth four-year plan, begun in 1965, is under way.

The underlying strategy in the consecutive series of plans is to achieve a balanced development of agriculture and industry, and to provide for the agricultural sector as a base for further development of the industrial sector. Formosa has avoided the mistake of a hasty decision to build heavy industrialization under forced draft. Considerable emphasis was initially put on agriculture and food processing industries. Through successful land reform, intensive research and experiment, as well as the expansion and consolidation of farmers' associations, Formosa's gross agricultural output per hectare is reported to be the third highest in the world.[4] The diversification of Formosa's agricultural products is shown by the changing composition of its exports. As the sugar industry plays an extremely vital role in the economic life of Formosa, the government has spared no effort to expand its role both vertically and horizontally. The annual export of sugar is a substantial portion of total exports measured in dollar value. Throughout Formosa, about 10 per cent of the population rely for their living either entirely or partially upon the activities of the Taiwan Sugar Company, which is owned and operated by the government. As a result of the successful development of agricultural production and the sugar refineries at an earlier stage, a solid foundation was laid for the subsequent series of industrialization programs.

The implementation of three consecutive economic plans from 1953 to 1964 has been acclaimed as highly successful and given wide publicity. According to official reports for the period, Formosa's real national income increased by 134.9 per cent and real per capita income by 59 per cent. The per capita income in 1964 was U.S. $163 (NT $6522). The average annual growth rate of real national income was 7.4 per cent and that of real per capita income 3.9 per cent, the high rate of population growth notwithstanding. During that period, agricultural output was reported to have increased by 78 per cent, and industrial output by 304 per cent, with an average annual growth rate of 4.9 per cent and 12.3 per cent respectively.

The achievement can also be attested by Formosa's trade

expansion in recent years. Realizing the inherent limits in the growth potential of the domestic market of an island economy, Formosa has expanded its export industry and trade. From 1954 to 1964, total exports rose from less than U.S. $100 million to more than $460 million, while total imports increased from $200 million to $400 million. Nineteen hundred and sixty-three was a landmark in the history of Formosa's export trade, with a foreign exchange surplus for the first time. From U.S. $238 million in 1962, total exports sharply increased to $357 million in 1963, and to $463 million in 1964. This was attributed partly to the unusual upsurge of world sugar prices in 1963 and partly to the increased and diversified output of agricultural and industrial products. It is remarkable to note that industrial exports, only 7 per cent of total exports in 1953, amounted to as much as 40 per cent in 1964. In terms of dollar value, total exports rose from U.S. $7 million in 1953 to U.S. $180 million in 1964. Trade areas have shown comparable expansion in recent years. Japan and the United States remain Formosa's most important trade partners. Next to them are Hong Kong, South Vietnam, Iran, West Germany, Thailand, Malaysia, Singapore, Philippines, South Korea, Australia, and Canada. New markets are being sought in Latin America and African countries.

These achievements, impressive as they were, are attributable in no small measure to United States aid. From 1951 to 1965, the Nationalist regime received a total of almost $1.5 billion in economic aid (in addition to $2.5 billion in military assistance) from the United States. Annual obligations average almost $100 million over the fifteen-year period 1951–1965, and deliveries averaged about $80 million over the eighteen-year period 1951–1968. On a yearly average, U.S. aid amounted to $10 per capita, 6.4 per cent of Formosa's GNP, 34 per cent of its gross investment, and covered 91 per cent of its aggregate net import surplus of goods and services. Although economic aid was terminated in June 1965 (except $178 million previously committed through 1967), mili-

tary assistance will continue as usual under the direct administration of the U.S. Defense Department. By 1962 U.S. grant aid
to Formosa had virtually ended, and was replaced by loans re-
payable in United States currency, with interest. From the first,
United States aid programs were geared to the basic needs of
Formosa's economy. Until 1956 the aid fund was primarily used
to help realize the goals of economic rehabilitation and stability
on a short-term basis. At the initiation of the second four-year
plan (1957), emphasis was put on long-term economic development through the diversification of agricultural and industrial
products and the promotion of export trade. Since 1961 priority
has been given to the development of Formosa's capacity for
self-sustaining growth, with special emphasis on the private sectors.
In a word, the sequence of emphasis was from monetary stabilization to agricultural production, building of infrastructure, and
finally to private industrial investment.

It goes without saying that it is U.S. aid that helped carry the
burden of Formosa's vast military expenditures under the Nationalist regime. On an average, the government deficit amounted to
26 per cent of total expenditures, which was primarily covered
by allocations of local currency generated by U.S. aid. The Agency
for International Development stated: "National defense expenditures take up virtually 100 per cent of the central government
domestic revenue excluding aid-generating currency. Defense expenditures account for 65 per cent of consolidated central and
provincial domestic revenues. The U.S. aid has to play a part as
much as 25–40 per cent of the total consolidated expenditures of
the central and provincial governments. Without foreign grants
the average deficit in budget would have reached about 25 per
cent for the period from 1956 to 1962."[5]

The ratio of deficit before foreign grants to total expenditures
is reported as follows: 22 per cent (1956), 25 per cent (1957),
24 per cent (1958), 21 per cent (1959), 32 per cent (1960), 28
per cent (1961) and 30 per cent (1962). This brief account

demonstrates vividly the role played by United States aid in the recent growth of Formosa's economy. Indeed, it has contributed significantly to price stability and helped mitigate balance of payments problems. The unceasing efforts of the Joint Commission of Rural Reconstruction, which consists of five members, three appointed by Formosa and two by the United States, made possible at an early stage a successful comprehensive land reform. Moreover, it was reported that United States aid accounted in the past years for 68 per cent of the total investment in public utilities, 28 per cent in transportation and communication, and 24 per cent in manufacturing.

No less important is the contribution of United States aid to the rapid growth of Formosa's private enterprises. Formosa's economy is basically a mixed one. As we noted earlier, when the Nationalist government occupied Formosa at the end of World War II, it took over all the industries, utilities, and banks previously owned by the Japanese government and people, including a number of manufacturing enterprises, and placed them under government control or monopolization. Aside from exclusive control over the "essential industries," such as electric power, railroad, petroleum, the government has had a monopoly over sugar, tobacco, and alcoholic beverages. Except for the transfer of the total shares of four government corporations—cement, paper and pulp, industrial and mining, agricultural and forestry—to landlords in partial payment for land taken under the land reform program, despite its repeated declarations the government is reluctant to sell other holdings to the private sector. This is attributable to a combination of factors, notably the so-called vested interests of the ruling elites, a basic distrust of private capitalists, and a pressing need for tight government control for planning and revenue purposes. However, under the persistent urging of American aid officials, the regime has increasingly emphasized the growth of the private sector, while remaining loyal to Sun Yat-sen's "principle of livelihood" (in essence, a combination of socialist and capitalist programs). Not only has it refrained from expanding into new enterprises in competition with the private sector; the regime has fostered private industry since the commencement of the third four-year plan (1961). As a result the overall picture of Formosa's economy has been significantly altered. According to official reports, while the contribution of the private sector to the *nation's total industrial production* amounted to only 39.5 per cent in 1952, it rose as high as 68.9 per cent in 1964.

The "spectacular" achievement of Formosa's economic development in the past thirteen years has been widely publicized by the Agency of International Development as well as by the Nationalist government. We have no disposition to doubt that considerable progress has been made by the Nationalist regime, but we have some reservations about the extent of actual progress as asserted in the official statistics.[6]

However, it is important that the fundamental difficulties of Formosa's economic development be realistically faced. The crippling trend of Formosa's stock market and the decrease in export trade after the termination of U.S. aid in June 1965 seemed to be a warning against a false sense of security and misguided optimism. Despite the short-term gains, there is a danger to Formosa's economy as long as the Nationalist regime continues to proclaim its determination to reconquer the mainland. The Nationalists assert an ultimate goal of the recovery and reconstruction of the mainland; Formosa's economic development, therefore, is an instrumental and "transitory" objective of policy. The "planning commission for the recovery of the mainland" (comprising over seventeen hundred members) has been set up to work out a blueprint for future reconstruction of a reconquered mainland. As the proposed invasion requires huge manpower, 600,000 members of the effective labor force are diverted to preparation for "killing" rather than production. The expenditure needed for maintaining an armed forces of 600,000, even with substantial U.S. aid, is out of proportion to Formosa's economic capability. It eats up a substantial portion of the capital needed for industrial investment. Under the present regime the annual budget on national defense is consistently maintained around 85 to 90 per cent of the total national expenditure.

Furthermore, to give some credibility to the claim that the Nationalist government is the only authoritative government representing all China, a duplicate set of government structures has been maintained. On the theory that Formosa is only one of the provinces of China, and despite the fact that the "Republic of China" and the "province of Taiwan" are practically identical in terms of authority and control over people and territory (except Quemoy and Matsu), two layers of governmental structures are kept in being: one is called the "national government," and the other the "Taiwan provincial government." Aside from foreign affairs and national defense (plus so-called Tibetan and Mongolian affairs), all the functions of a national government can well be discharged by the Taiwan provincial government. Aside from contributing to administrative inefficiency and irresponsibility, the duplex system has been used to justify a huge number of unnecessary and unproductive government employees.

Accordingly, a priority task for Formosa's economic development after independence is the overall reorientation of economic policy exclusively toward the development of Formosa, abandoning provocative assertions of the goal of reconquering the mainland. Only when this fundamental change is effected and accepted can there be realistic long-term planning that makes possible to the fullest extent the utilization of Formosa's economic potential. The reduction of government expenditures through the simplification and consolidation of government agencies, and the gradual reduction of national defense expenditures can cut the nation's outlay for nonproductive purposes, and contribute to the formation of capital for industrial expansion. The new capital can be used to spur the development of the economy; it can also be effectively mobilized to solve the problems arising from the conversion of displaced military personnel to civilian employment, and of discharged governmental employees to industrial jobs; in connection with both operations new employment opportunities can be opened up and retraining programs made effective on an appropriate scale.

The fundamental reorientation of Formosa's policy that would result from the discontinuation of the perennial threat to reconquer mainland China can be counted on to create a climate genuinely conducive to international investment. The Nationalist regime has in recent years through legislation or executive orders undertaken measures to encourage the flow of foreign capital into Formosa. These measures include a five-year tax holiday for approved new investments; reduction or elimination of various business taxes; guaranteed profit remittance and capital repatriation for foreign enterprises; industrial parks for preplanned factory sites; financial aid to private investors through the China Development Corporation; and special services to investors rendered by the newly established institutions such as the Industrial Development and Investment Center, the Productivity and Trade Center, and China Technical Consultants. Very recently, a "tax-and-duty-free industrial processing zone" has been established in Kaoshung for the purpose of spurring international investment for export trade.

With the creation of a congenial environment for international investment, a forward looking policy is necessary in order to channel the available resources in the most constructive direction. Besides continuing the attention needed by the agricultural sector, policy will undoubtedly operate on the assumption that industrial expansion is the key to Formosa's economic growth.

Situated at the center of air and sea routes between Japan, the Philippines and Hong Kong—three of the most prosperous trading areas in East Asia—Formosa promises to have a bright economic future. It is a ruggedly mountainous island, densely populated along the west coastal plain, about 240 miles from north to south and 60 to 80 miles wide. Actually natural resources are neither numerous nor extensive. Only about 25 per cent of the land area (35,834 sq. km., or about 3,600,000 hectares) is arable, but agriculture is highly productive, supplying abundant food for domestic consumption and a substantial export surplus. To overcome the inherent limitation imposed by the shortage of arable land, efforts have been made to diversify production, with special emphasis on the growth of some high-value crops that require relatively small amounts of land and can be processed for export without interfering with basic food production.

The largely untapped forest resources of Formosa, although costly to develop, offer the best potential for future development, with good prospects for lumber processing and paper manufacture. Another important resource is the fisheries—pond, inshore, and deep sea. The deep-sea fishing industry is growing fast, and is active in the Atlantic, South Pacific, and Indian oceans.

The coal resources, characterized by narrow seams and high-cost mining, are important to Formosa's economy as a whole. They provide not only the fuel for power but also the coking quality coal essential to the development of an integrated steel industry. Natural gas has recently been discovered and is being developed, giving promise for further development of the chemical industry. Not well endowed with industrial minerals, Formosa does nonetheless have some good deposits of nonmetals, including limestone, dolomite, and silica sand, which are well developed and extensively used.

Located in the midst of the east Asian monsoon system, Formosa has an ample water supply that has been utilized for irrigation. Its swift-moving mountain streams provide dam sites for generating low-cost hydroelectricity for industrial use. With the completion of the Shihmen Dam, both the Tachien reservoir and Chen-wen reservoir projects are under construction to meet the pressing needs of industrial expansion.

Formosa's greatest resource, it must be emphasized, is its thirteen million manpower. With a low mortality and a high birth rate, Formosa's population shows a 3½ per cent increase annually. The labor supply is intelligent and trainable, and labor disturbances are rare. However, the labor force is extremely underutilized: only 31 per cent of the total population is economically active, which is very low indeed when compared with other industrialized nations.

The industrial sector has already reached the so-called take-off phase for sustained growth. Manufacturing is more highly developed in Formosa than in other nations with comparable per capita incomes. As the domestic market is small, Formosa's industry is dependent upon exports and hence is export-oriented. Food processing, textiles, and ceramics are largely responsible for absorbing the labor force in industry. However, chemicals, plastics, and other technically based industries are growing rapidly. Too often the existing industries are fragmented into too many producing units and are characterized by overcapacity and inadequate equity capital. This has the adverse effect of retarding the establishment of well-financed, economical modern plants that can meet the quality standards of the export market.

In the light of the preceding summary, it appears that in projecting a new direction for Formosa's future industrial development special attention should be paid to factors such as employment opportunities for both skilled and nonskilled workers, export potential, attractiveness to foreign investors, potential of related investment, potential import reduction, and effective use of Formosa's available raw materials and resources. While the Nationalist regime avoided the mistake of making a hasty decision to develop a steel industry, it is now time to move ahead with an integrated steel industry, as a means of providing real muscle for Formosa's economy in the long run. The chemical and plastics industries also should be developed, followed by metal fabrication and the manufacture of light machinery and consumer appliances. In any event, as Formosa has to trade to live, the government should endeavor to help strengthen existing industries by improving the quality of product, heightening the level of efficiency in manufacturing, modernizing packaging and merchandising techniques, and encouraging a sounder financial structure. In new industries, it is desirable to nurture a few sound, well-financed plants which, through quality of product, are capable of participating effectively in export as well as domestic markets.

Another problem is the effective utilization of manpower, the human resources, in Formosa. Despite the laudable achievements of the Nationalist regime in the economic sphere, a very serious problem of unemployment and underemployment exists—probably more serious than governmental officials are inclined to admit. Although in recent years the average growth rate of Formosa's economy amounted to 7 per cent in terms of gross national product, the comparable increase in the rate of employment was less than 1 per cent in the same period. In his comprehensive study on "U.S. Aid to Taiwan," Dean Jacoby states:

> Notwithstanding astonishing increases in production and employment, Taiwan suffered from rising unemployment during 1951–65. Apparently, 300,000 to 400,000 persons, representing from 8 to 9 per cent of the labor force, were unemployed during 1951–62; and, by 1964, unemployment increased to between 450,000 and 500,000, representing about 10 per cent of the labor force (p. 93).

The problem has shown no sign of abatement, partly because of an annual population increase rate of 3½ per cent. The density of population in Formosa is 341 persons per square kilometer, exceeded only in the Netherlands.

This rate of annual increase is just too high, and has to a large extent canceled the advantages of Formosa's economic development in terms of real improvement in the standard of living. The Nationalist regime has been inhibited from taking effective measures by its adherence to the goal of mainland reconquest and reconstruction. The annual rate of increase of Formosa's population should be reduced by a rational policy. As this problem is closely related to family planning and to both urbanization and industrialization, we shall explore population policies further in the section dealing with these topics.

In view of the pressure of unemployment and underemployment we have stressed the necessity of developing labor-intensive industry in the near future. Indeed, there are no significant opportunities for the agricultural sector to absorb the unemployed and underemployed, since agriculture is already saddled with hidden unemployment. Any effective solution must come from an industrialization program of major magnitude. In this connection a peculiar phenomenon emerges: while unemployment is very serious, industrial entrepreneurs not infrequently find it difficult to find manpower with the skills for their particular enterprises. There is a wide gap between the skills transmitted by the educational system and the skills appropriate to new industry. Despite the quantitative increase at all levels of education, the present regime has failed to produce a younger generation with the skills needed in an economy of accelerating industrialization. The primitive and narrow scope of "apprenticeship," on-the-job training, and other practical training methods must be expanded and supplemented. The message is clear: a fundamental solution to the manpower problem is through a reformed system of education.

Meanwhile, the manpower problem comes properly within the sphere of our proposed council on economic development. The question of effective utilization of present and potential human resources should be continuously studied and assessed by an independent institution composed of experts who can approach the problem contextually and make integrated and coordinated planning possible. They can translate economic development plans into manpower terms and eventually bring the supply of manpower into phase with requirements. The manpower gap can also be bridged by manpower markets better geared to the emerging needs of industrialization.

So far, our focus has been on the problem of fostering optimum production. No less important, however, is the problem of distribution. At an early stage of industrialization, some sectors necessarily develop at a faster tempo than others. New entrepreneurs, innovative and willing to take risks, provide needed savings for investment and reinvestment, and play a leading role in overall development. Yet the rise of a new enterprising class may also mean a widening gap between upper and lower income brackets. This problem is more acute in Formosa because of the inequitable tax system. One must not lose sight, in the midst of economic growth, of the unbalances that appear if a privileged few are allowed to perpetuate themselves without substantially improving the wealth position of the rest of the community.

Formosa's present tax system, largely a carryover from the mainland, consists of various levies made on behalf of the three levels of government—national (central), provincial, and local. The so-called national tax consists mainly of income tax, commodity tax, customs duty, estate tax, and stamp tax. The "provincial tax" includes land tax, business tax, harbor dues, and defense surtax. The principal "local taxes" are house (property) tax, household tax, vehicle license tax, entertainment and amusement tax, deed tax, and slaughter tax. Many of the revenues are shared by the three layers of government. There are also revenues from state monopolies of tobacco and liquor, which are generally included along with the tax revenues in governmental budgets. Custom duties and the state monopolies of tobacco and liquor are administered by independent agencies, which transfer revenue to the central and provincial governments. All other taxes are collected by the Taiwan Provincial Government on behalf of all levels of government through twenty-two chief tax offices and a number of suboffices. Responsible for the enforcement of all relevant tax laws and regulations, these offices issue assessment notices, conduct interrogation, and receive and act on complaints.

Of the total tax revenues for the national government, about

80 per cent are an "indirect tax" in the form of a commodity tax and custom duties (including revenues from monopoly). As practically all these indirect taxes are transferable to consumers, the large proportion of indirect taxes has the effect of reducing the already very modest purchasing power of the low income class. The Nationalist regime has neither the self-confidence nor the determination required to collect substantial revenues from the rich by a graduated direct tax that is actually enforced. Under the present regime, tax administration is riddled with corruption: the rich and those with "good connections" can usually evade their obligations by bribery or collusion. The whole operation is also made inefficient by loose financial supervision that tolerates the widespread practice of "fraudulent accounting." A member of the Legislative Yuan recently pointed out that Formosa's present tax system is a "double-three system".[7] That is to say, a businessman keeps three sets of accounting books: one for revenue officers, one for bankers, and one for personal records; and revenues are divided evenly into three portions: a third to the public treasury, a third to the pockets of tax collectors, and a third to businessmen. The business community in general complains that the present tax burden is too heavy and too manifold, and any strict compliance would at once drive them into bankruptcy. "No tax evasion, no survival" has become an article of faith in the ranks of business. Indeed, burdened by vast military expenditures, taxes in Formosa today appear to have reached a saturation point. The general public is reminded from time to time of "Taiwan Wan-swei!" ("Long Live Taiwan!" or "Taiwan, the island of ten thousand taxes").

Accordingly, a pressing task after independence is a comprehensive tax reform to mitigate the imbalance of income distribution and conserve the purchasing power of low-income people. Indirect taxes should be substantially reduced and replaced by a reasonable graduated income tax. The rate of taxation levied on businesses should be reasonably reassessed so as not to cause undue hardships or to jeopardize their operations. Only when the assessment realistically and equitably corresponds to the ability of an enterprise to pay can compliance be assured. The point is to eliminate the existing gap between paper assessment and actual compliance. It is preferable to impose a lower assessment that promises full compliance rather than an unrealistically heavy burden that encourages general evasion, and penalizes honest and law-abiding citizens. The entire reform will need to be executed by efficient tax administrators who have reasonable motivations to be honest. Clearly it will be essential to encourage sound accounting systems as part of the program.

Finally, the government must endeavor to improve the plight of the poor by providing more adequate public services, social security, better working conditions, better universal education, and other welfare programs. Formosa's present expenditure on social security schemes (in percentage of gross national product) is nearly the lowest among all the nations whose data are available.[8] The farmers' gain during recent years can be truly consolidated by abolishing the notorious system of compulsory exchange of rice for fertilizer at artificial rates, and by lifting unreasonably harsh control over the relative price of farm products, particularly rice. The principal sources of insecurity among Formosan farmers are the calamities caused by typhoon and flood. While weather conditions are at present beyond human control, it seems worth while exploring the possibility of initiating a system of comprehensive coverage against disaster; this, at least, is fully within man's reach.

Communication and Plural Associations

AS THE policy sciences of development gain in depth and scope, it is increasingly recognized that nation-building involves all value-institutions of the social process. The interaction of the social process is a pattern that goes beyond the simple fact that one factor affects another. In an interaction, two sequences can be distinguished from one another: communication and collaboration. Communication accelerates interaction; it brings symbols into the present that refer to events which, though not part of the present, can influence the behavior of individuals and groups. Effective communication within a body politic is essential to generate common awareness of the full dimensions of the development task, and initiate effective and timely coalitions of all participants in the pursuit of common goals. In this light, nation-building is primarily a matter of communication.

Basic to an effective communication process in Formosa is the problem of an "official language." Coming from different parts of the mainland, the mainland Chinese on Formosa speak a variety of dialects, but all of them share the use of Mandarin Chinese. The story is somewhat different for the native Formosans.

Their ancestors migrated to Formosa from the southeastern part of mainland China in the late seventeenth and early eighteenth centuries. They were principally of two kinds: "Ho-lo-lang," whose ancestors migrated to Formosa from the southern part of Fukien; and "Ke-lang" whose ancestors came from the eastern part of Canton. The difference in origin meant difference in spoken language: the Ho-lo-lang spoke Ho-lo-way (commonly referred to as Taiwan-way, i.e., the Formosan dialect) and the Ke-lang spoke Ke-way. Of the total population of native Formosans today, descendants of Ho-lo-lang are a substantial majority. (The ratio of the Ho-lo-lang and the Ke-lang is roughly 3 to 1.) Not only are spoken Ho-lo-way and Ke-way both sharply different from Mandarin Chinese, but also essentially different from each other. Those who speak Ho-lo-way do not comprehend those who speak Ke-way, and vice versa. (In written form, all Chinese use essentially the same language, despite the great diversity of dialects from region to region.) Also about 1.5 per cent of the total population are aborigines who speak their own language. And many of the older generation of Formosans were educated under Japanese rule and still feel more at home using Japanese, even though they are not handicapped by lack of proficiency in Mandarin Chinese. Because of their deprivations under the Nationalist regime they look back with nostalgia to "the good old days"—and the use of Japanese is one way of voicing their protest against the regime and of coping with tension and frustration.

In the initial period of the Nationalist occupation of Formosa after World War II, a serious problem of communication resulted from the absence of a common language. Through the regime's conscious effort, the general level of literacy, the small size of Formosa, the frequency of social interaction facilitated by rapid urbanization, and transportation and communication, Mandarin Chinese became within a reasonably short time an official language widely shared and used by all the people, including aborigines, in the Formosan community. At present, it has become an important tool in all sectors of life, particularly in education and government. The Formosan dialects (including both Ho-lo-way and Ke-way) are still widely used among native Formosans, but are mostly confined to private contexts.

With a view to arousing Formosans' sense of identity, some leaders dedicated to the cause of independence have advocated that Taiwan-way (the Formosan dialect) replace Mandarin Chinese as the official language, once the new Republic is born. The use of the native language is considered a decisive means of dramatizing the sense of pride and identity of Formosans and of fostering unity in the pursuit of common goals. Some have sought to systematize the Formosan language and make it fully operational for use in a modern industrial society.

No matter how much sentimental justification this view may evoke, we consider the proposition too costly to merit support. Two million mainland Chinese generally do not speak Formosan dialects. Even among the native Formosans, there is no single Formosan dialect uniformly shared by them all. Ho-lo-way and Ke-way are distinctly different; to make a choice one way or another would create division among native Formosans as well as complicate the whole matter. In this connection, the tragic lesson of India is instructive. Both Ho-lo-way and Ke-way are far from being fully adapted to the needs of a modernizing society, and neither has yet evolved into an efficient and refined tool of communication for all purposes and occasions. While we do not subscribe to the idea that some languages are inherently too primitive to express advanced concepts, we do counsel careful weighing of the relative gains and costs that may be involved in any change of the existing official language. In order to make a Formosan tongue fully operative, a great deal of work would have to be done. An enormous investment of scholarly manpower would be needed to create the handbooks, dictionaries, and translations required to overcome present deficiencies. As Mandarin Chinese is a ready-made medium of communication understood throughout Formosa, the sudden imposition of a new language would greatly disrupt existing administrative routines, as well as educational and business practices. Far from forging a new sense of attachment, people in general would feel uprooted and alienated under the new system of public order. Such a far-reaching adverse impact is not to be dismissed lightly.

Throughout this study, we have consistently emphasized that it is in the common interest of all the Formosan people—mainland Chinese as well as native Formosans—to cooperate and integrate fully in building a new Republic of Formosa. United, they can form a viable nation; divided, they will be in chaotic, bloody, and continuing crisis. The prime task after Formosa's independence is generally agreed to be the protection of the two million mainland Chinese minority. We emphasize again that unless these people are individually assured of equal and effective participation in politics, and in the other sectors of social life, the prospect of building a successful Formosa is dim. Hence our concern with policies that provide such assurance in fact as well as in form.

If the new Republic continues to use Mandarin Chinese, these two million are bound to have a stronger sense of attachment and identity than would otherwise be possible. Indeed, it can be a very effective unifying factor. For the native Formosans, this "concession" would certainly do no harm, and such a policy would demonstrate that the emerging Formosan elites are well balanced, moderate, and responsible in their approach; hence, no accusation of either extremism or parochialism could be substantiated.

Most strikingly, perhaps, the act would show that Formosa's search for independence does not imply a sweeping rejection of the Chinese cultural heritage. What the new elites would be rejecting is a political process that denies general participation and relies on coercion, and absurd government structures and ideologies —not the long-cherished Chinese culture itself. On the contrary, they would demonstrate that they are genuinely concerned with the creation of a thoroughly modern body politic where science, technology, and democracy are flourishing, and where the fundamental virtues of Chinese civilization are challenged to express themselves under new conditions. The creativity of the great tradition can continue to flourish at a time when this is made virtually impossible on the mainland under the pressure of Communization.

At present Mandarin Chinese is the common language of nearly one-fourth of the world's population. A major language, it is used in diplomacy, cultural diffusion, and business transactions. By continuing to employ a language shared by one fourth of the world's citizens, Formosa will benefit tremendously in her dealings with others. If one projects into the future, it is probable that the relation between mainland China and Formosa will improve in due course, notwithstanding the intransigent hostility thus far exhibited by the Communists. Should that day approach and relations based on mutual respect are normalized, contact between Chinese on the mainland and the Formosan people can be made most fruitful as a result of the shared use of a basic tool of communication.

The proposal to retain a world language such as Mandarin Chinese is in harmony with a trend among new states since the end of World War II. Between the two World Wars newly emancipated people were loath to continue the language of the former rulers. The task of promoting native languages was pursued with the same zeal characteristic of the nineteenth century. In the post-World War II period, that trend has been largely reversed. Recognizing the practical value of international languages in a world of accelerating interdependence, the emerging nations of the Afro-Asian continents have not let their sense of nationalism stand in the way of the continuing use of the mother tongues of their former colonial rulers, notably English and French.

In short, while we feel very strongly the importance of fostering a sense of national identity and unity among all Formosans, the proposal to change the official language from Mandarin Chinese to a Formosan dialect is not the right answer. Given the present level of literacy and political awareness, the principal strategy for forging national unity is enlightened political education and civic participation. It is unnecessary to waste human resources on language improvement and inculcation when talent might be applied directly to the most pressing tasks of nation-building. The point is particularly persuasive when the final result would be a permanent barrier to facile international intercourse, notably to the cultivation of the world market or to grasping the opportunities offered in world affairs. Nation-building calls for a proper sense of priority and proportion. By the time the so-called new Formosan language was fully installed, there might well be no "independent Formosa" to build.

The choice of Mandarin Chinese is a fundamental question of communication policy, not only because language is the principal instrument of communication, but because the instrument is itself an object of identification for the self. The formation of a national identity is, of course, shaped by experiences that depend on the contents of the media employed in transmitting intelligence among

the members of the national community. We must give further
attention to the management of the media as tools of national
identity and unity. The flow of media content can and should be
employed to clarify common goals and to articulate the common
interest of all in the life of the new nation. A related task is ex-
pounding the magnitude and complexity of the problems involved
in national development. Too often the general population cher-
ishes the thought that as soon as independence is attained, everything will change for the better. It tends to be impatient and to
overlook the fact that such an outcome depends on the willingness
of the citizens to contribute through the years to the process. To
prevent rising expectations from becoming rising frustrations, it is
not enough to pinpoint the complexities and difficulties of the
problem, since this may create a general sense of impotence. It has
to be made clear that while the problem is far from simple, it is
after all a manmade challenge that can be solved by man, provided
that all intellectual skills are used, all resources are mobilized, and
all important moves are realistically planned. Hence it is important
to present to the public the most comprehensive map of nation-
building humanly possible. Such a map would cover the underlying goals of development and the conditions essential to their
attainment. Emphasis would be on the role that individuals can
play, outlining both the sacrifices and the outcomes, individual
and collective, that can be expected from timely and effective
cooperation. Communication is an indispensable means of wiping
out the noxious effects of mass indoctrination under the old regime, and of reorienting old myths to new realities.

The strategies of political and civic education aimed at building
a new Formosa call for the adaptation of the fundamental message
to the predispositions of group audiences, and to a balanced network of channels. Audience receptivity to mass media varies by
culture, class, interest, personality, and crisis level. Among the
cultural differences contrast between the rural and urban population is significant. Any process that accelerates social change is

likely to arouse defense mechanism among the rural population, who may not comprehend the advantages to them of the total process. It may appear to the rustic mentality as another conspiracy to establish and support urban supremacy.

As industrialization accelerates, and the advantages become more obvious, the traditional outlook is eroded, and the climate becomes more hospitable to innovation. With skilled use of every instrument of communication the lag between old and new perspectives can be greatly shortened. The essential point is to think in terms of the equivalence of human experience and to discover the symbols that present the new in categories comprehensible in the symbolic context of the old. No one needs to convince the farmers or any other element in society that rising income or better health, for example, are desirable. The problem is to find a parallel in past experience to the innovations required to achieve the ends, and to provide an immediate, present experience that establishes a strong presumption in favor of adopting a specific new technique. Modern television can mobilize all the senses to comprehend a new method of raising plants, a new way of cooperative buying or selling, or a new way of doing housework. The pace of enlightenment and of skill acquisition can be accelerated by adapting television to the task.

Television is an important medium of national growth when properly used, but it must be supplemented by organized chains of human contact that lead from every individual, family, and village to the nation as a whole. The development of plural associations is vitally important. A nation in transition usually suffers a wide gap between the ruling elites and the masses. The intermediate level may be a social vacuum. An urgent task is to develop and consolidate this intermediate layer through the cultivation of pluralism based on a wide variety of private associations devoted to many interests. An enormous training school in political and civic action is provided by an active network of private associations. By participating in the decision process of such organizations the individual can acquire the skills essential to collective action. To some extent these skills are communicative. But they go much farther since they include the skills required to collaborate on tasks that call for a division of function within a frame of policy. Pluralistic associations reach outside the boundaries of primary groups (family and school), while remaining close enough to sustain the personal touch. An organization of this kind provides interlocking situations in which a genuine if somewhat impersonal communication process can be initiated and strengthened.

When effectively organized and functioning, private associations are useful intermediaries between the ruling elites at the top and bottom of society. They help elucidate government policies and programs to the people to obtain their sympathetic understanding and timely support. The people, in turn, show greater concern and interest in political participation because of the "visibility" and "comprehensibility" of their influence in groups that crystallize particular interests and demands. Plural associations help avert or mitigate the "crisis of miscommunication" that may result from the direct confrontation of ruling elites and the rank and file.

At present, there are some associations such as labor unions, farmers' associations, fishermen's associations, and so on in Formosa. But these are strictly controlled and regulated by the government; they are instruments of central power, not of representation. The Nationalist regime is basically oriented toward the centralization, concentration, and monopolization of power. Hence Nationalist policy has prevented the growth of subcenters of power by imposing drastic limitations on the permissible functions of pluralistic groups. Internal decisions are dominated by key KMT members, which means that the government has assumed the principal responsibility for articulating and aggregating the group interests throughout Formosa. The individual member sees little relation between his participation in associations and the decisions taken within or beyond their boundaries. The entire network operates, not from the bottom to the top, but from the apex of the regime to the bottom. Their instruments of communication are speaking tubes for the ritualized communiqués of the KMT.

After Formosa's independence, it is important to make sure that the development of plural associations will be effective, not formalistic. Their existence must be external to the government and outside the political parties. Only genuine, not token, associations can carry on a meaningful dialogue with parties and official agencies, and contribute to national development. When functioning at their optimum, plural associations serve the common interests of government and society. On the one hand they inhibit any totalitarian trend and protect the initiatives taken by individuals and small groups everywhere in the community. On the other hand they protect the government from gross mistakes and from catastrophic upheavals that result from years of accumulated grievances.

Under a system where a plurality of private associations effectively exists, the pursuit and realization of their respective demands will be conducted not in a context of isolation, but in interaction with one another and with political parties and government. Through the process of nonviolent claims, they eventually come to terms with the fact that the harmonious accommodation of competing interests is a basic fact of human experience and political life. When this intricate interrelation is widely perceived and reflected in national politics, the general sense of tolerance and moderation, essential to a working democracy, gains strength and flourishes.

A Nonpartisan Military

AN ESSENTIAL condition of national development is national security. Hence practically all new nations, regardless of their resources and economic capacities, give top priority to the military establishment. In some developing nations, the military is the most progressive element in the community, and plays a leading role in modernization. The relations between the military and civilian components of government are often complex and variable during the course of national growth.

Having pacified initial armed resistance, the Japanese eventually established public order in Formosa in 1902 and maintained it well thereafter. Not until the outbreak of World War II were Formosans recruited to serve in Japanese armed forces. During the War, although Formosa was used as a base for the advance southward, the conscripted natives were assigned primarily to the labor services of the Japanese forces. The Formosans' role in combat duty was limited, for the obvious reason that the Japanese did not fully trust their loyalty to the Empire. During the period of Japanese control, Formosa was saved from the long-drawn-out confusion of warlordism and civil strife on the mainland.

When the Nationalist forces took over, native Formosans greeted them with some expectations, simply because they were glad to be emancipated from colonial control. Their expectations were soon shattered, however. To the Nationalist soldiers, the advanced stage of Formosa's progress was too startling to believe. And from the very beginning of their landings in Formosa, Nationalist forces acted more like conquerors, pointing their guns toward the greeting audiences, than "brothers from the motherland" who professed to "deliver their compatriots from misery and oppression." The looting, violence, and ruthlessness of the Nationalist forces had brought within a few months more scourges to Formosans than had been inflicted upon them during the course of the War. By their own barbarous acts, the Nationalists succeeded in alienating themselves from the local population, and the 1947 massacre was the climatic event that reinforced the Formosans' contempt and hatred.

Upon the Communist takeover of the mainland in October 1949, Chinese Nationalists exiled to Formosa numbered about 600,000 soldiers (who came to Formosa not by choice, but by order) and 900,000 civilians. The hands-off policy of the United States was soon abandoned when the Korean war broke out in June 1950. The outdated and weary Nationalist forces were given a breathing spell for recuperation, reorganization, and modernization, thanks to extensive United States assistance. Since then the Nationalists have been alleged to operate as a powerful counterweight against the expansion of Communist Chinese in the Western Pacific.

While it has never been made public officially, it is generally estimated that the total number of Nationalist forces in Formosa has been maintained around 600,000. It is also estimated that as many as one-fifth of the total number are officers and about four-fifths rank and file. The number of generals and admirals is notoriously huge (about 1600 and 200 respectively)—as if the Nationalist regime were still ruling all of mainland China. The Nationalist army has approximately 400 more generals and 700 more colonels than the U.S. army, which is three times the former in size. As years pass, both the officers and men who were evacuated from the mainland in 1949 are aging and retiring. While the officer corps to an overwhelming extent is still composed of mainland Chinese those who have had combat experience have sharply decreased. Of the rank and file 80 per cent are native Formosans conscripted to serve terms of one to three years.

This massive armed force—the highest in the world proportionate to population[9]—has been acclaimed the best armed forces in Asia by Chiang's government. The alleged achievement, if true at all, is largely attributable to massive United States assistance in training, renovation and equipment. Under the leadership of Chiang Kai-shek, these forces are not only indoctrinated with the mission of defending Formosa and the Pescadores, but also of recovering mainland China.

Chiang Kai-shek has kept agitating that invasion of the mainland is "imminent" and "the promised land is just around the corner."[10] He is restrained, of course, by the well-known disap-

proval of the United States. In giving military aid to the Nationalist forces, the United States Military Assistance Advisory Group
(MAAG) has seen to it that none of it is used for purposes other
than those mutually agreed upon. The United States has made
clear its "defensive" purpose in Formosa, and given no encouragement whatsoever to the invasion goal.[11] Presumably, if Chiang
could find sufficient means outside the U.S. aid program he could
"go it alone," as he has so often threatened. In order to invade
the mainland, he needs naval transport, air cover, and massive
logistic support; yet he has only enough amphibious craft to land
10,000 men on the mainland. The basic thinking that underlies
Chiang's strategy toward the United States seems to be that if
only the United States gives him a green light for an initial landing on the mainland coast, the United States would inevitably
be dragged deeper and deeper into a large-scale confrontation with
Communist China. This strategy has not paid off so far, but
Chiang is persistently hopeful, particularly in the light of escalation in the Vietnam conflict. By this time his slogan is probably
more political than military, since he is always able to use the
United States as the scapegoat to justify his inaction to the minority of extreme fanatics in the party.

As far as native Formosans are concerned, most of them see
only too clearly that Chiang's professed goal of mainland reconquest is a political lie designed to perpetuate his monopoly of
power at the expense of native Formosans. Deeply attached to
their home island, Formosan soldiers will pay any price, bear any
burden, in the defense of Formosa. But they want no part as
stooges in a suicidal attempt to overthrow a regime that is in
effective control of over 700 million people.

For the past seventeen years Generalissimo Chiang Kai-shek
has been the unchallengeable military leader on the island. Though
he is not regarded as a "revolutionary" leader with far-reaching
historical vision, he is widely considered to be shrewd and ruthless
in consolidating and manipulating personal power. Having sur-

vived a long struggle with a series of warlords and with the Chinese Communists on the mainland, Chiang is accustomed to take complex measures to prevent the growth of military leaders who may effectively challenge his position. Aside from the favorite technique of playing one off against another, Chiang has introduced a strict tenure and rotation system for top command posts and a comprehensive set of political commissars. To prevent any general from establishing a personal clique as a base of power, the term of appointment of the chief of general staffs, commanders-in-chief of the army, navy, air and combined services is two years, and no one can be appointed more than twice for the same office. No commander can expect to challenge Chiang by obtaining sufficient loyalty and support from his subordinates or the local people in so short a time.

The structure of the political department in the armed forces is patterned after the political commissar system of the Communists. Political commissars are charged with the functions of intelligence, security, political indoctrination, and supervision. As distinguished from military officers, they belong to an independent channel of communication and command under the ultimate control of Chiang Ching-kuo. As "loyalty" to Chiang Kai-shek and the KMT is paramount, promotion is based less on individual merit than on connections with the political department or political commissars. The overall morale and efficiency of the military is thus gravely undermined. Underneath the surface calm is a deep-rooted tension between the officer corps and the political commissars. In private, some officers make no secret of their sentiment: "If fight we must one day, we shall have to kill the agents of the Political Department first."[12]

Aside from the professed goal of mainland recovery, a principal concern of Chiang Kai-shek is the effective performance of the internal police function. Should there be a revolt, for whatever cause, he is ready to crush it promptly and without mercy. Every precaution is taken. Native Formosan soldiers are being sent in large number (estimations ranging from 100,000 to 150,000) to Quemoy and Matsu. There is no danger that they will defect to the mainland, and they constitute no threat to the established internal order amid crises. For those stationed inside Formosa, access to live ammunition is carefully denied.

The absence of any prominent military leaders to challenge Chiang Kai-shek and his son Ching-kuo, while insuring the prolongation of the Chiang dynasty, may well be a blessing in disguise for the Formosan people, should Formosa become an independent nation by overthrowing the Chiang dynasty. For according to our tentative projection of future development, Formosa's attainment of independence is most likely to occur in a context where international crisis generates revolutionary changes within Formosa, culminating in a popular uprising with rapid success. Far from being the work of any single general, its success would seem to lie in a spontaneous coalition of several elements—mainland Chinese as well as native Formosans, elites at home as well as abroad, the military as well as civilians. Once Chiang is pushed aside no single general, native Formosan or mainland Chinese, can expect to emerge from the crisis as the sole and unchallengeable strong man with popular support. (Provided, of course, that every precaution is taken to forestall any possible attempt on the part of generals of mainland origin to seize power and align with Communist Chinese.) This is an important factor in avoiding "warlord politics" in Formosa during the crucial period of transition. Instead of displaying loyalty to any single hero as an alternative to Chiang, the public can proudly identify with and show allegiance to the new Republic.

However, this sanguine possibility does not assure a smooth path for a newly independent Formosa. Desirable as it is to have a nonpartisan military oriented solely to national defense, no constitutional provision, even when coupled with the absence of strong men, necessarily guarantees civilian supremacy in a new nation. Particularly when one turns to many newly independent nations around the globe, it is hardly a surprise to discover that the military seizes power.

Unlike nineteenth-century Europe, where the military was predominantly "aristocratic" in origin and outlook, in newly developing nations today the military is typically drawn from far broader layers of the population. Disciplined by a single purpose —"victory, nothing but victory"—and accustomed to a strict hierarchy of authority, military professionals tend to display basic distrust of civilians and to have little taste for party politics. They may be intolerant of the practical operation of "dirty politics," and often mean by this disparaging phrase the accommodation of competing interests that is an invariable fact of life. Since some members of the military profession have a grasp of modern science and technology, they may also be exposed to the complexity of mobilizing the mass and group support required to generate a modern nation state. They tend to line up against whatever vested interests retard industrialization, or seek to exclude some elements of the nation from contributing to the common task of development. Thus the military contains elements whose role can be progressive. At the same time they are cross-pressured by traditional loyalty to the established order.

The perpetual crisis of world insecurity keeps alive the preconditions favorable to the garrison-police state, in which the role of the military, specialized in the management and skill of violence, is dominant. As modern organization techniques are perfected, the military has not been immunized from their impact. Within the military establishment, the control system is based on a highly disciplined hierarchy that also relies on loyalty and group cohesion. When these features are coupled with charismatic leadership, the military is able to exert a special leverage in a world where the expectation of violence shows no sign of decrease, particularly where civilian supremacy is yet to be established.

The critical period for a new body politic is the time immediately following independence when expectations, exaggerated by preindependence promises, are unduly high. If a civilian regime is in charge, it typically operates under extraordinary stress. At a time when only quick tangible returns can satisfy, the task of nation-building is often handicapped by the complexity of the problems, the shortage of trained personnel, and the lack of practical experience. The new elites are badly in need of the unified effort of all concerned. Unfortunately, the unity displayed in the preindependence phase tends to disappear soon after independence, and to disintegrate into factionalism. Hence sharp critical ups and downs often characterize the life of a new nation. Inefficiency, corruption, and the dogmatic defense of vested interests act as brakes on national development. Though not initially inclined to the acquisition of civilian power, the military, secure in its practical monopoly of skills of violence, cannot be expected to hesitate indefinitely from taking advantage of crises of frustration by seizing power.

The effects of a military junta are more often than not damaging and disruptive. While it is suggested that in some nations (particularly in Latin America) a successive series of "reform coups" is a healthy way of achieving reform and progress, any move in that direction at an early stage of Formosa's independence would be a tragedy. While it is possible to transfer certain military skills such as organization and management to the civilian arena, the reverse is not likely to be true. The military is, by its very nature, not trained in public political communication and integration of interests. The military is apt to seek a simple and clearcut solution to a complex problem that requires a disciplined contextual sense if common interests are to be clarified and brought to fruition through a delicate balancing process.

The failure of a civilian government is often a result of its inability to obtain an effective coalition of wide segments of the population. A military takeover does not automatically solve this problem. The task of arousing popular concern, participation, and cooperation in national development is multidimensional: it is not achieved but postponed by the strict imposition of military discipline. To be successful, a military junta no less than a civilian government must obtain wide public support. In the face of growing discontent and opposition, the military is bound to devote more and more national assets and resources to the task of consolidating its power: the result more often impedes, rather than fosters, the immense task of national development in the name of which the seizure of power was originally justified.

In some nations the nonmilitary sector is so far behind that only the military can provide the leadership needed to move the nation forward. The society may be so closed that a military career is the only practical avenue for social advancement and mobility for the underprivileged. Where these conditions occur the effects of military takeover of the civilian decision process are to be viewed in a different light. But Formosa is not a tradition-bound tribe, nor is it an enclave of feudal lords and ignorant serfs. As our analysis has shown, the fundamentals of an impressive national growth are already realized. No military tutelage is necessary; but at the same time the military is sorely needed for its properly specialized role of national defense. Compared with other professions, a military career continues to suffer from remarkably persistent disadvantages—inherited from the past when a Chinese soldier was cast in the role of a thug.

It is imperative that the miltary in Formosa be "nonpartisan" and oriented solely to the defense of national security. With a view to upholding civilian supremacy in deeds as well as in words, we submit the following proposals.

First, *a realistic reorientation of the fundamental goal of national security—from the offensive goal of reconquering mainland China to the defense of Formosa.* The entire defense complex should be adjusted accordingly. The armed forces ought to be reduced substantially on a gradual basis, with proper attention to the shift from military to civilian employment. It seems reasonable to estimate that an armed force of 100,000 men would be ample to defend Formosa. It may be argued that such a small number is altogether insufficient for a nation in the periphery of Communist China. However, let us make no mistake about it: the security of Formosa in the past seventeen years is not attributable to an armed forces of 600,000, as claimed by the Nationalists, but to the continuing presence of the United States Seventh Fleet in the Formosan Straits. Withdraw U.S. forces from the Formosa area, and the Nationalist regime would collapse in twenty-four hours. In view of the massive military buildup on the other side of the Straits, an armed force of 600,000 is too small to make any headway on the mainland, yet too large to be sustained by Formosa's resources. In the foreseeable future, as in the past, Formosa's national security must continue to rely heavily on collective bilateral and multilateral security arrangements.

Second, the principle of civilian supremacy should be embodied in the constitution. The President (chief executive of the state) ought to be the commander-in-chief of the armed forces, and endowed with ultimate authority for defense decisions and military appointments. Such prescriptions, while nothing novel, will serve as a focal point around which community perspectives can stabilize through time.

Third, the political commissar system must be abolished. Political parties should be strictly prohibited from meddling in military affairs. Political education for soldiers is not a partisan matter.

Fourth, a distinct line should be drawn between the defense of national security against external foes and the police function of maintaining internal order. When the military is employed to play these two roles, the probability of military intervention in internal politics increases. In attempting to reduce this probability to a minimum, it is useful to set up a separate police force, charged with sole responsibility for the performance of the internal police function. By divorcing one from another, both military and the police are likely to check excessive power tendencies of both services. In this connection, the role of the military police must be made clear: to carry out the police function exclusively within the framework of the military establishment, under the chain of military command. If its role remains obscure, the military police tend to trespass their jurisdiction.

Finally, we would like to underline the point that in the final analysis, there is no substitute for an effective and responsive decision process. All the preceding proposals would be of no avail were the civilian government unable to act effectively to meet the needs of the nation. As we have elaborated at some length, the military professional is not deliberately oriented toward the seizure of power: he is, however, often provoked to act, when the civilian government fails to measure up to its responsibility. The military reacts to crises. Hence while we have no way of inventing a crisis-proof system, it is possible to reduce the probability of military interposition to a minimum by eliminating conditions likely to lead to crises. In a word, the surest way to uphold the principle of civilian supremacy rests with the establishment of a civilian process of decision capable of creative, realistic problem solving in pursuit of a rising level of participation in all values.

High Levels of
General Enlightenment

AS IN THE building of the "Great Society," education is the most fundamental task in developing a new nation. Without denying the importance of meeting the pressures and strains of daily events that require immediate attention, it must be conceded that the long-term solution to nation-building problems lies in educating the rising generations, who need to be equipped with adequate skills and progressive perspectives conducive to national development. Educational policy must be harmonized with other programs of national development.

Under Japanese rule, education in Formosa was oriented toward the needs of colonial administration. In order to consolidate its rule by obtaining the understanding support of the masses, the Japanese government did a commendable job in raising the level of literacy in Formosa at a time when most Asian nations were bogged down in mass illiteracy. But educational opportunity for the most part was limited to elementary and secondary education. As far as higher education was concerned, there was little opportunity for access and advancement even for the rich, to say nothing of the poor. Even the areas of study were limited, and severe restrictions were imposed on the study of the social sciences and the humanities. Anything that might contribute to the growth of a Formosan's political consciousness was systematically suppressed. As a result, we witnessed a peculiar phenomenon in Formosa. Virtually all gifted talents, when given a chance, were encouraged to pursue a medical career—a profession with a humanitarian mission that afforded the least danger of political consciousness.

When Japan surrendered at the end of World War II, practicing physicians as well as landlords were the only elite groups in Formosa with considerable command of local influence. While the landlords' influence has sharply diminished as a result of land reforms, practicing physicians still play an important role in Formosa's local politics. Lately there has been a new trend for physicians to give up medical practice and to engage in industrial enterprises.

The unique status of the medical profession has strong repercussions among native Formosans of today. Highly cherished in practically every civilized community, in Formosa the medical profession is pursued with a zeal seldom seen elsewhere. This can be testified by the nerve-wracking competition for admission to medical schools at the annual unified college entrance examination for high school graduates. To be admitted to medical schools is highly regarded as a status symbol and an impressive credential for a young man. Unfortunately, the choice of a medical career

is more often than not prompted less by the applicants' own dedication, interest, and temperament than by the misguided persuasion of parents. It has led to an imbalanced allocation (or mis-
allocation) of high-caliber human resources. The outlook of adults
is attributable to a combination of factors—a long-cherished tradition, the present status of physicians, and more importantly, a
deep sense of insecurity and apathy toward careers that touch
politics.

When the Nationalist regime took over Formosa, the level
of education was higher there than in mainland China. Since then,
there has been by and large equal opportunity for the education of
all Formosans; and the educational system has expanded considerably at all levels under Nationalist rule.[13] Inheriting the Confucian tradition of placing a high value upon education, parents,
rich and poor, have generally given it top priority. It is widely
accepted as the key to survival and success in a changing world
of rigorous competition—indeed, as the logical and practical avenue
to power, wealth, and respect, among other valued outcomes. The
community expectations about education are such that any discrimination in this sector is likely to lead to massive resentment.
Whereas the people may not be sophisticated enough to comprehend fully the complex absurdity of Nationalist power structures
and political myths, they are fully competent to judge problems
that directly reach their personal and immediate spheres.

In terms of quality, however, Formosa's education is subject to
critical reappraisal and reform. The most serious problem is the
systematic political indoctrination conducted by the Kuomintang
at all levels, which stifles creative thinking among the younger
generation as well as among "established scholars." Education is
highly politicized. Without exception, all school administrators
are dominated by the KMT machine, and teachers feel constrained to join the KMT en masse. (Even high school students
are targets of membership recruitment.[14]) Hence the entire educational process has virtually become an extension of the KMT's
ideological campaign.

"The Three Peoples' Principles" (San Min Chu I), KMT's basic ideology invented by Sun Yat-sen, is being taught intensively in elementary and high schools, in college, and even after college. It is a required subject for all kinds of examinations—college entrance, civil service, advanced study abroad, and so on. Every essay is expected to conclude with a reference to San Min Chu I (or the policy of mainland recovery), even when the relevance is remote or absurd. (A former minister of education, Chang Chi-yun, a pious preacher of the gospel of San Min Chu I, once traced the origin of modern atomic theory back to the teachings of Confucius, which is supposed to be the source of Dr. Sun's inspiration.)

In mainland China today every individual is taught that all the answers to the complex problems of our time are in the writings of Chairman Mao Tse-tung. Similarly, the San Min Chu I is claimed to be all-inclusive. The political indoctrination based on the San Min Chu I and the slogan of mainland recovery has set a boundary of thought and expression for both academic and nonacademic contexts, with a parochializing effect on the frame of reference.

The task after independence is abundantly clear: to cultivate creative thinking and free expression by doing away with stagnant doctrines and procedures of thought. Creativity can flourish best in an environment of freedom. The task is not easy, but can be tackled with hope once a basic national goal is realistically postulated. It is amazing to see how radically the thinking of Formosan students—all victims of the Kuomintang's mass indoctrination—change, once they are exposed to different opinions in foreign lands. Indeed, the Nationalist regime can hardly find this situation comforting.

At present, Formosa is confronted with an acute crisis of physical fitness among the pupils enrolled in elementary and secondary schools. As population increases at a tempo of 3½ per cent annually, Formosa undergoes a critical shortage of facilities and teachers. Two-shift (or sometimes three-shift) instruction in elementary schools is common. Formosa's present educational system is "6-3-3-4"—six years of elementary school; three years of junior middle school (corresponding to the American junior high school); three years of senior middle school (corresponding to the American senior high school); and four years of college. As compulsory education is confined to the elementary school, admission to the junior middle school and up is based on highly competitive entrance examinations.

Competition at entrance examinations is so severe that "passing examinations" has become the central and sole concern of educators as well as the educated. Under the unbearable pressure of the "examination hell," school life is reduced to a succession of examinations. Burdened by an all-pervading anxiety for their children's future, parents no less than the children, look upon examinations as a matter of life and death. It is inhumane that boys and girls in their formative years are saddled with 16 hours of work a day, and seven days a week, for a sixth grade pupil (8 hours for regular class attendance, 4 hours for cram courses after school, and another 4 hours for homework). Readers can draw their own conclusions about the physical condition of these precocious scholars.[15]

Physical fitness is indispensable to a strong, vital mind, and a harmonious development of mind and body is the key to creative intelligence. The strength of Formosa rests, in the final analysis, upon the well-being of its citizens. It must therefore become a matter of high priority that the children of the new Formosa are assured the benefit of physical as well as intellectual development. The fundamental solution lies in the adoption of a rational population policy to arrest the rapid rate of increase and to make more funds available for education by reducing military expenditures. This is well within the realm of policy when the offensive goal of mainland recovery is reoriented to the defensive goal of Formosa's national development.

Another proposal is to extend compulsory education from six to nine years. This step would not only eliminate the crisis of transition from elementary to junior middle schools, but also contribute constructively to the solution of the unemployment problem. As indicated, even at the present stage of industrial development, Formosa has a problem of surplus manpower to deal with. Unemployment is particularly acute for the less educated and less skilled people. To meet the needs of Formosa's accelerating industrialization for the next decade or so, a minimum of nine years of education is essential to the formation of a useful labor force. It is as usual a matter of priority in the allocation of limited resources; but this step would no longer be delayed on the ground of finance, if the mainland chimera is relinquished.

An important factor that aggravates Formosa's unemployment difficulties is the divorce of formal education from the pressing needs of expanding industrialization. Ironically the outcry over unemployment (and underemployment) is matched by the outcry over the shortage of skilled workers needed in industry. The gap will continue to widen unless appropriate steps are taken. Part of the difficulty, of course, comes from the fact that in an epoch of accelerating change, the training that fits men for today may unfit them for tomorrow. The crux of the problem on Formosa, however, is the fundamental misorientation of the present system. Under the pressure of "examination, nothing but examination," the teachers' role is sadly reduced to a coach who unceasingly prepares students to write entrance examinations. The number who pass competitive examinations of all kinds has become the test of excellence for teachers. Very little attention is paid to the prior question, which is whether the subject matter makes sense, or whether examination writing is the most realistic skill to be inculcated by the educational institutions of developing nations.

As Formosa's industrialization accelerates, the need for skilled and semiskilled workers will be greater than ever. Hence a comprehensive and intensive program of junior technical colleges and vocational schools, coupled with practical training programs, is urgently needed. The scope of the present program must be greatly expanded, and made far more diversified and flexible. By relating education to the practical needs of the nation through the transmission of adequate skills, the gap between manpower requirements and supplies can be bridged.

In the course of vocational and other education, conscious effort should be made to cultivate a new perspective about the significant role of technicians and industrial workers. A time-honored bias in Chinese society is to look upon manual work as degrading; whereas mental work is the proper concern of the learned, manual work is the monopoly of the less educated and the uneducated. Our strong expectation is that as industry provides better career opportunities for the people, the traditional zeal in the excessive pursuit of a public career (supposedly non-manual work) will gradually diminish.

The crises sketched above do not stop at elementary and secondary levels. If anything, they are even more serious for higher education. Instead of a place where creativity and thinking flourish, universities become hothouses for the preparation of more examinations—notably civil service examinations for jobs at home and examinations for studying abroad.

To survive in a society where "graduation means unemployment," a person without connections or background must pass civil service examinations of some sort after receiving his college diploma in order to qualify for a job in public agencies, including government enterprises. The ratio of success in these examinations is normally as low as one in ten. Recruitment practices in the private sector are to a certain extent affected by this tradition of examination. The capacity of the private sector to absorb college graduates is limited, partly because of limited openings, and partly because of lack of adequate skills on the part of applicants.

The problem of unemployment and underemployment for college graduates, if left unchecked, could well lead to the formation of a hard-core group of frustrated and rebellious intellectuals who may endanger the existing order that does so little for them. However, in the midst of rising frustrations, a last hope still remains: to study abroad. As doors at home are closed, young men look elsewhere for new opportunities—particularly to the New World. Experience has shown that once Formosan youths are exposed to the outside world, they are highly susceptible to change. We have called attention to the fact that generally speaking, they begin to feel betrayed by the Nationalist regime, hence they are seized by a sense of indignation. They begin to visualize an independent Formosa and want no part in irresponsible talk about mainland reconquest.

The Nationalist regime is not blind to this potential danger. (Hence the so-called "professional students" of the KMT are quite active around major U.S. and Japanese campuses to supervise the political utterances and behavior of Formosan students.) But the regime has wisely kept the door open for advanced study, evidently recognizing that it also operates as a safety valve. Aside from some relief to the problem of unemployment, the regime has much to gain by the physical absence of many discontented young intellectuals from Formosa. Whatever opposition may sooner or later emanate from abroad, it is believed to be distant; such a threat is certainly more remote than the disaffection that would result from an organized opposition appealing to internal discontent. So long as the door to foreign lands is kept open, a discontented person finds that it pays to "get the hell out of Formosa" rather than to take the risk of attempting to overthrow a tightly controlled police state.

The continuing exodus of college graduates on a massive scale (more than 2,000 annually in recent years), while having the side effect of slightly easing the unemployment, is a great loss to Formosa. They are the intellectual cream of Formosa, and less than 7 per cent return on completion of graduate study abroad. Those who come to the United States (an overwhelming majority) find their talents and skills easily absorbed by the American economy after a fairly brief period of training. This is a source of personal gratification for the successful, but consider the huge investment of Formosa in having educated them for the first 25 years.

The reluctance of these young men to go home, aside from the attraction of better pay and better working conditions abroad, is principally prompted by their basic uncertainty about Formosa's political future. Would they not be required to make the sacrifices called for by Chiang Kai-shek's madness? To them, the war of mainland invasion is not a sacred mission but rather the obsession of an irresponsible politician who could not care less about the welfare of "his thirteen million subjects." The Formosans with an education or a job abroad wonder whether they can become reconciled to being retrapped in Chiang's police regime, especially after having experienced freedom. They are puzzled and worried, and to many of them the wisest course is to wait and see.

The phenomenon of mass exodus of first-rate talents takes place at a time when Formosa itself is badly in need of young blood to vitalize quality education at undergraduate and graduate levels. Formosa has been characterized by foreign observers as a cultural desert, alluding partly to the stagnation of creative thinking caused by political indoctrination and partly to the absence of a successor generation able to carry on with vigor and distinction.

Much of the increase in quantity of education has been at the expense of quality. The graduate study programs in Formosa today are still in an infant stage. The limited resources available are thinly dispersed, rather than concentrated in one or two top universities with proper conditions for advanced study and research. As long as Formosa relies primarily on foreign institutions to give advanced training to its talented youth, it must expect a "brain drain" as students fail to return. Recent government efforts to invite Chinese scholars living abroad to give lectures in Formosa on short-term visits, though perhaps better than nothing, have had little impact upon the quality of education in the country.

The dilemma will continue as long as the basic orientation of the government remains ambiguous and uncertain. A straightforward reorientation of basic national policy would promptly result in adequate solutions for many of Formosa's seemingly insoluble problems. The effective remedy is the attainment of Formosa's independence. Once Formosa becomes independent and the offensive goal toward mainland China is renounced, Formosan intellectuals abroad will gladly return on the completion of their training.

A massive inflow of top talent, endowed with a shared perspective and determination, when properly channeled can lead to a breakthrough in the search for quality in education. Top priority should be given to the concentrated development of one or two university centers that would measure up to international standards in scholarship and research. Pooling the best minds of the nation would not only eliminate unnecesssary waste, but also accelerate fruitful interactions within the intellectual community. When a supportive environment for higher learning is firmly established at home—with the capacity for self-renewal—the pursuit of advanced scholarship and research can be related to the effective problem-solving processes of the national community. By contributing to the practical solution of emerging problems, the intellectual community will command more respect from the public and set a pace in national development. This, in fact, is the key to self-sustaining growth in higher education.

The attainment of self-sustaining growth does not mean a move toward isolation from the outside world; Formosa cannot afford to lose touch with the outside environment. The programs for sending students abroad, though on a smaller scale, should continue; but they will be two-way. No longer fearful of returning to their country, Formosan students who study abroad can be expected to relate their pursuit of knowledge more closely to the pressing needs and problems back home.

A major university center in Formosa will stimulate a two-way operation at another level. Chinese Communists are engaged in the radical reorientation of all phases of life on the mainland, Formosa ought not forfeit its opportunity to conserve the Chinese cultural heritage. Outside the orbit of Communist China, no place in the world is more fitting than Formosa to provide a center where basic Chinese culture can be authentically studied in an atmosphere of freedom. Honolulu and Hong Kong have been suggested as such a center; but Honolulu lacks a general background of Chinese culture, and Hong Kong is still handicapped by British rule, geographical proximity to the mainland, and an extreme emphasis on commerce and industry.

The task, however, is not only to continue and conserve, but also to renew and innovate. Overall education can and should be modernized through the introduction and extensive use of modern scientific methods and new instrumentalities, including film, radio and television, and other "audio-visual" aids. The computer too is revolutionizing not only the productive capacity of human society, but the whole educational process. While the cybernation revolution is principally centered in the United States, its impact has reached far beyond the industrial world. The effectiveness of machine computation promises to liberate man-hours and to open up new outlets for trained personnel. Formosa has a reservoir of thousands of scientists and engineers who have obtained experience in this field in the United States.

Contemporary educational methods are also being influenced by simulation models. For years it has been necessary for engineers to use models in the shape of wind tunnels, bridges, dams, electric generators, and transmission towers. But social scientists in general have been slower in perceiving the full potentialities of model building. This comes, in part, from failure to bridge the theoretical gap between the "thinglike" character of a bridge or an engine and the "symbolic" dimensions of a decision process. Model building has itself become a cultural device of enormous potential for the reconstruction of education. The underlying strategy in enlightenment for Formosa is not emphasis on the individual device, but the integrated and coordinated application of all available instruments.

Bureaucratic Reform

AS A RESULT of the rapid and worldwide expansion of governments and nations, the role of government administration has become more important than ever before. The task of building a new nation, involving all phases of life, calls for the cooperative efforts of all segments of the community. While private initiative is essential to the task, the private sector in newly emerging nations, unlike the advanced nations, is relatively weak. Thus the public sector bears a special responsibility. Not only does it have at its disposal vast resources, trained personnel, for example, but it is mainly responsible for the overall planning and the implementation of development programs. Its role has reached far beyond what is considered the traditional domain of bureaucracy, or the administration of law and order.

During the half-century of Japanese control, native Formosans participated in the administration of local affairs on a very modest scale. They were predominantly confined to the lower positions. When the Japanese surrendered Formosa at the end of World War II, the vacuum left by Japanese bureaucrats was filled by Chinese Nationalists. When the Nationalist regime was exiled to Formosa in 1949, the Central Government of the "Republic of China," with its skeleton kept intact, was placed above the "Taiwan Provincial Government," even though their sphere of jurisdiction (except Quemoy and Matsu) is identical.

The duplication in government structures for governing the same people in the same territory has caused frequent conflicts of jurisdiction as well as administrative inefficiency. According to the administrative hierarchy, decisions made by the Provincial Government of Taiwan can easily be overruled by the Central

Government. Hence the autonomy of the Taiwan Provincial Government is virtually nonexistent. The continuing existence of two layers of administrative structures has enabled the regime to put a large number of mainland refugees on the government payroll. At present every government agency continues to be overstaffed with employees: it is a conservative estimate that what one man can do is now being done by three.

At the national level of government agencies, including public enterprises, mainland Chinese predominate; Formosans' participation is insignificant. In the sphere of provincial and local adminitration, participation by Formosans is substantial in terms of numbers. Yet apart from some department heads of the Provincial Government (for window dressing) and some elected mayors and magistrates (whose authority is eroded by their respective "chief secretaries"—key KMT members), key administrative positions (managerial positions) are also dominated by mainland bureaucrats.[16]

When the swollen bureaucracy took shape in Formosa in 1949, a refugee mentality was prevalent among mainland Chinese. As they saw it, they would either reconquer the mainland within a few years (Chiang Kai-shek had repeatedly assured them at most *five* years) or they would soon be wiped out by Chinese Communists. They did not identify Formosa as their own land or native Formosans as their fellow countrymen, nor did they expect to stay in Formosa for two decades. Perceiving Formosa as a conquered territory up for "grabs," mainland bureaucrats seized every advantage offered by their offices for personal advantage. In an insecure world, a government office, high or low, was a base for the accumulation of personal wealth. The notorious practices of corruption and graft, which were partially accountable for the Communist takeover of the mainland, were repeated in Formosa. Native bureaucrats followed the practices of their mainland colleagues. The Formosans, however, were handicapped by the low offices they held, their primitive "graft-craft," and above all, the lack of an ultimate power elite as a shield.

In any event, at the very outset of the Nationalist rule in Formosa, irreparable damage was done to public administration, since the public lost confidence in the bureaucrats. As the dream of returning to the mainland grows dim with every passing year, there is a growing demand among all elements to identify with Formosa; hence deepening concern is voiced about the detrimental effect of corrupt practices. There has been some outcry for reform, for instance, the imposition of more severe sanctions on offenders; but it is too late. The perspectives and operational techniques of "corrupt bureaucrats" are deeply ingrained in every phase of administration. Short of a radical change, such as independence, no effective remedy is feasible.

Uncertainty about the future, accentuated by the myth of mainland reconquest, has increased the demand for personal security. Faced with the prospect of being overtaken by a younger generation of native Formosans, mainland bureaucrats are extremely sensitive to any sign of change in the status quo. Obsessed with the preservation of "vested interests" (in this connection the same office), they stick rigidly to conventions. The automatic strategy of a stereotyped bureaucrat is to preserve his security by inaction and evasion of responsibility. The living motto that is epidemic among the bureaucratic community is: "The more one does, the more mistakes one makes. The less one does, the less mistakes one makes. And no action, no mistake."

In addition to this damagingly passive perspective, present practices in regard to retirement and promotion have practically ruled out any possibility of administrative vitality. Overburdened by military expenditures, the Nationalist regime has not been able to allocate an adequate pension fund to provide retired employees a minimum standard of living. Hence the retirement system exists only on paper. In 1965 out of a total of 220,000 government employees 5,156 persons were supposed to retire, but only 333 actually did. In 1966 an additional 6,392 was required to retire.[17] Nonenforcement of the retirement system means the continued occupation of key managerial positions by aging mainland bureaucrats and the consequent deprivation of promotion for junior officials. Hence the low morale prevalent among bureaucrats in Formosa today. The "merit system" is an empty slogan.

Each unit of officialdom operates in an arena in which superordinate, coordinate, and subordinate units are involved. As a defense mechanism, bureaucrats are notoriously loath to communicate with other coordinate units lest their own sphere should be encroached. As for the vertical relation, it is full of silent tension. Superiors and subordinates eye each other suspiciously and guardedly. The superiors view their subordinates as potential foes who are conspiring to usurp their posts; the subordinates blame their superiors for blocking the way to promotion. Inter-elite and intra-elite communication is thus strictly formal and imperfect, with the result that mutual withholding of information has gravely undermined administrative efficiency.

The best prospect of improvement again lies in the attainment of independence. Once the offensive goal toward mainland China is replaced by the realistic and constructive goal of developing Formosa, bureaucratic symptoms can be cured. Logically, the first step is to consolidate and simplify the existing administrative structures. Through consolidation and simplification, clarity of authority and responsibility horizontally and vertically can be achieved among various government agencies. Clarity of jurisdiction and responsibility is obviously indispensable to an efficient administrative process.

As a result of consolidation, the present overblown government expenditures can gradually be reduced to half of the present level. What is saved can be used for a much needed pension fund to provide realistic and reasonable implementation for retirement programs. With the opening of new promotional opportunities, a new sense of commitment to high standards may come to life.

One of the most intriguing problems likely to arise in some

newly independent nations is the relationship between "politicians" and "administrators," as understood in conventional usage.

Generally speaking, before the attainment of independence top administrators come from the colonial government. Some local people are also recruited, mainly from the upper classes. They have the advantage of higher education, and they tend to self-perpetuate from generation to generation. Grouping together, administrators become a very special class with shared experience and perspectives during the colonial era. Appointed by the colonial government, they are not responsible to the people and have no popular bases of support. Even as the administrators fail to identify themselves with the people, the people fail to identify with the administrators. During the period of agitation for independence, while not altogether indifferent to the cause of their own countrymen, they usually refrain from committing themselves, partly because of the delicate position in which they find themselves, partly because of their own vested interests.

Accustomed to an administrative process that emphasizes efficiency, authority, hierarchy, and rationality, they consider gradual and orderly advancement as a logic of life. During the colonial rule, as the colonial government was the ultimate source of power with a monopoly of the prescribing function, there were no significant internal politics. Hence they tended to equate bureaucratic administration with the entire political process, which greatly exaggerated their own role. In the transitional period following independence, their skills and services are badly needed, but they suddenly find themselves operating in a very different context, and one to which they are poorly adapted.

The attainment of independence brings to prominence and power a new group of "politicians." Unlike the administrator, the politician's role emerges after independence. The social background of the politicians is more diverse than the administrators'. During the years when they worked for independence, they were denounced as "traitors" and operated either underground or abroad. Their prime task was to agitate and organize the masses, hence they are closely identified with the people and have popular support. Their new role, as they see it, is to articulate and represent the demands and interests of the newly sovereign people.

Since many administrators had displayed indifference or timidity toward the cause of independence, politicians have misgivings about their loyalty and dependability. Inspired by sudden success in obtaining power, they are confident that they can manage the same miraculous performance again in the new task of nation-building. They aim big, and they want quick and bold action. They tend to dismiss the role of administrators as "backward, routine, trivial, and inconsequential."

Because of the basic differences in their perspectives as a result of different life experiences, administrators and politicians tend to have little appreciation of the necessity of an effective working relationship with one another. Instead of acting as partners in nation-building, they tend to become hostile rivals. Their clashes more often than not paralyze the decision process, which paves the way for military intervention in civilian affairs.

Is such a clash between politicians and administrators likely to occur in Formosa after independence? The possibility cannot be ruled out, but hopefully effective measures can be undertaken to anticipate and to cope with the problem.

First of all, it has to be made crystal clear that after independence the job security of present administrators will be assured, except those who are subject to compulsory retirement. This is necessary to assure at least minimum stability and the cooperation of administrators during the changeover; and to retain useful skills and services pending orderly replacement.

Secondly, as indicated before, an important task after independence is to consolidate and reorganize administrative structures. Reorganization would call for the termination of redundant agencies affiliated with the Provincial Government of Taiwan and the Central Government of the "Republic of China," and the creation of new agencies. The termination of old organizations means the liquidation of "the old frontiers" of established bureaucrats. The creation of new ones provides an excellent opportunity for reshuffling key personnel. The selection of key personnel to fill managerial positions should be carefully done by special reference to an individual's competence and ideological commitment. Insofar as top administrative positions are occupied by those who share the essential perspectives of the newly established public order, a more efficient working relation can be worked out between politicians and administrators in their common pursuit of national development.

Encouraging progressive perspectives among bureaucrats is a continuing task that requires every conscious effort. With a closer relation between politicians and administrators—a closer supervision over administrators by elected officials—administrators can be expected to be more responsive to the needs of the people. Under Nationalist rule, as the administrative process is dominated by KMT's party machine, administrators are covertly responsible to the ruling party rather than the people. Meanwhile, as the Formosan people have been denied effective influence over the prescribing (legislative) function, popular access to the government is mainly confined to the application phase of the decision process. The people, in their confrontation with administrators, more often than not feel frustrated, because they seem to be at the mercy of the "public servants." Accordingly, since the people cannot escape from the power implications of the government, and government functions are all-pervasive, they have little inclination to identify positively with the government. An apathetic public is a notorious source of weakness. A new sense of civic responsibility may emerge when the people have access to prescribing as well as applying functions, and when their elected officials keep an eye on administrators. In the final analysis, no serious analyst would deny that an enlightened and responsible public is the true strength of a working democracy.

A Rational Family Program

IT IS COMMONLY recognized that the family is the basic unit for political socialization; and in the early formation of children's personality and civil perspectives no other institution exerts a more far-reaching impact than the family. The close link between childhood experience and adult behavior is well known. Psychoanalytic theory indicates that the perspectives an individual gains at an early age are usually most enduring, even when they are exposed to differing contexts and other cultures at later stages of life. Early experience in childhood tends to provide a basic frame of reference for the selection and incorporation of facts and concepts at later stages of development. Recent study also indicates that an individual's political orientation shows a strong tendency to stabilize at early adolescence.

An established public order is most likely to perptuate itself when sustained by citizens with shared perspectives—shared identifications, demands and expectations—from generation to generation. The task of preparing to stabilize shared perspectives across generations is particularly crucial for a new nation, since its public order has only come into being. And the proper starting point is the family.

The long years of Japanese rule, despite official efforts on behalf of "Japanization," had little impact upon the basic pattern of family life in Formosa—a legacy of ancient Chinese cultures. As Formosa was an agricultural society, the traditional big family continued to prevail throughout the island. Three or sometimes four generations, bound together by close kinship, lived under one roof, headed by the senior male member of the family. The family, operated as a miniature community, was the center of existence. Submissiveness toward senior authority in the family, justified by the Confucian ethics of filial piety, predisposed people to absolute obedience of absolute authority. Hence Confucianism was as much indulged (and exploited) by Japanese colonial rulers as by generations of Chinese emperors. A paternal relation was sought between the colonial rulers and the ruled in the exercise of authority.

The big-family system operated smoothly in an agricultural setting. The family usually was an individual's focal center, where enlightenment, skill, wealth, power, respect, affection, and rectitude were transmitted from generation to generation. Traditionally the Formosan family was responsible for the religious education of its members; instead of going to the temple, families generally conducted their own religious ceremonies. While senior members exercised highly arbitrary authority, they did in turn provide basic security and opportunity for other members of the family. The family absorbed all of its own labor force. The larger the family, the higher its productivity.

But as industrialization and urbanization accelerate, this pattern of family relations is confronted with dilemmas. Aside from shaping and sharing affection and rectitude, the family finds itself no longer able to perform its traditional functions effectively. Not only is it unable to provide minimum economic security and opportunity for its members, but the tasks of transmitting enlightenment and skill are taken over by institutions of the larger community. This profound change, however, does not easily bring about corresponding modifications of perspectives within the family. The older generations especially find it hard to reconcile themselves to the new realities, even though their reduced role and growing ineffectiveness are evident to any candid observer. Senior members of the family continue to assert traditional authority, without the corresponding capacity to provide basic protection and opportunity for their juniors. The gap (and sometimes the clash) between generations is principally attributable to this fact. Formosa's entire family system is undergoing a profound transformation.

In the process of transformation, perplexing problems arise. Whereas the "struggle for life" becomes more tense than ever, the family is not properly directed to family programs based on an enlightened and realistic population policy. A rapid increase of population (annual rate 3½ per cent) not only offsets the gains of economic growth in recent years, but also aggravates the problems of "undereducation" and "unemployment." In Formosa there are no religious reasons that inhibit family planning. The principal impediment to the candid acceptance of such programs is the offensive goal of mainland reconquest projected by the Nationalist leaders. Recent surveys indicate that the Formosan people, under the severe stresses of life, are generally receptive to the idea of family planning, although they have not altogether discarded the concept of a big family. The initiative for family planning has been taken by private organizations, but without unambiguous government guidance and support, the outcome is more exploratory than substantial. Apparently the Nationalist regime gives this support without compromising the mythical goal of mainland reconquest and reconstruction which is alleged to require a huge supply of manpower. However, as soon as the basic national goal is oriented to the development of Formosa, an enlightened and realistic policy of population control by means of proper family planning can be systematically encouraged.

Lately, it has become increasingly apparent that the traditional family system does not adequately prepare an individual for modern adult life in general or for political participation in particular. Within a big family overemphasis on senior authority has led to a dependency relation within the family. Junior members as a rule have little sense of initiative, independence, and responsibility, since they are denied participation in the consideration of family affairs that affect their own welfare. This is particularly true in the case of women, who have been taught, according to the Confucian ethics, to obey "fathers before marriage, husbands after marriage, and sons after the death of husbands." Modern psychocultural research suggests that not only do childhood experiences have great bearing upon adult behavior, but experiences with authority figures in the family setting also affect responses to authority in subsequent political participation in the larger community. It seems too much to expect an individual who lacks a sense of initiative, independence, and responsibility to play an active and responsible role in the democratic process.

In a big family, as the family is the shelter of one's existence, one always feels secure at home and highly insecure when away from home. Contrasted with the family, the outside world appears unkind and even hostile. Hence one is predisposed to withdraw from interaction with others as much as possible, and a large part of leisure time is spent within the group setting provided by the family. Probably the traditional isolationism of the family exerts a permanently limiting effect on empathy with strangers, including the larger national community. The individual is trained not to allow his generous impulses or his curiosity to extend beyond the circle of the family. While family solidarity grows, basic trust toward other human beings is weakened. And the basic trust is vital to the formation of functional associations as well as the task of nation-building.

Therefore, we strongly urge that every conscious effort be made to foster the trend toward egalitarianism in the form of smaller families. The new model family—the nuclear family—will be centered on parents and unmarried children; the key emphasis ought to remain on affection and rectitude—the sphere in which Formosan families were most successful in the past. An affectionate family life is an indispensable source of strength and security in a world of personal insecurity. In the framework of an egalitarian family affection between family members is spontaneous and mutual. Children are likely to be consulted in solving problems that affect their welfare. Parents are bound to display a keener sense of voluntary responsibility for the many-sided growth of children; and children early assume a responsible attitude toward parents. Such a family circle would help prepare children for democratic and responsible participation in future political life.

It is evident from contemporary Chinese political and social history that a fundamental barrier to modernization is an individual's strong personal loyalty to the family at the expense of the larger community and the nation. The omnipotence of the family was understandable when it performed manifold functions in meeting the essential needs of an individual and was the center of his existence. Yet in the contemporary context, a nuclear family can no longer be a shelter in which one is securely isolated from the rest of the community. As interdependence deepens, interaction with others becomes more frequent. Less burdened with family obligations, one finds more time to associate with persons other than one's own relatives, and the individual learns to adjust to the life of the larger community, not to withdraw from it. The new emphasis is likely to have a constructive effect on one's ability to trust and associate with other human beings on both a personal and a relatively impersonal basis. Such a capacity is essential to the ready development of functional associations; and the growth of pluralism in turn aids in expanding an individual's frontier of loyalty to intermediate communities and the nation.

In order to make of the family a viable unit for political socialization in the post-independence era, a campaign of enlightenment will be necessary to project a new image of the family, respecifying the authority of parents and the obligations of junior members. The new role of family members toward all communities must be clarified and stressed.

Parents bear a distinctive responsibility for the political education and orientation of their children. After independence, as politics becomes everybody's business because of general participation, political talk within the family will no longer be taboo, as it is now. The emerging civic interest in politics and modern mass media will expose children to political symbols at an earlier stage. From natural curiosity, they will ask all sorts of questions relating to politics. How parents will cope with the situation is of great significance.

As a result of Japanese colonial rule and Nationalist police control, Formosan parents are generally ambivalent toward politics. On the one hand they regard it as too risky to try, but on the other hand they are well aware of the implications of power for their lives. At present, as President Chiang Kai-shek is supposed to be "immortal," no parent is so indiscreet as to suggest openly that "everybody can be a President." But Formosan parents place a high value on a public career. What is fundamentally lacking seems to be rational optimism. If independence kindles a new sense of pride, opens up a new political frontier, and eliminates the pervasive atmosphere of an unnamed fear, we can be hopeful that Formosan parents will regain self-confidence as at least partial masters of their own destiny. And the self-confidence of children can and should be deliberately cultivated by self-respecting parents.

As the movement toward egalitarianism proceeds, new problems will arise, particularly in connection with the elders and juveniles of broken families.

Orientals see the plight of senior citizens in Western society as unusually harsh in its "spiritual life" (by which is meant affection and respect). However, this observation tends to be exaggerated. No longer an economic burden to children or grandchildren, the elderly in the West are motivated to make themselves interesting and attractive to the younger. Normally a close and affectionate relation can be maintained on a voluntary basis. Senior citizens in the West are well prepared psychologically and materially early in life as to what to expect from their descendants in later years. As the small family system takes shape, the economic security of the elderly would ultimately depend on the social security system and other welfare programs, rather than on their descendants.

Formosans Abroad

ACUTELY aware of the sheer magnitude of the task of nation-building, we have in these pages submitted some fundamental

guide lines for an independent Formosa. Our proposals are necessarily brief and tentative; but they have put our recommendation for "one China, one Formosa" in a proper and responsible
perspective.

We have defined the fundamental task as establishing a public
order in which all values are widely shaped and shared, and genuine pluralism finds expression within the framework of an effective
decision process. At a time when the process of communization is
going forward on mainland China, Formosa may be able to renew
as well as conserve the distinctive cultural heritage of all Chinese
in an environment of freedom.

Structural changes are indispensable in establishing a new public order. But they are sterile and ephemeral unless the people are
able to mould an appropriate character. To some extent a stable
public order fosters the appearance of personality types that har-
monize with the regime; and conversely a new form of personality
facilitates the eventual modification of a constitutional system.

Those who remained in Formosa over the years have accumulated invaluable experience under the trying conditions of Nationalist repression, and they can inject a sense of realism into
future planning and action. Those who have been abroad may take
a while to reorient themselves to the conditions inside Formosa.
But with their educational backgrounds and wider exposure to the
outside world, they can provide much needed innovation and a
broader perspective.

Inside Formosa today political agitation and communication
must go underground. The internal audiences are largely cut off
from political communications with their countrymen abroad because of the Nationalists' severe censorship of correspondence. At
present, therefore, no concrete alliance between external and internal participants could come to the surface. If the cause of Formosan independence is to prosper, Formosan youths abroad must
play a responsible part. With appropriate tact, they can liberate
themselves from the bonds of old and obsolete tradition, without

rejecting the viable elements of the great inheritance of all Chinese. It would be a deplorable waste of talent if they allowed themselves to become an isolated and cynical group. Above all, they must prepare themselves ideologically to lead on the basis of accepted merit, not privileges, as has so often been true of intellectuals in the past. A sense of identity with the common fate is a requisite of strong democratic leadership.

As a means of fostering common perspectives and of contributing to the future, new intellectual methods ought to be applied where possible. More concretely, Formosan intellectuals abroad can make fruitful use of the "decision seminar" technique. A decision seminar is a "problem solving" enterprise. Such seminars would focus on the policy problems of building a Formosan nation state. Special attention must be paid to the questions that are likely to arise in the period of transition. A fact of political life is that the functions of planning (intelligence) and appraisal can be adequately performed by intellectuals even without access to power (i.e., before independence).

Problem solving calls for a contextual procedure that guides the focus of attention back and forth between part and whole. Appropriate to this end is an agenda of periodic meetings among competent and like-minded persons. Initially participants will be selective and limited. But as a seminar progresses, its scope gradually expands. Such activities are quite practicable at least in the United States, Canada, and Japan, where many Formosan intellectuals are gathered. Decision seminars are relatively costless. They can be conducted at convenient locations on major campuses, cities, or regions, and they can be informal in style. As the prospective participants are well educated (they have either completed or are completing graduate degrees) and familiar to one another through past or present shared experiences, they can be expected to work smoothly with each other. One task of a seminar is to clarify the overriding goals of the participants and to translate these into objectives for the short term, the mid term, and the long term. Trained in a variety of disciplines, participants can be expected to bring an interdisciplinary approach to bear on practical problem solving.

Such an interacting process may be a fresh and exciting experience for many Formosan youths. The rewards are more immediate than national problem solving itself, and will surely improve the capability of the participants to articulate and reason together, and also to lead and to follow.

A crystallized consensus among Formosan intellectuals about the course of Formosa's future development is indispensable in establishing genuine communication between Formosan and mainland intellectuals. We have emphasized that in the long run a genuine understanding between these two groups is in the common interest of all. Its success or failure will be determined largely by whether the two million mainland Chinese in Formosa will be accorded genuine equality after independence. The existing crisis —a virtual breakdown of political dialogue between mainland Chinese and native Formosans (whether inside or outside Formosa)—is a reminder of the magnitude of the task. Inside Formosa there is no effective communication, and off the island Formosan and Chinese intellectuals have deliberately avoided political confrontations from a sense of sheer futility exacerbated by contempt and suspicion. But these facts must not be allowed to overshadow the possibility of establishing political communications between Chinese and Formosan intellectuals abroad.

There are more mainland Chinese abroad than Formosans. Although their experiences in Formosa up to the completion of their college education parallels that of native Formosans, mainland Chinese usually do not identify with Formosa, partly because of a mystical Chinese "superiority complex," and partly because of Chiang's myth of mainland reconquest. While liberal elements who echo the proposition of Formosa's independence are not lacking among mainland intellectuals, their perspective is profoundly different from what is generally prevalent among native Formosans.

An independent Formosa, as they see it, will be a temporary relief from Chiang's totalitarian control—and also a temporary escape from Mao's Communist rule. Once Chiang and Mao pass from the political scene, they think it is inevitable that Formosa will once again be part of mainland China. They strongly believe that China is destined to be the center of the universe, and see the cycle of "split—union—split" as an iron law of Chinese political history.

The perspective of nonliberals and antiliberals about Formosa's independence is colored by distortion, contempt, and panic. Formosa's independence movement is denounced as a conspiracy—ironically, of either Communist China or the United States, and its participants are called, impartially, stupid and ambitious politicians exploited by Communists, or puppets of the United States imperialists. To them, Formosa's independence is treasonable, a betrayal of all that China has always stood for. They fear that an independent Formosa will be only for native Formosans; mainland Chinese will be "buried in the Pacific Ocean." It is inconceivable to them that Formosa can be a viable independent nation, separated from mainland China, without being somebody's puppet. Underneath all the dogmas and distortions lies a deep-rooted fear: when mainland Chinese read the angry indictments of systematic Nationalist brutality toward native Formosans, their fear of possible retaliation equals the Formosans' resentment of the Nationalists.

In balanced perspective it appears that the atrocities of the past were the work of a handful of irresponsible Nationalist bosses. Most mainland Chinese are as innocent as native Formosans: both are fellow victims of a degenerate Nationalist rule. Genuine cooperation and integration between native Formosans and mainland Chinese is both possible and imperative, stemming from enlightened self-interest. At stake is survival and freedom. For mainland Chinese who cling to the dream of sharing the glory of the Chinese Communist empire, it is well to bear in mind that children whose parents happen to have been affiliated with the Nationalists in the past are still being discriminated against in schools on the mainland for having "reactionary blood," although they belong to the new breed born and brought up after the Communist takeover.

If mainland Chinese are presented with a constructive and comprehensive blueprint for a future Formosa by responsible, moderate Formosan leaders, it will be apparent that they cannot dismiss Formosa's independence movement as nothing more than an international conspiracy. They can begin to see that Chinese culture has a real chance of self-renewal in an environment of freedom. And they will gradually discard obsolete political bonds and become proud citizens of a new Formosa. Beyond question that path is long and hazardous, calling for patience as well as tact; the Chinese, it may be recalled, are famous for their patience.

According to an ancient Chinese proverb, "A journey of a thousand miles must begin with a single step." After the first step, which depends on small-group initiative, comprehensive campaigns of enlightenment are necessary in the mass media. Such campaigns must include a complete map of the goal values and institutions of a free Formosa, conjoined with necessary specifications.

In human resources, economic development, standards of literacy, communication networks, and many other assets, Formosa is much better off than a great many of the member states of the United Nations. The shadow of Communist China, though omnipresent, is no reason to counsel retreat. Separated from the European continent by the Strait of Dover, twenty-one miles wide, Great Britain became a first-rate sea-oriented power, not a continental satellite. The Straits of Formosa are a hundred miles wide.

A Viable Prospect

AMERICAN foreign policy is evidently preparing to cope with the approaching emergence of a Chinese Communist leadership beyond the "Yenan generation." The decision-makers of many countries other than the United States are evincing a willingness to take a fresh look at an old problem in the light of changed conditions. Hence the presumptive timeliness of our re-exploration of the "Chinese-U.N.-U.S." tangle, and the policy relevance of the proposal to abide by the "one China, one Formosa" formula. According to this recommendation, Communist China would occupy "China's" seats in both the General Assembly and the Security Council in place of the Nationalist delegation; and simultaneously Formosa would be assured membership in the United Nations upon attaining independence through self-determination.

It is not far-fetched to expect the United Nations to become the champion of Formosa's self-determination, as it has in fostering decolonization. Handicapped by the uncertain scope of its authority and by the scarcity of resources actually at its disposal, the U.N. may find it exceedingly difficult, if not impossible, to overcome Nationalist resistance against holding an impartially administered plebiscite inside Formosa. Nevertheless—and this is a policy-relevant consideration—the moral endorsement by the U.N. of a just cause cannot fail to give decisive encouragement to the suppressed aspirations of the overwhelming majority of Formosans.

Once the United Nations insists on applying the principle of self-determination to settle the *indeterminate* status of Formosa— hence simultaneously to solve the Chinese participation question —the self-help movement among Formosans can be relied upon to generate conditions essential to Formosa's survival as an independent state.

Independence would raise new though manageable problems, and the threat of Communist China would not vanish overnight. As long as the United Nations falls short of being a centralized agency for effective peace-keeping, the security of Formosa would best be assured by continuing the twelve-year alliance with the United States. The public order of an emerging national movement calls for a decision process that facilitates both effective action and widespread participation while the Nationalist power structure is disintegrating. The common challenge is to build in Formosa a democratic body politic that would enable Chinese culture to achieve creative expression in a modern pluralistic society and would act responsibly in the world arena.

As an independent nation in law and in fact, the new Formosa-oriented polity will abandon any obsessional and fictional claims to represent 700 million Chinese on the mainland, and cease offering dangerous and futile provocations to mainland China. Freed of the fantasies and abuses of Chiang's dictatorial leadership, the new Formosa can become a viable and responsible member of the world community. By relying more and more fully on the collective self-help of the people a durable Formosan republic will persevere until the Chinese Communists bury their claims to Formosa.

That a genuinely popular and viable state of Formosa is the key to unlock the China impasse may become increasingly apparent as future events unfold. Should the people of Formosa demonstrate that independence is neither a personal affair of Chiang's nor an artificial outcome of United States strategy, but rather the crystallized expression of popular aspirations, many more members of the world community, including eventually the leadership that emerges in Peking, can be expected to incline favorably toward Formosa's new status. The viability of Formosa's independence can thus eliminate the root problem that besets Washington and Peking, and their mutual relations can be progressively normalized. As world community expectations about Formosa's independence are stabilized, an explosive threat to world security in the Far East is eliminated.

The conclusion is that the "one China, one Formosa" policy, as distinguished from the "two Chinas" formula, is the solution offering the greatest promise of clarifying and serving the common interest of the United Nations, the people of Formosa, the United States, and ultimately the people of mainland China. This policy will hasten the day when the Chinese "representation" question will be a thing of the past.

Bibliography and Notes

For the sake of the general reader we have kept bibliographic citations to a highly selective minimum. At the beginning of the notes for each chapter there is a short list of titles. The notes themselves are extremely condensed and are intended, among other considerations, to provide a guide to points of public or scholarly dispute.

Unless otherwise specified, general references to the pertinent literature in Chinese are omitted. For the account of daily events on Formosa, we have relied primarily on *Central Daily News* (international edition), the official newspaper of the Kuomintang, *United Daily News* (overseas edition), and *China Post*, all published in Taipei. The former two are in Chinese and the latter in English.

Chapter 1 China in the United Nations

A convenient way to become familiar with the question of Chinese participation in the U.N. is the *Yearbook of the United Nations*, published by Columbia University Press in cooperation with the United Nations and by the U.N. Office of Public Information. The interested reader will find there pertinent documentary references to the annual China debate in the Assembly. Other introductory reference works include: W. Chamberlin, T. Hovet, Jr., and

E. Hovet, *A Chronology and Fact Book of the United Nations, 1941–1964* (Dobbs Ferry, N.Y.: Oceana, 1964); "Issues Before the General Assembly," *International Conciliation* (various dates); C. Eagleton and R. N. Swift, eds., *Annual Review of United Nations Affairs* (New York: New York University Press, various dates); Office of Public Information, United Nations, *Everyman's United Nations*, 7th ed. (New York, 1964).

Useful guides to Chinese participation in the U.N. include M. S. McDougal and R. M. Goodman, "Chinese Participation in the United Nations: The Legal Imperative of A Negotiated Solution," 60 *Am. J. Int'l L.* 671 (1966); *China, the United Nations and United States Policy* (New York: UNA-USA National Policy Panel, 1966); L. M. Tondel, Jr., ed., *The International Position of Communist China* (Dobbs Ferry, N.Y.: Oceana, 1965); F. B. Schick, "The Question of China in the United Nations," 12 *Int. & Comp. L. Q.* 1232 (1963); R. Higgins, *The Development of International Law Through the Political Organs of the United Nations*, Pt. III (London: Oxford University Press, 1963). For earlier treatment, S. Appleton, *The Eternal Triangle? Communist China, the United States and the United Nations* (East Lansing: Michigan State University Press, 1961) and T. Lie, *In the Cause of Peace: Seven Years with the United Nations* (New York: Macmillan, 1954).

The literature on the United Nations is vast. Standard treatises are: L. M. Goodrich, *The United Nations* (New York: Crowell, 1959); I. L. Claude, Jr., *Swords Into Plowshares: The Problems and Progress of International Organization*, 3d rev. ed. (New York: Random House, 1964). See also A. Ross, *The United Nations: Peace and Progress* (Totowa, N.J.: Bedminster Press, 1966); N. J. Padelford and L. M. Goodrich, eds., *The United Nations in the Balance: Accomplishments and Prospects* (New York: Praeger, 1965).

An incisive analysis of the dynamic process of the U.N. is O. Schachter, "The Relation of Law, Politics and Action in the United Nations," 109 *Hague Academy Recueil des Cours* 169 (1963). R. B. Russell and J. E. Muther, *A History of the United Nations Charter: The Role of the United States, 1940–1945* (Washington: Brookings Institution, 1958), is indispensable for understanding the shared expectations of the framers of the U.N. Charter. The U.S. view on major U.N. issues is expressed in R. N. Gardner, *In Pursuit of World Order: U.S. Foreign Policy and International Organizations*, rev. ed. (New York: Praeger, 1966).

Concerning the changing role of the General Assembly, see L. M. Goodrich and A. P. Simons, *The United Nations and the Maintenance of International Peace and Security* (Washington: Brookings Institution, 1955); B. V. Cohen, *The United Nations: Constitutional Developments, Growth, and Possibilities* (Cambridge: Harvard University Press, 1961); and H. G. Nicholas, *The United Nations as a Political Institution*, 2d ed. (New York: Oxford University Press, 1963). See also G. Rosner, *The United Nations Emergency Force* (New York: Columbia University Press, 1963); J. G. Stoessinger et al., *Financing the United Nations System* (Washington: Brookings Institution, 1964).

On the trend toward universality of membership, see R. M. MacIver, *The Nations and the United Nations* (New York: Carnegie Endowment for International Peace, 1959); E. Stein, *Some Implications of Expanding United Nations Membership* (New York: Carnegie Endowment for International Peace, 1956).

On bloc politics in the U.N., see H. R. Alker, Jr., and B. M. Russett, *World Politics in the General Assembly* (New Haven: Yale University Press, 1965); T. Hovet, Jr., *Bloc Politics in the United Nations* (Cambridge: Harvard University Press, 1960); R. O. Keohane, "Political Influence in the General Assembly," *International Conciliation*, No. 557 (1966).

The Sino-Soviet rift has lessened the support of Peking's participation from Moscow; see the classic D. S. Zagoria, *The Sino-Soviet Conflict, 1956–1961* (Princeton: Princeton University Press, 1962) and W. E. Griffith, *The Sino-Soviet Rift* (Cambridge: MIT Press, 1964).

For the Nationalist-Communist competition in seeking support of the African members, see G. T. Yu, "Peking Versus Taipei in the World Arena: Chinese Competition in Africa," 3 *Asian Survey* 439 (1963); L. M. S. Slawecki, "The Two Chinas in Africa," 41 *Foreign Affairs* 398 (1963).

On the double veto, see L. Gross, "The Question of Laos and the Double Veto in the Security Council," 54 *Am. J. Int'l L.* 118 (1960); E. Jimenez de Arechaga, *Voting and Handling of Disputes in the Security Council* (New York: Carnegie Endowment for International Peace, 1950).

1. The procedures for approving credentials are grounded in the Rules of Procedure for each organ. See Rules 27–29 of the Rules of

Procedure of the General Assembly, as amended during the 18th session by Resolution 1990, U.N. Doc. A/520/Rev. 7 (17 Dec. 1963); Rules 13 to 17 of Provisional Rules of Procedure of the Security Council, U.N. Doc. S/96/Rev. 4 (1952).

2. The United States, though still a champion of the Chinese Nationalist regime, has shifted its position from the admission theory to the representation theory in its effort to block Peking's participation in the U.N. The shift took place at the 16th Assembly in 1961.

3. In 1962, for example, the issue of Chinese participation was dealt with by the Trusteeship Council, Committee on Arrangements for Conference for Purpose of Reviewing Charter, Commission on Human Rights, Statistical Commission, Social Commission, Commission on Status of Women, and Commission on Narcotic Drugs (1962 Yearbook of the United Nations, p. 117).

4. A notable exception was the decision of the Universal Postal Union to seat Peking in May 1950, which was soon reversed when the Korean war broke out. See G. A. Godding, Jr., The Universal Postal Union (New York: New York University Press, 1964), pp. 92–95.

5. Chairman, U.S. Delegation to the U.N. Conference on International Organization, San Francisco, 1945, Charter of the United Nations: Report to the President on the Results of the San Francisco Conference (Dept. of State Pub. No. 2349) (Washington: Government Printing Office, 1945), p. 60.

6. Gen. Ass. Resolution 377A(V), 3 Nov. 1950.

7. In Claude's view, "the veto has assumed larger proportions in the minds of cynical critics and disillusioned idealists than in the workings of the United Nations. The size of the veto problem cannot be accurately measured by tabulating the instances of its use." Swords Into Plowshares, p. 141.

8. 226 United Nations Treaty Series 3 (1950); and 248 id. 213 (1956).

9. We use "public order" in the same sense as in M. S. McDougal, H. D. Lasswell, and I. Vlasic, Law and Public Order in Space (New Haven: Yale University Press, 1963). "Public order" is distinguished from civic order. By minimum public order is meant the prevention of unauthorized coercion, and by maximum public order the promotion of the greater production and wider distribution of all values.

10. "United States Policy on Nonrecognition of Communist China" (Dept. of State Memorandum to Missions Abroad), 39 *Dept. State Bull.* 385, 387 (1958).

11. Former U.S. Assistant Secretary of State Harlan Cleveland was reported to have made such a suggestion (*New York Times*, Nov. 3, 1961, p. 9). William R. Frye also observed: "The Soviet Union curiously helped build up the United States' margin of victory by insisting upon posing the question in such an extreme manner that fence-sitters were driven into the American camp, or prompted to hold aloof" (*Christian Science Monitor*, Dec. 16, 1961, p. 1).

12. Gen. Ass. Resolution 500 (V), adopted on the report of the First Committee, at the 330th plenary meeting (fifth session), 18 May 1951.

13. Article VI of the Treaty. For text see 31 *Dept. State Bull.* 899 (1954).

14. 69 *Stat.* 7 (1955).

15. *China and the Asian-African Conference (Documents)* (Peking: Foreign Languages Press, 1956), p. 28. These five principles are: (1) respect for each other's sovereignty and territorial integrity, (2) mutual nonaggression, (3) noninterference in each other's internal affairs, (4) equality and mutual benefit, and (5) peaceful coexistence.

16. *New York Times*, June 29, 1956, pp. 1–2. In its intensified campaign to obtain Nationalist defections, Peking went so far as to offer the Nationalists amnesty, rewards for "meritorious services," jobs on the mainland, and the right to visit their mainland homes, including the right to return to Taiwan (*id.*, Jan. 31, 1956, p. 1).

17. See *id.*, Nov. 23, 1958, p. 32.

18. *Peking Review*, Aug. 9, 1960, p. 14.

19. K. Mehnert, *Peking and Moscow* (New York: Putnam, 1963), p. 452.

20. *November 1965: African nations having diplomatic relations with* Communist China: Algeria, Burundi, Central African Republic, Congo (Brazzaville), Dahomey, Ghana, Guinea, Mali, Morocco, Kenya, Senegal, Somalia, Sudan, Tanzania, Tunisia, Uganda, United Arab Republic, Zambia; with Nationalist China: Cameroon, Chad, Congo (Leopoldville), Gabon, Ivory Coast, Liberia, Libya, Madagascar, Mauritania, Niger, Rwanda, Sierra Leone, Togo, Upper Volta, South Africa; with neither: Ethiopia, Malawi, Nigeria, Gambia. *November 1966: African nations having diplomatic relations with*

Communist China: Algeria, Congo (Brazzaville), Ghana, Guinea, Mali, Mauritania, Morocco, Kenya, Somalia, Sudan, Tanzania, Tunisia, Uganda, United Arab Republic, Zambia; with Nationalist China: Botswana, Cameroon, Chad, Congo (Democratic Republic of), Dahomey, Gabon, Ivory Coast, Lesotho, Liberia, Libya, Madagascar, Malawi, Niger, Rwanda, Sierra Leone, South Africa, Togo, Upper Volta; with neither: Burundi, Central African Republic, Ethiopia, Gambia, Nigeria, Senegal.

21. *U.N. Doc.* A/AC.38/L.21 (1950).

22. *U.N. Doc.* A/L.360 (1961).

23. *U.N. Doc.* A/L.375 (1961).

24. *U.N. Doc.* A/L.500 (1966).

25. MacIver, *The Nations and the United Nations*, p. 55.

26. Having charged Peking's aggression against India, the representative of India concluded that "the only effective way to check Chinese military adventurism is to make it accept its responsibilities as a member of the world Organization and thereby be subject to the views and disciplines of this august body" (17 *U.N.* GAOR 597, 1962).

27. 16 *id.* 899 (1961).

28. See 11 *id.* 50–52 (1956) (remark of the Nationalist delegate).

29. See Lin Piao, "Long Live the Victory of People's War!" *Peking Review*, Sept. 3, 1965, pp. 9–30; the text can also be found in *New York Times*, Sept. 4, 1965, p. 2.

30. 16 *U.N.* GAOR 905 (1961).

31. *Ibid.* at 1046 (remark of U.S. representative).

32. "U.S. Policy on Nonrecognition of Communist China," 39 *Dept. State Bull.* 385, 387 (1958).

33. 16 *U.N.* GAOR 905 (1961).

34. At a press conference on September 29, 1965 (*Peking Review*, Oct. 8, 1965, p. 12).

35. 16 *U.N.* GAOR 998 (1961).

36. For the remarks at the 16th Assembly, see *ibid.* at 926–29, 997–1000, and 1018–20 (Nigeria, Sierra Leone, and Federation of Malaya). For the 17th Assembly, see 17 *id.* 618–19, 626–27, 644–45, 647–48 (1962) (remark of Japan, Cyprus, Central African Republic, Federation of Malaya). Concerning the 18th session, see *U.N. Gen. Ass. Off. Rec., 18th Sess., Plenary* 6–7, 16–17 (A/PV.1247), and 16–18 (A/PV.1248) (1963) (remark of Liberia, Central Afri-

can Republic, Senegal). For the 20th Assembly, see particularly the statement by Jamaican representative: *U.N. Gen. Ass. Provisional Verbatim Record, 20th Sess., Plenary* 22–30 (A/PV.1379) (16 Nov. 1965).

37. On the Canadian statement, see *U.N. Gen. Ass. Provisional Verbatim Record, 21st Sess., Plenary* 2–17 (A/PV.1475) (23 Nov. 1966). See also *ibid.* at 66–70 (A/PV.1478) (25 Nov. 1966, Netherlands); *ibid.* at 71–86 (A/PV.1479) (28 Nov. 1966, Malaysia); *ibid.* at 58–65 (A/PV.1479) (28 Nov. 1966, Trinidad and Tobago); *ibid.* at 2–6 (A/PV.1479) (28 Nov. 1966, Ireland).

38. On the eve of annual debate on the Chinese participation question by the General Assembly the Committee of One Million has customarily bought space in a few leading newspapers to publicize a declaration opposing Peking's participation and a list of the congressional endorsers. The last political advertisement of the kind appeared in the *New York Times* of October 31, 1966 (p. 12). Most recently Senator Jacob K. Javits has publicly withdrawn from membership in the Committee "in the interest of [his] duty as a United States Senator to retain freedom of action regarding Communist China." In his view the Committee's inflexible position toward Communist China "forecloses even the hope of negotiation" with Peking. He was reported to have sent copies of his letter of withdrawal to 49 other senators and 284 representatives who are members of the Committee. On the same day Senator Javits withdrew, Marvin Liebman, the Committee's Secretary, reputedly sent a memorandum to all congressional members, indicating that the use of their names on letterheads and Committee publications would be discontinued (*New York Times*, Dec. 18, 1966, p. 1).

39. *Gen. Ass.* Resolution 490 (V), 19 Sept. 1950.

40. These nations are: Cameroon, Central African Republic, Chad, Congo (Brazzaville), Dahomey, Gabon, Ivory Coast, Madagascar, Niger, Senegal, Togo, Upper Volta (all former French territories), and Congo (Leopoldville), Liberia, Libya, Rwanda, South Africa.

41. These 34 nations are: (a) those having diplomatic relations with Nationalist China: Belgium, Bolivia, Brazil, Canada, Chile, Colombia, Congo (Democratic Republic of), Ecuador, Greece, Guatemala, Italy, Jamaica, Japan, Liberia, Libya, Luxembourg, Malawi, Malta, Mexico, New Zealand, Nicaragua, Panama, Peru, Turkey, United States of America, Uruguay, Venezuela; (b) those having diplomatic relations with Communist China: Israel, Morocco, Netherlands, Tunisia; and (c) those having diplomatic relations with neither: Iceland, Ireland, Trinidad and Tobago.

42. The relevant provisions are Articles 60, 85, 87; 61(1), 86(1), 97; 64(1), 66, 85(1); 101(1); 17; and 88, 98.

43. 11 *U.N. Conf. Int'l Org. Docs.* 711, 714 (1945).

44. The Spanish question was concerned with the Polish request of April 1946 that would have the Security Council declare the existence of the Franco regime a threat to international peace and security, and call on all members of the Organization to sever diplomatic relations with it. The Greek question dealt with Greek complaints against Albania, Bulgaria, and Yugoslavia for aiding guerrillas in northern Greece. The issue of double veto arose when the Council was asked to vote on a United States proposal purporting to have the dispute transferred to the General Assembly for consideration and recommendation. The Czechoslovak question was concerned with the request for an investigation of events preceding and succeeding the change of government in Czechoslovakia in February 1948. The negative vote cast by the Soviet Union defeated a proposal to appoint a subcommittee to receive and hear evidence.

45. 5 *U.N. SCOR*, 507th meeting 5–8 (1950).

46. 14 *id.*, 848th meeting 22, 23 (1959).

47. 11 *U.N. Conf. Int'l Org. Docs.* 711, 712 (1945).

48. Commenting on the Laos question, Kellogg points out that "The real danger lies in adopting a practice, unsupported by the Charter, under which a substantive matter will be treated as procedural by disregarding the substantive nature of the vote on the preliminary question and turning it into a procedural vote by presidential ruling" ("The Laos Question: Double What Veto?" 45 *Va. L. Rev.* 1352, 1360 (1958)). Note also the nationalities of the presiding President connected with the exercise of double veto in the past: the Mexican representative (the Spanish question), the Soviet representative (the Greek question), the French representative (the Czechoslovak question), the British representative (the Formosa question), and the Italian delegate (the Laos question).

49. In 1967, in addition to the five permanent members, the ten nonpermanent members of the Security Council are as follows: Argentina (1967), Bulgaria (1967), Japan (1967), Mali (1967), Nigeria (1967), Brazil (1968), Canada (1968), Denmark (1968), Ethiopia (1968), and India (1968) (terms of office expire on

December 31 of year given in parentheses). France, U.S.S.R., United Kingdom, Bulgaria, Mali, Nigeria, Denmark, Ethiopia, and India voted to seat Peking at the 21st Assembly in 1966. Canada abstained from voting. The positive support for the Nationalist regime, excluding itself, was four votes only—the United States, Brazil, Japan, and Argentina.

50. Gen. Ass. Resolution 2030 (XX), 29 Nov. 1965.

51. *Peking Review*, Jan. 29, 1965, pp. 5–6; *Washington Post*, Sept. 30, 1965, p. A1; *New York Times* (international edition), Sept. 30, 1965, p. 1.

52. U.N. Note No. 2991, 22 Oct. 1964, Secretary-General U Thant's press conference.

53. In its advisory opinion concerning competence of the General Assembly for admitting a member, the world court concluded that "the admission of a State to membership in the United Nations, pursuant to paragraph 2 of Article 4 of the Charter, cannot be effected by a decision of the General Assembly when the Security Council has made no recommendation for admission, by reason of the candidate failing to obtain the requisite majority or of the negative vote of a permanent Member upon a resolution so to recommend" (*1950 I.C.J. Reports*, p. 4, at 10).

54. Appendix in A. T. Steele, *The American People and China* (New York: McGraw-Hill, 1966), pp. 254, 274–76.

55. It may be noted that should it be decided that contemporary mainland China is not the same state as the "Republic of China" which was a founding member of the United Nations, then our argument for Formosa becomes even stronger. If Communist China is not the "Republic of China," a fortiori it cannot claim the benefit of the Cairo Declaration or the Potsdam Declaration or any other commitment that Formosa should be returned to that state. For the development of this thesis, see M. S. McDougal and R. M. Goodman, "Chinese Participation in the United Nations: The Legal Imperatives of a Negotiated Solution," 60 *Am. J. Int'l L.* 671 (1966).

56. This position is well known. However, it is interesting that Peking once accused the Nationalist regime of plotting "two Chinas": "Under U.S. pressure, the Chiang Kai-shek gang has lately become increasingly shameless: in an attempt to maintain its precarious existence as a protégé, it has switched over from opposition to 'two Chinas' to actively collaborating with the U.S. imperialists in their plot to create 'two Chinas.'" People's Daily, "No 'Two

Chinas' Scheme Will Be Tolerated" (Aug. 20, 1962), in *Peking Review*, Aug. 24, 1962, p. 5.

57. *Old Myths and New Realities and Other Commentaries* (New York: Vintage, 1964), p. 59.

Chapter 2 Self-Determination
for an Independent Formosa

For the early history of Formosa, see J. W. Davidson, *The Island of Formosa, Past and Present* (London: Macmillan, 1903); W. A. Pickering, *Pioneering in Formosa: Recollections of Adventures among Mandarins, Wreckers, & Head-hunting Savages* (London: Hurst & Blackett, 1898). A classic in Chinese, Lien Hung's *Tai-wan tung shih* ("The History of Taiwan") (2 vols), first published in 1921, was reprinted by the Committee of Chinese Collections, Taipei, in 1955. Testifying to the loose Chinese control over Taiwan in the nineteenth century, see E. H. House, *The Japanese Expedition to Formosa* (New Haven, 1963. Photocopy made by Yale University Library Photographic Services of the original edition published in 1875).

Formosans' perspectives about their past are presented by: Shih Ming, *The Four Hundred Year History of the Formosans* (Tokyo: Otoba Shobo, 1962); Ong Joktik, *Taiwan* (Tokyo: *Kyobun Do*, 1964) (both in Japanese).

For Formosa's conditions after World War II, particularly during early Nationalist occupation, see the excellent study by George H. Kerr, *Formosa Betrayed* (Boston: Houghton Mifflin, 1965). See also J. W. Ballantine, *Formosa, A Problem for United States Foreign Policy* (Washington: Brookings Institution, 1952); F. W. Riggs, *Formosa Under Chinese Nationalist Rule* (New York: Macmillan, 1952). On the contemporary scene, see Mark Mancall, ed., *Formosa Today* (New York: Praeger, 1964).

The controversial nature of Formosa's status is reflected in a flow of publication. See especially Tung Pi Chen, "Legal Status of Formosa," 4 *Philippine Int'l L. J.* 99 (1965); J. P. Jain, "The Legal Status of Formosa," 57 *Am. J. Int'l L.* 25 (1963); D. P. O'Connell, "The Status of Taiwan and the Chinese Recognition Problem," 50 *id.*, 405 (1956); F. P. Morello, *The International Legal Status of Formosa* (The Hague: Martinus Nijhoff, 1966).

On the acquisition of territory, see R. Y. Jennings, *The Acquisi-*

tion of Territory in International Law (Manchester: Manchester University Press, 1963); Y. Z. Blum, *Historic Titles in International Law* (The Hague: Martinus Nijhoff, 1965); N. L. Hill, *Claims to Territory in International Law and Relations* (London: Oxford University Press, 1945). A comprehensive survey of contemporary boundary and territorial problems around the globe is contained in Vol. 2 and 3., M. M. Whiteman, *Digest of International Law* (Washington: Government Printing Office, 1964).

Regarding proscription of force as a means of change, see L. P. Bloomfield, *Evolution or Revolution? The United Nations and the Problem of Peaceful Territorial Change* (Cambridge: Harvard University Press, 1957); M. S. McDougal and F. P. Feliciano, *Law and Minimum World Public Order* (New Haven: Yale University Press, 1961); I. Brownlie, *International Law and the Use of Force by States* (Oxford: Clarendon Press, 1963); C. H. M. Waldock, "The Regulation of the Use of Force by Individual States in International Law," 81 *Hague Academy Recueil des Cours* 455 (1952). For dissent, see J. Stone, *Aggression and World Order* (London: Stevens, 1958).

On the Japanese peace treaty, see Dept. of State, Pub. No. 4392, *Conference for the Conclusion and Signature of the Treaty of Peace with Japan, Record of Proceedings, San Francisco, 1951* (1951).

On claims relating to domestic jurisdiction, see *Repertory of Practice of United Nations Organs*, vol. 1 (1955); *Supplement*, No. 1, vol. 1 (1957); *Supplement*, No. 2, vol. 1 (1964). See also M. S. Rajan, *United Nations and Domestic Jurisdiction*, 2d ed., (New York: Asia Publishing House, 1961); R. Higgins, *The Development of International Law Through the Political Organs of the United Nations* (London: Oxford University Press, 1963).

On the U.N. role in self-determination, see *Repertory of Practice of United Nations Organs*, vol. 1 (New York, 1955); *Supplement*, No. 1, vol. 1 (1958); *Supplement*, No. 2, vol. 1 (1964); E. J. Sady, *The United Nations and Dependent Peoples* (Washington: Brookings Institution, 1956); Office of Public Information, *The United Nations and Decolonization* (New York: United Nations, 1965); B. Rivlin, "Self-Determination and Dependent Areas," *International Conciliation*, No. 501 (1955). See also R. Emerson, *From Empire to Nation* (Cambridge: Harvard University Press, 1960); J. Plamenatz, *On Alien Rule and Self-Government* (London: Longmans, Green, 1960); A. Cobban, *National Self-Determination* (London: Oxford University Press, 1945).

A classic study on plebiscites is S. Wambaugh, *Plebiscites Since the World War* (2 vols.) (Washington: Carnegie Endowment for International Peace, 1933).

Finally, a note on the important documents referred to in this chapter is in order. The sources of the texts are: the Treaty of Shimonoseki, 1 *Am. J. Int'l L. (Supp.)* 378 (1907); Cairo Declaration, 9 *Dept. State Bull.* 393 (1943); Potsdam Declaration, 13 *id.* 137 (1945); Instrument of Japanese Surrender, 13 *id.* 362 (1945); Peace Treaty with Japan, 25 *id.* 349 (1951), 136 *U.N. Treaty Series* 45 (1952); Japanese peace treaty with the Republic of China, 138 *id.* 3 (1952), *China Handbook, 1952–1953,* at 154 (Taipei: China Pub. Co., 1953); Mutual Defense Treaty between the U.S. and the Republic of China, 31 *Dept. State Bull.* 899 (1954); 248 *U.N. Treaty Series* 213 (1956).

1. 22 *Dept. State Bull.* 79 (1950).

2. 23 *id.* 5 (1950).

3. "Mutual Defense Treaty with the Republic of China," *Senate Executive Report,* No. 2, 84 Cong., 1st Sess. (1955), p. 6.

4. 69 *Stat.* 7 (1955).

5. For the Communist Chinese position, see *Important Documents Concerning the Question of Taiwan* (Peking: Foreign Languages Press, 1955); The Chinese People's Institute of Foreign Affairs, *Oppose U.S. Occupation of Taiwan and "Two Chinas" Plot* (Peking: Foreign Languages Press, 1958). More recently, see People's Daily, "The Chinese People are Determined to Liberate Taiwan" (June 27, 1965), in *Peking Review,* July 2, 1965, pp. 9–10; People's Daily, "China's Sovereignty over Taiwan Brooks No Intervention" (May 12, 1964), in *id.,* May 15, 1964, pp. 6–8. Nationalist views on the issue have been expressed annually before the General Assembly during the debates on the Chinese participation question. See also President Chiang Kai-shek's address on February 8, 1955: *Free China Review* (Taipei), March 1955, pp. 49–54; Han Lih-Wu, *Taiwan Today* (Taipei: Hwa Kuo Pub. Co., 1951); Wen Lin, *Wo-men te Tai-wan* ("Our Taiwan") (Taipei: Hai Wai Pub. Co., 1965). The Soviet view on Formosa's status, echoing Peking's position, can be found in the Official Records of the General Assembly relating to the annual debate on Chinese question (see, e.g., 16 *U.N. GAOR* 892, 895, 1961).

6. 5 *U.N. SCOR,* 527th meeting 10 (1950) (remark of Wu

Shiu-chuan, special representative of the People's Republic of China).

7. *Important Documents Concerning the Question of Taiwan,* p. 161.

8. The Chinese People's Institute of Foreign Affairs, *op. cit.,* p. 16.

9. Chou En-lai remarked on February 25, 1964 that "with regard to this inalienable Chinese territory of Taiwan, there can simply be no such questions as whether it is of indeterminate status, whether there should be a plebiscite, and so on." "Isn't it ridiculous," added Chen Yi, "that Chinese should hold a plebiscite to decide whether they are Chinese?" (*Peking Review,* March 6, 1964, p. 18, at 19.). In the Nationalist view, a plebiscite ought to be held on the mainland, not in Formosa. Thus Tingfu Tsiang, late Nationalist representative to the U.N.: "We read in the papers the suggestion that a plebiscite might be held on the island of Formosa to determine its future. This line of talk furthers Communist aggression from the offshore islands to Formosa itself. People who make that suggestion forget to say what should really be promoted is a plebiscite on the mainland of China to find out whether the 450,000,000 people there want or do not want Communism. . . . The idea of a plebiscite on the island of Formosa is, of course, a fellow-traveler idea." "Recent Developments in the Far East," *Free China Review,* (March 1955), p. 6, at 7.

10. 23 *Dept. State Bull.* 959, 960 (1950).

11. *U.N. Gen. Ass. Provisional Verbatim Record, 21st Sess., Plenary* 42 (A/PV.1480) (28 Nov. 1966).

12. *New York Times,* April 24, 1964, p. 4.

13. The U.S. deems it expedient not to raise the issue of Formosa's status; even Dulles, a valued friend of the Nationalists, stated that "technical sovereignty over Formosa and the Pescadores has never been settled" (31 *Dept. State Bull.* 896, 1954). The Canadian and Australian governments expressed similar views; see 26 *Current Notes on International Relations* 57, 127, 176 (1955). For the Irish view, see *U.N. Gen. Ass. Provisional Verbatim Record, 21st Sess., Plenary* 2–6 (A/PV.1479) (28 Nov. 1966). Regarding Formosans' perspectives on the status of Formosa, see Li Thian-hok, "The China Impasse: A Formosan View," 36 *Foreign Affairs* 437 (1958); Ko Kiansin, "The Legal Status of Formosa from the Viewpoint of International Law," 1 *Formosan Quarterly* 37 (1962).

14. Great Britain, *Parl. Deb.* (Hansard), House of Commons,

Official Report, vol. 536, col. 159 (written answers) (Feb. 4, 1955).

15. Gen. Ass. Resolution 1514 (XV), 14 Dec. 1960.

16. M. S. McDougal, H. D. Lasswell, and I. A. Vlasic, *Law and Public Order in Space* (New Haven: Yale University Press, 1963), p. 146.

17. By an "interest" we mean a value demand—a "preference" or "volition"—formulated in the name of an identity and supported by expectations that the demand is advantageous. Since events and demands are not always congruent, we distinguish the expectation component from the demand component of an interest, and consider how realistic the expectation is. The interests sought by effective elites can be classified into two categories: common interests whose fulfillment will benefit the entire community and special interests whose fulfillment will benefit one segment of the community at the expense of the rest. Common interests are considered to be *exclusive* if they primarily affect single participants and *inclusive* when they primarily affect more than one participant. See *id.*, Pt. II; H. D. Lasswell and A. Kaplan, *Power and Society* (New Haven: Yale University Press, 1950), pp. 16–28.

18. 1 L. F. Oppenheim, *International Law*, H. Lauterpacht ed., 8th ed., (London: Longmans, Green, 1955), p. 576.

19. Jennings, *The Acquisition of Territory in International Law*, p. 23.

20. What the Covenant actually asked members of the League to do was to submit a serious dispute between them to arbitration, judicial settlement, or inquiry by the Council, and not to resort to war until three months after the award of the arbitrators, the judicial decisions, or the report of the Council. A further restriction was not to resort to war against a state which complies with the unanimous recommendation of the Council or the Assembly. See Articles 12, 13, 15 and 16 of the Covenant.

21. 1 M. O. Hudson, *World Court Reports* (Washington: Carnegie Endowment for International Peace, 1934), p. 143, at 156.

22. 54 *Congressional Record* 1742 (Jan. 22, 1917).

23. 7 *U.N. GAOR*, 3d Comm. 157 (1952) (remark of British representative).

24. See the Annexes to General Assembly Resolutions 567 (VI) (18 Jan. 1952) and 742 (VIII) (27 Nov. 1953), which deal with "factors indicative of the attainment of independence or of other separate systems of self-government."

25. General Assembly Resolution 1514 (XV), referred to as the "Colonial Resolution," was adopted by 89 to 0, with 9 abstentions (the U.S., Australia, Belgium, the Dominican Republic, France, Portugal, Spain, Union of South Africa and U.K.).

26. Gen. Ass. Resolution 1803 (XVII), 14 Dec. 1962.

27. According to Oppenheim and Lauterpacht, "If a cession of territory is the outcome of war, it is the treaty of peace which stipulates the cession among its other provisions" (1 *op. cit.*, at 548). Quincy Wright observed that "the Japanese surrender [based on the Cairo and Potsdam declarations] was not a definitive renunciation of the islands but a commitment to renounce them in the Treaty of Peace." "The Chinese Recognition Problem," 49 *Am. J. Int'l L.* 320, 332 (1955). Putting aside the imperative requirement for settlement through the peace treaty for a moment, we note that efforts have been made to repudiate the validity of the Cairo and Potsdam Declarations on the ground that they were "merely a statement of common purpose" or "an expression of intent" and were "not couched in the form of a legal instrument." A further argument is by invoking the doctrine of *rebus sic stantibus*. For an exposition of this thesis, see T. P. Chen, "Legal Status of Formosa," 4 *Philippine Int'l L. J.* 99, 131–38 (1965).

28. On December 27, 1950, the United States stated: "The Cairo Declaration of 1943 stated the purpose to restore 'Manchuria, Formosa and the Pescadores to the Republic of China.' That Declaration, like other wartime declarations such as those of Yalta and Potsdam, was in the opinion of the United States Government subject to any final peace settlement where all relevant factors should be considered. The United States cannot accept the view, apparently put forward by the Soviet Government, that the views of other Allies not represented at Cairo must be wholly ignored. Also, the United States believes that declarations such as that issued at Cairo must necessarily be considered in the light of the United Nations Charter, the obligations of which prevail over any other international agreement." 24 *Dept. State Bull.* 65–66 (1951). The cases of Korea's independence and of the Kuriles Islands and South Sakhalin are useful examples.

29. In dismissing the U.S. position that Formosa's status remains undetermined, Peking likes to quote the statements made by President Truman and Secretary of State Acheson in January 1950. In Acheson's words, "The Chinese have administered Formosa for four years. Neither the United States nor any other ally ever questioned that authority and that occupation. When Formosa was made a province of China nobody raised any lawyer's doubts about that. That was regarded as in accordance with the commitments." All the Allied participants to the San Francisco Peace Conference with the exception of the Soviet Union, Poland, and Czechoslovakia, signed the treaty. All signatories, except the U.S. and the U.K., were parties neither to the Cairo nor to the Potsdam Declaration; evidently they were not legally bound by the terms of these declarations. As for the claim that no government voiced protest against the Nationalist act to incorporate Taiwan as a "province" of China: in 1958 the Spanish government informed the Secretary-General that it "possesses no non-self-governing territories, since the territories subject to its sovereignty in Africa are, in accordance with the legislation now in force, considered to be classified as provinces of Spain," and sought to exclude U.N. supervision. This contention was dismissed by the U.N. When the Nationalist government changed Taiwan into a province, other governments lodged no protest, primarily because of the general understanding that like all other territories under Allied occupation, Formosa's legal status could not be changed by any single occupying power.

30. *Treaty of Peace with Japan (Record of Proceedings)*, p. 93.

31. "Mutual Defense Treaty with the Republic of China," Report of the Committee on Foreign Relations, Senate Executive Report No. 2, 84th Cong., 1st Sess. (1955), p. 6.

32. 31 *Dept. State Bull.* 896 (1954).

33. It might be suggested that the U.N. Charter proscription of the acquisition of territory through "conquest" is not retroactive. Since the Nationalist postwar occupation of Formosa took place before the United Nations Charter became effective in October 1945, the "Republic of China" could thus be exempted from the Charter proscription. This argument is easily dismissed on the ground that Nationalist control over Formosa in 1945 was clearly an exercise of the right of belligerent occupation of the Allied powers, not of the right of conquest. Japan surrendered Formosa to the Allied powers as a whole, not General Chiang alone. Equally, the assertion that the "Republic of China" possesses title over Formosa by "prescription" is untenable. Nationalist control over Formosa was initially authorized by the Allied Command. Even if the more basic dimensions of the issue could be set aside, the length of Nationalist control over Formosa is too brief to warrant prescriptive acquisition.

34. Directorate-General of Budgets, Accounts and Statistics, Executive Yuan, *Statistical Abstract of the Republic of China, 1965* (Taipei, 1965), pp. 648–49, 676–77, 772–73.

35. 1 Liu Shih-wu, *Chung-hua ming kuo shing hsien shih* ("The Constitutional History of the Republic of China") (Taipei: Chinese Cultural Publishing Commission, 1958) pp. 28–33, 100–01; 2 *id.*, at 302–303.

36. A recent example was the conviction in 1965 of Ming-min Peng, an air law specialist, and two of his former students. They were secretly arrested by security police on September 20, 1964, and their arrest was not made known for over a month. After a one-day hearing by a military court on March 27, 1965, they were sentenced to 8–10 year terms. Their crime lay in having drafted a declaration whose gist was: (1) there is one China and one Formosa, each distinct from the other; (2) Chiang Kai-shek's dream of "Return to the Mainland" has been used by him to perpetuate the rule of the Chinese minority in Formosa; (3) the Chiang regime, because of its commitment to recapture the mainland, is not interested in planning a long-range economy of the island, and its huge military expenditures have drained the island's valuable resources; (4) Formosa should seek a new constitution, concentrating on building a small but prosperous nation, and should join the U.N.; and (5) gradualism is not the way to attain these goals. Nor is the democratization of the Chiang regime feasible under existing conditions. The aim is to replace the present regime with a completely new government. Because Professor Peng had an international reputation and influential friends abroad, Chiang Kai-shek granted him amnesty in November 1965; and in the summer of 1966 the terms of imprisonment for the two students were reduced by half.

37. *New York Times*, Oct. 30, 1961, p. 1; Feb. 7, 1962, p. 40.

Chapter 3 The Transition to Independence

Concerning the analytical method we use in this chapter, see H. Eulau, "H. D. Lasswell's Developmental Analysis," 11 *Western Political Quarterly* 229 (1958). Consult also H. D. Lasswell, *World Politics Faces Economics* (New York: McGraw-Hill, 1945).

On general conditions in Formosa today, besides the work of

Kerr, Mancall, and Ballantine cited in the preceding chapter, see especially Whiting and Scalapino, in Thorp, ed., *The United States and the Far East*, 2d ed. (Englewood Cliffs, N.J.: Prentice-Hall, 1962); J. K. Fairbank, *China: The People's Middle Kingdom and the U.S.A.* (Cambridge: Harvard University Press, 1967); and W. J. Lederer, *A Nation of Sheep* (New York: Norton, 1961). Samples of useful articles are: M. A. Plummer, "Taiwan: 'The Other China,' " 51 *Current History* 165 (1966); J. K. Kallgren, "Nationalist China: The Continuing Dilemma of the 'Mainland' Philosophy," 3 *Asian Survey* 11 (1963); D. Wurful, "Taiwanese Nationalism: Problem for U.S. Policy," in R. Sakai, ed., *Studies on Asia* (Nebraska: University of Nebraska Press, 1963).

The articles in *Independent Formosa* (formerly the *Formosan Quarterly*) published six times a year by United Young Formosans for Independence (the Formosan Association) in Tokyo, though emotionally charged, reveal the side of Formosa that the Nationalists try to suppress. The special issue on "Chinese Refugees in Formosa" (*Formosan Quarterly*, vol. 1, no. 4, April 1963) analyzes the plight of mainland Chinese in Formosa.

The literature on Communist China is vast. For works oriented to its external process, see, generally, A. D. Barnett, *Communist China and Asia* (New York: Council on Foreign Relations, 1960); H. C. Hinton, *Communist China in World Politics* (Boston: Houghton Mifflin, 1966); A. L. Hsieh, *Communist China's Strategy in the Nuclear Era* (Englewood Cliffs, N.J.: Prentice-Hall, 1962); M. H. Halperin, *China and Nuclear Proliferation* (Chicago: Center for Policy Study, University of Chicago, 1966).

For books dealing with internal affairs, see R. Adams, ed., *Contemporary China* (New York: Vintage, 1966); F. H. Schurmann, *Ideology and Organization in Communist China* (Berkeley: University of California Press, 1966); J. W. Lewis, *Leadership in Communist China* (Ithaca: Cornell University Press, 1963); J. Chen, *Mao and the Chinese Revolution* (London: Oxford University Press, 1965); R. North and I. DeS. Pool, "Kuomintang and Chinese Communist Elites" in H. D. Lasswell and D. Lerner, eds., *World Revolutionary Elites* (Cambridge: M.I.T. Press, 1965). For an insight to the comparative study of Russian and Chinese Communism, see D. W. Treadgold, ed., *Soviet and Chinese Communism: Similarities and Differences* (Seattle: University of Washington Press, 1967).

For works on U.S. policy toward mainland China and Formosa,

see "U.S. Policy with respect to Mainland China," *Hearings before the Committee on Foreign Relations,* U.S. Senate, 89th Cong., 2d Sess. (March 1966); A. D. Barnett, *China After Mao* (Princeton: Princeton University Press, 1967); L. W. Pye, "China in Context," 45 *Foreign Affairs* 229 (1967). A series on "The United States and China in World Affairs" published for the Council on Foreign Relations by McGraw-Hill includes: A. M. Halpern, ed., *Policies toward China: Views from Six Continents* (1965); A. T. Steele, *The American People and China* (1966); A. Eckstein, *Communist China's Economic Growth and Foreign Trade* (1966); R. Blum, *The United States and China in World Affairs* (1966); L. E. Williams, *The Future of the Overseas Chinese in Southeast Asia* (1966).

Concerning a Nationalist-Communist deal, see O. E. Clubb, "Sino-American Relations and the Future of Formosa," 80 *Political Science Quarterly* 1 (1965).

On the ticklish issue of Quemoy and Matsu, see J. W. Lewis, "Quemoy and American Policy," 2 *Asian Survey* 12 (1962); T. Tsou, "The Quemoy Imbroglio: Chiang Kai-shek and the United States," 12 *Western Political Quarterly* 1075 (1959). See also DeW. Copp and M. Peck, *The Odd Day* (New York: William Morrow, 1962).

Concerning the China lobby in the U.S., see "Activities of Non-Diplomatic Representatives of Foreign Principals in the United States," *Report on a Hearing before the Committee on Foreign Relations,* 86th Cong., 1st Sess. (March 1963); C. Wertenbaker, "The China Lobby," *The Reporter,* April 15, 1952, pp. 4–24, and April 29, pp. 5–24; F. Greene, *A Curtain of Ignorance* (Garden City, N.Y.: Doubleday, 1964). For Americans' disillusion with the Nationalists at the end of war, see T. Tsou, *America's Failure in China,* 1941–50 (Chicago: University of Chicago Press, 1963); T. H. White, ed. *The Stilwell Papers* (New York: William Sloane, 1948).

1. *China, the United Nations and United States Policy* (New York: UNA-USA National Policy Panel, 1966), pp. 28–29, 36.

2. New Year Message of 1967: *Central Daily News,* Jan. 3, 1967, p. 1; Jan. 4, 1967, p. 1. See also *New York Times,* Feb. 15, 1967, p. 10.

3. As early as 1950 then Secretary-General Trygve Lie suggested that Formosa be placed under U.N. Trusteeship for five years, to be followed by a plebiscite by the inhabitants on the island (*In the*

Cause of Peace, pp. 264–65). At the Bandung Conference Sir John Kotelawala, Ceylon's Prime Minister, urged the convocation of conference comprising Burma, Ceylon, India, Indonesia, Pakistan, Philippines, Thailand, and Communist China to settle the Formosa question. The Ceylonese Premier intended to propose a five-year trusteeship by either the U.N. or the Colombo powers over the island, to be followed by a plebiscite by the Formosans (*New York Times*, April 22, 1955, p. 1).

4. See the excellent article by A. Axelbank, "Chiang Kai-shek's Silent Enemies," *Harper's Magazine*, September 1963, pp. 46–53; see also the London *Economist*, May 11, 1963, p. 536.

5. In response to Edgar Snow's question, "Would China refuse to sit in the United Nations as long as any kind of Taiwan government were allowed to represent Taiwan separately there?", Premier Chou En-lai flatly stated: "If the so-called 'Taiwan Clique' is to appear in the United Nations, under whatever form and in whatever name—be it the Chiang Kai-shek clique or some other clique—we will definitely refuse to take part in the United Nations and sit together with them, so as not to create a situation of 'two Chinas.'" (*Look*, Jan. 31, 1961, p. 98).

6. A recent dispatch by David Oancia of *The Globe and Mail*, Toronto, indicates that for years Peking's leaders perceive the liberation of Taiwan as primarily a political rather than a military matter, and "as part of the struggle against United States influence" (*New York Times*, Feb. 14, 1967, p. 14).

7. Peking's Foreign Minister stated in June 1964: "We are convinced that U.S. imperialism's manipulation of the United Nations will sooner or later break down and the Chiang Kai-shek gang will sooner or later be ousted from it. The lawful seat of the People's Republic of China in the United Nations will sooner or later be restored. This, of course, takes time. We are not in a hurry, we can wait. Under no circumstances will we barter away principles and sovereignty; any attempt to make the restoration of China's seat in the United Nations a bait for our acceptance of the 'two Chinas' scheme is doomed to failure" (*Peking Review*, June 26, 1964, p. 6, at 7).

8. For Peking's applause of Indonesia's withdrawal from the United Nations and the specialized agencies, see *Peking Review*, Jan. 15, 1965, pp. 5–12; Jan. 29, 1965, pp. 8–9.

9. Tingfu Tsiang, then Nationalist permanent representative to

the U.N., stated that the Nationalist government would have withdrawn if the U.N. had decided to seat Peking (*New York Times*, Oct. 9, 1961, p. 1). Chen Cheng, then Vice President of the Nationalist regime, also said that his government "would quit the United Nations rather than share Chinese representation there with Red China" (*New York Herald Tribune*, July 6, 1961, p. 3). In November 1965, immediately after the General Assembly voted to reject Peking's participation by the narrowest margin in its history (47 for Peking, 47 against, and 23 abstentions and absences), the Nationalist newspaper, the *Central Daily News*, began to prepare the people of Formosa for any future eventuality. The central theme of the Nationalist newspaper is, so its editorial ran, that the day Peking is seated in the U.N., it would mean the "moral bankruptcy" of the U.N. And any honorable and righteous people will certainly want no part in such a "bankrupt" Organization.

10. In the view of Nationalist spokesmen the only "native Formosans" are 200,000 aborigines of Malay stock who are for the most part scattered around the mountainous area of the island. They prefer, if called upon, to label the eleven million native Formosans as "Formosan Chinese."

11. Since Nationalist defense expenditures are classified, estimates on their actual figure vary. We adhere to the figure in Neil H. Jacoby, *U.S. Aid to Taiwan* (New York: Praeger, 1966), a comprehensive study commissioned by AID (p. 93).

12. Chiang Kai-shek's Double Tenth Message, *China Post*, Oct. 11, 1963.

13. Premier C. K. Yen's statement, *id.*, Feb. 24, 1965, p. 6. See also "Prodigal Son's Homecoming," *China Yearbook, 1965–66* (Taipei: China Pub. Co., 1966), pp. 16–18.

14. Li Tsung-jen, once Acting President of the "Republic of China," who defected to Peking in 1965 after a 16-year exile in the U.S., explained in 1961: "To agree to such a proposal ['two Chinas' or 'one China, one Formosa'] would stir up uneasy feelings in its leaders even beyond their graves. For after all these leaders of the Nationalist Government are Chinese, and they cannot be unmindful of what future generations may think of them and of their position in history. As long as they are making their present stand, comic as it may appear, they will be respected and honored in history as being men of conviction or even as patriots. The moment they agree to the formation of a separate government, detached from China, they will

be regarded as traitors to their own land, and that would be the most horrible verdict for them to bear. . . . Rather than subscribing to such a plan, the leaders in Taiwan would prefer, the moment they feel that the destruction of China's territorial integrity is becoming unavoidable, to turn over the island to Communist control. They would then at least have the merit of having suffered an honorable defeat and not a dishonorable surrender. I do not have to go into any details on this possibility; the CIA, with its superb organization and unrivaled knowledge, should have information to substantiate it." "Memorandum on the Chinese Question" (Appendix A), in Chang Hsin-hai, *America and China: A New Approach to Asia* (New York: Simon and Schuster, 1965), pp. 244–45.

15. Peking's Foreign Minister Chen Yi was quoted as saying: "Chiang Kai-shek and Chiang Ching-kuo are also welcome to join in this cooperation as Mr. Li Tsung-jen has done. Taiwan Province and any individual or group in Taiwan are welcome to come back to the embrace of the motherland and join in this cooperation. Only one condition is required: To break away from U.S. imperialist control and be loyal to the motherland. There are no other conditions. In my view, the possibility of Kuomintang-Communist cooperation is great and is moreover increasing" (*Peking Review*, Oct. 8, 1965, p. 7, at 12).

16. *The Observer* (London), Aug. 12, 1962, p. 1. A summary account of Bloodworth's dispatch can also be found in *New York Times*, Aug. 12, 1962, p. 31.

17. "Peking Takes the Plunge—Dialogue with Formosa," *Link* (New Delhi), Dec. 8, 1963; quoted in O. E. Clubb, "Sino-American Relations and the Future of Formosa," 80 *Political Science Quarterly* 1, 15–16 (1965).

18. The fear of a separate peace between the Nationalists and Japanese was a significant factor that dictated President Roosevelt's policy toward China during World War II: "[President Roosevelt] believed that there was no chance that the Chinese Communists would surrender to the Japanese as long as Russia was in the war against the Axis, whereas there was always the possibility that the Kuomintang might make a separate peace." Robert E. Sherwood, *Roosevelt and Hopkins* (New York: Harper, 1948), p. 740.

19. Commenting on the defection of General Li Tsung-jen to Peking, the *Washington Post* said in an editorial entitled "China Invisible" (Oct. 3, 1965, Sec. E, p. 6): "Former Vice President Li

Tsung-jen of Nationalist China, who recently defected to the Communist regime after 15 years in the United States, has illustrated one
of the anomalies that threaten the continued separate existence of
Taiwan. At a Peking press conference devoted to blasting the American role, the defector asserted that Taiwan (or Formosa) is 'an
inalienable part of China.' Much the same line was taken here last
week by Gen. Chiang Ching-kuo, the Nationalist Defense Minister
often regarded as heir apparent to his father, President Chiang Kai-
shek. The Nationalist government, he made clear, still bases its official hopes on return to the mainland and rejects any concept of an
independent Taiwanese state. General Chiang also in effect endorsed
the Communist government's claims in the border dispute with
India. This extraordinary pull of the motherland, irrespective of
ideology, is a phenomenon that has haunted some American policy-
makers who privately have feared that one day the government on
Taiwan might defect *en bloc.*"

20. Lederer, *op cit.*, at 55.

21. John Israel observed that the U.S. is "so far committed in
Formosa that nothing short of documentary proof of a Taipei-Peking
accord would turn us against Chiang. Mere rumors will, if anything,
simply make the US more anxious, and hence subservient to his
demands." "A Deal Between the Two Chinas?" *The New Republic,*
Oct. 1, 1962, p. 10, at 11.

22. Lei Chen was the editor of the *Free China Fortnightly,* the
most outspoken journal in Formosa under Nationalist rule. The
journal was able for about a decade to maintain a highly critical
posture toward the Nationalist policies, until 1960 when Lei Chen
was engaged in (along with Li Wan-chiu) organizing a new opposition party that would consist of liberal mainlanders and influential
Formosan leaders. Aware of the implications of such a coalition, the
Nationalists imprisoned Lei for having harbored an alleged Communist agent and for some of the articles that had appeared in his
journal. As Lei Chen went to jail, the movement to organize a new
opposition party collapsed, and his journal was suppressed (see *New
York Times,* Oct. 9, 1960, p. 1; Nov. 24, 1960, p. 2). Li Wan-chiu's
frequent criticisms of the regime's policies in his newspaper had been
tolerated until 1960 when he too was involved in the plan to form a
new opposition party. As a consequence, he was compelled to surrender his control of the newspaper under the systematic harassments
and intimidations of the KMT (see *id.,* March 6, 1961, p. 13; Jan.

1, 1962, p. 11). Li died in April 1966 at age of 64.

23. Mark Mancall wrote: "Taipei, it is true, is full of new modern hotels and taxis. But little of this has reached the people. The rise in per capita income, particularly in urban areas, has been offset by rising taxes to meet the enormous defense budget and by a slow but steady inflation unaccompanied by rising wages. People of all but the highest class have to work harder to maintain a lower standard of living than they did three years ago. The same appears to be true in agriculture. Statistically the land reform program was a success. In the ten years following 1949 the number of farmers owning their own land jumped from about 210,000 to more than 470,000, and agricultural output rose about 40 per cent. A growing population, rising prices, and rising taxes prevented any real increase in the peasants' standard of living." "The Two Dilemmas of Chiang Kai-shek," *New York Herald Tribune*, Dec. 8, 1963, sec. 1, p. 31.

24. See *United Daily News*, from August to November 1966, particularly Aug. 4 (p. 2), Aug. 5 (p. 2), Aug. 6 (p. 1), Aug. 9 (p. 1), Aug. 14 (p. 1), Aug. 24 (p. 2), Oct. 5 (p. 2) and Nov. 9 (p. 2). See also *Central Daily News*, Aug. 4, 1966, p. 2; Nov. 9, 1966, p. 3.

25. In 1956, the number was 519. From 1956 to 1964 the total number of students going abroad was 10,390, of whom 643 returned to Taiwan. In the 1950's those who left Formosa to study in the U.S. were predominantly mainland Chinese; in the 1960's, however, the number of native Formosans increased rapidly, contributing decisively to the large increase of all students studying abroad in the last few years. (Directorate-General of Budgets, Accounts and Statistics, Executive Yuan, *Statistical Abstract of the Republic of China, 1965*, Taipei, 1965, pp. 522–27).

26. C. Wertenbaker, "The China Lobby," *The Reporter*, April 15, 1952, p. 4, at 5.

27. 95 *Congressional Record* 12290 (1949).

28. "Military Situation in the Far East," *Hearings before the Committee on Armed Forces and the Committee on Foreign Relations, U.S. Senate, 82nd Congress, 1st. Sess.*, (May 1951), p. 2117. In "The United States and Taiwan" (in W. L. Thorp, ed., *The United States and the Far East*), A. S. Whiting and R. A. Scalapino state that "no foreign government in the world keeps such careful tabs on political trends and the voting records of individual congressmen as the Nationalists, nor does any foreign government take such pains in entertaining prominent American visitors, including many members of Congress and ranking Pentagon officials. Taiwan is one of the few areas where the aid funds have actually been increased by Congress over those requested by the administration" (p. 168).

29. See "Meet the Press: Guest, Madame Chiang Kai-shek" (Interview on NBC, October 31, 1965), vol. 9, no. 38 (Washington: Merkle Press, 1965). See also the *New York Times*, Sept. 12, 1965, Sec. E, p. 6, and Sept. 6, 1965, p. 19. The ambiguous status of Madame Chiang's last visit to the United States was officially questioned by Senator J. W. Fulbright; the State Department replied that she was in the U.S. on private visit (*New York Times*, Oct. 4, 1966, p. 94 and Oct. 5, 1966, p. 33).

Chapter 4 Goals and Strategies

A valuable guide to the policy sciences of national development (nation-building) is a series of publications, "Studies in Political Development," sponsored by the Committee on Comparative Politics of the Social Science Research Council and published by Princeton University Press. The series as of 1966 includes: L. W. Pye, ed., *Communications and Political Development* (1963); J. LaPalombara, ed., *Bureacracy and Political Development* (1963); R. E. Ward and D. A. Rustow, eds., *Political Modernization in Japan and Turkey* (1964); J. S. Coleman, ed., *Education and Political Development* (1965); L. W. Pye and S. Verba, eds., *Political Culture and Political Development* (1965); J. LaPalombara and M. Weiner, eds., *Political Parties and Political Development* (1966). Most of these contain comprehensive and useful bibliographies.

Consult also G. A. Almond and J. S. Coleman, *The Politics of Developing Areas* (Princeton: Princeton University Press, 1960); H. W. Peter, ed., *Comparative Theories of Social Change* (Ann Arbor, Mich.: Foundation for Research on Human Behavior, 1966); D. E. Apter, *The Politics of Modernization* (Chicago: University of Chicago Press, 1965); I. L. Horowitz, *Three Worlds of Development: The Theory and Practice of International Stratification* (New York: Oxford University Press, 1966); D. E. Novack and R. Lekachman, eds., *Development and Society* (New York: St. Martin's Press, 1964).

Concerning the problematic relation between industrialization and political development, see K. de Schweinitz, Jr., *Industrialization and Democracy: Economic Necessities and Political Possibilities* (New York: Free Press, 1964).

On the seven functions of decision we distinguish, see H. D.

Lasswell, *The Decision Process: Seven Categories of Functional Analysis* (College Park: University of Maryland Press, 1956); *idem, The Future of Political Science* (New York: Atherton Press, 1963).

1. "Bureaucratic and Political Development: A Paradoxical View," in LaPalombara, ed., *Bureaucracy and Political Development*, p. 120.
2. "The Higher Civil Service as an Action Group in Western Political Development," in *id.* at 62, 64.
3. See H. D. Lasswell, "The Emerging Policy Sciences of Development: The Vicos Case," *American Behavioral Scientist*, March 1965, pp. 28–33.

Chapter 5   The External
Process of Decision

Many of the works cited in Chapters 1–3 are relevant here and in following chapters, but will not be repeated. On the expanding role of regional and global functional organizations, see especially G. J. Mangone, ed., *U.N. Administration of Economic and Social Programs* (New York: Columbia University Press, 1966); J. Sewell, *Functionalism and World Politics* (Princeton: Princeton University Press, 1966); E. Haas, *Beyond the Nation-State* (Stanford: Stanford University Press, 1964); R. E. Asher and others, *The United Nations and Promotion of the General Welfare* (Washington: Brookings Institution, 1957); D. Wightman, *Toward Economic Cooperation in Asia: The United Nations Economic Commission for Asia and the Far East* (New Haven: Yale University Press, 1963).

Comprehensive and useful guides to the affairs of overseas Chinese are: V. W. W. S. Purcell, *The Chinese in Southeast Asia*, 2d ed. (London: Oxford University Press, 1965) and L. E. Williams, *The Future of the Overseas Chinese in Southeast Asia* (New York: McGraw-Hill, 1966). On the problem of their status, see Huang Cheng-ming, *The Legal Status of the Chinese Abroad* (Taipei: China Cultural Service, 1954); D. E. Willmott, *The National Status of the Chinese in Indonesia, 1900–1958*, rev. ed., (Ithaca: Cornell University, Modern Indonesia Project, 1961). For a sample case study according to nation, see G. W. Skinner, *Chinese Society in Thailand* (Ithaca: Cornell University Press, 1957).

1. The reference is to *United States Relations with China* (Dept. of State Pub. No. 3573).

2. Notes exchanged between the U.S. Secretary of State and the Nationalist Foreign Minister on December 10, 1954, shortly after the Mutual Defense Treaty was signed, declare: "In view of the obligations of the two Parties under the said Treaty, and of the fact that the use of force from either of these areas by either of the Parties affects the other, it is agreed that such use of force will be a matter of joint agreement, subject to action of an emergency character which is clearly an exercise of the inherent right of self-defense." 32 *Dept. State Bull.* 150, 152 (1955).

3. *New York Times*, June 27, 1962, p. 1; June 28, 1962, pp. 1, 12.

4. See E. Mauerer, "Legal Problems Regarding Formosa and the Offshore Islands," 39 *Dept. State Bull.* 1005 (1958).

5. In making this proposal, we are not unconcerned with the destiny of the civilian population on these two islands. The total area of the 14 Quemoy islets is 69 sq. miles. Matsu consists of 19 islets whose total land area is merely 10.5 sq. miles. The shortest distance from Quemoy to the Communist-held territory is 1.44 miles, from Quemoy to Formosa (Kaoshung) it is 174.9 miles. Quemoy and Matsu have a total civilian population of 67,000. The total military population, is of course a matter of strict confidence, but is estimated at around 200,000. In urging the return of these islands to mainland China, we nevertheless propose that each civilian on the islands be granted an opportunity to determine freely whether to remain there or emigrate to Formosa. Should he choose the latter, the new Formosan republic should render the necessary assistance.

6. In terms of percentage of GNP of each member state, Nationalist China's U.N. payment is the highest. In 1961 payments to the U.N. as per cent of GNP was as follows: China (Nationalist), .489; Sweden, .068; United Kingdom, .051; Canada, .044; United States, .038; France, .035; and U.S.S.R., .021. Of the regular U.N. budget, the U.S. provides 32.51%, U.S.S.R. 13.62%, the U.K. 7.78%, France 6.40%, and China (Nationalist) 5.01%. N. H. Padelford, "Financial Crisis and the Future of the United Nations," 15 *World Politics* 531, 538–39 (1963).

7. Overseas Chinese call themselves "hua-chiao"—sojourning Chinese—with the implication that their stay in foreign lands is only temporary. For the total figure of overseas Chinese and their geographical distribution, see *China Yearbook, 1965–66* (Taipei: China Publishing Co., 1966), pp. 266–67.

8. Article 98 of the Constitution of the People's Republic of China reads: "The People's Republic of China protects the proper

rights and interests of Chinese residents abroad." And Article 141 of the Constitution of the Republic of China provides: "The foreign policy of the Republic of China shall . . . protect the rights and interest of Chinese citizens residing abroad . . ."

9. *Central Daily News*, Jan. 8, 1966, p. 4.

Chapter 6   The Internal Decision Process: Constitutional Structures and Functions

The literature in English on the constitution of the Republic of China is scarce. Hsieh Kwan-sheng's *A Brief Survey of the Chinese Constitution* (Taipei: China Cultural Service, 1954) is concise and useful. A guide to the constitutional structures and functions of the Nationalist government during the mainland epoch is Ch'ien Tuan-sheng, *The Government and Politics of China* (Cambridge: Harvard University Press, 1961).

Designers of Formosa's constitution can benefit greatly from an adequate knowledge of comparative politics and governments. Particularly useful for this purpose is A. J. Peaslee, ed., *Constitutions of Nations*, 2d ed; 3 vols. (The Hague: M. Nijhoff, 1956), which compiles in English the texts of the constitutions of the various nations of the world, together with summaries, annotations, bibliographies, and comparative tables. Concerning our approach here, see G. H. Dession and H. D. Lasswell, "Public Order under Law: The Role of the Advisor-Draftsman in the Formation of Code or Constitution," 65 *Yale Law Journal* 175 (1955). See generally H. Finer, *The Major Governments of Modern Europe* (Evanston, Ill.: Row, Peterson, 1960); H. Eckstein and D. E. Apter, eds., *Comparative Politics: A Reader* (New York: Free Press, 1963); D. V. Verney, *Analysis of Political Systems* (New York: Free Press, 1959). On British system a great classic is *The English Constitution* by Walter Bagehot, 1867, available in paperback by Cornell University Press, Ithaca, New York. On German system see E. Plischke, *Contemporary Government of Germany* (Boston: Houghton Mifflin, 1961). On French system, see M. Duverger, *The French Political System* (Chicago: University of Chicago Press, 1958). On the presidential system of the United States, see H. J. Laski, *The American Presidency* (New York: Harper, 1940); R. E. Neustadt, *Presidential Power: The Politics of Leadership* (New York: Wiley, 1960).

The literature on guarantees of civil liberty is voluminous. See especially H. D. Lasswell, *National Security and Individual Freedom* (New York: McGraw-Hill, 1950); T. I. Emerson, D. Haber and N. Dorsen, *Political and Civil Rights in the United States*, 2 vols. (Boston: Little, Brown, 1967); H. Street, *Freedom, the Individual, and the Law* (Baltimore: Penguin Books, 1963). On the protection of minorities, see J. A. Laponce, *The Protection of Minorities* (Berkeley: University of California Press, 1960). On political parties, see especially R. A. Dahl, ed., *Political Oppositions in Western Democracies* (New Haven: Yale University Press, 1966).

1. When the five major scandals were exposed in 1966, Hou Ting-tu, a member of the Legislative Yuan, said that almost one fourth of the national legislators were holding concurrent positions either as board chairmen or trustees of business firms, excluding those engaged in business in a clandestine capacity; and more than half of them were practicing law as well (*United Daily News*, Aug. 5, 1966, p. 1).

2. See Sun Yat-sen, *San Min Chu I, The Three Principles of the People*, F. W. Price, transl., and L. T. Chen, ed. (Shanghai: Commercial Press, 1928), Part II, particularly Lecture 6. In Dr. Sun's usage "*Cheng Chuan*" and "*Chih Chuan*" are also referred to as "*Chuan*" and "*Nen*." While "*Chuan*" connotes the "sovereign right" of the people, "*Nen*" connotes the "ability" of a government to manage public affairs on behalf of the people. Since no standard equivalents are available, English translation of these two terms varies according to each individual. For instance, Price employed "sovereignty" and "ability" to mean "*Chuan*" and "*Nen*" respectively (*id.* at 319).

3. The Constitution of the Republic of China went into effect on December 25, 1947. Although the constitution as a whole reflects essentially the teachings of Sun Yat-sen, there has been a chronic and embittered debate among commentators as to how much the constitutional provisions as they now stand deviate from the original design of Dr. Sun.

4. See *New York Times*, March 22, 1966, p. 8; *Central Daily News*, March 29, 1966, p. 3.

5. *United Daily News*, Nov. 3, 1965, p. 1.

6. *Chung-hua ming kuo hsien fa lun*, 10th ed. (Taipei, 1963), pp. 153–156.

7. The "garrison state" hypothesis was put forth originally by one

of the authors in 1937 and expanded in 1941. For the expanded version, see H. D. Lasswell, *The Analysis of Political Behavior* (London: Kegan Paul, Trench, Trubner, 1947), pp. 146–57.

8. From Tillman Durdin's unpublished manuscript for the Council on Foreign Relations, *Taiwan and the National Government*, as quoted in Kerr, *Formosa Betrayed*, p. 395.

9. A. Axelbank, "Chiang Kai-shek's Silent Enemies," *Harper's Magazine*, September 1963, p. 46, at 49–50. See also *United Daily News*, Oct. 17, 1966, p. 1.

10. See letter of K. C. Wu, in Kerr, *Formosa Betrayed*, pp. 480–86.

11. *McCulloch v. Maryland*, 17 *U.S.* (4 *Wheat.*) 316, 415 (1819).

12. The total membership of the National Assembly was "legally" set to be 3045 in 1947 and the actual figure in 1964 was 1521. As of today the number is even smaller.

Chapter 7   The Internal Decision Process: Selected Problems

The literature on economic development is prolific. See generally W. W. Rostow, *The Stages of Economic Growth: A Non-Communist Manifesto* (Cambridge: Cambridge University Press, 1960); A. O. Hirschman, *The Strategy of Economic Development* (New Haven: Yale University Press, 1958); W. A. Lewis, *Development Planning: The Essentials of Economic Policy* (New York: Harper & Row, 1966).

The figures concerning Formosa's economic growth in this study derive primarily from the official sources of the Nationalists, including *Industry of Free China*, a monthly in both English and Chinese, published by K. T. Li, Minister of Economic Affairs; *Statistical Abstract of the Republic of China*, published annually in both English and Chinese by the Directorate-General of Budgets, Accounts, and Statistics, Executive Yuan; *Taiwan Statistical Data Book*, published annually by the Council for International Economic Cooperation and Development, Executive Yuan; and *Foreign Trade Quarterly*. Other valuable sources are: *Economic Bulletin for Asia and the Far East*, by Economic Commission for Asia and the Far East, United Nations, in Bangkok; *Far Eastern Economic Review* published in Hong Kong. The Quarterly and a series on *Taiwan Studies* (both in Chinese) published by the Bank of Taiwan are more scholarly in analyzing Formosa's economy than any other periodicals available on the island.

For Formosa's economic development during Japanese rule, see G. W. Barclay, *Colonial Development and Population in Taiwan* (Princeton: Princeton University Press, 1954). For a comprehensive and competent appraisal of the effects of U.S. aid to Formosa, see N. H. Jacoby, *U.S. Aid to Taiwan: A Study of Foreign Aid, Self-Help, and Development* (New York: Praeger, 1966). Concerning Formosa's recent growth in agriculture, see T. H. Shen, *Agricultural Development on Taiwan since World War II* (Ithaca, N.Y.: Comstock Publishing Associates, 1964). On the unemployment problem, see Kowie Chang, *The Measurement of Employment and Unemployment in Taiwan* (Taipei, 1964). For a study of Formosa's rural life, see B. Gallin, *Hsin Hsing, Taiwan: A Chinese Village in Change* (Berkeley: University of California Press, 1966).

On communication and national development, see especially D. E. Apter, ed., *Ideology and Discontent* (New York: Free Press, 1964). Concerning the function of plural associations, see V. O. Key, *Politics, Parties and Pressure Groups*, 5th ed. (New York: Crowell, 1964); W. Kornhauser, *The Politics of Mass Society* (New York: Free Press, 1959).

On the role of the military in the emerging nations, for an incisive comparative analysis, see M. Janowitz, *The Military in the Political Development of New Nations* (Chicago: University of Chicago Press, 1964). See also J. J. Johnson, ed., *The Role of the Military in Underdeveloped Countries* (Princeton: Princeton University Press, 1962).

On education and national development, see F. H. Harbison and C. A. Mayers, *Education, Manpower, and Economic Growth: Strategies of Human Resource Development* (New York: McGraw-Hill, 1964); A. Curle, *Educational Strategy for Developing Societies: A Study of Educational and Social Factors in Relation to Economic Growth* (London: Tavistock, 1963).

For a broadly comparative treatment on bureaucracy, see R. Braibanti, ed., *Asian Bureaucratic Systems Emergent from the British Imperial Tradition* (Durham: Duke University Press, 1966).

On the family and political socialization, see F. I. Greenstein, *Children and Politics* (New Haven: Yale University Press, 1965). See also H. Hyman, *Political Socialization: A Study in the Psychology of Political Behavior* (Glencoe, Ill.: Free Press, 1959); H. D. Lasswell, *Power and Personality* (New York: Norton, 1948). Two articles by D. Easton and R. D. Hess are especially useful: "Youth and the Political System," in S. M. Lipset and L. Lowenthal, eds., *Cultural and Social Character* (New York: Free Press, 1961); "The Child's

Political World," 6 *Midwest Journal of Political Science* 229 (1962).

A research project on family planning in Taiwan financed by the Population Council and the Ford Foundation is jointly sponsored by the University of Michigan Population Studies Center and the Taiwan Provincial Health Department. Samples of its preliminary reports include R. Freedman and J. Y. Takeshita, "Studies of Fertility and Family Limitation in Taiwan," 12 *Eugenics Quarterly* 233 (1965); B. Berelson and R. Freedman, "A Study in Fertility Control," *Scientific American*, Vol. 210, No. 5 (1964), pp. 3–11; R. Freedman, J. Y. Takeshita and T. H. Sun, "Fertility and Family Planning in Taiwan: A Case Study in the Demographic Transition," 70 *American Journal of Sociology* 16 (1964).

For a comprehensive survey of worldwide family planning, see B. Berelson and others, *Family Planning and Population Programs: A Review of World Developments* (Chicago: University of Chicago Press, 1966).

1. "Formosa in Transition," 4 *World Today* 209, 213 (1948).

2. According to the Bank of Taiwan wholesale price indexes, based on June 1937, the advances from November 1945 to January 1947 were as follows: foodstuffs, 634%; clothing, 426%; fuel, 1463%; fertilizers, 27,021%; and building materials, 1434%, Dept. of State Pub. 3573, *United States Relations with China* (1949), p. 924.

3. For the official perspective about Formosa's land reform, see Chen Cheng, *Land Reform in Taiwan* (Taipei: China Pub. Co., 1961).

4. FAO, *The State of Food and Agriculture 1963* (Rome, 1963), p. 110.

5. AID, Aid Form 10–120 (7–62) on Taiwan, pp. 11, 1.

6. Formosa's current statistics, as principally processed by the Government's Directorate-General of Budgets, Accounts, and Statistics, though lagging behind the standards of the more advanced nations, are considered to be all right. The most serious deficiencies, however, are found in the statistics concerning government expenditures as well as employment and labor.

7. *United Daily News*, Nov. 4, 1965, p. 4.

8. ILO, *The Cost of Social Security, 1958–1960* (Geneva, 1964), pp. 243–48.

9. See B. M. Russett, et al., *World Handbook of Political and Social Indicators* (New Haven: Yale University Press, 1964), pp. 72–81.

10. This theme is evident on even a cursory reading of Chiang's annual messages on New Year's Day and the Double Tenth or other important occasions. See, e.g., *New York Times,* Oct. 26, 1965, p. 31.

11. In the midst of the second offshore islands crisis, Secretary of State Dulles and President Chiang issued a joint communiqué on October 23, 1958, reaffirming that the American military assistance to the "Republic of China" was for defensive purposes, stressing that the basis for the recovery of the mainland lay in "the minds and the hearts of the Chinese people," not "the use of force." The precise meaning of that statement has been a subject of controversy. (*Id.,* Oct. 24, 1958, pp. 1, 3).

12. "Dr. K. C. Wu's Views on the Police State and General Chiang Ching-kuo" (Appendix II), Kerr, *Formosa Betrayed,* p. 481.

13. Equal opportunity for education means the opportunity for all children to participate in the competitive entrance examinations. But mainland Chinese virtually monopolize key positions in educational institutions. Quantitative data from 1952 to 1966 can be found in Council for International Economic Cooperation and Development, Executive Yuan, *Taiwan Statistical Data Books, 1966* (Taipei, 1966), pp. 145–55.

14. More than 95 per cent of the freshmen at the Taiwan Provincial Normal University (Class of 1969) were constrained to apply for membership to the KMT during the orientation program for freshmen. *Central Daily News,* Aug. 31 (p. 2), Sept. 1 (p. 3), 1965.

15. The Education Bureau of Taipei Municipal Government disclosed in March 1965 that 68 per cent of primary school children in Taipei suffered from one disease or another (*China Post,* March 22, 1965, p. 4). Similarly, a medical survey conducted by the chairman of the Taiwan Provincial Medical Association indicated that in 1965 myopia had increased five-fold for sixth graders over 1945. (*id.,* May 7, 1965, p. 6). Further, children in Formosa today are shorter than their counterparts in Japan, even though the reverse was true before.

16. For instance, in 1963, it was reported that there was not a single native Formosan among 24 directors of the police bureaus, and only 5 among 120 directors of the police subbureaus throughout the island. U.S. Information Service, *Press and Publication Summary,* No. 1385 (Taipei), (translated from *Tzu Chih,* Mar. 1, 1963), p. 3.

17. *Central Daily News,* Jan. 11, 1966, p. 3.

Appendix

WE HAVE SUGGESTED that any group seriously concerned with the future of any participant in the political process will find it useful to initiate or to join a continuing inquiry (a decision seminar) designed to apply a policy sciences approach. Such an approach can be concisely summarized as *contextual, problem-oriented,* and *multi-method.* It is contextual because of the insistence on examining every specific detail in relation to the entire social process of which it is a part and with which it is in perpetual interaction. The approach is problem-oriented, since it emphasizes the importance of the clarification of value *goals,* the description of past *trends,* the analysis of explanatory *conditions,* the *projection* of probable developments, and the invention, evaluation, and selection of policy *alternatives* designed to define the middle range and immediate objectives and strategies appropriate to optimum goal realization. We refer to the approach as multi-method in order to emphasize the point that all methods available to science and scholarship are to be mobilized to the task in hand.

Among helpful tools of continuing inquiry are visual aids, such as charts and maps. As part of a permanent display in a decision seminar room they are reminders of past discussions and hence of features of the context that must be open to frequent reconsideration.

We shall not undertake to present a collection of exhaustive visual materials that bear on the complex issues in hand. Our generalized model of social process refers to "man" pursuing preferred outcomes ("values") through "institutions" affecting "resources." As indicated elsewhere in this book, we use eight categories to designate the value-institution sectors of the model (power, enlightenment, wealth, well-being, skill, affection, respect, rectitude); and analysis will show that specific issues have been at least provisionally, though partially, related to each dimension of the process model. We make available here a handful of tables and charts whose importance for the principal problems at hand is very great.

Of direct concern is trend data about the decisions taken by the General Assembly on the question of Chinese participation. The voting record is presented to call attention to a principal factor that conditioned the result, and hence is highly relevant to explanatory propositions about world politics. Voting alignments both register the configuration of power in the political arena and contribute to its alteration. For instance, some outcomes favorable to a participant may be obtained at the cost of restricting his freedom of action on other matters; or the effects of a success may backfire if resentment grows at the highhanded strategies employed to win. Resentment is directed against the "other" for having inflicted a value deprivation on the "self" contrary to what is perceived as a prescriptive norm. Thus acts of coercion—naked power—may be perceived as violations of legality (power), respect, and decency (rectitude).

By reporting U.N. votes in terms of pro- or anti-U.S. positions, we give prominence to a major conditioning factor, namely, the total impact of the principal superpower. At the same time the chart raises questions about the future of U.S. power. Has the cost of United States policy on the "participation question" risen, not only in terms of immediate "trade-offs," but in cumulative resentments that will presently render the costs prohibitive? This study cannot deal comprehensively with these questions. It does, however, provide some pertinent information that confirms the view that previous U.S. policies are "pricing themselves out of the arena." The chart by territorial grouping points toward the participants whose "cost" (to the United States) is rising (Charts 1–3).

One index of the relative strength of nation states in the world arena is the universality of their acceptance by other bodies politic, reflected in diplomatic recognition and exchange of missions. The rivalry between Nationalist China and Communist China is shown in Chart 4.

Since we look beyond the immediate situation of the inhabitants of Formosa to factors that condition future possibilities, it is relevant to highlight the principal points. Fundamental to any body politic is the nature of the balance among people, resources, and value shaping and sharing. The dynamic and unstable situation of Formosa is indicated by the high rate of population growth. Instability can be expected to increase unless value formation continues to accelerate, and distribution patterns move toward value sharing. Because food supply and agriculture are critically important, we emphasize the relationship between population and arable land (Charts 5, 6). At present a disproportionate percent of Formosa's resources and values is devoted to military preparations justified by the KMT's myth of reconquering the mainland. Even though a large part of the burden is carried by the United States, it is obvious that manpower and assets otherwise available for the values of civilian society are diverted from these purposes. Charts 7 and 8 show the manpower drain, and that drain as a percentage of G.N.P.

Formosa has more of certain base values at its disposal than a great many members of the U.N.—and more than most Asian countries. Enlightenment and skill levels are roughly indicated by literacy, higher education, medical competence, and access to mass media. Because of the importance of economic level, and the availability of G.N.P. data, we also characterize Formosa's position in G.N.P. terms. Seen in the context of "stages" between "traditional" economies and "high production, high consumption" economies, Formosa occupies a "transitional" position (Chart 9).*

If Formosa does in fact achieve independence, it will come as a strong reaction to the tyranny of a coercively supported regime of narrowly held power. Hence there will be an intense demand for popular government, for relatively noncoercive, widely shared participation in power. Chart 10, outlining the present structure of the Nationalist government, provides a reminder of the situation that has prevailed up to the present.

---

* Charts 5 to 9 are based on data in B. M. Russett, et al., *World Handbook of Political and Social Indicators* (New Haven: Yale University Press, 1964). We should like to point out, as does the *Handbook*, that these data have their limitations. They are subject to inaccuracy and imprecision because of: difficulties in classification and measurement; unreliability in the published data; deliberate distortion by governments; and statistical error. Nevertheless, they reflect general relationships, and they illustrate the use of charts in a decision seminar.

Chart 1. Chinese Participation: Total General Assembly Vote, 1950–1966

Year	Type of Draft Resolution	Total Membership	Pro-U.S. Position	Anti-U.S. Position	Abstention and Absence
1950	N	59	33	16	10
1951	M	60	37	11	12
1952	M	60	42	7	11
1953	M	60	44	10	6
1954	M	60	43	11	6
1955	M	60	42	12	6
1956	M	79	47	24	8
1957	M	82	47	27	8
1958	M	81	44	28	9
1959	M	82	44	29	9
1960	M	99	42	34	23
1961	I	104	61	34	9
	R	104	48	37	19
1962	R	110	56	42	12
1963	R	111	57	41	13
1964	(No vote taken)	114			
1965	I	117	56	49	12
	R	117	47	47	23
1966	I	121	66	48	7
	R	121	57	46	18
	S	121	34	62	25

N: The Indian draft resolution to seat Peking on the basis of its effective control.

M: A moratorium proposal to postpone consideration of the substance of the question at a given session.

I: A draft resolution to have the General Assembly decide that any proposal to change the "representation" of China in the United Nations is an important question.

R: A draft resolution to have Peking replace the Nationalist delegation in the United Nations.

S: The six-power proposal to establish a study committee.

Source: *Yearbook of the United Nations, 1950–1964; U.N. General Assembly Provisional Verbatim Record (Plenary Meetings),* 20th and 21st Sessions (1965 and 1966).

Chart 2. Chinese Participation: Roll Call Votes 1950–1966

U: Pro-U.S. positions.
P: Anti-U.S. positions.
A: Abstentions and Absences.
N, M, I, R, S: See Chart 1.

Member States	Year and Type of Draft Resolution										
	1950	1951	1952	1953	1954	1955	1956	1957	1958	1959	1960
	N	M	M	M	M	M	M	M	M	M	M
Afghanistan	P		A		A	A	P	P	P	P	P
Albania							P	P	P	P	P
Algeria											
Argentina	A		U		U	U	U	U	U	U	U
Australia	U		U		U	U	U	U	U	U	U
Austria							U	U	A	A	A
Belgium	U		U		U	U	U	U	U	U	U
Bolivia	U		A		U	U	U	U	U	U	U
Botswana											
Brazil	U		U		U	U	U	U	U	U	U
Bulgaria							P	P	P	P	P
Burma	P		P		P	P	P	P	P	P	P
Burundi											
Byelorussian SSR	P		P		P	P	P	P	P	P	P
Cambodia							A	A	P	P	P
Cameroon											A
Canada	A		U		U	U	U	U	U	U	U
Central African Rep.											A
Ceylon							P	P	P	P	P
Chad											A
Chile	U		U		U	U	U	U	U	U	U
China	U		U		U	U	U	U	U	U	U
Colombia	U		U		U	U	U	U	U	U	U
Congo (Brazzaville)											A
Congo (Leopoldville)											A
Costa Rica	U		U		U	U	U	U	U	U	U
Cuba	U		U		U	U	U	U	U	A	P
Cyprus											A
Czechoslovakia	P		P		P	P	P	P	P	P	P

404

Year and Type of Draft Resolution

1961		1962	1963	1964	1965		1966			Member States
I	R	R	R	R	I	R	I	R	S	
P	P	P	P		P	P	P	P	P	Afghanistan
P	P	P	P		P	P	P	P	P	Albania
		P	P		P	P	P	P	P	Algeria
U	U	U	U		U	U	U	U	A	Argentina
U	U	U	U		U	U	U	U	P	Australia
A	A	A	A		A	A	A	A	A	Austria
U	U	U	U		U	U	U	U	U	Belgium
U	U	U	U		U	U	U	U	U	Bolivia
							U	A	P	Botswana
U	U	U	U		U	U	U	U	U	Brazil
P	P	P	P		P	P	P	P	P	Bulgaria
P	P	P	P		P	P	P	P	P	Burma
		P	P		A	A	P	P	P	Burundi
P	P	P	P		P	P	P	P	P	Byelorussian SRR
P	P	P	P		P	P	P	P	P	Cambodia
U	U	U	U		A	A	A	A	A	Cameroon
U	U	U	U		U	U	U	A	U	Canada
U	A	U	U		P	P	U	U	P	Central African Rep.
P	P	P	P		P	P	P	P	P	Ceylon
U	A	U	U		A	A	A	A	A	Chad
U	U	U	U		U	A	U	U	U	Chile
U	U	U	U		U	U	U	U	P	China
U	U	U	U		U	U	U	U	U	Colombia
U	A	U	U		P	P	P	P	P	Congo (Brazzaville)
U	A	U	U		U	A	U	U	U	Congo (Leopoldville)
U	U	U	U		U	U	U	U	A	Costa Rica
P	P	P	P		P	P	P	P	P	Cuba
A	A	A	U		A	A	A	A	A	Cyprus
P	P	P	P		P	P	P	P	P	Czechoslovakia

Chart 2. Chinese Participation: Roll Call Votes 1950–66 (Cont.)

Member States	*Year and Type of Draft Resolution*										
	1950	1951	1952	1953	1954	1955	1956	1957	1958	1959	1960
	N	M	M	M	M	M	M	M	M	M	M
Dahomey											A
Denmark	P		U		P	P	P	P	P	P	P
Dominican Republic	U		U		U	U	U	U	U	U	U
Ecuador	A		U		U	U	U	U	U	U	U
El Salvador	U		U		U	U	U	U	U	U	U
Ethiopia	U		U		U	U	U	U	U	A	P
Finland							P	P	P	P	P
France	A		U		U	U	U	U	U	U	U
Gabon											A
Gambia											
Ghana								P	P	P	P
Greece	U		U		U	U	U	U	A	U	U
Guatemala	A		A		U	U	U	U	U	U	U
Guinea										P	P
Guyana											
Haiti	U		U		U	U	U	U	U	U	U
Honduras	U		U		U	U	U	U	U	U	U
Hungary							P	P	P	P	P
Iceland	U		U		U	U	U	U	A	A	A
India	P		A		P	P	P	P	P	P	P
Indonesia			A		A	P	P	P	P	P	P
Iran	U		U		U	U	U	U	U	U	U
Iraq	U		U		U	U	U	U	P	P	P
Ireland							U	P	P	P	P
Israel	P		A		U	A	A	A	A	A	A
Italy							U	U	U	U	U
Ivory Coast											A
Jamaica											
Japan								U	U	U	U
Jordan							A	U	U	U	U
Kenya											
Kuwait											
Laos							A	A	A	U	A

			Year and Type of Draft Resolution							
1961		**1962**	**1963**	**1964**	**1965**		**1966**			**Member States**
I	R	R	R	R	I	R	I	R	S	
U	A	U	U		A	A	U	U	P	Dahomey
P	P	P	P		P	P	P	P	P	Denmark
U	U	U	U		U	U	U	U	A	Dominican Republic
U	U	U	U		U	U	U	U	U	Ecuador
U	U	U	U		U	U	U	U	A	El Salvador
P	P	P	A		P	P	P	P	P	Ethiopia
P	P	P	P		P	P	P	P	P	Finland
U	U	U	U		P	P	P	P	P	France
A	U	U	U		U	U	U	U	A	Gabon
					U	U	U	U	P	Gambia
P	P	P	P		P	P	P	P	P	Ghana
U	U	U	U		U	U	U	U	U	Greece
U	U	U	U		U	U	U	U	U	Guatemala
P	P	P	P		P	P	P	P	P	Guinea
							U	U	A	Guyana
U	U	U	U		U	U	U	U	A	Haiti
U	U	U	U		U	U	U	U	A	Honduras
P	P	P	P		P	P	P	P	P	Hungary
U	A	A	A		U	A	U	U	U	Iceland
P	P	P	P		P	P	P	P	P	India
P	P	P	P				U	P	A	Indonesia
U	U	U	U		A	A	A	A	A	Iran
P	P	P	P		P	P	P	P	P	Iraq
U	U	U	U		U	U	U	U	U	Ireland
U	A	A	A		U	U	U	U	U	Israel
U	U	U	U		U	U	U	U	U	Italy
U	A	U	U		U	U	U	U	P	Ivory Coast
		U	U		A	A	U	A	U	Jamaica
U	U	U	U		U	U	U	U	U	Japan
U	U	U	U		U	U	U	U	P	Jordan
					P	P	P	P	P	Kenya
				A	A	A	P	A	A	Kuwait
U	U	P	P		U	A	U	A	A	Laos

Chart 2. Chinese Participation: Roll Call Votes 1950–66 (Cont.)

Member States	1950	1951	1952	1953	1954	1955	1956	1957	1958	1959	1960
	N	M	M	M	M	M	M	M	M	M	M
Lebanon	A		U		U	U	U	U	U	U	U
Lesotho											
Liberia	U		U		U	U	U	U	U	U	U
Libya							A	U	A	A	A
Luxembourg	U		U		U	U	U	U	U	U	U
Madagascar											A
Malawi											
Malaysia							U	U	U	A
Maldive Islands											
Mali											P
Malta											
Mauritania											
Mexico	U		U		U	U	U	U	U	U	U
Mongolia											
Morocco							U	P	P	P	P
Nepal							P	P	P	P	P
Netherlands	P		U		U	U	U	U	U	U	U
New Zealand	U		U		U	U	U	U	U	U	U
Nicaragua	U		U		U	U	U	U	U	U	U
Niger											A
Nigeria											P
Norway	P		U		P	P	P	P	P	P	P
Pakistan	P		A		U	U	U	A	U	U	U
Panama	U		U		U	U	U	U	U	U	U
Paraguay	U		U		U	U	U	U	U	U	U
Peru	U		U		U	U	U	U	U	U	U
Philippines	U		U		U	U	U	U	U	U	U
Poland	P		P		P	P	P	P	P	P	P
Portugal							A	A	A	A	A
Romania							P	P	P	P	P
Rwanda											
Saudi Arabia	A		A		A	A	A	A	A	A	A
Senegal											P

Year and Type of Draft Resolution										Member States
1961		1962	1963	1964	1965		1966			
I	R	R	R		I	R	I	R	S	
U	A	A	A		U	A	U	A	A	Lebanon
							U	U	A	Lesotho
U	U	U	U		U	U	U	U	U	Liberia
U	U	U	U		U	A	U	U	U	Libya
U	U	U	U		U	U	U	U	U	Luxembourg
U	U	U	U		U	U	U	U	P	Madagascar
					U	U	U	U	U	Malawi
U	U	A	U		U	U	U	U	A	Malaysia
					A	A	U	A	A	Maldive Islands
P	P	P	P		P	P	P	P	P	Mali
					U	U	U	U	U	Malta
U	U	U	A		P	P	P	P	P	Mauritania
U	U	U	U		U	U	U	U	U	Mexico
P	P	P	P		P	P	P	P	P	Mongolia
P	P	P	P		P	P	P	A	U	Morocco
P	P	P	P		P	P	P	P	P	Nepal
U	A	A	A		U	A	U	A	U	Netherlands
U	U	U	U		U	U	U	U	U	New Zealand
U	U	U	U		U	U	U	U	U	Nicaragua
U	A	U	U		U	U	U	U	P	Niger
A	A	A	A		P	P	P	P	A	Nigeria
P	P	P	P		P	P	P	P	P	Norway
A	P	P	P		P	P	P	P	P	Pakistan
U	U	U	U		U	U	U	U	U	Panama
U	U	U	U		U	U	U	U	P	Paraguay
U'	U	U	U		U	U	U	U	U	Peru
U	U	U	U		U	U	U	U	P	Philippines
P	P	P	P		P	P	P	P	P	Poland
U	A	A	A		A	A	A	A	A	Portugal
P	P	P	P		P	P	P	P	P	Romania
		U	U		P	A	U	U	P	Rwanda
U	A	A	A		A	A	U	U	A	Saudi Arabia
U	U	U	U		P	A	P	P	P	Senegal

Chart 2. Chinese Participation: Roll Call Votes 1950–66 (Cont.)

Member States	Year and Type of Draft Resolution										
	1950	1951	1952	1953	1954	1955	1956	1957	1958	1959	1960
	N	M	M	M	M	M	M	M	M	M	M
Sierra Leone											
Singapore											
Somalia											A
South Africa	U		U		U	U	U	A	U	U	U
Spain							U	U	U	U	U
Sudan							P	P	P	P	P
Sweden	P		P		P	P	P	P	P	P	P
Syria	A		A		A	A	P	P			
Thailand	U		U		U	U	U	U	U	U	U
Togo											A
Trinidad and Tobago											
Tunisia							A	A	A	A	A
Turkey	U		U		U	U	U	U	U	U	U
Uganda											
Ukraine SSR	P		P		P	P	P	P	P	P	P
U.S.S.R.	P		P		P	P	P	P	P	P	P
United Arab Republic	A		U		A	A	P	P	P	P	P
United Kingdom	P		U		U	U	U	U	U	U	U
United Republic of Tanzania											
United States	U		U		U	U	U	U	U	U	U
Upper Volta											A
Uruguay	U		U		U	U	U	U	U	U	U
Venezuela	U		U		U	U	U	U	U	U	U
Yemen	A		A		A	A	P	P	P	P	P
Yugoslavia	P		A		P	P	P	P	P	P	P
Zambia											

Source: *Yearbook of the United Nations*, 1950–1964; *U.N. General Assembly Provisional Verbatim Record (Plenary Meetings)*, 20th and 21st Sessions (1965 and 1966).

Year and Type of Draft Resolution

1961		1962	1963	1964	1965		1966			Member States
I	R	R	R	R	I	R	I	R	S	
A	P	P	A		P	P	A	U	A	Sierra Leone
					P	P	P	A	P	Singapore
A	P	P	P		P	P	P	P	P	Somalia
U	U	U	U		U	U	U	U	P	South Africa
U	U	U	U		U	U	U	U	P	Spain
P	P	P	P		P	P	P	P	P	Sudan
P	P	P	P		P	P	P	P	P	Sweden
P	P	P	P		P	P	P	P	P	Syria
U	U	U	U		U	U	U	U	P	Thailand
A	A	A	U		U	U	U	U	P	Togo
		A	A		U	A	U	A	U	Trinidad and Tobago
P	A	P	P		P	A	P	A	U	Tunisia
U	U	U	U		U	U	U	U	U	Turkey
		P	P		P	P	P	P	P	Uganda
P	P	P	P		P	P	P	P	P	Ukraine SSR
P	P	P	P		P	P	P	P	P	U.S.S.R.
P	P	P	P		P	P	P	P	P	United Arab Republic
U	P	P	P		U	P	U	P	A	United Kingdom
A	U	P	P		P	P	P	P	P	United Republic of Tanzania
U	U	U	U		U	U	U	U	U	United States
U	A	U	U		U	U	U	U	P	Upper Volta
U	U	U	U		U	U	U	U	U	Uruguay
U	U	U	U		U	U	U	U	U	Venezuela
P	P	U	P		P	P	P	P	P	Yemen
P	P	P	P		P	P	P	P	P	Yugoslavia
					P	P	P	P	P	Zambia

Chart 3. Chinese Participation: Voting by Territorial Grouping

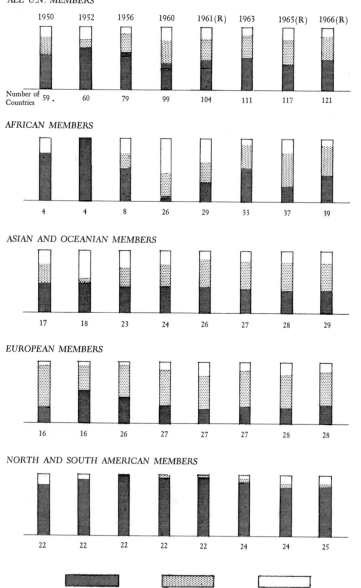

ALL U.N. MEMBERS

| 1950 | 1952 | 1956 | 1960 | 1961(R) | 1963 | 1965(R) | 1966(R) |

Number of Countries: 59, 60, 79, 99, 104, 111, 117, 121

AFRICAN MEMBERS

4, 4, 8, 26, 29, 33, 37, 39

ASIAN AND OCEANIAN MEMBERS

17, 18, 23, 24, 26, 27, 28, 29

EUROPEAN MEMBERS

16, 16, 26, 27, 27, 27, 28, 28

NORTH AND SOUTH AMERICAN MEMBERS

22, 22, 22, 22, 22, 24, 24, 25

Pro-U.S. Positions   Anti-U.S. Positions   Abstentions and Absences

Source: *Yearbook of the United Nations*, 1950–1964; *U.N. General Assembly Provisional Verbatim Record (Plenary Meetings)*, 20th and 21st Sessions (1965 and 1966).

Chart 4. Chinese Nationalist-Communist Rivalry

Adhering to the myth of "one China," both Chinese Nationalist and Communist regimes have since 1949 made it a policy not to establish diplomatic relations with those who maintain diplomatic relations with the rival regime. Hence some U.N. members recognize and maintain diplomatic relations with the former, and some with the latter. Some grant recognition but fall short of exchanging envoys. Some have switched their diplomatic relations from one side to the other. Others have recognized neither. As of March 1967, the relations of U.N. members with both Nationalist and Communist China are as follows:

Members which recognize the Republic of China (59):

AFRICA: Botswana, Cameroon, Chad, Congo (Democratic Republic of), Dahomey, Gabon, Ivory Coast, Lesotho, Liberia, Libya, Malagasy Republic, Malawi, Niger, Rwanda, Sierra Leone, South Africa, Togo, Upper Volta (18);

ASIA AND
OCEANIA: Australia, Iran, Japan, Jordan, Kuwait, Lebanon, Maldive Islands, New Zealand, Philippines, Saudi Arabia, Thailand, Turkey (12);

EUROPE: Belgium, Cyprus, Greece, Italy, Luxembourg, Portugal, Spain (7);

NORTH AND
SOUTH
AMERICA: Argentina, Bolivia, Brazil, Canada, Chile, Colombia, Costa Rica, Dominican Republic, Ecuador, El Salvador, Guatemala, Haiti, Honduras, Jamaica, Mexico, Nicaragua, Panama, Paraguay, Peru, United States, Uruguay, Venezuela (22).

Members which recognize the People's Republic of China (50):

AFRICA: Algeria, Burundi, Central African Republic, Congo (Brazzaville), Ghana, Guinea, Kenya, Mali, Mauritania,

413

Morocco, Senegal, Somalia, Sudan, Tanzania, Tunisia, Uganda, United Arab Republic, Zambia (18);

ASIA: Afghanistan, Burma, Cambodia, Ceylon, India, Indonesia, Iraq, Israel, Laos, Mongolia, Nepal, Pakistan, Syria, Yemen (14);

EUROPE: Albania, Bulgaria, Byelorussian S.S.R., Czechoslovakia, Denmark, Finland, France, Hungary, Netherlands, Norway, Poland, Romania, Sweden, Ukrainian S.S.R., U.S.S.R., United Kingdom, Yugoslavia (17);

NORTH AND
SOUTH
AMERICA: Cuba (1).

Members which have recognized neither the Republic of China nor the People's Republic of China (12):

AFRICA: Ethiopia, Gambia, Nigeria (3);

ASIA: Malaysia, Singapore (2);

EUROPE: Austria, Iceland, Ireland, Malta (4);

NORTH AND
SOUTH
AMERICA: Barbados, Guyana, Trinidad and Tobago (3).

	Members recognizing Nationalist China 48.76%	Members recognizing Communist China 41.32%	Members recognizing Neither 9.92%
Africa	14.87%	14.87%	2.48%
Asia and Oceania	9.92%	11.57%	1.65%
Europe	5.79%	14.05%	3.31%
North and South America	18.18%	0.83%	2.48%

Source: Treaty Section, Ministry of Foreign Affairs, Republic of China.

414

Chart 5. Annual Rate of Population Increase

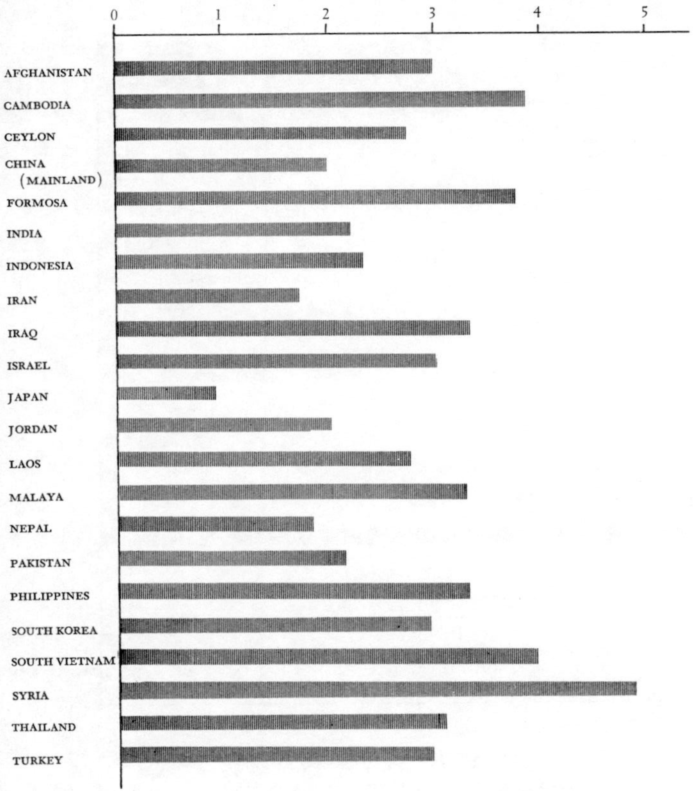

0
1
2
3
4
5
AFGHANISTAN
CAMBODIA
CEYLON
CHINA (MAINLAND)
FORMOSA
INDIA
INDONESIA
IRAN
IRAQ
ISRAEL
JAPAN
JORDAN
LAOS
MALAYA
NEPAL
PAKISTAN
PHILIPPINES
SOUTH KOREA
SOUTH VIETNAM
SYRIA
THAILAND
TURKEY

Chart 6. Population per 1000 Hectares of Agricultural Land

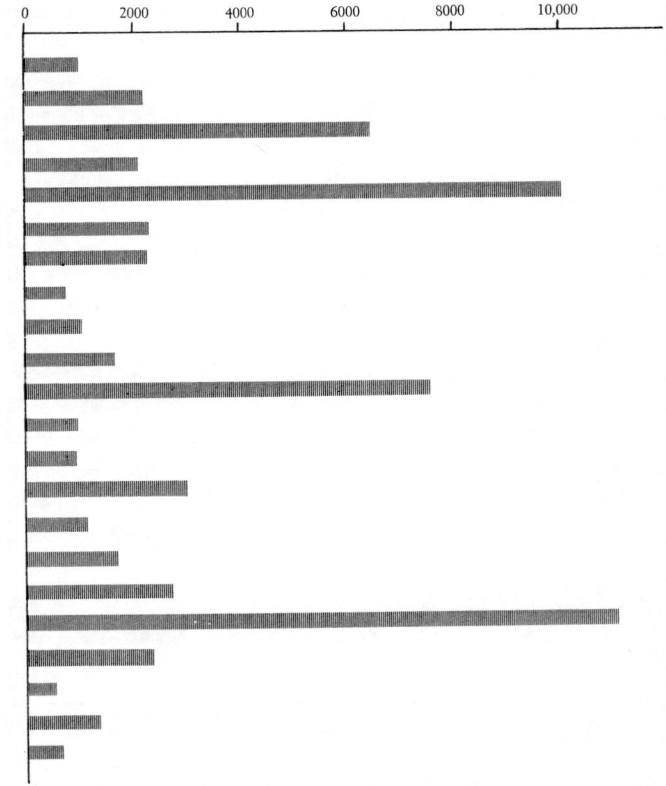

0
2000
4000
6000
8000
10,000

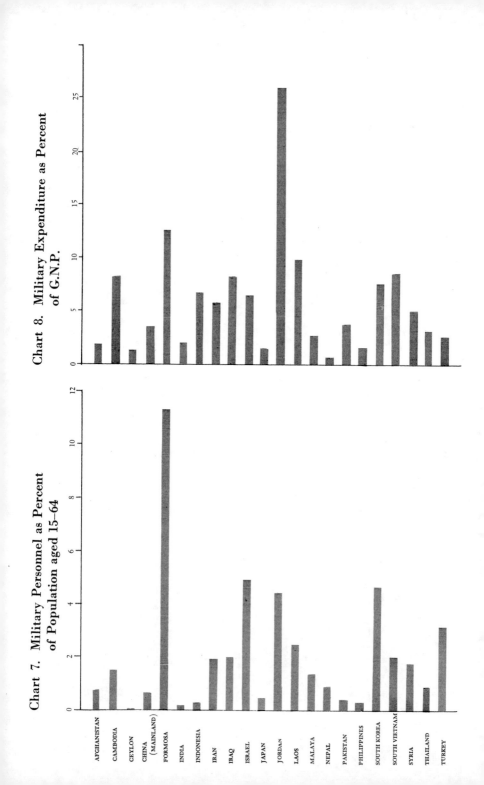

Chart 7. Military Personnel as Percent of Population aged 15–64

Chart 8. Military Expenditure as Percent of G.N.P.

Chart 9. Formosa's Economic and Political Development Compared with Other Asian Countries

Country	G.N.P. per Capita	% Urban (20,000)	% Adult Literacy	Higher Educ. per 100,000	Inhabitants per Physician	Radios per 1,000
Nepal	45	4.4	5.0	56	72,000	
Afghanistan	50	7.5	2.5	12	41,000	1.7
Laos	50	4.0	17.5	4	100,000	8.0
Burma	57	10.0	47.5	63	15,000	5.6
Pakistan	70	11.8	13.0	165	8,670	3.0
China (Mainland)	73	10.0	47.5	69	8,700	
India	73	12.0	19.3	220	5,200	5.0
South Vietnam	76		17.5	83	29,000	8.9
Thailand	96	7.7	68.0	251	7,500	6.2
Cambodia	99	16.0	17.5	18	95,000	6.5
Iran	108	21.0	15.0	90	3,800	65.3
Ceylon	129	11.4	63.0	56	4,500	38.4
Jordan	129	25.5	17.5		5,800	37.7
Indonesia	131	9.1	17.5	62	48,000	7.4
South Korea	144	18.5	77.0	397	3,700	
Iraq	156	23.6	10.0	173	5,600	21.2
Formosa	*161*	*24.0*	*54.0*	*329*	*1,500*	*69.5*
Saudi Arabia	170	9.5	2.5	6	13,000	12.1
Syria	173	38.8	27.5	223	4,600	57.3
Philippines	220	12.7	75.0	976	5,555	22.3
Turkey	220	18.2	39.0	255	2,800	52.5
Japan	306	43.1	98.0	750	930	106.7
Malaya	356	22.7	38.4	475	6,400	36.5
Lebanon	362	23.0	47.5	345	1,100	60.8
Singapore	400		50.0	437	2,400	88.3
Israel	726	60.9	93.7	668	400	194.0

Source: B. M. Russett, et al., *World Handbook of Political and Social Indicators* (New Haven: Yale University Press, 1964).

Chart 10. The Present Government Structure of the "Republic of China"

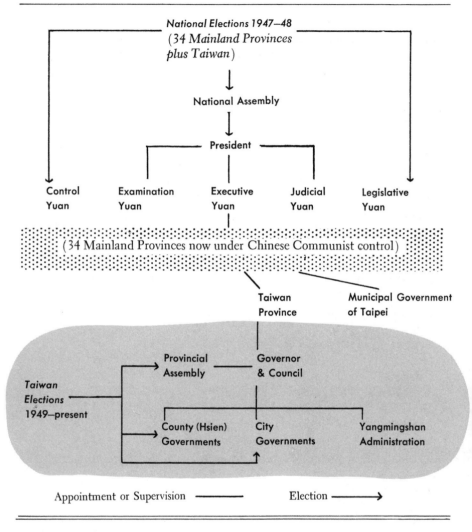

Native Formosans' share of representation in the top level decision-making ("Congressional representation")

	Mainland Chinese	Native Formosans
Formosa's present population	2,000,000	11,000,000
Representation in National Assembly (1964)	1,503	18
Representation in Legislative Yuan (1964)	467	6
Representation in Control Yuan (1964)	77	5

Source: Executive Yuan, *Statistical Abstract of the Republic of China, 1965* (Taipei, 1965).

Index